ON CELESTIAL MUSIC

Also by Rick Moody

Garden State

The Ice Storm

The Ring of Brightest Angels Around Heaven

Purple America

Joyful Noise: The New Testament Revisited
(coeditor, with Darcey Steinke)

Demonology

The Black Veil

The Diviners

Right Livelihoods

The Four Fingers of Death

ON CELESTIAL MUSIC

AND OTHER ADVENTURES IN LISTENING

RICK MOODY

BACK BAY BOOKS
LITTLE, BROWN AND COMPANY
New York   Boston   London

Back Bay Books / Little, Brown and Company
Hachette Book Group
237 Park Avenue, New York, NY 10017
www.hachettebookgroup.com

First edition: March 2012

Back Bay Books is an imprint of Little, Brown and Company. The Back Bay Books name and logo are trademarks of Hachette Book Group, Inc.

The publisher is not responsible for websites (or their content) that are not owned by the publisher.

Quotation from "A Coney Island of the Mind" is copyright © 1958 by Lawrence Ferlinghetti. Reprinted by permission of New Directions Publishing Corp. Excerpt from "First Party at Ken Kesey's with Hell's Angels" is from Collected Poems 1947–1980, copyright © 1965 by Allen Ginsberg. Reprinted by permission of HarperCollins Publishers.

Library of Congress Cataloging-in-Publication Data
Moody, Rick.
   On celestial music : and other adventures in listening / Rick Moody.—1st ed.
      p. cm.
   Includes index.
   ISBN 978-0-316-10521-7
   1. Music—History and criticism.   I. Title.
   ML160.M693 2012
   780.9—dc23   2011030556

10 9 8 7 6 5 4 3 2 1

RRD-C

Printed in the United States of America

For my mother, Peggy Davis,
And for Hannah Marie Marcus

Contents

Music and Literature: An Introduction   3

Against Cool (1997/2004)   11

On Meredith Monk (2002)   57

Thirty-One Love Songs (2003)   72

How to Be a Christian Artist: On the
Danielson Famile (2004)   89

Five Songs (By Wilco) (2004)   106

Guilty Pleasures (2005)   131

Some Propositions Concerning the
Lounge Lizards (2006)   158

The Pete Townshend Fragments (2006)   176

Two Weeks at Music Camp (2007)   234

On Celestial Music (2007)   265

The Problem of Impairment (2008)   283

The New York Underground, 1965–1988 (2009)   301

Europe, Forsake Your Drum Machines!: A Genealogy
(2010)   352

Acknowledgments   419

Index   421

ON
CELESTIAL
MUSIC

Music and Literature

An Introduction

Here's a passage I have always loved, from *Molloy*, by Samuel Beckett: *I had say sixteen stones, four in each of my four pockets these being the two pockets of my trousers and the two pockets of my greatcoat. Taking a stone from the right pocket of my greatcoat, and putting it in my mouth, I replaced it in the right pocket of my greatcoat by a stone from the right pocket of my trousers, which I replaced by a stone from the left pocket of my trousers, which I replaced by a stone from the left pocket of my greatcoat, which I replaced by the stone which was in my mouth, as soon as I had finished sucking it. Thus there were still four stones in each of my four pockets, but not quite the same stones. And when the desire to suck took hold of me again, I drew again on the right pocket of my greatcoat, certain of not taking the same stone as the last time. And while I sucked it I rearranged the other stones in the way I have just described. And so on.*

And here's another, from *Varieties of Disturbance*, by Lydia Davis: *When I describe this conversation to my husband, I cause in him feelings of disturbance also, stronger than mine and different in kind from those in my mother, in my father, and respectively claimed and anticipated by them. My husband is disturbed by my mother's refusing my brother's help and thus causing disturbance in him, and by her telling me of her disturbance and thus causing in me disturbance greater, he says, than I realize, but also more generally by the disturbance caused more generally not only in my brother by her but also in me by her greater than I realize, and more often than I realize, and when he points this out, it causes in me yet another disturbance different in kind and in degree from that caused in me by what my mother has told me, for this disturbance is not only for myself and my brother, and not only for my father in his anticipated and his present disturbance, but also and most of all for my mother herself, who has now, and has generally, caused so much disturbance, as my husband rightly says, but is herself disturbed by only a small part of it.*

These passages have in common not only their beauty, their attenuation, their long lines, their complexity, which are estimable in an era of prose that grows ever more abbreviated, ever more fragmentary; these passages also have in common that the prose writers who fashioned them were (*are*, in Lydia Davis's case) *musicians*. Beckett played piano avidly. And Lydia Davis, like Beckett, is a lifelong player of keyboard music and an advocate of the musical classics.

There are many such examples among writers of literature. James Joyce was a gifted singer, as was Thomas Bernhard, who was held back in music by the fact of his tuberculosis. Allen Ginsberg played the harmonium. Nicholson Baker, the author of *The Mezzanine, Double Fold, Human Smoke,* and other works of startling diversity, studied music composition when he was an undergraduate at Haverford. George Saunders, also a stylist of a most limpid prose, is a guitar player of some note; Myla Goldberg, author of *Bee Season*, plays flute, banjo, and accordion; Paul Muldoon, the excellent Irish poet, writes songs and plays rhythm guitar in a band. David Gates, of *Jernigan* fame, plays old time and is learning the pedal steel guitar. There is my friend the novelist Wesley Stace, who also plays music and records under his stage name, John Wesley Harding. Wells Tower, noted short-story writer, played in a band; Jonathan Lethem wrote lyrics for any number of musical projects. Nick Cave, the Australian musician, writes novels and screenplays, and his novel-writing voice, far from being declarative and untutored, despite the absence of an MFA, is rich, decadent, and full of linguistic excesses of just the sort I admire. And that's just off the top of my head.

There is a link, I mean to suggest, between literary writing and music—a very specific link, a link of great relevance, which finds itself in the fact that literary writing is an aural phenomenon, though it appears on the page. The origin of literature is in the oral tradition, in what is spoken. That is, literature that avoids its sonic register does so at its peril. Literature that never lived in someone's mouth, or someone's ear, is *desiccated literature*. And that's part of why a lot of writers have also played music (leaving aside the fact that music is delightful and it often gets you out of the house). Playing music encourages you to listen more closely, playing music makes you more concerned with the musical component of your prose, and for my money, this makes you a more interesting writer, a writer who is not engaged with how a page looks or how a plot advances itself but is engaged instead with how a line sounds in the ear, how it gets *sung*.

As I say several times in the essays that follow, my house, growing up, was not musically erudite, but it was musically passionate. For this I owe my mother a great debt, as she had been schooled in piano from her earliest childhood and could make her way through some Debussy with real grace. She sang, too, and does to this day. My sister played guitar, not terribly well (she didn't practice enough), but because she was three years older than I, she was the recipient of much attention around the house—attention verging on adulation—for her picking away at "What Shall We Do with the Drunken Sailor?" on her nylon-stringed guitar, circa 1969. Even my father had a couple of songs in his piano repertoire, and he had friends who liked to come around our place in the suburbs and bang on the baby grand, mangling show tunes. *Show tunes!* Those abominations that indicated a certain upwardly mobile artistic appreciation in the fifties and sixties. My family had all of those recordings, from *South Pacific* to *Man of La Mancha* to *1776*, and on the slightly drunken nights, my parents and their friends could often be heard warbling away at "The Impossible Dream" or "Send in the Clowns."

Though we sang a lot, it didn't really occur to me that I might study music myself until I was in middle school and my parents were divorced, and my mother, among her other melancholy preoccupations, was attempting to learn Beethoven's "Moonlight Sonata," which, though I was mostly interested in the Top 40 of the time (the early seventies), I found mysterious, austere, and beautiful. That and Scott Joplin, who was experiencing a renaissance (owing to the score for *The Sting*), converted me into a music student briefly. Well, I remember also that we had weekly assemblies in the auditorium of my middle school and that a great number of these assemblies involved certain kinds of musical performance—African music, big bands, marching bands, music that was considered beneath contempt by my friends. I could not hide the way I reacted when there was music around, whether with tapping feet, or with impulsive singing, or with jubilation more egregious. Perhaps there were even shameful tears, because there were songs and varieties of music (bagpipes!) that caused weeping, and I can't really list all of these, because weeping to music ought to be a private affair, a tendency that I wasn't always sure I wanted people to know about. And so I prepared myself to try to learn something about music.

This involved, at this juncture, the piano, and a Russian guy who taught in a little office building in downtown New Canaan, Connecticut. And because I found the whole thing intimidating, embarrassing—being alone in a room with the Russian guy—because all my worldly, suburban friends thought that piano playing was somehow unmasculine, I was powerfully casual about my lessons (and I am embarrassed to say this, but I was *twelve*); there was the skipping of the recital on the day of the big town fair in New Canaan, after which I made up one story for my mother and another story for the Russian, who in due course sent home a note to my mother observing that though I had musical aptitude I didn't practice or give anything back at all. Soon the lessons lapsed. As the violin lessons had lapsed in the fourth grade, as the singing lessons lapsed the next year (when I was thirteen), as the piano lessons started and lapsed again (when I was seventeen), as the violin started and lapsed again (when I was forty-three).

What remained was passionate listening. These essays,

which were composed over so many years now, nearly fifteen years, are a record of that pursuit, and they return to the site of the first revelation of music as though there really were a *first* revelation and not an entire lifetime of listening. These essays try to explain what it is that so overwhelms this writer in song and instrumental music. It bears mentioning: the inability to *stop* trying to explain this imprinting, this mark that music has made on me, is why some of these pieces are longer than essays normally are. I can't stop. What these songs have done to me, in remaking me, is open me up to certain kinds of feelings and perceptions, even when much of what's in the world opposes any opening up at all.

Literature, exactly like certain moments in song—like that moment in "Hey Jude" when the Beatles get ready to sing the long coda, like that moment in "Celebrated Summer," by Hüsker Dü, when the acoustic guitar breaks through the wall of noise for a minute and reminds you that it's *recollection* that the song recommends unto you—literature, like music, wants openness, wants experiences, experiences of consciousness, experiences of sensation, and it wants these described in a way that is felicitous and sweet. Sweetness, gracefulness, these must be auditory phenomena when we are talking about prose, and if English is not the handsomest tongue, it has its moments, and these moments are literary moments or they are moments of song, and we are improved in these instances, made more charitable, more generous, and the two are therefore the same phenomena, music and literature, or so it seems to this writer, as if there is a certain order in these things, an order such as what J. S. Bach thought he heard when he made, over a great many years, what he so laboriously made. Literary effects are like harmonic intervals are like metrical feet are like time signatures are like cycles per second.

I always return to writing—in the harder moments; I come back to these alphanumerical keys here, as if it's only with words that I can make sense of the travails of consciousness. And yet when I come back to these keys, I find that music often comes with me. Much has changed, and the kinds of things I'm listening to are nothing like what I loved when I was first listening to the AM transistor radio under the sheet; now I find that sentimentality always drives me off, and a lot of what I like is music that most people would find hard to enjoy, but the experience is the same; I could still easily pass a whole night just spinning tunes on the stereo, and I could talk the ear off a friend, indulging in the little shades of differences between certain approaches to the popular song, certain recordings. I feel very excited and happy when I encounter a person with whom I can go on in this way, and you, consumer of books, are that person today.

The suspended fourth! Why so beautiful? The major seventh! Why so beautiful? And how do these instances of sonic beauty relate to that paragraph from Nabokov's "Signs and Symbols" that struck such a chord with me back when I read it in my undergraduate years *(She thought of the endless waves of pain that for some reason or other she and her husband had to endure; of the invisible giants hurting her boy in some unimaginable fashion; of the incalculable amount of tenderness contained in the world; of the fate of this tenderness, which is either crushed, or wasted, or transformed into madness; of neglected children humming to themselves in unswept corners; of beautiful weeds that cannot hide from the farmer and helplessly have to watch the shadow of his simian stoop leave mangled flowers in its wake, as the monstrous darkness approaches)*, though Nabokov himself professed a nearly complete estrangement from music? Now that I have been playing music more seriously for almost ten years, in a band, now that I know a tiny bit more about the architecture of the song, I am even more helpless in my admiration. And this book is my attempt to compile my musical affiliations and, in the explaining, to say to other passionate listeners, *Did you hear this? And did you hear it the way I heard it? And isn't it amazing? And do you have in your collection similar things that I should hear too?* I can think of no better place to put all these obsessions than in this volume. The best books are like albums of songs. Books and albums are of one vital substance. And I hope that vital substance is apparent here.

Against Cool

DISCLAIMERS FIRST! Whatever *cool* is or was—that term bandied about relentlessly from the 1950s to the present (by teens, by hipsters, by cultural critics, by baby boomers), that term which lately concludes many arrangements made between young people ("So I'll see you on St. Marks Place at seven? Cool")—I, your narrator, *do not now consider myself cool and never have been cool.* As a teenager, when questions about cool are at their most rigorous, when a lack of cool implies the possibility of future psychotherapy, I wore Levi's corduroys in the rainbow shades—yellow cords, red cords, powder-blue cords; I wore flannel slacks, Oxford button-downs, tweed jackets; my hair was not long enough to be beatnik or short enough to be clean-cut, and it *poofed* in ways that best recall Michael Landon during the *Little House on the Prairie* years; I liked to mix plaids; I loved my parents and was all broken up about the divorce; I preferred, where music was concerned, Cat Stevens, Yes, Jethro Tull, and other bands even more embarrassing to enumerate, when all around me was Grateful Dead and Rolling Stones; I went to boarding school;

I came from the suburbs; I read science fiction—for example, Frank Herbert's Dune trilogy, Isaac Asimov's Foundation books, everything Kurt Vonnegut ever published; I cried easily, was sentimental, loved New England autumns, made elaborate protestations of love from my high school radio show, fell in love as swiftly as I contracted head colds. In an area of inquiry where *credibility is everything*, where credentials are essential, where any deviation from this orthodoxy of the unstated and recondite is actionable, I was and am an interloper. I am, in fact, uncool.

This fact suggests an initial axiom on the subject: *If you have to talk about cool, you are not it.*

Second disclaimer: There is no Platonic category of *coolness*. As with what movies endure (your *Forrest Gump* is my *One Flew Over the Cuckoo's Nest*, or vice versa), as with what novels define an era, what is cool is often in dispute, quickly outmoded, neglected soon thereafter. The very proposition that we might say what *cool* exactly denotes is risky, inadvisable from the outset, since cool, in a sort of pop culture version of Heisenberg's uncertainty principle, alters what it pleasing finds. This book or record or movie or trend, hitherto cool, becomes precipitously irrelevant in the inexorable march of time. Cool, therefore, is not a moral question (like what is virtuous or what is beautiful), although its slipperiness may be of interest. Cool, in fact, is probably more easily reckoned by its absences than its presences (Del Close and John Brent made the same point on their 1959 Mercury album, *How to Speak Hip:* "It's easier to say what *isn't* cool"). Would we not all agree that if a school of thought or a trend becomes the subject of a feature in *Sixteen* or *People* or in like purveyors of mass trends, it is clearly *no longer cool?* Would we not agree that whatever *cool* is, it is not what the Sears catalogue once said was fashionable (foul-weather gear, camouflage pants), nor is cool apparent, in even the most infinitesimal degree, in the complete output of Michael Bolton, Barry Manilow, or Barbra Streisand, unless, and this is surely a disagreeable possibility, irony is cool?

Yet, as was once noted of the pornographic, *don't we know it when we see it?* We do. We do know *cool* when we see it. Or we can get pretty close. And therefore a discussion of its history is potentially useful. Because in an absence of clearly delineated American ethics, in a period of cultural relativism, in a political environment in which both American parties have amplified their rhetoric to such a degree that the other side is *beneath contempt,* in which religion seems no longer able to rationally or effectively deploy its messages except through moral intimidation or force, in which families are no longer the ethical bulwarks they felt themselves to be in the past—in such a millennial instant, cool has become *the* system of ethics for the young in America. Cool, it seems, is one thing that kids believe in. Cool is what they talk about, cool is what motivates them, cool is what they occasionally live and die for, at least in some precincts. So what are they saying, these kids, when they say something is *cool?*

Well, the *OED* gives us early Teutonic and Anglo-Saxon derivations for the word: *cólian, cole* (as in *Merlin, or the early history of King Arthur,* circa 1450: "As they that wolde ride in the cole of the mornynge"); *colen, kola, cule, cull, coole* (Coverdale, 1535: "Like as the winter coole in the harvest"), prior to our first modern usages (as in Addison, 1713: "But see where Lucia, . . . / Amid the cool of yon high marble arch, / Enjoys the noon-day breeze"). The word was in play throughout the nineteenth century, first as a description of temperature and then figuratively as a term (noun or verb) that might connote *mood* as well, as in Lord Macaulay's *History of England* (1848): "The lapse of time which cools the ardour of friends whom he has left behind"; it also turned up as a synonym for impudence, in, e.g., Durivage and Burnham's *Stray Subjects* (1846): "You are the coolest specimen of a genuine scamp that it has ever been my ill luck to meet with." There were any number of slang idioms making use of *cool: cooling one's coppers*, in which we treat the dehydration from a prior night's drinking; *cooling the heels*, or waiting, dating back to the mid-eighteenth century; *cool as a cucumber*, from 1700 on; a *cool* sum of money (*a cool million*, e.g.), from the 1720s; *cool pleasure*, from the 1820s on, as in Cather's *Death Comes for the Archbishop* (1927)—"He took a cool pleasure in stripping the Indians of their horses"—and *cool crape*, which has connoted a funeral shroud since the early nineteenth century. Perhaps it's not *church* or *door* in the pantheon of often-employed Anglo-Saxon words; nonetheless *cool* has had a real popularity since the dawn of our tongue.

The contemporary usage, the one with which we're concerned here, seems to date from the end of World War II (only ninety years or so after Lord Macaulay) and, like so many twentieth-century English-language phenomena, to find its initial articulation on this side of the Atlantic in popular culture. In particular, what was *cool*, after the globe had finished its convulsions, was a moment in the history of jazz. In the late 1940s, Miles Davis, who was until then most prominently known as a sideman in Charlie Parker's band, convened an ensemble, with Gil Evans and Gerry Mulligan as arrangers (Davis and Evans would later go on to work on seminal orchestral jazz albums like *Porgy and Bess* and *Sketches of Spain*), designed to address some problems with the form in which they were working. The Miles Davis Nonet, as it came to be known, featured six horns (trumpet, trombone, French horn, tuba, alto and baritone sax), piano, bass, and drums, and was conceived as a reaction against bebop. This bebop style, which was preeminently influential at the same time and which is credited mainly to Davis's former boss, Charlie Parker, and to Dizzy Gillespie, was fast and technically virtuosic, as Davis himself points out in his autobiography, *Miles:* "Bird and Diz played this hip, real fast thing, and if you weren't a fast listener, you couldn't catch the humor or the feeling in their music.... Bird and Diz were great, fantastic, challenging—but they weren't sweet."

Davis's nonet, and the sessions that came out of it, had a different intent. Sweetness and melody were their ambition, a less fiery tone. The results, dubbed *Birth of the Cool* by Pete Rugolo, an A&R man at Davis's record company, were, according to no less an authority than Count Basie, "slow and strange but good, really good." Davis himself says, "We shook people's ears a little softer than Bird or Diz did, took the music more mainstream. That's all it was." Davis sees this softness in the *Birth of the Cool* sessions as a gambit to ensure the safety of *white* listeners in an idiom that was primarily African American, but this seems now to understate unnecessarily the accomplishments of *Birth of the Cool.* The jazz of Miles Davis's nonet is evocative in its restraint, is supple and sure-footed, both in the composed passages and in the way Davis's solos eschew vibrato and begin to articulate the vulnerability and the ferocity that came to characterize his playing later. This jazz is *cool,* then, in Davis's devotion to expression first, to the emotional center of jazz, rather than to athleticism, rather than to mastery of an instrument.

Would Rugolo's offhand title for the nonet sessions be the first reference to this ubiquitous term as we hear it so much these days? There are a lot of opinions on the subject. Eric Partridge's *Dictionary of Slang and Unconventional English* gives the sense of *cool* as "good and modern" as a term in jazz circles since 1945, but can give no source but an article from the *Observer* of 1956. Partridge also offers *cool* as "(of a singer) slow and husky," since 1948, or coeval with the Miles Davis sessions. *Harper's Magazine,* in an article of 1950, is meanwhile *hip to the craze,* noting "the Bop musician's use of 'cool' instead of 'hot' as a word of the highest praise." But this usage may predate the Davis sessions by years, as in Charlie Parker's 1947 recording of "Cool Blues," or in Doris Day's 1941 recording of J. P. Johnson's "Keep Cool, Fool." Gary Giddins says, "Black musicians in the 1930s used *cool* in the literal sense, to contain feeling, to play with restraint." Still, toward midcentury, jazz and popular music begin to affect the meaning of the word *cool* finally and permanently, so that Macaulay or Addison would have been surprised by its connotation à la mode. Partridge makes this transition abundantly clear, quoting F. E. L. Priestley: "*Cool* became a word of praise when *hot* ceased to be one; that is, when hot jazz went out of fashion to be displaced by bop or bebop, a later—a 'progressive' or 'modern jazz.'"

There's an implicit cultural fusion in this way of speaking. That is, a white arranger and A&R man (Rugolo) coins the term to describe sessions by a black musician (Davis), who is himself attempting a music that fuses elements of a black idiom (jazz, and especially the style and form of bebop) with a white style (a jazz slower and more given to melody than to loose improvisation). This is the way words are generated in America, I'm trying to say, by use and reuse, by experiment and malapropism, across a great spectrum of cultures and subcultures and communities ("hot" jazz originated in France, and "cool" jazz was reactively American), and so in this usage jazz serves not only as the locus for the meaning of the word *cool*, but also as a laboratory for the way in which the term gets disseminated: spontaneously, loosely in an improvisatory fashion, as a delineator of passions and moods and styles. Which is to say that if *cool* is an example, our American popular argot is now finally multiethnic and vigorous across boundaries of race, class, and religion. We chatter, and chatter is good, and in the groove of chatter words become flexible and porous and intoxicating, and they perform a breathy *ars nova*.

Given this kind of energy coming out of the jazz world (there wasn't rock and roll yet), it's not surprising that the next group to champion the term *cool* and to make it a part of the daily language, at least according to myth, was a mostly white group of writers and thinkers who brought to the term a long-lasting value and meaning in the margins of postwar America. I mean the Beats. Those coiners and harvesters of new locutions, of *hip* and *gone cat*, etc. Their appearance in American culture had quite a bit to do with *cool*.

Oddly, though, Jack Kerouac, who in 1948 articulated the term *beat* to describe his generation (borrowing it from Herbert Huncke), infrequently employed the word *cool* himself. Using up-to-the-minute and very *cool* technology—a recent CD-ROM publication on Kerouac and the Beats entitled *A Jack Kerouac ROMnibus*—I have been able to do a full-scale search on the appearance of the term in a large sampling of Kerouac works. Although I can find few appearances in selections of his poems, or in selections from *The Subterraneans* or *The Town and the City*, his later work, *The Dharma Bums*, does have eight incidental appearances of the word *cool*, seven of which are used in connection with weather descriptions ("The trail would suddenly come into a *cool* shady part" or "Then as it got *cool* in the late afternoon" [italics mine]). Only one passage seems tangentially to address the issue of contemporary cool, yet it is far from conclusive: "Whenever people dropped in to visit us at the cottage, I'd always put my red bandana over the little wall lamp and put out the ceiling light to make a nice *cool* red dim scene to sit and drink wine and talk in." (By way of a control sample, I also checked for the word *hip* in *Dharma Bums*—three mentions, of which two had to do with an anatomical part—and the word *beat*, of which all eight mentions had to do with drumming or fistfights.) I did find, however, that the Viking Press advertisement for *Dharma Bums* used the word *cool* in its plot summary, in the contemporary fashion: "They come swinging down to San Francisco—hot girls and cool jazz, to wild parties and wild poets…"

Meanwhile, in a passage toward the end of *On the Road*—Kerouac's sloppy, joyous, and fabulously passionate rant about youth in the late forties—the author does begin to articulate what *cool* might mean in a broader, nonmusical context, apart from the idiom of jazz. The passage in question takes place in chapter four, in the third section of the book, which begins with encomiums about the jazz written and played then by African Americans. Black jazz. The scene is San Francisco (to which city "cool" jazz migrated later in its existence) and features Dean Moriarity (a.k.a. Neal Cassady, who in any true account of *cool* must be said to carry the torch from the Beat years to the "hippie" enclave of Ken Kesey, the Merry Pranksters, and the Grateful Dead) and Sal Paradise, a.k.a. Kerouac. Here they are visiting a jazz club on the Barbary Coast:

> Out we jumped in the warm, mad night, hearing a wild tenorman bawling horn across the way…. The behatted tenorman was blowing at the peak of a wonderfully satisfactory free idea, a rising and falling riff that went from "EE-yah!" to a crazier "EE-de-lee-yah!"… Uproars of music and the tenorman *had it* and everybody knew he had it.

What is the celebrated *it* of this formulation? Kerouac doesn't take up the question right away, because he is busy with further descriptions of jazz soloing: "The tenorman hauled back and stamped his foot and blew down a hoarse, laughing blast, and drew breath, and raised the horn and blew high, wide, and screaming in the air.... Dean was in a trance." And later, during a ballad: "Here we were dealing with the pit and prune-juice of poor beat life itself in the God-awful streets of man, so the tenorman said it and sang it, 'Close—your—' and blew it way up to the ceiling and through the stars and on out—'Ey-y-y-y-y-es.'" The values of jazz, the intangible values of the music, abstractions about spontaneity and feeling, are in the process of being transferred by Kerouac from the music onto the players of the music. What's cool about jazz has become a characteristic of jazzmen. This becomes clearer as the scene begins to involve carousing around town with the aforementioned tenorman ("Yes! Ain't nothin I like better than good kicks!") rather than listening to him play. Here, as in Kerouac's fanciful prose, jazz becomes a way of life rather than a musical idiom; jazz is a process, jazz is a series of intentions, jazz is a style.

Thus, in the next scene, *cool* does turn up—in a nascent stage—and it's during a rather homophobic passage (though "Carlo Marx," the Ginsberg character, and "Old Bull Lee," who stands in for William Burroughs, as well as Neal Cassady and perhaps even Kerouac himself, were practicing homosexuals with varying frequency, Kerouac was certainly not *gone* enough yet to find gay life *cool*):

We saw a horrible sight in the bar: a white hipster fairy had come in wearing a Hawaiian shirt and was asking the big drummer if he could sit in.... The fairy sat down at the tubs and they started the beat of a jump number and he began stroking the snares with soft

goofy bop brushes, swaying his neck with that compla-
cent Reichi-analyzed ecstasy that doesn't mean anything except too much tea and soft foods and goofy
kicks on the *cool* order. But he didn't care. He smiled
joyously into space and kept the beat.

A similar and less troubling usage appears in a 1950 letter
from Kerouac to Cassady: "A raw mind and a cool mind are
two different minds. The raw mind is usually associated with
the physical life, whether athletic, work, or just beat...; the
cool mind is the intellectual emphasis and the physical counterpart of it is a kind of gracefulness...a gracefulness that is
almost effeminate."

Cool here mirrors the difficulties of the "cool" jazz style
after Miles Davis's *Birth of the Cool*. What is cool, after Miles
moved on to his Gil Evans collaborations and then on to his
terrific quintet (with John Coltrane et al.), is what's white,
what's deracinated, what's goofy, perverse, cerebral. The jazz
of Chet Baker, with (as Gary Giddins puts it) "his movie-star
good looks"; Dave Brubeck's academic, intellectual jazz: odd
time signatures and Middle Eastern modalities. And yet,
despite these judgments, directly after Kerouac's brief invocation of the term *cool* in chapter four of *On the Road*, he takes on,
at last, the task of defining the "it" his tenorman "had" at the
opening of the passage, for the simple reason that these
values—*cool* and the ineffable IT—are related, are harmoni-
ous, are consonant:

I wanted to know what "IT" meant. "Ah well"—Dean
laughed—"now you're asking me impon-der-ables—

ahem! Here's a guy and everybody's there, right? ... All of a sudden somewhere in the middle of the chorus he *gets* it—everybody looks up and knows, and they listen; he picks it up and carries. Time stops. He's filling empty space with the substance of our lives, confessions of his belly button strain, remembrance of ideas, rehashes of old blowing. He has to blow across bridges and come back and do it with such infinite feeling soul-exploratory for the tune of the moment that everybody knows it's not the tune that counts but IT."

"Then," Kerouac says, "I begin talking; I never talked so much in my life."

This is *cool*, finally, in its transitional moment, in which it is embodied in Kerouac; he is cool, IT is cool; and cool crests, perhaps not yet in the explicitly modern usage of the word, but rather as a way of carrying oneself, a way of marking an attitude that extends beyond language and the capacity of language to denote, that preempts the civilizing and hypocritical layers of *straight culture*, that focuses instead on a deportment, an ephemeral and unstable aspect, a perfume of the infinite, a wisp of the spiritual, in which improvisation and spontaneity enable numinous predisposition, access to the ether. IT's not a product or an extract or a medication; IT is cool, and cool is an approach characterized by feeling, by passions, and you find it in the riotous voice of Kerouac's narratives, as well as in the riffing of Ginsberg's poems in the later fifties. Among his catalogue of great minds *destroyed by madness* are included "angel-headed hipsters":

who bared their brains to Heaven under the El and saw
Mohammedan angels
    staggering on tenement roofs illuminated,

who passed through universities with radiant cool *eyes*
hallucinating...

As you also find *cool* in the withering comedy of William
Burroughs, in his *lapsed idealism* (as Mary McCarthy put it);
even the opening of *Naked Lunch* (1959), in its recoiling from
the warmth, seems to prefigure the rising of cool as a reptilian
cultural imperative: "I can feel the heat closing in, feel them
out there making their moves, setting up their devil doll stool
pigeons, crooning over my spoon and dropper I throw away at
Washington Square Station, vault a turnstile and two flights
down the iron stairs, catch an uptown A train." *Heat* is slang
for the authorities (dating to about 1936, according to Partridge, or only slightly ahead of the whole "hot" and "cool"
jazz issue), but here it's *heat* that is opposed by the narrator, and
this narrator is *cool*—as any reader would agree who has drifted
through the icy nightmare of *Naked Lunch*, one of the century's great examples of sangfroid. Yet it is also a novel beautiful
and irate in its melancholy:

America is not a young land; it is old and dirty and evil
before the settlers, before the Indians. The evil is there
waiting. And always cops: smooth college-trained state
cops, practiced, apologetic patter, electronic eyes
weigh your car and luggage, clothes and face; snarling

big city dicks, soft-spoken country sheriffs with something black and menacing in old eyes color of a faded gray flannel shirt.

Burroughs, that "gone cat" in *On the Road*, opposes the power of the state with the renegade but slightly detached passions of individuals. Cool individuals. The state usually wins, but the logic, as in Kerouac and Ginsberg, is passionately individualistic. Thus, in Burroughs we get an implied articulation of *cool* as (again according to Partridge) "retaining compete control—or so the addict believes—while 'turned on' (drug exhilarated)" and, by extension, staying *cool* when the cops come for the bust.

I loved this Beat writing as a young reader. The velocity and spirit, the opposition to the stuffiness of academic writing (to the monolithic sobriety of New Criticism), the sheer, dizzy glee. What the great Beat writers did for American letters was appropriate America's one truly indigenous music form, jazz, and fuse the lessons of that music with the transcendentalism that had been irrigating American literature for a century. The Beats yoked Miles and Bird to Whitman and Emerson. And by the late fifties and sixties, the cool Beat idiom had become as frankly spiritual as its transcendentalist models. The theme becomes explicit in their work, as in Kerouac's 1960 journal entry: "Anybody can become a 'hipster' O Mailer... Broyard,... et al., but even the dumbest college kid who believes in God is beat, beatific and blessed." Unfortunately, the ambition concealed in this "transcendentalist" message was ultimately lost on Kerouac: the later journal entries, from the mid- to late sixties, by which time he was *drinking around the clock*, are grueling to read, it must be said. Kerouac squandered his talent fantastically. Perhaps the process ("First thought, best thought," as Ginsberg said) and the freedom of Beat activity, the blissful singularity of it, couldn't be sustained for long. Both Burroughs and Kerouac (and Cassady later) resorted to considerable amounts of drugs to catalyze their work, and the cost was the highest of all costs. They left their best work behind while young.

Meanwhile, *cool*, through its relationship to the movement of the Beats, began to assume its new shape in other efforts. For example, in the person of Gwendolyn Brooks, an African American poet writing in 1959: "We real cool. We / Left school. We / Lurk late. We / Strike straight." Or in Lawrence Ferlinghetti's *A Coney Island of the Mind*, adapting (in 1958) the narrative of Christ's passion to a Beat vocabulary: "You're hot / they tell him / And they cool him / They stretch him on the Tree to cool / And everybody after that / is always making models / of this Tree / . . . Only he don't come down / from His Tree / Him just hang there / on His Tree / looking real Petered out / and real cool." In Ferlinghetti's poem (which, in earlier stanzas, also makes use of *hip* and *cat* in the retelling of the Galilean odyssey) all the possible *cools* intersect, the cooling-down cool, the cool of jazz, "the cool of self-possession," as Partridge gives it. The Lamb of God *unites meanings*, makes contemporary slang stick, as in Kerouac's beatification of the Beat. *Jesus Christ, one cool, hep cat.*

By 1960, though, the Beats, with their jazz and their tea and their smack and their cross-country driving escapades, were like Neanderthals in the era of the Cro-Magnon. Something had happened in the intervening years, something had diverted the fickle attentions of young people, and I mean, of course, *the idiot bastard cousin* of "cool" jazz or bebop—the dread menace of rock and roll. Antimusic, devil's spawn. Music of hellions. If jazz was a fertile crescent for American colloquial language, rock and roll, its very name a slang term for *getting it on*, would prove to be a hothouse, a *bop a loo bop a lop bam boom*. From rock and roll and its culture came terminology like *boogie, boogaloo, doo-wop, shang-a-lang, mojo, punk, bump and grind, hardcore, hip-hop*, and *grunge*, and many other manic turns of phrase, sacred and profane. Therefore, rock and roll has much to say about cool.

Jerry Leiber and Mike Stoller, who (in the period before artists wrote their own material) were the preeminent mythicists and fabulators of rock and roll, invoked the sociology of cool occasionally. *Cool* is in one of their hits written for Elvis Presley, "Fools Fall in Love": "Fools fall in love in a hurry / ... Oh! They got their love torches burning / When they should be playing it cool"; and it's in one of their finer tunes for the black vocal group the Coasters, "Three Cool Cats" (a prominent early cover for the Beatles): "Three cool cats... / Parked on the corner in a beat-up car / ... Three cool chicks... / Are walking down the street." Danny and the Juniors, in the 1958 number one "At the Hop," had a little to say about *cool*—"You can swing it, you can groove it / You can really start to move it at the hop / Where the jockey is the smoothest / And the music is the coolest"—as did the Del Vikings in their 1957 hit, "Cool Shake." And if you'll pardon a few anachronistic examples, I can finish the catalogue: the Beatles lifted the "playing it cool" formulation from "Fools Fall in Love" for their hit "Hey Jude," the bestselling single for the entire decade from 1960 to 1969 ("For well you know that it's a fool who plays it cool / By making his world a little colder"). There's "Cool Jerk," the infinitely covered classic. And, on the margins, the Stooges with "Real Cool Time," composed in 1970 and consisting mainly of repetitions of the line "We will have a real cool time tonight." There's the Hollies, with their "Long Cool Woman (In a Black Dress)"; there's Kool and the Gang; there's the Little River Band, with "Cool Change," and Pablo Cruise (in 1981), with "Cool Love." There's Squeeze, with "Cool for Cats." Rickie Lee Jones, "Coolsville." There's the Blues Brothers gorging themselves on a "cool water sandwich." There's John Cale's "Indistinct Notion of Cool." Queen punned on rockabilly cool in the 1980 hit "Crazy Little Thing Called Love": "She gives me hot and cold fever / Then she leaves me in a cool, cool sweat." Bruce Springsteen raised the issue in his account of Vietnam vets coming home, "Born in the U.S.A.": "I'm a long gone daddy in the U.S.A. / . . . I'm a cool rocking daddy in the U.S.A." David Bowie used it in "Diamond Dogs"; Sparks used it in "Cool Places"; Devo used it in their awesome satire "Through Being Cool." There are many other examples.

But though rock and roll, since the fifties, had and has a lot to say *about* cool, it doesn't much *embody* the tricky concept. Not in the way Miles Davis or John Coltrane or Jack Kerouac embodied cool. Here we have to venture forth with a number of finely tuned discernments. Notwithstanding the Sun sessions version of "Mystery Train" or the spontaneous portions of the 1968 "comeback" special in which he jammed with

Scotty Moore et al., *Elvis, it turns out, was not entirely cool.* He was alluring, erotic, intense, but for the purposes of this argument he didn't have IT. I make this judgment, in part, after having spent an afternoon reading Elvis's lyrics in their entirety (A to Z) and after having ruminated over the vexing fact of Elvis *after* the 1968 special, the Elvis who sang "America the Beautiful" and "When the Saints Go Marching In," the Las Vegas Elvis, the Elvis who accepted a special citation from President Nixon, the Elvis of the later movies, the Elvis who presided, in his last tours, over the very kind of hack musicianship that rock and roll was designed to slay. *Elvis was not cool.* Elvis was an entertainer with a grand sentimental streak. An entertainer capable of mesmerizing and delighting. But he wasn't cool. And you know what? The Beatles, except for few fleeting moments ("Strawberry Fields Forever," "Dear Prudence," "Twist and Shout," side three of *The White Album,* most of *Revolver*), even when they got *beyond fab,* were not really cool either. Anything having to do with Paul McCartney, it should be clear at this late date, is not and cannot be *cool,* no matter how hummable the melodies. John struggled valiantly to forge a credibility for his fellow Liverpudlians, but even he ("[Just Like] Starting Over") ultimately succumbed to professionalism. The Rolling Stones are not now cool (although they may have been in one song: "Gimme Shelter"), and the Who are not now cool (Broadway!), and the Clash were not terribly cool, and Talking Heads were not cool, though David Byrne in his 1985 book version of *True Stories* used the word *cool* often enough that his editor, Nan Graham, had to suggest alternatives. In fact, rock and roll (and by extension most popular music), by virtue of its relation to the promotion and business of large multinational entertainment providers, has, since the sixties, when the British artists first trammeled our shores, traded in the possibility of *cool* for a longevity associated with paychecks. Rock and roll has become a job opportunity for younger people not otherwise gifted with business acumen. Thus we arrive at that captioned American postcard from the eighties of the kid with the green mohawk: "Too cool for school, too dumb for the real world…Guess I'll start a band."

Myself, I lived by rock and roll; I learned as much from it as I did from *Moby-Dick* and *The Scarlet Letter*, I wept over certain songs and albums, I waited breathlessly for new releases, I quoted song lyrics when asked to quote poetry in English class, I learned about the passions through the passions of forty-fives. But lately the ecstasy of three minutes and fifteen seconds of guitar racket is elusive. Where did the promise go? Where is the deliverance, the goofy, cool intoxication rock and roll once accomplished? Where is a rock and roll about which might be said, as Richard Meltzer opined in his (1970) *Aesthetics of Rock*, "For an experience to be artistically viable, it must be 'cool,' that is, it must be serious enough to attract reflective interest and primary emotional response and yet contain a tinge of the comic or benign just great enough to prevent overindulgence in this seriousness."

Well, there are a few examples left. There is some vestigial *cool* in the old battered idiom. These exceptions have to do, mainly, with the conjunction of Beat process with aspects of jazz and American transcendentalism, with the beatified emphasis on the spontaneous and the ephemeral and the excitable and the spiritual, and the way in which these things stew with the counterculture of the late sixties. Bob Dylan, Jerry Garcia, Joni Mitchell, Neil Young, Patti Smith, the Velvet Underground, Marvin Gaye, Nina Simone, were *cool* in the rock era. The Bob Dylan of "Subterranean Homesick Blues": "Don't follow leaders / Watch the parkin' meters." The Bob Dylan who said, "To live outside the law you must be honest," who said, "I came out of the wilderness and just naturally fell in with the Beat scene." The Marvin Gaye of "What's Going On?" The Patti Smith of *Horses.* The Velvet Underground of "Sister Ray." The Jerry Garcia of *Live/Dead.*

That these rock-and-roll artists became very popular, that *cool* became with them pandemic among the American young— these facts demonstrate the *metastasis* that took place in the realm of youth culture during the sixties. In my history of cool, the sixties are when the word *cool* goes from being meaningful to becoming depleted. As Thomas Frank notes in his fascinating (if uncool by virtue of excessive theorizing) *Conquest of Cool,* this has everything to do with the attention of straight society, with articles in *Time, Life,* and *Mademoiselle* ("Flaming Cool Youth of San Francisco Poetry"), with Leonard Bernstein's *West Side Story* (and its theme entitled "Cool"), with Maynard G. Krebs (the televised Beatnik of *The Many Loves of Dobie Gillis*), with the mass attention that signified the creative exhaustion of the Beat revolution, and with this exhaustion the advent of the time in which merchandisers and advertisers began to define cool culture as a demographic and began to sell things to this group, as well as to make of it a commodity in itself, a category of status that America might find a way *to purchase:*

> Before the 1960s, young people had always been an established part of marketing and a staple image in advertising art, largely because of their still unformed tastes and their position as trend leaders. This was especially true in the 1920s. But during the 1960s, this standard approach changed. No longer was youth merely a "natural" demographic to which appeals could be pitched: suddenly youth became a consuming position to which all could aspire.

Frank's account—for example, of Pepsi's shift toward an image of "Pepsi hip" in the late sixties—captures an essential aspect of the way youth culture is deployed in business. There is, in Frank's view, an inextricable link between "straight" culture and the hip margins: "Now the copy [in 1966] is smart-alec in tone rather than inviting, and the overt explanations of 'Pepsi-ness' are replaced with hip phrases and anti-establishment wit. An ad depicting surfers describing them as 'Board members / of the Pepsi Generation.'"

But, while effectively accounting for the way merchandising concepts get reproduced in our civilization of signs, Frank fails to deal exhaustively with the *meaning* of a word like *cool* (which, beyond the title, doesn't get much treatment in *The Conquest of Cool* anyhow, not like *hip*, which gets *charts:* "Hip Appliance Advertising, *Life* Magazine, as a Percentage of All Appliance Advertising, 1958–1972"). Frank's book avoids describing what was being marketed in the sixties and seventies so that it may instead concentrate on *how:* "Apart from certain obvious exceptions at either end of the spectrum of commodification (represented, say, by the MC5 at one end and the Monkees at the other), it was and remains difficult to distinguish precisely between authentic counterculture and fake."

It remains difficult to say what counterculture *means.* It remains difficult to define *cool.* It remains difficult to think of a tribe of underemployed hitchhikers, drug dealers, and poets, to take the square view, as *meaning much of anything at all.* Advertising, according to the scheme Thomas Frank describes, simply puts *cool* in play, and then, through a large-scale distribution, makes it accessible to a horde of Americans, in this way *moving some product.* Yet this process shouldn't imply that the condition of *cool* doesn't or couldn't, in some fertile way, *exist.* Just because a word is used to market a product shouldn't disqualify the word, shouldn't reduce it to mere signifier. If *cool* gets used, pragmatically speaking, it must get used to connote something. And maybe this is best demonstrated in an example, in the case of the American product most frequently associated with the word *cool* in the past three decades: the mentholated cigarette brand Kool, manufactured by Brown & Williamson.

Kool is B&W's flagship brand and has been marketed nationally in this country since the mid-thirties — or not long before the first appearance of the word *cool* in jazz subculture. At the dawn of its robust life, the Kool advertising campaign made no mention of *cool* in the contemporary sense (the name Kool probably referred to the taste of menthol). In fact, the original

Kool advertising copy merely reflected the fact that Kool carried coupons: "Free coupons bring handsome gifts." But in 1962, the advertising strategy for Kool cigarettes shifted suddenly toward—as an official B&W brand history terms it—a "problem/solution" approach. The problem addressed in the 1962 advertisements, according to these official communications, was a *lack of cool*, and the solution, obtainable through lighting up Kool cigarettes (which in 1962 had a 2.9 percent market share of total cigarette consumption), was "extra coolness." As B&W says, "Kool was the only U.S. domestic cigarette to make so specific and proven a claim."

If Kool cigarettes, by virtue of their title, somehow affected the word choice, the *cool*, of jazz cats in the late thirties and early forties (in "Keep Cool, Fool" etc.) through the conjunction of their mentholated brand and the dawn of bebop, and if Kool influenced the renovation of the old Anglo-Saxon word *cool* and from there seeped into the values and the subconscious of jazz subculture, by the late fifties the brand was nonetheless playing catch-up. Suddenly it was the Beats and the kids who were deploying the slang. In the late fifties and early sixties, Kool was symbiotically pitching itself back to these very wordsmiths it had first influenced. By 1969, for example, the linkage between *cool* and Kool was entirely explicit in the brand's courting of women smokers with the "Lady Be Cool" line (rekindled in the 1997 hip-hop-oriented "B Kool" billboard campaign). Kool cigarettes, it was now clear, provided *cool*. That's how they were sold. Then, in 1975, in a gesture of unmitigated postmodernism, Kool sponsored its first jazz festival, yoking the music to the cigarette once and for all. The festival has existed ever since.

The proof of all this adroit word choice has been in the bottom line: the Kool "problem/solution" campaign of 1962 resulted in an additional percentage point of the market share, as well as an additional 4.5 billion units sold. At their peak, in the late seventies, after two decades of sales increases, total Kool sales were on the order of 59.4 billion units per annum.

All of which is to say that in the sixties, *cool* continued to be a major site for linguistic play. As in the postwar years, when a jazzy spontaneity was evident in the way the word was used, by the mid-sixties any number of *cool* idioms had become abundantly popular in the argot of kids. *Keep cool, cool it, cool out, cool in, cool hand, cool cat, cool as a virgin, cool beans, coolcock, in the cooler, cool off, cool one*, were all part of the hip dictionary. From a term that mainly described a certain kind of music in 1945, *cool* had multiplied and subdivided, like the various constituencies using it, geometrically, exponentially. Corporations tried to co-opt the tongue of the kids, as above, by making use of *cool*, but the kids were acting simultaneously to co-opt the language of business for their own comic revolutionary ends. As is most often the case when there is real enthusiasm and real love of language, meaning proved more powerful than merchandise. Street language, street impulses, the vigorous solecisms of folks, won. You also see this kind of revenger's energy in the case of Kool-Aid, which, in the sixties, became important to American cool culture in a very novel way.

Tom Wolfe's *Electric Kool-Aid Acid Test* (1968) is a good primary text for tracking the motility of *cool* in the sixties, not only because Wolfe himself deploys the term—in frank imitation of the lingo he heard at the time—but also because he quotes it frequently among interview subjects: writer Ken

Kesey and his band of mid-sixties LSD-dropping Day-Glo Merry Pranksters, who, for a brief couple of years, wrought a very cool havoc on the west side of the American continent and stirred up, in the process, a bona fide *alternative lifestyle*. Wolfe, for all his bravado, is attuned to the movement of ideas and to their tectonic shiftings. And perhaps for this reason, he opens *Electric Kool-Aid* with a witty pun: "That's good thinking there, Cool Breeze. Cool Breeze is a kid with three or four days' beard sitting next to me on the stamped metal bottom of the open back part of a pickup truck." Cool Breeze, who turns up but once more in *Electric Kool-Aid*, is here not only a signifier for the slightly awkward but ambitious *cool* of the Pranksters, but, as a hippie primitive, he is also faintly comic amid the run-down technology of a good old American pickup truck.

And that's just at the outset. Wolfe uses the word *cool* a lot: "The Chief; out on bail. I expect the whole random carnival to well up into a fluorescent yahoo of incalculably insane proportions. In fact, everybody is quiet. It is all cool." Or: "Some of the old Perry Lane luminaries' *cool* was tested and they were found wanting"; "Chuck is one of the nicest people in the world and Sandy can trust him. If only he can remain cool." Etc.

In addition to using the word, Wolfe does a fine job of getting at the cool of Kesey's ideas, at their Beat origins. Here he is certainly amplifying Kerouac's notion of the unstated IT of cool as it was expressed in the California of the mid-sixties:

The Life—that *feeling*—The Life—the late 1940s early 1950s American Teenage Drive-In Life was *precisely* what it was all about—but how could you tell anyone about it?

But of course!—the *feeling*—out here at night, free, with the motor running and the adrenaline flowing, cruising in the neon glories of the new American night—it was very Heaven to be the first wave of the most extraordinary kids in the history of the world— only 15, 16, 17 years old, dressed in the *haute couture* of pink Oxford shirts, sharp pants, snaky half-inch belts, fast shoes—with all this Straight-6 and V-8 power underneath and all this neon glamour overhead, which somehow tied in with the technological superheroics of the jet, TV, atomic subs, ultrasonics—Postwar American suburbs—glorious world!

Wolfe is rendering a late-night drug-induced rant of Kesey's. It's a spirited and funny monologue (which goes on for about three pages), and it's clearly indebted to Kerouac's high style, with a Kerouacian emphasis on the evanescent, uncanny aspect of life ("It couldn't be put into words anyway"). But there are a few telling alterations to the Beat construct of cool as it is recycled in Kesey's posse. Though Neal Cassady, the Dean Moriarty of *On the Road*, was present in this band of Merry Pranksters— he was the driver of the famous Prankster bus (and otherwise seemed to stand mainly on the fringes of the action)—and though Ginsberg turned up periodically at Kesey's house, though even Kerouac made an appearance in the Pranksters' "movie" (when the Pranksters were in NYC)—"Here was Kerouac and here was Kesey and here was Cassady in between them, once the mercury for Kerouac and the whole Beat Generation and now the mercury for Kesey and the whole—what?—something wilder and weirder out on the road"—in spite of a perfect Beat pedigree, there was wide-eyed optimism somehow missing from the Pranksters' activity, especially later on. The Beat process was somewhat intact ("Kesey's explicit teachings were cryptic, metaphorical; parables, aphorisms"), but not the *meaning.* Wolfe says of the hippie kids of the period, "They had no particular philosophy, just a little leftover Buddhism and Hinduism from the *beat* period." The message got a little incoherent, a little malevolent, a little *white.* But that's the least of it.

With a movement among the Pranksters toward vagueness and inactivity and, on occasion, even pathology (Sandy Lehmann-Haupt's psychotic break on the bus that no one quite bothered about), the notion of cool also slid sideways, so that some activities that would not have been *cool* earlier, in the fifties, were now routinized, made tolerable. The meaning of cool shifted slightly, away from the *spiritus mundi.* There are two passages in *Electric Kool-Aid* that depict this transition. The first has to do with the meeting between Kesey's Pranksters and the motorcycle gang called the Hells Angels.

Kesey met the Angels through Hunter S. Thompson, Wolfe tells us, and took to them right away. Kesey's lumberjack charm apparently didn't put off the Angels either—"Kesey was a stud who was just as tough as they were"—and they accepted an invitation to party with Kesey's group immediately. The Angels, as they arrived at Kesey's domain, were a little reticent at first, but soon they fused with the loose, unpredictable flow of things, so much so that even Wolfe seems nearly tolerant at the ensuing carnival, at least initially: "The Hell's Angels party went on for two days and the cops never moved in. Everybody, Angels and Pranksters, had a righteous time and no heads were broken." While the democratic principles of this meeting seem honorable according to a Beat sort of cool—even an Angel was an *angel* if he was *on the bus*—the passive acceptance of, for example, a gang rape scene that took place at the powwow chilled my readerly affections for Prankster activity considerably:

> The girl had her red and white dress pushed up around her chest, and two or three would be on her at once, between her legs, sitting on her face in the sick ochre light of the shack with much lapping and leering and bubbling and gulping through the furzes of pubic hair while sweat and semen glistened on the highlights of her belly and thighs and she twitched and moaned, not in protest, however, in a kind of drunken bout of God knew what and men with no pants on were standing around, cheering, chiding, waiting for their turn, or their second turn, or the third until she had been fenestrated in various places at least fifty times.

Given that the woman in question was drunk or drugged or both, not at the peak of her decision-making capabilities, young and vulnerable, one wonders if she still, to this day, views this particular *afternoon delight* as consensual, or if *gang bang* (as Wolfe terms it) is really the correct terminology. Whatever the scene was, it sure wasn't *cool*. Nonetheless, in concluding the passage, Wolfe uses the word again, as if out of an anxiety about the whole violent Angels scene: "The Angels respected [Kesey] and they weren't about to screw around with him. He was one of the coolest guys they had ever come across."

As a footnote, it's worth noting that Ginsberg, too, whom the Angels tolerated (according to Wolfe) as a sort of wise freak, an imponderable, wrote about this cultural event in "First Party at Ken Kesey's with Hell's Angels":

Cool black night thru the redwoods

. . . .

at 3 A.M. the blast of loudspeakers
hi-fi Rolling Stones Ray Charles Beatles

. . . .

a little weed in the bathroom, girls in scarlet
tights, one muscular smooth skinned man
sweating dancing for hours, beer cans
bent littering the yard...

I'd suggest that the tights here, with their inflamed hue, are a tacit admission of the sexual coercion taking place on the premises, while the revolving squad car lights at the poem's close anticipate the encircling force arrayed against a *cool* that had begun to veer a little too close to felony, a felonious cool, a *cool* that was no longer so inviting.

Not long after the Angels party, Kesey went on the lam, fleeing drug-related charges, and the Pranksters began to fray, though they remained coherent enough to begin a string of large-scale, organized LSD raves, in Los Angeles and elsewhere, in a subterranean effort to disseminate further their mad charm. It's here that the word *cool*, the cool of the

Pranksters, collided with a squeaky-clean American food product, *a soft drink and its history*, with truly strange results.

Like many great American beverages, Kool-Aid began its life making somewhat spurious medicinal claims. According to Kraft Foods, owners of Kool-Aid's Perkins Product Company since 1953, the initial inventor of Kool-Aid was one "E. E. (Edwin) Perkins of Hendley, Nebraska," who, in 1914, "established a printing office and mail-order business, offering household remedies." Perkins's company later moved to Hastings, Nebraska (the Hastings Museum, "home of Kool-Aid," is now located there), and "expanded to include the manufacture and distribution of about 125 flavorings, spices and household products." In 1927, Kool-Aid became a powder, instead of a syrup, and assumed its present name. The name, I should point out, is roughly coeval with Kool cigarettes and, again, not too far ahead of the great blossoming of *cool lingo* in the late thirties and forties. In 1931, Kool-Aid became the sole product of the Perkins Product Company, after which Perkins sold out, in the fifties. Since then, Kraft has "innovated the Kool-Aid business with presweetened Kool-Aid Bursts (1991), Kool-Aid Island Twists (1995), and Mega Mountain Twists (1997)."

(I love the excessive names of American products! I love all derangement of language in merchandising! I love all hype and bluster and exaggerated language! And I'm especially taken with the very Beat names of some of the recent Kool-Aid varieties, with their "wild, twisted-up flavors": Oh Yeah Orange-Pineapple, Man-O Mango Berry, Soarin' Strawberry Lemonade, Kickin' Kiwi Lime, etc.).

The *very, incredibly cool* Kool-Aid Frequently Asked Questions site on the World Wide Web catalogues some factoids about the beverage that are important to compile at this juncture: (1) Kool-Aid has been used effectively as a hair dye for children. (2) Unofficial taste tests by soft-drink-obsessed Internet consumers indicate that Kool-Aid's "super-fruity" designation of recent vintage is identical to the so-called regular Kool-Aid of old. (3) However, it is *not* true, as previously supposed, that James Jones and the People's Temple members committed mass suicide (in Jonestown) by dissolving cyanide in grape Kool-Aid. "The followers of Jones," according to the Kool-Aid FAQ, "drank cyanide-laced Flavor-Aid, a cheap imitation of Kool-Aid." (4) Kool-Aid in Great Britain is sometimes sold on the black market, at seventy-five cents a packet—a significant markup. (5) And, *irrefutably true, though subject to total suppression by all Kraft Foods materials that I was able to gather*, is that in 1966 the Merry Pranksters, under the de facto leadership of Kenneth Babbs (while Kesey was a fugitive), held their famous "Electric Kool-Aid Acid Test" in Compton, Los Angeles (not far from where, less than six months earlier, the Watts riots had raged)—at which the catalytic drug of the evening was tendered in a solution made with the famous medicinal beverage of E. E. (Edwin) Perkins, *Kool-Aid*.

A product made *cool* by virtue of its name.

Tom Wolfe thus describes the *love potion*, quoting an acid-test participant called Claire Brush:

> The [Pranksters' home movie] continued, some slides were shown of flowers and patterns, this and that... then a large trash can, plastic, was carried to the middle of the room, and all were invited to help themselves

to the Kool-Aid it contained.... Since Kool-Aid is a staple in the homes of Del Close and Hugh Romney and other friends of mine, I thought it was a natural thing to serve.

The Compton acid test continued in the usual fashion, with a fair amount of mayhem and mystery and boredom and carnage, with police ceaselessly monitoring the activity (LSD wasn't yet illegal, and thus the Pranksters couldn't be busted on a lysergic rap). But soon Wolfe's description takes a sinister turn. A particularly bad trip by one female attendee was captured by a microphone and broadcast over a loudspeaker by Babbs and other Pranksters in a seminal moment at the LA test:

> Babbs is getting it all over the microphone to make it *part of the test*—not an isolated event—but All-one, anachoretic freakout—*Who cares!* Romney looks at Babbs and Who cares!—well, Babbs cares, with one part of him, but with another his devotion is to the Test, to the Archives...Who Cares in the Prankster Archives, and the cry wails over the hall, into every brain....Romney can't get this insane cry out of his head, *Who cares*...and he is back at the microphone, with his mission now, his voice furrowing into the microphone: "Listen, this girl's brains are coming out! And who cares?"

Few attended to the woman's cries, or perhaps her panic subsided (as bad trips often do), but the ennui of the acid tests had begun, at which point one kid asked the police for a cigarette and, amazingly, the cop slipped out for smokes and came back with *a pack of Kools*, but the fun had gone out of the expedition, the passion of Kesey had gone out of it, a passion itself deracinated when compared to the joy advocated by Kerouac, *no one particularly cared any longer*, though caring, and the passions in general, had once (in an elegant way) been integral to the mission of cool. There was division among the Pranksters about the leadership of Kenneth Babbs; there was division about the nature and purpose of the Pranksters. By the end of the Electric Kool-Aid Acid Test, the Pranksters as a community were threatened, perhaps terminally so. They may have lingered, persisted, but the mantle of cool had passed beyond them. When Kesey returned from Mexico he began talking about going "beyond acid," and his new caution and his retrospection about the bus and its inhabitants was palpable (in Wolfe's account). Cool, as a social experiment, was wearing out its time.

Thus, with the end of the Pranksters, *cool* became a term primarily and mostly related to drug chatter — is he *cool* (does he smoke)? Was it *cool* (was the location free of cops)? — in the precise sense that Del Close and John Brent discussed the word *cool* in *How to Speak Hip* (1959): "[To be cool is to] protect yourself from police intervention." The energy around *cool* had shifted away from jazz, away from black Americans (as Wolfe says: "The big thing with spades on the hip scene has always been the quality known as *cool*. And LSD freaking well blows that whole lead shield known as cool, like it brings you right out front, hang-ups and all"), away from writers, away even from Kerouac and Kesey. Cool, instead, had become something that was possessed by drug users and free-love espousers and rock-and-roll musicians. In fact, among the standard-bearers for several years would be the house band from the Prankster acid tests at Kesey's house, viz., the Grateful Dead. For example, Jerry Garcia, of the Dead, in a posthumous collection of interviews (*Garcia*, by the editors of *Rolling Stone*), uses the word *cool* a couple of times, first in connection with his album *Workingman's Dead:* "After we got busted [in New Orleans in 1971], we went home to make our record. And while we were making our record, we had a big, bad scene with our manager. Actually, making the record was the only *cool* thing happening—everything else was just sheer weirdness" (italics mine). And, later, in discussing the legacy of the Beatniks in San Francisco, as perceived by Garcia's generation: "They liked...*jazz*. You know: 'Jazz, man. Dig it.' Rock & roll wasn't *cool*, but I *loved* rock & roll. I used to have these fantasies about 'I want rock & roll to be, like, respectable music.' I wanted it to be like art."

These instances for the word presage entirely the meaning that we associate with *cool* now. *Cool*, once it had passed into the early seventies, meant not much more than *modern and good*. And potentially much less. This was the *cool* of the Dead, and it had a vestigial spontaneity, a jazz and Beat spontaneity, it had *space*, it had throw weight, at least until the mid-seventies, when the Dead went "disco," when they fossilized, and as went the Dead, so went the word, at least for a time.

And this is when I come into the story as an observer. This is the beginning of the *cool* of my growing-up years. A cool America in which we were taught that LSD would enable you to change the traffic light from red to green *at will*, that you should not take LSD, therefore, because *it would cause traffic accidents*, an America that learned to accept as routine that a man holding the highest office might use skulduggery or tape recordings to discredit his enemies, an America in which the coolest thing, the free concert, carried the possibility of murder (Altamont, 1969), in which military incursion into neutral countries was considered explicable, in which the free expression of youth culture was circumscribed, in which youth culture had conspicuous traces of *hard luck* upon it, a cool America in which *Billy Jack* was cool, or *Walking Tall* was cool. My America. I personally thought that Elton John was *the man*, or Al Pacino in *Serpico*, or Gene Hackman in *The French Connection*, or just about anybody in *The Poseidon Adventure*. (I thought that the end of *The Poseidon Adventure*—in which the Gene Hackman character *asks God to take him so that others might live* as he lets go of the steam valve in the belly of the cruise liner and drops to his death—was *really cool*.)

Yet, by the mid-seventies, when the singer-songwriter school was wearing thin and with it the whole flaccid enterprise of California rock and roll, people were nonetheless realizing that literature had once again become cool, suddenly, with the words "a screaming comes across the sky," in the mad, cabalistic invention of *Gravity's Rainbow*, in the fury of Donald Barthelme's unequaled experiments in short prose, in John Ashbery's poems, or in the tremendous innovative assault of the Living Theatre (a pride of New York artists walks into a theatrical space, takes off its clothes, and *just starts talking*— without script or theme or character), or in the violent electric period of Miles Davis (who probably comes closer, in his life's work, to *embodying cool* than any other single American artist). About the time I came into the story, cool was poised to make one last effort at a comeback.

I didn't know about any of this. I was trying to get comfortable among my contemporaries. My time was spent, hours of it, attempting to make myself presentable, shucking layers of clothing, donning new ones, trying to mat my absurd hair, committing acts of home surgical intervention upon skin blemishes. I amounted to a desperate series of premeditated strategies for fitting in, none of them successful. However, when I went away to school, in New Hampshire, I suddenly began to learn, intuitively, that there was such a thing as *cool*, and that it was a quality I might ape, or aspire to. It was around me in the upperclassmen and -women, and, oddly enough, *it was completely synthesized and represented in the person of one of my coevals there*, a guy from the Philadelphia area named Jamie Neilson.

From ninth through twelfth grade, Neilson was a one-man sideshow of creativity, comedy, malice, and charm. He was blond and attractive (later it seemed that every woman I knew had been involved with him); he wrote great poetry — according to my standards at the time; he was no slouch as an athlete. According to rumor, he consumed legendary amounts of drugs and alcohol; he flouted all "major school rules"; he swam naked at the dam; he broke curfew; he swiped my copy of *Freak Out!* by the Mothers of Invention; he did ribald skits at chapel; he acted; he sang; he was everywhere at once, tormenting people, praising them, visiting them in their dreams; he was, by the standards of my school, a cool work of art.

There's one of these guys at every high school.

So I decided, in completing this investigation of *cool*, to see what Benjamin R. Neilson Jr., himself now an instructor in English at a boarding school as well as a dean of the senior class, a husband and father, a regular citizen, thought of *cool* now. I asked Jamie first about Kerouac and that ancient Beat model of cool, and then about whether he thought about the term now. So here's the onetime urchin of cool as he would describe himself now:

> Whatever we thought was cool was miles from anything Kerouac had in mind. What he thought of as cool was a lot more *difficult* than what we did. By the time we got to cool it had lost all of its earnestness and it had an almost complete lack of self-awareness.
>
> And the unfortunate thing about cool in our era was that it wasn't very nice. Being cool was about distance. Sparring, in that verbal kind of way, conferred cool. If possible, frighten all fuckers away from ever *thinking* about judging you.
>
> I didn't perceive until I had been away from school for years that trying to be cool was about selling out in the worst way. We were trying desperately to be distant, to have a critical detachment that would allow us to sit in judgment. And as anti-establishment as we styled ourselves, that wish to be the one doing the judging was strictly generic arrogance.
>
> As you may have inferred from the foregoing, my career as a Cool Guy is somewhat painful for me to contemplate.

Neilson's cultural analysis mirrors the difficult realities of the *last gasp of cool* in America, as he and I both experienced it, which is to say the punk rock upheavals of the late seventies. Out of a few stray particles of Beat and jazz and hippie energy—Richard Hell and the Voidoids swiping a line from a 1959 song called "The Beat Generation" and coming up with their version, "Blank Generation"; Patti Smith updating the Burroughs style for her monumental album *Horses*; Ginsberg recording with the Clash—a rock-and-roll style was formulated in London and New York that seemed, for a moment, to change everything. What was degraded and unattractive, perverse and inept, was celebrated and accorded the highest respect of all. Guys and women (finally) who could scarcely play their instruments called attention to all the scabs and sores of contemporary society, in a style that featured wit, energy, and inventiveness. Punk *included anyone*. There was no in-crowd or out-crowd. The more marginal you were, the better. (At a Devo concert I went to, on New Year's Eve of 1978, the area where the disabled people were clustered in their wheelchairs seemed to be the most important section of the theater. The disabled were *more* Devo, more plugged into the sinister contradictions of the straight life, the tyranny of beauty.) Almost overnight, many at my boarding school went from the groovy tie-dyed threads of the Grateful Dead to the giddy vindictiveness of the Sex Pistols ("We're pretty vacant! /...And we don't care!").

Never was a cultural movement so quick to extinguish itself. As a dramatic evocation of the transition, I think most often of Exene Cervenka's commentary about the punk scene in Los Angeles, as depicted in part six of the Time Life *History of Rock 'n' Roll*. Cervenka describes the initial community spirit of punk and the way that community quickly became permeated by a sinister edge: "Everything went along just great until at some point the audiences went from being relatively intelligent and understanding people to being kinda young scary kids who liked to spit at the band a lot.... We kept begging them to stop spitting at us." There were earlier signs of trouble, too, for example in one of the Stooges' last shows, in the mid-seventies, in Detroit (as described by Iggy Pop in *Please Kill Me*):

> This guy kept whipping eggs at me. I had on this little ballerina costume and a G-string and everything and I just got sick of it. It was a biker hangout, you know? So I finally just stopped everything and I said, "Okay, I'm calling the fucker down!" Everybody clears out and here's this guy, about six foot three.... You know, I had little ballet shoes on, and it was just like seeing a train coming.... He just got me. But he didn't deck me, he couldn't knock me down, it was weird. Finally, the blood got to be too much for him so he just stopped and said, "Okay, you're cool."

Some of this—performers assaulting the audience, audience assaulting performers—was play, was innovation, but some of it was no cooler than the gang rape at Kesey's house or the "who cares" desolation of the late acid tests. Some of this was contempt for fellow men. By the end of the seventies, there was already developing an *us and them* of cool, divisions within divisions, bickering, lack of ambition, careerism, heroin addiction, death. By the time punk burned itself out, cool was a way to constitute community, but mostly this was a community *that kept others out*—as in the opening sequence in Woody Allen's 1980 film, *Stardust Memories*, in which the filmmaker, whom Allen portrays, imagines himself on a train (one of those brokenhearted locals that run to the end of the line) full of sad, destitute, homely Americans, the elderly, the obese, the disabled, a train running exactly parallel to another train, this other full of happy, beautiful, charming, cool people. Allen looks from his car, the train of the bereaved, into the cool car, desperate for a way to effect passage from here to there.

If the seventies were bad, the eighties were worse, and I refuse on principle to admit that the eighties contributed anything at all to the history of *cool*. Or to much else, excepting the national debt. The connotation of the word *cool* in this dark period didn't change (one friend of mine, a writer well known in the eighties, protested, when I asked about it, "I used 'cool' to describe the weather!")— *good and modern*, in the Partridge sense; *satisfactory and acceptable*, according to the *Random House Historical Dictionary of American Slang* (which cites, for example, a 1980 University of Tennessee freshman theme: "There are a couple of cool guys on my floor. The rest are a bunch of shitheads"). Otherwise, in the eighties, there is little viable youth culture that is not being wholly and entirely controlled by *multinational entertainment providers*. The most conservative president of the postwar era occupies the Oval Office. *Crack cocaine* contributes a compelling new example of alliteration to the national vocabulary. *Cool* is isolated in pockets like indie rock (Hüsker Dü, the Replacements), advanced semiotics and cultural criticism (Slavoj Zizek, Jane Gallop, Greil Marcus), independent cinema (Jim Jarmusch, Steven Soderbergh). Meanwhile, the culturally accepted notion of cool, ever more powerful over the margins, adheres in *Slaves of New York*, *Less Than Zero*, and *Bright Lights, Big City*. Jill Eisenstadt uses *cool* in one of the period's finer coming-of-age novels, *From Rockaway*: "You can say anything to Seaver; he's cool," or " 'I's cool, ma'am,' says Sloane. 'You ain't gotta worry, we're his friends.'" But elsewhere there is an unbelievable paucity of self-knowledge masquerading as *cool*. The second-person narrator of Jay McInerney's *Bright Lights, Big City*, for example, says of himself, in a moment of high introspection,

> [In college] you succeeded in faking everyone out, and never lost the fear that you would eventually be discovered a fraud, an imposter on the social circle. Which is just about how you feel these days. Even now, as you puff yourself up with tales of high adventure in magazine publishing, you can see Elaine's eyes wandering out over the room, leaving you behind.

When the Ironman Nightlife Decathlons lurch to a close, the architects of eighties cool begin to wonder what lies beneath. It is clear, in these moments of candor, how far we have fallen from the cool of the forties and fifties. This *cool, in the most dramatic shift in the whole history of the word*, has again become *literally cool*. Devoid of feeling, or noteworthy only for its nostalgia about the time—way back—when human emotions mattered. You see it preeminently in the work of Bret Easton Ellis, in the deliberately flattened affect of his chef d'oeuvre:

> I don't like driving down Wilshire during lunch hour. There always seem to be too many cars and old people

and maids waiting for the buses and I end up looking away and smoking too much and turning the radio up to full volume. Right now, nothing is moving even though the lights are green. As I wait in the car, I look at the people in the cars next to mine.

Literally cool. From a cool that was meant to be evocative and emotionally dexterous (Miles Davis's cool jazz), to a cool that was cerebral and goofy (Burroughs and Ginsberg), to a cool that was at first rigorously opposed to state power and straight culture (Kesey, the Pranksters, the hippies), to the all-inclusive insurrection of the seventies (Sex Pistols, X, Patti Smith), we have, in the eighties, a cool that means *dead inside.* Chilled-out cool, to use nineties locution. Flat, lifeless, dim, empty, dead cool.

And that's about where things remain. Here's cool as described in some recent tongue-in-cheek catalogue copy *for a lava lamp:* "The key to being cool: Wear clothes as black as the base of this pop icon. Watch the primordial goo rise up through the illuminated blue liquid....Note how this is just like life. Order another espresso and decide you are deep and should go back to writing beat poetry. Cool, Daddy-O!" Here's cool from a *New York Times* article about smokeless cigarettes: "But smokers must lift the device to their lips for each puff, as if smoking a kazoo. This is not exactly the cool image of Humphrey Bogart." A recent General Foods International Coffees coupon extols "Cool Ways to Unplug: Lusciously flavorful delightfully easy recipe ideas." At the close of the Tommy Lee Jones vehicle *Volcano* ("The Coast Is Toast!"), Jones asks his screen daughter how she liked watching LA's Beverly Center being detonated by a bomb squad. Her reply: "It was cool, Dad."

Are any of these examples legitimately cool? Even one?

A last-chance cottage industry of *cool* has sprung up in the world of hip-hop, in the jive of inner-city and faux-inner-city entertainers, the cool of Kool Herc, Kool Moe Dee, Cool Nutz, Kool Keith, Kool G Rap, LL Cool J, and Coolio. Since this represents the dialectical weight of cool swinging back toward black Americans, I find it temporarily exciting and interesting. When a slang term gets neglected by one mob of citizens, it is often elsewhere the site of rehabilitation. As an example of this, I find Coolio's *Gangsta's Paradise* album, like the really terrific hip-hop albums of old (*Fear of a Black Planet, Straight Outta Compton*), a genuinely moving evocation of the difficulties of urban life, featuring "gangsters and thugs," like "Young n—— fighting the case with public defenders," as well as "His little girl just now taking training wheels off her bike / While her daddy gets twenty-five to life," in addition to a grand cast of innocent bystanders, of which Coolio observes, "Be your own good ride / Right right / These are the geto highlites [sic]." His line of cool is also the cool of the detached observer, the distant relation of the low-affect Bret Easton Ellis cool, and perhaps not unlike the cool of blues musicians of the thirties who played with elegiac restraint amid burdens of racism and poverty, where cool is all survival, where cool is *beating the rap*, living to tell.

Cool is a "grunt of assent," as my former classmate Jamie Neilson put it. It's meaningless. It's no better than *neat* or *keen* or *sweet* or any of the other shifters in the pantheon of Anglo-Saxon single-syllable grunts of assent whose only reason to be is phatic, to ensure the continuity of communication, the insistence on noise, the bluster of a Young America that is no longer certain what it means or what it wants to mean or if it is capable of meaning at all. "Like...cool," Beavis says to his cartoon sidekick, Butt-Head, as they gaze at some meager television fare, at some forgettable output from the *medium cool* ("Some like it cold," as Marshall McLuhan says), and his rap is funny and devastating and sad, all at the same time. What does *he* think it means?

Sisters and brethren, kids all grown up now, adults of America (kids with kids of your own), remember those chambers where we once kicked back, avoiding homework or the first years of our nine-to-fives—in sudden, comical embraces, hoisting early-morning beers, drinks stolen from our parents, or later, the convenience apartments in which we worried about income and outflow, worried about our futures, what were we going to do, about the ineffable thing that we all wanted to have, that quality that seemed to slip away from us, out of reach, like a mooring line fraying and slipping, briefer than the neutrinos, briefer than the subatomics, this thing that others seemed to have, this *unknown tongue* (as Richard Meltzer calls it), the unknown tongue of a cool that made the opening of *Lolita* perfect, or the moment when James Dean says, "You're tearing me apart!" in *Rebel Without a Cause*, or the gum-snapping cool of Grace Paley's voice in *Enormous Changes at the Last Minute*, or the cool of Aretha Franklin shouting, "Respect," the cool of Neil Young's "Cortez the Killer," the cool of the Ramones? Where is the cool hidden in all these moments of bliss that are past now, moments when we felt suddenly vitally *here* and *good* and *modern* and *happy* and ready to go, to drive, like roadrunners, like continental explorers, across the impediments of a continent? Where is the cool we once thought we had or thought we wanted? Shimmering interstate mirage, never to materialize? Cultural spook of a credulous age?

Gone, gone, long gone. Cool is spent. Cool is empty. Cool is ex post facto. When advertisers and pundits hoard a word, you know it's time to retire from it. To move on. I want to suggest, therefore, that we begin to avoid *cool* now. Cool is a trick to get you to buy garments made by sweatshop laborers in Third World countries. Cool is the Triumph of the Will. Cool enables you to step over bodies. Cool enables you to look the other way. Cool makes you functional, eager for routine distraction, passive, doped, stupid. I would like now to suggest some alternatives. For the young people, lest the words they know are words that refer only to *adjustable-rate mortgages* and *price-earnings ratios* and the like. My initial thought was *lucid*, but too many syllables, too hard to say; so then I worked with *sublime* for a while: still too many syllables, but it has the right drift. *Sublime* points at the beyond, the way *cool* once did, the way Miles did, the way Coltrane did. Similar problems with *humble*. *Humble* gets at the disappearance that was at the heart of cool, the selflessness, but doesn't sound active enough. What about *meek* or *warm* or *cooked* or *brum* (it used to refer to prostitutes) or *raw* or *spared* or *fraught?* I like the sound of *the Fraught Generation. We belong to the Fraught Generation!* The records I like are *fraught!* Kurt Cobain, though not cool, was certainly *fraught!* Or how about *goss*, the nineteenth-century slang word short for gossamer? These times are *goss*. Or how about *guff?* Or *crass?* Or how about *dorf, euchred, flint, prim, sleek, tranced, scrag,* or *relinquent?* How about *pipient?*

But the job is best left to you, users of the American tongue. Seize control of your splendid language. Work your alchemical *mumbo jumbo.* Mix up your slang. Blow your innumerable horns. Play well. Play with feeling.

On Meredith Monk

In college I was in love with a dancer. It was a mess—as college romances often are. It was a mess even after college, flaring up in conflagrations that left both of us sad. Couldn't stay together exactly, nor could we part. Now she's a social worker and psychologist, with kids and a lawyer husband. A friend recently ran into her, in that Upper West Side citadel of kitchen gizmos, Zabar's. I don't know what she was buying. Her account of our time together would differ from mine, obviously. Back in college she was a dancer and she was spectacularly beautiful and I was in love with her. She was tiny and thin. She'd had a struggle with anorexia. She never finished reading books. There was always a stack of half-finished books on her night table. She liked Roland Barthes and Michel Foucault, and I think she was for a while the subtenant of Sylvère Lotringer, editor of *Semiotext(e)*. These things didn't help her finish any book that I ever saw.

Whereas I had known nothing about dance in high school, beyond the occasional auditorium presentation of ballet at which my attendance was compulsory and at which I was mostly bored, I now learned a lot about dance. My problem with dance, prior to this crash course, had to do with *tote bags.* I didn't want to end up one of those people with a *tote bag* that I was lugging around to cultural events, expatiating on how great the ballet was.

It's the condition of youth to imagine that its time, its era, is of unprecedented ferment. All is possibility, and the intellectual ideas to which you are being exposed suggest infinite permutations, all of them impressive. I'm sure it was true for Lee, and it was true for me. I remember (heatedly) suggesting to her one night that she had to make a dance where the only accompaniment was *the amplified sound of the dancers breathing.* She said it had been done. Instead, Lee choreographed a piece for dancers with tennis rackets. I don't think she had played a racket sport since her unrewarding teen lessons at the country club in Mamaroneck. Yet somehow she made the tennis racket, in the context of a dance studio, look like a Greco-Roman shield.

Another choreographer of our acquaintance, David, was at the same time making a piece for nondancers, in which I performed myself. This was noteworthy because I had almost no natural grace, and I was unable to commit movement combinations to memory. Lee once attempted to teach me a phrase from a master class she'd been to: I couldn't even raise one arm and jump simultaneously. Luckily, the piece David was making consisted *entirely* of Sufi spins, a movement strategy favored by contemporary choreographers for its elegance and simplicity. To put it bluntly, all I had to do onstage was spin around and around and around and try to avoid falling over. There were a number of things you could do in order to avoid falling over while doing Sufi spins. The Sufis had been doing it for centuries, after all.

The text of our piece was from Gertrude Stein, "As a Wife Has a Cow: A Love Story." It was an opaque but hilarious Stein composition that was musical and fanciful in equal measure: *Nearly all of it to be as a wife has a cow, a love story. All of it to be as a wife has a cow, all of it to be as a wife has a cow, a love story.* And so forth. There was some unison recitation at the beginning of the dance, and then each of us (Lee, David, myself, a guy called Ed) recited a paragraph, and then there was again some unison at the end. It was almost impossible to memorize Stein, I found, because it didn't *mean anything* in the usual way. I had memorized a lot of dramatic writing in college, I'd acted in various plays, and if you had a sense of where you were going, you could, in the course of things, memorize the words. In Stein, you had *no idea* where you were going, so remembering the prose was a matter of counting repetitions: *We feel we feel. We feel or if we feel if we feel or if we feel. We feel or if we feel. As it is made made a day made a day or two made a day, as it is made a day or two, as it is made a day. Made a day. Made a day.* Even typing it is hard. The good news was if you got lost in the Stein text, you could just repeat what you were saying for a while. No one would notice.

Actually being able to dance, even in this very primitive, ritualistic way, is one of the happy memories of college for me. But just as galvanizing as the experiencing of trying to do Sufi spins while reciting Stein was rehearsing. David always encouraged us to improvise in order to get warmed up, and there were certain records that were really good for improvising to in the dimly lit dance studio at my college, with its fabulous sound system, and these albums are themselves records of this particular time of ferment: *Music for 18 Musicians*, by Steve Reich and Musicians; *Einstein on the Beach*, by Philip Glass; *The Name of This Band Is Talking Heads*, by Talking Heads; *My Life in the Bush of Ghosts*, by David Byrne and Brian Eno; and *Dolmen Music*, by Meredith Monk.

Lee had just given me *Dolmen Music* for Christmas, Christmas of 1982. I remember a disclaimer: *Seems like it might be something you'd like.* So the record was part of our conversation, part of our *hocket*, which is a form that Meredith herself has used, a duet in which the two singers finish parts of each other's musical lines, as in Meredith's duet with the singer and musician Robert Een, where the two voices are so carefully listening to each other that you aren't always sure who's singing what, nor who is finishing for whom. In Baroque music it was considered very funny, the hocket. It was part of the human comedy.

Dolmen Music blew through my life like an intercessory voice from the musical beyond. To say I had never heard anything like it was probably not entirely true, because there are a few things that were not *absolutely* unlike it, some of Yoko Ono, maybe a few jazz singers, like Ella Fitzgerald, maybe some early Joni Mitchell or Laura Nyro. But these examples represent just a small piece of the technical strategy in Meredith Monk's music, and they don't get, at all, to the mood of her pieces, which always comes first. In fact, even *mood* is the wrong word, because it would be like saying that *black rage* is a mood, or *unrestrained grief* is a mood, or *the ecstasy of the spirit* is a mood. Often, in Monk's music, several of these moods coexist or overlap. As in the case of *Dolmen Music*, which begins with a piece called "Gotham Lullaby." This song, since it is just soloist and piano, begins with an iteration of the chords, the accompaniment on piano, after which Meredith joins, in one of her unrestrained lyrical modes, singing something like a conventional statement of the melody, but without words, or rather with words in some tongue otherwise unknown, twice through thus, and then she launches herself up into the high end of her soprano, doing some staccato quarter tones over the piano part (which never changes), then back to the melody as stated at the outset. Something ghostly hovers over the piano in the distance, a faint cello part? The piano plays through its cycle of chords one more time, and the lullaby is over. At the end of the piece, you can hear Meredith's foot slip off the sustain pedal. It's a spectral, affecting performance. Somehow the song completely breaks through whatever impenetrabilities you have erected around yourself. In its wordlessness, maybe. Which is probably why Monk almost never sets texts. Or maybe it has to do with the microtonality of the middle of the song, with the way she flirts with and resists the tonal home of the key in which the piece is composed. Or maybe it has to do with the folk music repetitions and simplicity of "Gotham Lullaby."

I came from a rock-and-roll youth, and for a while rock and roll was vital and it did the thing I wanted it to do. I wanted to be astonished by music, I wanted to have important certainties of my life called into question by music, I wanted whole civilizations to be founded on the ominousness of music, and I don't mean that I wanted what particularly good guitar solos do (although these were sometimes nice), or what a good funk band can do (although Funkadelic was great), I mean that I wanted my life changed somehow. I wanted a music that had been passed down through many generations like religious arcana; I wanted a music that had its cabalistic secrets.

There weren't too many records that did this for me, really. But even opening the packaging of *Dolmen Music*, which was one of those moody ECM jackets with the clear plastic sleeves, seemed ritualistic. After I graduated, I took the record, or at least a cassette edition of it, with me to California, where I lived for a while in an apartment with the novelist Jeff Eugenides and a theater director called Mark Pleasant. I had only a few cassettes with me in San Francisco, *Dolmen Music* among them, and so I often played Meredith Monk when I wrote. I'm pretty sure it was playing the night of the earthquake, which wasn't a big one. I was working on my Smith-Corona, on some long-lost short story, and the floor of my bedroom looked as if it were *rippling* for a second, and there was that cello part, the cello in just intonation that inaugurates the long suite called "Dolmen Music." I ran out into the hall. *Hey, you guys, are you hearing what I'm hearing?*

A few months later I was in Ireland, with my mother on an ancestral tour, when I saw my first actual dolmen ring. You drove down a certain street, took a left, passed a couple of old lorries, walked through some laundry flapping semaphorically in the breeze, and there, in a yard by itself, was this annular arrangement of stones, as in Stonehenge, erected for a purpose now forgotten, but generous with access to the past, to its losses and jubilances and anxieties, the kinds of things summoned in the song "Dolmen Music," the kinds of things summoned by Meredith Monk's wordlessness, the kinds of things that music has to do and doesn't do enough. One of the first adventures I undertook when I got back from this traveling was to go see Monk perform at Carnegie Hall.

Soon I was in the wilderness of writing my first novel, and then my second, and for both of these books I had superstitious notions about what kind of music I was supposed to listen to while composing, and this music had to be very narrowly applicable to the works themselves. So, while I was writing *Garden State*, my first novel, I was listening to a lot of Jersey bands, like the Feelies and Yo La Tengo and other bands associated with the Hoboken sound. With *The Ice Storm*, my obsessions were pretty much of the same narrowness, except that it was music from the early seventies. In fact, I'd actually started buying records when I was a kid during just those years (*Don't Shoot Me I'm Only the Piano Player*, *Led Zeppelin IV*, *Made in Japan*, *The Dark Side of the Moon*), so it was pretty easy to reenact this list. I wasn't listening to much *new music* for a good five or six years, and on the rare occasions when I was, it was all Hüsker Dü, the Replacements, the Minutemen, Pere Ubu, and other stalwarts of the indie rock movement.

Until I became bored. Boredom with the popular song, which seems inevitably to overtake you in your late thirties, is a bittersweet thing. It happens incrementally, so it's easy to rationalize or set aside at first: *This must just be a really bad time for rock and roll*, you say. When a Whitney Houston or a Mariah Carey comes along, you say, *This must just be a really bad time for popular music*. When faced with a Sammy Hagar or a Stone Temple Pilots, or a Tool or a Live, or any of the mediocre bands of today, you are bored, or you are bored with their bubblegum counterparts, maybe because the melodies just suck, or because the canned electronics sound like car commercials, or because they *are* car commercials, or the hip-hop guys, no matter how important you might think it is giving voice to disenfranchised political groups, the lyrics are about beating on a *ho* or shooting up the place; it's boring. All this stuff stopped speaking to me, see, and maybe I was wrong when younger to believe that my time was epochal and that all this music was going to transform the world; maybe it was wrong to believe that Sonic Youth was going to change the world, that the best *high-art stuff* and the awesome cultural penetration of popular music were going to meet at some point in the middle, whereupon we would have America realizing how great and creative its artists were instead of churning out the same leaden drum sound in the same leaden fours, saying the same thing over and over; even when I started listening to stuff that many people would consider unlistenable, when I contented myself with heading out onto that promontory of Alvin Lucier and La Monte Young and Terry Riley or Robert Moran or Ingram Marshall or Carl Stone or Stockhausen or Cage or Morton Feldman or Pauline Oliveros, I was still getting older and I still felt like all I was saying was *Turn down that noise.* I started listening to a lot more vocal music, especially extended-vocal-range stuff, like David Hykes, the overtone singer, and Nusrat Fateh Ali Khan and Youssou N'Dour, and Tuvan throat singing, and American sacred harp singing. Sacred harp singing was a way to teach church congregations with no organ to sing hymns. It was big in the South for a long time. It's also called shape note singing, because instead of notating the parts the way you would see them on a G clef, etc., the specific parts were indicated with little shapes, each for a spot in the old scale *do re mi fa.* As far as I can tell, they didn't even use a pitch pipe to start the sacred harp pieces; a group leader would just pick a starting note out of thin air. In its primitiveness, sacred harp singing is some of the loveliest folk music ever made in this country.

All this singing, all this vocal music, led me back to Meredith Monk.

In 1999, a German magazine wanted to know: if I could do a dual interview with any artist on earth, who would it be? They had run a series of these features, mostly pretty obvious pairings, actors picking other actors, and so forth, John Turturro and Susan Sarandon. I'm sure they expected me to pick a writer, to pick a William Gass or a Don DeLillo, and these guys are great, of course, and they have helped me a lot by their example and their accomplishments, but since I think of what I do as owing a lot to music, as owing something to singing and to kinds of improvised rhythms that are very musical, meant to be heard in the ears instead of seen with the eyes, I wanted to pick a musician, so I picked Meredith Monk.

Naturally, we were being tape-recorded and photographed by a crew of unnecessarily organized German nationals, and after a couple hours of it (the photographs took longer than the interview itself), it was hard to feel much except a sense that Meredith Monk's time was being wasted and that I didn't really deserve the honor of this conversation. It was satisfying to note, however, that Meredith and I had a lot to say about politics for the German magazine, about the mercilessness of the Giuliani administration, the hideousness of Tom DeLay, and so forth. Still, I left feeling as if I had met a mahatma, and that my job was amazing because it provided opportunities to meet great artists.

Though I believed I had imposed on her more than I wanted to, Meredith and I made an effort to stay in touch. Which is to say that I kept writing to Monk occasionally, and she replied and I watched her movies and tapes of her performances and I listened to her records, because the records had been made even more impressive by the fact of Meredith's personality, because for all her approachable warmth as a person, it was still impossible to understand where her talent came from, except that it was *everywhere* in her. I guess it's an impossible question, really, where talent comes from, like that old question about the seat of the soul; it's just there, and you can ask all kinds of questions about the early life of a person like Meredith Monk and talk about the movement-oriented musical program she learned as a child, called Dalcroze eurythmics, but in the end talent just seems impenetrable and awesome.

A strange coincidence was involved with all of this, in that my late sister's name was Meredith, too, and she had a monogram pretty close to Meredith Monk's, obviously, since her surname was the same as mine, and I am always acutely aware of friends who are women who are older than I, of not wanting to burden them with the projections of that lost relationship, but one day I was home and playing the messages on the answering machine, sitting on a couch, letting them sing out into my empty house, when a voice said, *Hey, Rick, it's Meredith*... At first, everything that came after these words was lost; in my confusion and my disorientation, I thought she was back, my sister, as in those Hollywood narratives where you get to experience the dead all over again. Then there was a period of terrible letdown, when I realized it wasn't *her*, though maybe it was, subliminally or emblematically. Maybe I have admired Meredith Monk since then precisely in a sentimental way, because now the unstated message of Monk's phonemic melodies is an injunction to remember that other Meredith.

The story moves toward its crescendo in the second half of 2000, when WNYC asked if I'd like to do something for a Sunday morning show they had called *The Next Big Thing*. I said that I was always looking for ways to work with music and musicians, and would it be possible, maybe, to set one of my stories to music? Some parameters for such a collaboration were discussed, and then they asked me which composer I would like to work with, and I said, without hesitation, *Could we get Meredith Monk?*

I mean, I couldn't imagine that she would want to do this thing with me, set my story "Boys," but it's worth dreaming sometimes, right? Meredith agreed to do the piece when the radio station called, but when I talked with her on the phone later on, she admitted, of course, that she was frantically busy, she didn't know if she would have time to do anything new, but I could use existing recordings as accompaniment for my story, sure. This seemed like generosity enough, especially when it included dinner with Meredith. We had a long chat about sustaining creativity, among other things, as she has done for almost forty years now, always expanding her range and her investigation. I said lots of things about how her music had changed my life and my work, even though this stuff always feels hollow when you say it. (But I'm writing these lines to "Do You Be?" from one of her very first recordings, *Key*, and in the conjunction of the sustained organ chords and the fluttering birdsong soprano vocal line, I know I *am* different since I learned of this work.) It was a nice dinner, of the sort I always hoped I'd be having one day, and the waitstaff at the restaurant, which was right near Meredith's loft, knew her and treated her with incredible reverence. So much so that they actually seemed to think *I* was important, simply because I was with Meredith. Next day, I got an incredible telephone call from Meredith Monk saying that she had gone home and started messing around with her four-track and had already come up with some short pieces, all revolving around the word *boys.*

I recorded the narration first, using a friend, the short-story writer and artist of metaphor Julia Slavin. Since the story is narrated from the point of view of a *mother* of boys, I wanted a voice that sounded as if it understood the material completely. Slavin and I went into the WNYC offices and she banged out her part fast. Almost immediately, I had a CD-R version of the recording. Whereupon I went home and, using a computer music program, went about the task of dummying up some of the text with *spot music,* as they do in rough cuts of films, marking where I thought the pauses might go, the silences, the spots where music might play without words of any kind. It was one of those obsessive tasks, like imagining which cuts could be removed from *The White Album,* and it took me several days, chopping up tiny bits of *Dolmen Music* and the two great instrumentals from *Turtle Dreams,* etc., fitting them underneath my words, underneath Slavin's reading, so that my words seemed far more lasting and important than they actually were. I wanted to be prepared when we went into the studio with the music and the producers. So that Meredith could do as much as she wanted and no more.

I'd only been in a digital studio one other time, to record a little piece of *The Ice Storm* for a Little, Brown and Company sales conference. My own voice, which is appalling to me, which I would have surgically altered if there were *cosmetic surgery for voices*, scarcely emerged from the speakers in the studio on that occasion. I advised more reverb. *A whole lot more reverb.* Nothing worked. I sounded like Willie Nelson on quaaludes, and there was nothing to be done about it. Yet my attitude about the studio, left over from analogue recording sessions with Jim Lewis when we were in a sequence of bands together in college and graduate school, was pretty much *Record the damn thing and get it over with*, or, as Brian Eno had it, *Honor thy error as a hidden intention*.

Meredith was kind of nervous, I understood later, because of her sometimes complicated relationship with the studio, even though she had with her her amazing studio engineer Scott Lehrer. Well, she was busy, too, and this was not a hugely remunerative gig, of course, for either of us. It was for the fun of it. All the more astonishing, then, when Meredith Monk went into the proverbial soundproofed booth of the digital recording studio and recorded three separate pieces of music, in two-, three-, and four-part harmonies with herself, including abstruse time signatures, infrequently visited intervals (the famous *diabla en musica*, or minor second interval), and unforgettable melodies, in forty-five minutes. It was one of those things that make clear how the engine of creation is variety; variety is the manifestation of possibility. Meredith Monk has arguably more *possibility* in her, as a singer, than any other singer *has ever had*. Perhaps there have been the likes of Maria Callas or Joni Mitchell or Captain Beefheart who could do particular things in an interesting way, but Meredith Monk really is alone in having incorporated *all* the possibilities of the voice into her output, summoning many cultures, many traditions, many emotions, some even imaginary.

We went on to fiddle with the rest of "Boys" for five or six hours. At first, my map of how to slug in the music was useful, and a number of my edits (including "Gotham Lullaby" from *Dolmen Music* and "Fat Stream" from *Key*) made it into the final recording, but somewhere around *hour five*, I could see Meredith getting kind of impatient. And since, even though she is incredibly kind and respectful, she never bullshits, she wasn't long about getting to the truth of the situation: *It's starting to get predictable to me. You have the words here and the music here, and the music is abstract and the words aren't.* It was getting late, and Meredith probably had to fly somewhere (she is often on her way to Hong Kong or Copenhagen or Berlin), and Dean Olsher from *The Next Big Thing* was tired, and in the exhaustion of the moment, it became clear to me that even though this was one of the most exciting projects I'd ever been involved in, a project that got nearer than I ever had to the kind of music that was in my head when I wrote a sentence, it was still pretty primitive compared to what Meredith was capable of doing, even with something as elemental as a pitch pipe or Jew's harp. By the time I had dealt with the force of this conclusion, we were already done, and I was still thinking about it when the show aired on the radio a week later, to some favorable responses. Your life can draw you up to a certain moment, you know; you can see how important a moment it is, and then still wake up and feel like you have a lot more work to do.

Or: All things come to their close, especially the feeling that your youth was epochal; this feeling comes to an end, the bright eyes of youth get dimmed, all that dancing around to certain soundtracks of youth, it passes away, and you are hurtling from one unfinished task to another and trying to keep creditors at bay. Love letters are outnumbered by bills. It was only a couple of weeks after the collaborative work with Meredith Monk that it seemed as if I had never done it at all, it was just some kind of dream I had, a rare alternative to dreams of teaching class without having prepared, which I have a couple of times a month. Now, predictably, I was back to my same long list of failures and inabilities, and this seems like *the situation*. There is no other. My youth was not epochal. I was just vain. And so what's left after? Elegy, requiem, nocturne, lullaby, all the musical idioms of late night? And what is the best instrument for all of these musical idioms—not the cello, though the cello is splendid, not the harpsichord, though it is good, not the harmonium, though the harmonium is very melancholy and summons the truths of the past. No, the best instrument for the music of loss, which is the best of all music, is a woman's voice.

Thirty-One Love Songs

It's the fate of the good work to belong to the public. It's the fate of the masterpiece to be bent out of shape, to be reimagined, remodeled by its audience. It's the fate of popular art to be scoured for clues, understood only in part or misunderstood, and this can't be controlled by the artist who came up with the work in the first place. The way a book or record or painting or movie thrives in the face of this barrage of refractions indicates its long-term durability. Those endless new translations of *The Odyssey* and *The Divine Comedy*, for example. "The Star-Spangled Banner," wrenched out of its casing by Jimi Hendrix. Joni Mitchell singing Mingus. If something works, it can stand a little misuse.

What about all those guys, and they are mainly guys, who have sat around winnowing *The White Album* down to a single disc? Well, first you get rid of "Revolution 9," which I happen to like a lot, and then you get rid of "Ob-La-Di, Ob-La-Da," despite the fact that one respects McCartney more as one grows older; out with "Bungalow Bill," out with "Wild Honey Pie," "Martha My Dear." Before long, you are left with a record that has on it "Dear Prudence," "Julia," "Happiness Is a Warm Gun," "Why Don't We Do It in the Road?," "While My Guitar Gently Weeps," "Helter Skelter," "Birthday," "Everybody's Got Something to Hide (Except Me and My Monkey)," "Cry Baby Cry," "Yer Blues." In short, you've got an unbelievably great rock-and-roll album. Does it do *the Beatles* a disservice? On the contrary. It indicates the bounty of material from which to choose. This is how some people pass an afternoon.

The subject of today's surgery is *69 Love Songs* by the band known as the Magnetic Fields. The Magnetic Fields, as I understand it, began, under various names and permutations, in the late eighties in the Boston area and hardened, more or less, into a group when Claudia Gonson, one of its singers and now manager of the band, was studying at Harvard. The other principals were also living in the area, first and foremost Stephin Merritt, singer, composer, guitarist, keyboardist, etc. The Magnetic Fields are the closest thing to a traditional band in the multiform career of Merritt, who has any number of other musical entities to which he occasionally turns his attention—the 6ths, the Gothic Archies, the Future Bible Heroes. Much of the time Merritt records all the music himself, at home. The Magnetic Fields, however, unlike most of his vehicles, list a little bit in the direction of the band-oriented idiom called *indie rock*. (A term I struggle with, and I expect Merritt would too.) The Magnetic Fields are not entirely electronic. They have two guitar players, Stephin and John Woo. They have a sort of a bass player in cellist Sam Davol. They occasionally have drums. Claudia Gonson can play the drums as well as the piano. Notwithstanding their denials, and there are many denials, the Magnetic Fields are sort of a rock-and-roll band. They occasionally play as an ensemble, and they leave their recordings somewhat unvarnished, in the tradition of bootleg, or in the tradition of low-fi, punk, or early folk, old time.

Prior albums by the Magnetic Fields were theme oriented. As Merritt himself points out, "Usually we do short records with some theme like travel or escape or Phil Spector or vampires." However, the concept on *69 Love Songs* was much more basic: *scale*. Initially intended to be a *hundred* love songs, the album was winnowed down, perhaps in a kind of exhaustion, though Merritt argues that the number sixty-nine was graphically satisfying. Perhaps he ran out of subgenres in which to compose. Perhaps he is saving the other thirty-one (though he has said that there are as many as fifty leftover tracks) for an expanded edition. In any event, the album now fits on three CDs, which, as with Guns N' Roses on *Use Your Illusion*, or those two Bruce Springsteen records, you can buy separately, if it suits you. The boxed version includes a lengthy exchange between Daniel Handler (a.k.a. Lemony Snicket, who occasionally serves as an accordionist for the Magnetic Fields) and Stephin Merritt that in some ways forecloses on all possible interpretive responses to the record:

> DH: Do you expect listeners to make tapes of their favorite songs and whittle it down to a smaller size?
> SM: I expect some people to hate particular songs.

I have taken these lines as an invitation, and before someone else does it, I now declare that I have made the definitive one-disc collection of songs from *69 Love Songs*. All others will now have to reckon with my version. I have done it because I love the band. I have done it because I love the album. I love the album as I have loved few pieces of so-called popular music in the past ten years. I love it so much that I had one of the songs sung at my wedding. I love it so much that I have given away any number of copies of it as gifts. I love it so much that I am still playing it almost four years later.* I love it so much that I can remember the lyrics, the harmony lines, and even some of the text in the exhaustive accompanying booklet. All because I love it.

Before I get to listing the tracks, however, I should admit, in the spirit of complete disclosure, that sometime in the midst of my romance with *69 Love Songs*, I got an e-mail message from Claudia Gonson herself, aforementioned singer and manager, asking if I wanted to *open* for the Magnetic Fields on a couple of tour dates they were about to undertake in Philadelphia and D.C. Open for them? A total shock. Apparently, Daniel Handler had done it, too, on the West Coast, and according to Claudia, it had gone "pretty well." This ought to have been a red flag. I knew enough about reading in public to know that rock audiences, with their need for spectacle, *ate writers for breakfast;* I knew enough to know that belittlement and heckling would be built in to this task, that not having a rhythm section up on stage with me would be the pinnacle of lunacy. And they wanted me to read for forty-five minutes, at first, and they wouldn't put me up in a hotel suite where I could throw the furniture out the window, and they wouldn't pay me

---

* I still feel this way, in 2010, although I have loved recent releases less fervently than this magnum opus.

much. I would be on my own recognizance. Like Victoria Williams, who nearly got shouted off stage opening a Neil Young show I saw. Because she was there. In short, it was a mixed blessing being proposed, probably in front of five hundred or a thousand people a night. I agreed.

It began this way: I walked into this old punk club in D.C., the 9:30 Club, home to many bands that I loved when I was younger. Everybody played there, I think. Black Flag, Big Star, the Replacements. Sort of nerve-racking to walk into an old punk club and to hear Claudia Gonson approximating the synthesizer line from "You're My Only Home" on the piano. There was an uncanny quality to it. And here I was, the only person in the audience during sound check. Me and the guy up in the booth, the Magnetic Fields' traveling sound guy. And I felt, uh, unworthy. I watched them do their sound check for half an hour. It was great. They had huge ring binders with all the songs in there. There were a lot of songs, of course, so there was a lot of music. I loved the way they fucked with rock show nonsense. Everyone sat, for example. John, the lead guitar player, had to be one of the least demonstrative guitar players ever in popular music. He made Robert Fripp seem like Steve Jones.

When they were done running through things, I nervously made my way toward the stage. This was when I learned what many had noticed before me: talking to Stephin Merritt is one of the hardest things you will ever do in your life. Many assume that it is difficult to talk to him because Stephin is acerbic, laconic, does not suffer fools gladly, etc. And these things, I believe, are true. I was destined, therefore, to be uncomfortable in the first place. But there is another issue.

Which has to do with the pauses. Handler, in the *69 Love Songs* booklet, refers to this tendency as the *trademark Stephin Merritt pause*. Does it come from a youthful obsession with Harold Pinter? Is it neurological? Is it a leftover expression of Merritt's childhood epilepsy? All I know is that Merritt takes longer to reply to a remark than anyone you know. He is two or three beats longer in reply than all your hard-core aphasics. You will be tempted to append further wasted verbiage to your initial remark. Do not do this. It will confuse things. Wait patiently. Then, at last, you will get the acerbic, laconic reply.

I was given a couple of minutes to test out the microphone, and then we all went upstairs and ate backstage food. I don't know what was in the Magnetic Fields' contract rider, nothing about M&Ms or vegan fare, but there was some fruit backstage, and a lot of beer. I don't drink or smoke, so I was in the minority there. I think Claudia is the only person in the Magnetic Fields who *doesn't* smoke, so Stephin and John, and sometimes Sam, were all sequestered in the smoking room, so designated by general agreement, where for at least part of the time Stephin was curled into a kind of fetal ball. Not because he was nervous. He just seemed comfortable that way.

The first night, I was so uncertain about what to expect onstage that Claudia and Stephin and Sam all followed me down the stairs to the very hem of the curtain, murmuring encouragement. They were as worried as I was. Apparently, "pretty well," Claudia's assessment of the Handler opening gigs, did not mean "without difficulty." I expected the worst. But the audience, at least the front third, listened somewhat. I read short things, rhythmical things, things that were almost musical, and this was probably a mistake. Probably I should have stood there and read like I believed in my form, the form of literature, like they were *lucky* to be hearing me. But yet this kind of confidence is not native to me. I did my job and got it done so I could go be in the audience like everyone else. That's where lovers of a record belong, in the audience.

The next night was Philadelphia. Stephin and Claudia were already spooked by Philly, before we even got there. They said they'd never had a good gig in Philadelphia, ever. One of my best friends lives in Philly, though, and my sister lived there for a while, and I know that *Eraserhead* was meant to suggest David Lynch's time there. And Philly has the Mummers Parade. How bad could it be? Pretty bad, it turned out. First, the club we were playing was enormous. Called the Trocadero, it seemed to hold thousands, in the upper levels, especially near the bar. Why people would want to pay to come to a Magnetic Fields gig and then just go up to the bar and *talk* is a mystery. But this is what happened.

For the Philly show, I made use of a songwriter friend from the area, Marc Beck. He was my guitar and keyboard accompanist. We were scared shitless, fair to say, but having an accompanist made the whole opening-act role a lot easier. I didn't care that the entire back of the room was talking and drinking, because at least there was an electric guitar wailing. I wasn't as naked as the night before. Unfortunately, the Magnetic Fields didn't get much more respect than I did. Claudia tried talking sense to the audience, offering the disclaimer that they *weren't a rock band*, etc. And Stephin, who can exude a punk rock irritability when he needs to, was pretty savage. But they played great and even, as a kindness to me, performed "Grand Canyon," one of my favorites on *69 Love Songs*. By the end of the show, though, everyone was short-tempered. They'd never play in Philadelphia again, it was a hellhole, and so forth.

The experience, for all its terrors, sort of changed my life. There is nothing harder than trying to bring fiction, literature, *words*, to the mass audience, even as refined an audience as the one that comes to a Magnetic Fields gig. After you have done this, after you have stood in front of a rock audience that just wants you to shut up and get the fuck off the stage, you are never again nervous about a reading. Well, maybe a reading on television. Television is still pretty traumatic. But the Magnetic Fields tamed the idea of the public performance for me once and for all. Which is not to say that the shows were *fun*. They were grinding, maddening, harsh. But I survived them, and I was stronger for it.

The first principle of reduction for the abbreviated *69 Love Songs* we will refer to as the principle of the self-hating bisexual. To the uninitiated, it's fair to say that one of the really joyful, wonderful things about *69 Love Songs* is the fact that it is extremely complicated from the point of view of gender and erotic cathexis. There are songs here about boys loving boys, there are songs about girls loving girls, there are songs about men loving women, and women loving men, and these are sung, more or less, by whoever has the right range. Claudia Gonson and Shirley Simms hold down the upper registers. In the male range, there's Stephin doing a lot of bass parts (some of these computer enhanced), and there are two other guys, Dudley Klute and LD Beghtol, in the upper-baritone and tenor ranges, respectively.

As Stephin points out in the *69 Love Songs* booklet, the album began as a contribution to the world of musical theater. You can feel the traces of this ambition in the finished project, in a number of songs that are closer to show tunes than to popular songs. I'm listening to one of these right now. It's called "How Fucking Romantic," from the first disc, and it's the song in which Dudley sings along with finger snaps and no other accompaniment. The composition is clever, simple, and it rhymes *moon* with "Rodgers & Hart tune." Who can dispute the mastery of the form? Who can dispute the clean energy of its bitterness? Who can dispute how smart it is? Nonetheless, I resist the song (even though Dudley is devastatingly handsome, as almost all my women friends observe). Another example? "Very Funny," from disc two, another ditty in which my-lover-is-probably-cheating-on-me to an incredibly beautiful cello part. Dudley works with the upper end of his range, and he has a little of that Marc Almond sexiness. And yet the composition seems more of a genre exercise than, say, "Fido, Your Leash Is Too Long," which deals with similar material but has an infectious groove.

The problem is that I hate show tunes. Not to mention musical theater. I don't find the American musical charming and funny and full of a canny brilliance. I find it embarrassing and overstated, and I resent all the old people filling the sidewalks in midtown on Wednesdays and Saturdays. I wish they'd go back to Long Island. I thought *Rent* was a debacle, especially the singing homeless guys. I don't like the vibrato in the conventional show tune voice. I find it cloying. Bernadette Peters sends me screaming from a room. Liza Minnelli is appalling, and so was her mom. And, while we're at it, I dislike opera too.

Having said this, I did have a past as a boy singer of Gilbert and Sullivan, and my first important experience with cross-dressing and festishization of cross-dressers occurred when, as a ten-year-old, I played one of the three little maids from school in a summer camp production of *The Mikado*. It's more than possible that my disaffection as regards the show tune, even the arty, insightful, and postmodern show tune, has to do with an attempt to eradicate the legacy of Broadway and light opera from my personality. I'm not proud of this disclaimer, but it is mine. Accordingly, I knew that the songs closest to the show tune idiom on *69 Love Songs*, the tunes largely sung by Dudley and LD, were first on the hit list.

For some reason, however, Stephin Merritt cannot sound like a show tune even when he lists in that general direction (on, e.g., "Let's Pretend We're Bunny Rabbits"). So I had fewer, if any, antipathies to his songs. And perhaps this is because of his gruff, cigarette-enhanced bass-baritone, which is always funny and world-weary. My fiancée,* Amy, dislikes a song called "Busby Berkeley Dreams" because of its Hollywood excess ("I haven't seen you in ages / But it's not as bleak as it seems / We still dance on whirling stages / In my Busby Berkeley dreams"), but in this case I would make a strict critical division between the ballad and the show tune. I have no problem with ballads. Ballads are heartfelt and moving, no matter their lyrical content. Show tunes are over the top and sentimental. Stephin Merritt is one of the best ballad singers on earth.

No problem at all with the women singers. Shirley's voice is incredibly sultry, with a faint southern twang. And even

---

* Now my wife, mother of my daughter, etc.

when she's singing something arch, like on "No One Will Ever Love You" ("If you don't mind / Why don't you mind?"), she sounds earnest. Probably the faux–Fleetwood Mac guitar parts by John add to the perception. Or what about the catchy "Washington, D.C.," where Claudia channels Up with People or the Bay City Rollers, but with an affectionate smirk? It's hilarious and beautiful, and Claudia can rock as well as anyone in the band. Her voice has a touch of Grace Slick to it. Sort of seductive and hoarse at the same time. If one of the hidden influences here is bubblegum, the songs for women's voices are the best examples.

However, I didn't really make decisions on what *shouldn't* be on the single-volume version of *69 Love Songs*. I made decisions on what *should*. I just picked the songs I liked. I didn't say "Epitaph for My Heart" is a little *too much*. What I did say to myself was how much I loved certain other songs. It turned out there were a lot of songs I loved. So, at last, I append the list, with the songs stripped off of their original CDs and sequenced at random, in keeping with Stephin's original design:

1. "Experimental Music Love"
2. "I Don't Believe in the Sun"
3. "Yeah! Oh, Yeah!"
4. "Reno Dakota"
5. "Come Back from San Francisco"
6. "The Book of Love"
7. "You're My Only Home"
8. "Fido, Your Leash Is Too Long"
9. "Boa Constrictor"
10. "Nothing Matters When You're Dancing"

11. "Punk Love"
12. "Wi' Nae Wee Bairn Ye'll Me Beget"
13. "Sweet-Lovin' Man"
14. "The Things We Did and Didn't Do"
15. "Roses"
16. "When My Boy Walks Down the Street"
17. "Busby Berkeley Dreams"
18. "Grand Canyon"
19. "If You Don't Cry"
20. "I Don't Want to Get Over You"
21. "A Chicken with Its Head Cut Off"
22. "My Only Friend"
23. "World Love"
24. "Washington, D.C."
25. "Kiss Me Like You Mean It"
26. "Time Enough for Rocking When We're Old"
27. "Papa Was a Rodeo"
28. "I Shatter"
29. "Acoustic Guitar"
30. "The Night You Can't Remember"
31. "Xylophone Track"

Though the organizing principle is nothing other than pleasure, it is possible, retroactively, to notice a few tendencies. Songs with really good piano parts: "I Don't Believe in the Sun," "My Only Friend," "Papa Was a Rodeo," "Busby Berkeley Dreams"; songs with live drums that repudiate disclaimers about how the Magnetic Fields are not a rock band: "A Chicken with Its Head Cut Off," "Punk Love," "Sweet-Lovin' Man," "When My Boy Walks Down the Street," "Washington,

D.C.," "Papa Was a Rodeo"; songs with John Woo playing guitar on them: "Reno Dakota," "Come Back from San Francisco," "Boa Constrictor," "Time Enough for Rocking When We're Old," "Acoustic Guitar"; songs with really catchy synthesizer lines that recall the early eighties: "I Don't Want to Get Over You," "Fido, Your Leash Is Too Long," "The Things We Did and Didn't Do," "Grand Canyon," "You're My Only Home"; songs with a modernist ambition: "I Shatter," "Experimental Music Love"; songs sung by Stephin; songs with incredibly inventive lyrics; songs that have a lot of space in them; songs that leave room for the listener and aren't fussy about arrangements; songs that are full of heartbreak.

Maybe this last quality, in fact, is the quality that draws me most to *69 Love Songs*, and I take pains here to point out that the perception of heartbreak in *69 Love Songs* is interpretation, not fact. Since Stephin Merritt remarks that he doesn't "want to say which ones are 'true' songs," there is no profit in going down that byway of pop criticism that insists on seeing songs as extracts from an autobiography. And yet I adhere to the delusion that there's something heartbroken and truthful and even *sincere* about a lot of these songs. *Sincere*, a word that doesn't come in for a lot of respect these days. I brought the point up with Claudia, by e-mail, and her response was "There's something about sincerity that nauseates me." I had the same reaction from Stephin himself. I did an interview with the *Philadelphia Inquirer* before opening for the Magnetic Fields, and when asked why I liked the band, I told the interviewer that I thought that Stephin's songs were, notwithstanding his denials, heartfelt and moving. Then I made the mistake of repeating this to Stephin backstage. His put-down was swift and complete. I can't re-create it exactly, but it was close to words like: "What incredible bullshit." And there was a pause after, to make sure I understood what he meant.

But if there's *not* something true and sincere about the complexity of human emotions on this record, why bother to keep listening to it? A record merits attention over four years or more because it means something about how people *live*. That's why no one really listens to Electric Light Orchestra anymore. Theirs were impeccably crafted pop songs that meant nothing at all. They were adept, and they were as compelling as Sheetrock. People listen to Burt Bacharach not for the tricky metrical changes and major seventh chords, although these are nice, but because of the conjunction of the music and the complicated pathos of the words.

After all, it's not called *69 Clever Songs* or *69 Songs with Extremely Dexterous End Rhymes* or *69 Songs in Which a Guy with a Lot of Talent Apes Other People's Musical Styles*. It does say "love songs" in the title, and I take the ambition to be as indicated. The word *love* is invoked in the title, and it turns up in ninety-nine one-hundredths of the songs—not as a mere signifier of the sort imagined by Stephin's beloved Ferdinand de Saussure, but because *love*, the word, the idea, speaks to an important, even exalted way that people interact. When this interaction has been effectively dealt with in the popular song ("All You Need Is Love," "Shelter from the Storm," "God Only Knows," "My Funny Valentine"), it has reached a place that is indelible to millions. To incline toward this word *love*, to incline toward this abstraction, with all the trouble and bliss that it causes, in sixty-nine different ways, is to be preoccupied—centrally, vitally—with what it means to be living here on earth. That we are still listening to the album is proof of its *meaning*, not proof of its inventiveness. Because inventiveness is *not* forever. Inventiveness lasts about fifteen minutes.

Remember when Mike Chapman was producing Blondie and he said, "If you can't make hit records you should fuck off and go chop meat somewhere"? The same could be said of love songs. If you can't tell the truth about love, then you might as well fuck off, etc. The Knack, also produced by Chapman, were clever and shallow, and they were the next Beatles for a few minutes in the late seventies. And where is Mike Chapman now? Doing some spots for a VH1 program in which he reckons with the fact that the popular taste has passed him by? *Why love songs?* What is it about love songs? Why all these love songs? Why not songs about war? Why not songs about death (like "Last Kiss" and "Teen Angel")? Is it simply because these are not affirmations and we would be unwise to spend our leisure on music that recoils from affirmation of any sort? Or is it because music, that incredibly powerful but largely abstract art form, is best and most practically married to subject matter that ennobles? Is desire the perfect catalytic agent for the abstraction of music? Is *music itself love*, as David Crosby once remarked in song?

The most beautiful moments on this collection of love songs, the most beautiful moments in the history of Stephin Merritt, are the moments when he is somehow alone with his ukulele or his guitar, and there's a lot of air in the recording, and he's seducing the listener with lines like "You can sing me anything," and the equipoise is between a distrust of love and the faint but stirring hope that maybe it will *turn out well* this time. The accompaniment, almost always written *after* the melodies, leaves a hovering uncertainty in the piece, a little bit of echo, a little bit of reverb. Unmistakable is the sensation that love is a thing of the atmosphere. It could go either way; there could be another dead end of acrimony and disputation or, and Stephin would deny it aloud, perhaps there could be harmony. Maybe he really does know something about it, even though he would claim to be a debunker ("Are you out of love with me? / Are you longing to be free? / Do I drive you up a tree? / Yeah! Oh, yeah!"); maybe, even though he'd prefer to allude to a certain bar where he writes while staring off languidly and listening to the Human League on the jukebox, there are these instants when affirmation and annihilation are *equally* part of love's system of uncertain futures. And this is an instant that is best captured in song. He says it right there in "The Book of Love": "The book of love has music in it / In fact, that's where music comes from."

That's the Magnetic Fields I adore.

Thirty-one songs, then, because it's a prime number, and because it's the same number as in that medieval classic, Andreas Capellanus's *The Art of Courtly Love*, which preserves such irrefutable complexities as #1: "Marriage should not be a deterrent to love," and #2: "Love cannot exist in the individual who cannot be jealous." Like Andreas, the Magnetic Fields, as preserved here, have fashioned a primer on the *complexities* of love. They have denied both their affirmations and their heartbreak in the press, sure, because to be vulnerable is hard, sad, thankless, and costly, as Andreas has himself advised (#13: "Public revelation of love is deadly to love in most circumstances"). But in their secret hearts, as we know from the songs, they betray how fervently they *are* lovers. Compare the medieval master in #14: "The value of love is commensurate with the difficulty of its attainment," with the songwriter: "Well, darling, you may do your worst / Because you'll have to kill me first." Or Andreas in #21: "Love is reinforced by jealousy," and Merritt, on disc one: "Fido, your leash is too long / You go where you don't belong." Thirty-one *love songs*, then, because love songs when they are true ("No one will ever love you honestly / No one will ever love you for your honesty") instruct us in suffering, school us in desire, remind us of our loss, foster in us our enthusiasm.

Of course, now I'm rethinking the whole project and wondering about the songs that got left off. Maybe I really made some mistakes here. I mean, it's stupid to overlook "Absolutely Cuckoo," which just sort of has to start the whole thing, as it does on the official release. "The Cactus Where Your Heart Should Be"? With its great guitar part? And what about the Modern English simulations of "(Crazy for You But) Not That Crazy"? LD's star turn on "The Way You Say Good-Night"? Or what about volume three? Initially it seemed kind of weak to me, but now I'm into "I'm Sorry I Love You," with Shirley's harmonies. How could I have been so stupid? And "Love Is Like a Bottle of Gin" and "Two Kinds of People." And Claudia singing "Zebra," the last song. I should have included them all. I should definitely do it over. But I promised a friend that next week I'd get *Decade* down to a single disc.

How to Be a Christian Artist

On the Danielson Famile

I like music that makes other people uncomfortable. I like Pere Ubu a lot, for example, and my favorite Pere Ubu album is *New Picnic Time*, an album that has sent many listeners screaming from the room. Captain Beefheart is another favorite, in which case I like *Lick My Decals Off, Baby*, an album of great rhythmic complexity and impressionistic lyrics. Rhys Chatham's out-of-tune guitar pieces. Tony Conrad's violin pieces for just intonation, La Monte Young's minimalisms, free jazz from the mid-sixties, the Sun City Girls, the Slits, Daniel Johnston, the Shaggs, Wesley Willis, Syd Barrett's most ominous solo work, the most experimental David Grubbs, etc. It's not that I think this music is interesting simply because it's *unusual*. This music brings me genuine pleasure. I like some pop songs, too, of course. But somehow the work that makes an indelible impression on me comes from a place of singularity. This work doesn't give up its secrets easily. It makes demands. In the process of reckoning with it, you feel as though you've helped make it what it is.

An example: a few years ago I was invited to a record club in lower Manhattan by a painter friend. The record club worked this way: each of the twelve members brought two songs that they were *in love with* at the moment, and, according to a sequence generated by randomly dealt playing cards, we circled the room in two rounds with everyone playing his or her songs in turn. Though I've never really been a book club sort of guy, I was taken with the spirit of this gathering right away.

On the Friday night in question, the record club was marching along, doing what it does, glancing off of jazz, electronica, Britpop, cabaret, country, when suddenly there emerged from the speakers the most strangled, desperate racket I had heard in ages.

The first problem was the singer's voice. The singer sang in a tortured falsetto, or most of the time he did. Sometimes he hovered just above and below the line that separated his chest voice from his falsetto. In the tenor range, he had a boyish drawl, sort of like Kurt Cobain, if Kurt had been raised in the Ozarks. But then there was his boy soprano, into which he lurched for various pitches, where he was silly and ghostly and a little bit shrill all at the same time.

Having taken note of this singer, I moved on to the accompanying ensemble: acoustic guitar, organ, celeste, two rather primitive drummers. The band would probably have sounded *adorable*, like the soundtrack to the tugboat in Mister Rogers' neighborhood, were it not for the structure of the song itself, which, I later learned, was entitled "Holy Kisser's Block Party."

It began with an alarm clock, followed by a section A, some kind of whispery chant in which Daniel Smith, the lead vocalist, and some girl backup singers intoned their rhetorical intention, "I do vow / Here and now / I will kiss again / It starts right now." This was followed by section B, in which the celeste, or chimes, dominated, and a very different melody was explored, followed by a section C, in which varieties of love were described and suggested by the narrator, "Begin your loving to the one who bothers most," this in turn followed by a section D, an actual chorus, in which piano propelled the rhythms, major triads, while above there hovered some really strange counterpoint between Daniel and the backup singers, his *sisters*. Did I not say that the band in question, the Danielson Famile, really are a family? Daniel on acoustic guitar and vocals, Rachel on vocals and flute and sometimes organ, Megan on bells and vocals, David and Andrew on drums and percussion, respectively. "Get your rear in gear, lend an ear, have no fear, draw near, my dear, bring the cheer, take time to hear." And then a section E, which was really section B, except in a minor key, consisting only of a repetition of the line "As coals of fire rest on their heads," with minimal accompaniment. Back to section A.

I thought it was some of the worst caterwauling I had ever heard. And I *like* caterwauling.

Record club always produces a little anthology — the minutes of the proceedings, if you will — and so I had opportunity to hear "Holy Kisser's Block Party" again, in my car, because that's often where I first listen to compact discs, and I confess I was a little shocked by the song. I resisted its complex demands. And yet when I stumbled on it periodically when playing the anthology of the record club event, I realized that I was beginning to think the song was indisputably great.

After a couple of years, I was invited again to the record club (visit their website: www.recordclub.org), this time along with my wife, Amy. By coincidence, Julia Jacquette, the painter who'd first issued the invitation to me, had *again* selected a Danielson Famile song, as though she'd been thinking of nothing else in the intervening years. On this occasion, the song was the hit, sort of, from the brand-new Danielson album, *Fetch the Compass Kids*, viz., "We Don't Say Shut Up," again composed of a bunch of rather diverse sections that in this case featured really great counterpoint writing between the piano and the acoustic guitar, and great vocal arrangements, etc. At first, I had no idea what the song was about, really, except that it extolled the notion of "quiet time," and the author of this "quiet time" seemed to be the "holiest of ghosts." However, with proximity and familiarity I was beginning to understand something quite fundamental about the Danielson Famile that had escaped my notice — they were evangelical Christians.

Julia Jacquette, my painter friend, had made a pilgrimage to see them perform live, and she said it was sort of an amazing thing. For example, the singer and acoustic guitar player, Daniel, performed the entire show from inside of a large papier-mâché tree, which must have made it rather difficult to play all the chords properly. The rest of the family wore medical garb. The motives for the costumes and props were not explained to the audience, but upon reflection it now appears likely that they had something to do with the laboriously worked out theology of songwriter Daniel Smith.

My first reaction to the evangelical dimension of the work

was, naturally, to resist. What I liked best was the *sound* of this album, which, frankly, was and is unlike anything else that is being produced today. Half innocent and half cultivated. *Compass Kids*, which was released in early 2001, was produced by Steve Albini, the man behind some of Nirvana, some of PJ Harvey, some of Will Oldham, and the most recent album by Godspeed You! Black Emperor. You can tell that a lot more thought went into the recording this time, since Daniel's voice is mixed back a little bit, as the vocal choir of Megan, Rachel, and others is brought forward. And: for a band that has no bass player, the album feels nicely bass heavy, with strange keyboard sounds and bits of distorted guitar filling in the low end. Also, some of the music writing on *Compass Kids* is divided between Daniel and the keyboardist, Chris Pallodino, with the result that the piano and acoustic guitar interact almost uncannily in spots, in a way that calls to mind the sublime Vince Guaraldi and his music for the *Peanuts* cartoons.

My wife became obsessed, too, and we bought *Fetch the Compass Kids* and played it for a long stretch. Yet, as with many such things these days, I never spent much time on the lyrics. Unlike in my youth, when I pored over the lyrics of albums (back then, I remember reading with intense disappointment an interview with Mick Jagger, wherein he remarked that lyrics were "just something to sing"), these days I tend to play things because I like how they sound, with an indifference to the "message." I never knew what Michael Stipe was singing, and I never cared; I never cared what Bob Mould was singing; I never cared what Paul Westerberg was singing; I certainly didn't care what Kurt Cobain was singing. Around our house, we played *Compass Kids* because the music rewarded attention, because the piano and acoustic guitar traded the downbeats in different verses, and because the time signatures were unusual, because the instrumentation was bizarre, and because there was something charming about the ominous innocence of the entirety.

Later, however, I did start to wonder about the lyrics. It was perhaps when my wife bought one of the earlier albums. On the first track from *Tell Another Joke at the Ol' Choppin' Block*, released in 1997, Daniel chants, "I love my Lord, I love my Lord, I love my Lord." Pretty straightforward, huh? And, later, on "Flesh Thang," I noticed the following: "It's a house of the Lord / It's a house of the Holy Ghost / But the house be speakin' at times / Haunted house is bein' tricky / You better only be hearin' the Holiest of Ghosts." Similarly, on "Smooth Death," the title of which acts as a leitmotif on *Choppin' Block*, there is an allusion to the wine of the Eucharist: "It's gonna be a smooth death, take it slow... / Take a bath in the blood." Maybe it's possible that I didn't notice the Christian dimension of the Danielson lyrics at first because I didn't *want* to have to think about Christian imagery in what is for all its eccentricity an example of so-called indie rock. But the specific musical characteristics of *Choppin' Block* made avoidance of the lyrics almost impossible. *Choppin' Block* was produced by the one-named Kramer, who also brought you Galaxie 500, Low, Bongwater, et al. It follows that the album rings with echo and reverb, with the repetition of open chords. The litanical reiteration of phrases like "I love my Lord," or "It's time to rest, my son," from the song entitled "Jersey Loverboy," falls naturally into this reboant space, with the spooky quality that we associate, perhaps, with a certain kind of psychedelia.

Daniel could just as easily be singing, "Father? Yes, son. I want to kill you."

Or: what is psychedelia but entry-level spiritual investigation? I first understood that the Danielsons were singing about God when I understood that the music on *Choppin' Block* sounded like they were singing about God. There's a misuse of the litanical in some rock and roll. There's a perversion of the litanical, and you hear it, for example, in Lou Reed, the reliance on the one-four progression, while you sing, for example, about heroin. In such a context, that is, the secular *is* spiritual. "Heroin," that is, is spiritual, or it wants to borrow from a spiritual tradition, in its repetitions and its life-or-death concerns. The narrator of "Heroin" does, after all, feel like Jesus's son.

Choppin' Block reaches a similar zenith of repetitions in "Quest for Thrills," a song largely composed of one chord, which advances a relentless and slightly humorous passion play over its drone: "Hungry humans / Rootless man / Just a number / Avoid the question / Of the truth / Get the injection / The good infection / Take a drink / Of spirited tunes / Of spirited pop / Of spirited tunes / Pop tunes / Poppy tunes / Fifth dimension / Belt of truth / Bible belt / ... Thirty minutes / After death / Something called E. coli / Is detected / In your nose / You'll be decomposing / In the dirt / And your cryin' / Yourself to sleep / ... Dead man's wishes / Is bein' sacred." Soon after, the song proceeds into a second droning passage where Daniel chants "Amen, brother" for a good couple of minutes.

Choppin' Block concludes with a longish instrumental (there is in its course just one brief flourishing of voices) actually recorded in a funeral home, consisting of an orchestra of tuba, flute, sax, and clarinet, all playing the big ominous drone that one imagines has everything to do with the idea of the *smooth death* enunciated earlier on the album, as if the cheerful demeanor of Daniel Smith here puts forth the inevitability of finding E. coli in his nose, postmortem, passing from there into the smooth death of evangelical experience, viz., the after-life. When the vocals finally break out at the end of the unnamed instrumental, they consist of the words "I believe," repeated ad infinitum.

In the African American tradition of musical evangelism, the ambiguity is between the spiritual and earthly love. God's *caritas* and *agape* are adjacent to the *eros* of the first world, so that when Al Green says, "Let's stay together," he could mean, *Let's you and I work this thing out*, or he could mean that he is spiritually frail and is in desperate pursuit of some kind of certainty about *divine* love, a certainty that is often framed in the context of doubt, because doubt is the human thing. You find this same evangelical origin in a lot of black popular music, of course—in Aretha Franklin, whose gospel roots are well-known, but even in Motown, where songs like "Ain't No Mountain High Enough" trade on the conflation of the earthly and the spiritual. The other salient feature of this African American musical evangelism is its lack of punitive imagery. There's little in these songs about the theology of hell.

The theology of (white) rock and roll is often much less forgiving. From "Great Balls of Fire," by Jerry Lee Lewis, which makes love and brimstone bedfellows, right up to the heavy metal theology of AC/DC (in "Highway to Hell" and "Hells Bells"), you feel that the spiritual in the rock-and-roll tradition is mainly obsessed with sin and penitence (or the lack thereof), with the downright *fallen* qualities of mankind, with doubt, with all that is harrowing about Christian experience, not a moment given over to forgiveness, except perhaps in that awful song by Don Henley, or in the bland affirmations of the contemporary "country" radio format.

The Danielsons sidestep all prior solutions to the problem of how to be evangelical recording artists. On the one hand, the Danielson Famile are so far from the gospel idea of a musical ministry that it's hard to consider what they do as being in the same league at all. There's none of the improvised *testifying* of an Al Green or a Solomon Burke here, none of the reliance on scriptural citation and pre-ordained Old Testament imagery that turns up again and again in the gospel music tradition. And, at the other extreme, notwithstanding their love of the occasional barre chord, the Danielsons avoid the bombastic cock-rock posturing of Creed and their brethren, wherein the evangelical involves the inevitable removal of the lead singer's shirt.

The Danielsons create something closer to a sonic equivalent of the genuine difficulty of contemporary faith, because they create music that is incredibly ungainly and awkward, as faith itself is ungainly and awkward, though no less fervent for its homeliness. Well, perhaps there *is* some consistency between the way that the Reverend Al Green uses his music and the way that Daniel Smith uses his in the aforementioned repetition of phrases. This has everything to do, believe it or not, with *Franny and Zooey*. You remember, of course, that Franny goes out to a luncheon on the day of the big game, and despite the loving and affable affection of her suitor, she *passes out* at lunch. The reason for this fainting spell is often given in literature classes as a *spiritual crisis* of some kind. In particular, it is said, Franny Glass faints because of her attempts to repeat the Jesus prayer: "Lord Jesus Christ, have mercy on me, a poor sinner." In fact, in *The Way of the Pilgrim*, the religious tract where this prayer technique was first given mass-market evocation, the idea is to repeat the prayer so constantly and so perfectly that your heart is able to say it with each muscular pulsation. When you get to that point, amazing things begin to happen—your life improves, your relationships improve, doors open that once were closed, etc.—and, I suppose, you experience loss of consciousness. This is the way the Danielsons use a phrase like "I believe." They use it as if the phrase had magical properties, and they use it as if they definitely believed, and as if they knew that if they repeated a phrase often enough, life would improve, the door would open that once was closed, etc.

Fetch the Compass Kids, the 2001 masterpiece of the Danielsons, came immediately after a two-album package called *Tri-Danielson Alpha* and *Tri-Danielson Omega*, in which Daniel Smith tries to play in three separate group contexts: (1) in a primarily acoustic guise, (2) with the Danielson Famile, as described above, and (3) with a sort of conventional rock group, replete with electric guitar. The trinitarian model is obviously fundamental on *Tri-Danielson*, though he's also being facetious, since the same Smith siblings and the same cast of side characters play in all three groups. The results vary more widely than on any other Danielson album. A hilarious song like "Rubbernecker," a dead ringer for the early B-52s, can be followed by something that really relies on Daniel's obsession with downwardly moving chromatic melodies, wherein there is no chorus and no hook. *Tri-Danielson* is hilarious and moving in spots, but it's also big and sloppy.

Not so *Compass Kids*. You emerge from the diffuse ambitions of *Tri-Danielson* into a record that is thoroughly composed, where the band is better equipped than ever before, where the young drumming Smiths suddenly seem to be first-rate drummers, and where the evangelical context of the album seems to be resolutely organized around a single idea, which is the pursuit of a moral compass in a dangerous and modern secular world. "It's an incredibly confusing time / Been told I must be in my prime," Smith observes on "Rallying the Dominoes." "It's too much of a confusing time / 'You forgot to eat again,' but I don't mind." Or elsewhere, on "Singers Go First": "Papa pushed me out the boat again / My morning face says I cannot swim / Did not eat again." Or on "The Wheel Made Man": "Fear comes where loves was / Then love comes where fear was / The wheel within wheel in the sky, who am I?" Of course there are the usual protestations of faith on *Compass Kids:* "We live each day as our last / Moved by what we see," or "Happy and sad / Gonna sing the wide and deep, oh Lord," or "In Him do we move and live and do become." And yet, in general, *Compass Kids* attempts a more subtle evocation of the frailties of the spiritual life. It attempts to evoke these frailties gently and compassionately, while it continues to demonstrate the evangelical properties of music and religious imagination, all of this in the context of a musical idiom that I suspect most people would find too strange for their listening delectation. The result is that the contradictions implicit in such an undertaking emerge as massive, overpowering, and, for me, incredibly interesting.

Which is to say that I find that I have come somehow to *identify* with the Danielson Famile. I identify with them, in that rock-and-roll way, and I am reassured by them. Here's why. Because in the literary community, at present, one of the worst career moves you can make is to admit that you are a person who *believes*, a person who goes to church and finds value in it. To say that you both go to church and consider yourself an intellectual is to court skepticism and even disdain from your peers. I have been asked by at least one editor not to talk about churchgoing because "people don't want to think about you as a churchgoer." And the reason for this is transparent: in some quarters *all* churchgoing has come to mean literalism or fundamentalism.

I should qualify my experience for the purposes of these remarks. I don't have particular adherence to Episcopalianism, the religion in which I was raised, to the extent of including or ruling out adherence to any other sect. I don't believe in Christianity as the one truth faith; I don't believe in the Christian God as the one true God, excluding all others. I don't believe that the ancient Abrahamic faiths are more correct than some druidic sun-worshipping commune in eastern Oregon. At various moments, I have been just as taken with the Quaker faith, or Tibetan Buddhism, as with Episcopalianism, and I am a fan of the Qur'an and Talmudic scholarship. A friend of mine sends me daily prayers from the Lubavitchers, and I think they're fabulous. While I find Madonna's obsession with the Kabbalah kind of self-congratulatory, I don't rule it out. I love the church of my birth because I love the ritual of the church of my birth, the bells, the censer, the sung liturgy, the emphasis on textual interpretation. Moreover, I like the repetition of certain kinds of rituals, simply because things repeated are pleasing. And I love that Episcopalianism is the locus of debates, now, about what scripture means on the subject of homosexuality. I love that my church has been brave enough to lead in the matter of ordaining gay bishops.

Do I believe every day? I believe every day, and I doubt every day. I cannot conceive of faith without doubt. I can't conceive of a relationship to the God of my faith without conceiving of terrifying overpowering silences that make me wonder what the hell it is I think I'm doing when I am praying and when I am addressing myself to the divine. I have never found that my faith has completely eliminated the fleshly appetites, and I don't even know if it's *meant to be* that faith eliminates these fleshly appetites—because we wouldn't have these bodies if we weren't meant to wrestle with the significance of having them.

Did I also say that I love the music of the church? As Dylan remarked of himself, I understand the spirit, whatever it is, through music. Music somehow actualizes belief in the face of doubt, in the face of the considerable secular pressures in my life and professional community, so that I feel myself made stronger by music and literature. And this seems to be the sort of thinking at the very center of *Compass Kids*, as when Daniel Smith says, "I will empty my accounts / To become a waiter on hand and foot and tend / To invisible hammers, guitars, and pens / Everything returns with purpose again."

What does music sound like when it is rendering these sorts of complexities? The paradoxes of belief in a modern age? It doesn't sound *easy*. Daniel Smith came up through the music department at Rutgers, and he learned composition, and his thesis was the first Danielson Famile album, *A Prayer for Every*

Hour, and even in that far more primitive recording, you can already feel him aspiring toward punk rock, prog, children's music, and the high-art tradition of contemporary classical music. Likewise, lyrically, he is already longing for an architecture of Christian symbolism that is not tainted by overuse, sentimentality, and tradition. In a way, Smith is like Dante, wanting to conceive of an imagination so rich that in understanding his words and his protagonists, you will have automatically worked through some of the mystery of Christianity: "Making a point of being disappointed / That rule of thumb will take you far in this life / 'Cause I know I'm always being disappointed / By my plans, by my boys and girls and by my plans / ... I now know I need, I now know I'm needy / I need to me [sic] a King. King of the Jungle / There's a good fire and a bad fire / My flame's burnin' at both ends / The one's gotta go, the other's gone wild / ... My wild fire is my feeling tank / My tank or heart is not mine / There's no me involved, man / It's the Great Comfort moving man / Amen, brother."* Already, the experience of listening to the music and coming to parse the lyrics is the experience of being faithful, which is an experience of much confusion, and much disappointment, and much that is *not* reassuring, and not simple, and not easy. Or, as a friend once preached at my parish in NYC, people would quit asking for angels to visit if they bothered to read up on when exactly angels turn up. Angels are terrifying. The appearance of angels always brings with it cataclysmic changes in life and circumstance. They aren't hovering outside to make sure that your tax return arrives promptly. They appear to tell

---

* The song is called "Feeling Tank," from *A Prayer for Every Hour*.

you that *you* are about to be impregnated by the power that created all space and time. Or they appear to tell you that the world as you know it is going to end, and that you may perish among the billions.

Consider the allusive quality of the most beautiful song on *Compass Kids*, "Can We Camp at Your Feet": "I get down from my sky high chair to / Camp at your feet / With what can I get away? / Your love will have your way with us / Anything that we can do? / Water all the gifts in my shipshape children / Bless this mess / Water all the gifts in my compass children / ... Feet of good news." There's nothing screechy about the music on this one, just a morose stillness to Daniel's harmony with one of his sisters. The pulse of a backbeat begins with the line "With what can I get away?," which, as anyone who has ever tried to be religious will tell you, is the line that your brain utters with greatest regularity: *Why should I bother to do this? I get very little respect for trying to do this here on earth, where the options are between some mindless adherence, which seems to involve wearing blinders and condemning everyone I love to a fiery eternity, and a slightly decadent secularism, why bother with the coffee hour with the Republicans after a church service in which they have ignored everything they have just heard, why should I bother, couldn't this possibly just pay off a little bit, couldn't the thing that I'm supposedly praying to, the thing that supposedly created all this stuff around me, just respond once to my pleas, couldn't it just one time, this thing, make life a little bit of easier, instead of making it more complicated? Isn't there a reward for people who go through with all this stuff and give away a lot of money because that's what you're supposed to do, isn't there one meager reward for doing this in terms of actual gifts given, or results conveyed, because if there's no reward, when everyone else is outside doing all the stuff they get to do, buying what they get to buy, sleeping in on Sunday, why should I bother to do this, because it really would be a lot more fun* not *to have to do it?* "Can We Camp at Your Feet" brings this difficulty into relief, suggesting what is frankly heretical in most sects of Christianity, that the believer should take his or her faith directly to the unnamed omnipotence (Christ is almost never mentioned in the entirety of the Danielson oeuvre, for example), *around* the intervening authorities, the bishops, ministers, etc., *around* the commentators who say it should be done this way and no other way. In doing so, the song proceeds toward a truly magnificent instrumental coda in which, after the line "Your love will have your way," there is a beautiful overdubbed *exhalation,* by the vocal chorus, and this exhalation, the breath of God, I guess, recurs through the chord progression, while the backup singers sing the word *good,* from the *good news* of the last line, and the drummers stop and start in some kind of martial style, with myriad snare rolls, and the song threatens to end three times, always with these exhalations, the breath of God, the thing worshipped brought near, away from the history of a religion, away from the religious controversies of the moment, away from the sectarianism, away from the battles between Christianity and Islam, away from the anti-Semitism of fundamentalism, and in a musical style that any smart kid on any college campus in this country would recognize and respond to, a musical idiom that is full of instruments actually being *played,* instead of machines being played, mistakes and awkwardnesses preserved, barely an amplifier turned on, all because this is the way things really are, they are insurmountable, they are irreconcilable; it's hard to get through any twenty-four-hour period, that's what it means to be a Christian artist, it means that you understand what it's like to be here, and you don't presume to know more, you presume to care about what other people think and feel, which is emphatically what most Christians do *not* do; that's how it is.

Five Songs
(By Wilco)

1.

The question before us is about the nature of evolution. The question before us is whether evolution, generally speaking, is smooth and proceeds at a certain rate, or whether this evolutionary business is full of abruptness and complexity, such that its rate is not fixed, nor its surface smooth. The question before us is whether the evolution of a certain kind of composition, a composition that looks on the surface as though it might be erratic and violent, is in fact more orderly than it appears. Or perhaps the question is whether a surface that appears relatively smooth and consistent can be, on its obverse, abrupt and disorderly. The question before us, a question whose response herein has five parts, is whether a thing can be itself and its opposite at the same time, and whether a composition can intentionally embody an ambition and its opposite, and, if so, what is the means for one attempting to apprehend or interpret this composition, as in the case of a listener attempting to get comfortable with a certain musical body of work.

The first release by the band called Wilco is entitled *A.M.*, and since the release has the picture of a radio on the front cover, it would be reasonable to assume that the record alludes to the AM band of American radio, the broadcast frequency of the childhood of members of the band called Wilco. In the New York metro area, the AM radio band, and thus popular music, was controlled by WABC radio and WNBC radio, and by disc jockeys like "Cousin Brucie" Morrow and Harry Harrison. Does *A.M.* allude to deejays of this kind? Deejays who used too much reverb on their broadcasts and who always talked over the beginnings and endings of songs? Does the *A.M.* of Wilco's title refer to this tender and nostalgic AM radio of our youth? Is the album's relatively *sunny* and *twangy* means of expression a reflection of this radio of our youth? Or is it not possible that *A.M.* means something else entirely? What if *A.M.* alludes to the 1900 transmission, over a distance of one mile, of the words *One, two, three, four, is it snowing where you are Mr. Thiessen? If it is, would you telegraph back to me?* by one Reginald Aubrey Fessenden? Does the *A.M.* of Wilco's title refer to this most primitive AM band? Or maybe, notwithstanding the photograph of the radio, is it not possible that we are instead referring here to AM as in ante meridiem, otherwise known as *before noon*, and thus is it correct to conclude that *A.M.* has the intention of being *sunny* and *twangy*—which it arguably is, on songs like "I Must Be High" and "Casino Queen" and "Passenger Side"—or are we more exactly speaking of a *morning* of composition, which is to say a *new day*, like the *new morning* of another folk rock troubadour? Or perhaps, to stretch the possibilities even further, we are speaking of *artium magister*, the Latin for *master of arts*, though I am not sure that the principals of the compositional entity called Wilco would make the claim that they are *masters of arts*, as this is maybe a little pretentious; no, perhaps *artium magister* goes too far as an interpretation, except that no interpretation goes too far with Wilco, even on the *sunny* and *twangy* album known as *A.M.*, because its very simplicity is also deceitful and ambiguous. Take, for example, the beautiful "I Thought I Held You," which contains the lines "I'm like a songwriter / You're the reason I've run out / Run out of metaphors." Meaning what exactly? Is the writer of the song *not* a songwriter? How can he be "like a songwriter," making use of the similitude of "like," when he *is* in fact a songwriter, the lines themselves serving as the proof? And when he says he has "run out" the first time, does he not mean "run out" as in abandoned, as in ended a *love relationship* (if you accept the prevailing interpretation, perhaps the narrator is alluding to having *ended a band*), such that he is both ending a *love relationship* and "running out" of or exhausting his metaphors (metaphors being somewhat different from similes), or is he simply extending a line so that it scans properly, so that it fits into the space allotted?

When the beautiful "I Thought I Held You" moves forward from its desperate similes, it moves forward into a chorus, which I would argue is written in direct address from the failed songwriter (I'm *like* a songwriter, so I'm *not* a songwriter but rather someone who is attempting to use simile as though I were) to the audience, who might think that this *sunny* and *twangy* song is just what it appears, *sunny* and *twangy*, when what it actually is is something altogether more desperate: "I don't even think you understand / I thought I held you by the hand / I thought I held you…" Which means what exactly? Does it mean the failed songwriter is abandoning a *love relationship* or *ending a band?* Or is it rather a very desperate and harrowing question about whether this endeavor, the endeavor of songwriting and band-making, the routine of writing, recording, and touring, is actually *connecting* songwriter and audience *at all?* Are you actually getting the meaning I'm attempting to send to you, in this failed system of transmission, the popular song, or is the system somehow faulty? And if it is faulty, with what shall we replace it?

For the purposes of a discussion of evolution, however, I didn't mean to talk about "I Thought I Held You," though like almost all of *A.M.* it is, in its way, perfect. Rather I meant to speak about the strangest and most out-of-place song on *A.M.*, the song called "Dash 7," which is not *sunny* at all, and though it has the ubiquitous pedal steel guitar of *A.M.*, the kind of thing that folk rock zealots manage to turn into a cliché that must appear on all records in order to ensure legitimacy, it doesn't *sound* like it has a pedal steel. Because the song does not capitulate to the one-four-five-with-relative-minors song structures that make the rest of *A.M.* so easy on the ears ("Can you keep it simple? Can you let the snare crack?"). Instead, "Dash 7" makes use of a modal tuning, and some passing chords, as a way to get at some really acute loneliness, like so much of the later and more self-evidently complex work by the band known as Wilco. Therefore, "Dash 7" appears to prefigure this evolution of which we speak. What "Dash 7" does is go from a one-four (D to G) progression to B minor, and then emphasize the possibility of a C chord, a half step up from B minor. It's a passing C, a diminished C triad with a suspended second, if it works the way it sounds, which is a chord that would shock most rock-and-roll ears. This is *difficult listening* to those who start with Chuck Berry and end with AC/DC. And because it's difficult it's evolutionary.

However, the question before us, with "Dash 7," is what is the song *about*—is the song really about a certain kind of propeller plane, one in the transport category, first manufactured in 1975, popular in Europe, discontinued in 1984 after a mere hundred of them were built? (Lately the Dash 7 has been used by the US Army for surveillance.) Because of the *slipstream* around the prop, the Dash 7 is known for *firm* landings, which are not necessarily easy on passengers, and "Dash 7" the song seems to take on the matter of the Dash 7 in the moment of landing. Yes, songs about touring are well-known, lamentations about touring, and at first glance, "Dash 7" would seem to allude to the endless travel of a musician's life: "Dash 7 in the air / Propped to the sun alone / Jets hum / I wish that I was still there / Props, not a jet, alone / Where the sun doesn't come down." Sure, it's probably just a song about touring. That would be obvious. At least until the chorus: "Because I've found the way those engines sound / Will make you kiss the ground / When you touch down." Is "Dash 7" about the way the engines sound in general, or about the possibility of engine failure, the possibility of calamity, and is the captain's announcement in the third verse ("Dash 7 pointed down / The captain's announcement / Doesn't make a sound") an intimation of *bad news*, and is its soundlessness part of a strategy to create in the listener a certain kind of *audition*, as John Cage called it? Because, without giving up its mysteries, "Dash 7" fades into twenty-five seconds of

looped rumbling—apparently the sound of airplane engines—
at its close. If evolutionary, the song is asking us to embark on
leaving behind the *sunny* and *twangy* surfaces of *A.M.* The song
is asking us to embrace completely abstract noise, and to find in
it the same poignancy that we might bring to the more accessible emotional core of the popular song. Indeed, the *later and
more complex* work of the band called Wilco discourages passive
listening, and the pristine, ominous, and melancholy "Dash 7"
begins this transition from *sunny* and *twangy,* even as it estab-
lishes a reputation for same, by first composing an old-timey
melody about the sound of plane engines, and then including
looped industrial noise at the melody's close.

One last coincidence on the matter of "Dash 7." This
involves the history of the electric chair. The first execution in
the electric chair involved a gentleman called Kemmler, whose
last words were thus: "I want only to say that a great deal has
been said about me that is untrue. I am bad enough. It is cruel
to make me out worse." In order to prepare to execute Kemmler, an audience of electricians had to test the technology on an
animal, a dog convicted of biting, a dog who first required 300
volts, and then 400 volts, and then 700 volts and who still
would not die, who tore his muzzle and menaced the crowd,
and the name of that dog was Dash.

2.

Beneath the *sunny* and *twangy* surface of *A.M* is something
else, and I have been trying to point in the direction of this
something else. Our job is to divine what Wilco is trying to

say, in these five fathoms down. Does supplemental material indicate the *obverse* of whatever is indicated in the *sunny* and *twangy* exterior of *A.M.*? The situation is like unto the voice of Wilco singer Jeff Tweedy. As with the memorable blues and gospel singers, Tweedy's instrument has gravelly overtones (partly owing to his consumption of the demon tobacco, no doubt). His voice is parched in that way that Paul Westerberg's was back when he was a Replacement. And yet Tweedy sings beautifully. His is a voice of yearning, loss, dry wit, occasional rage, impatience, and almost none of these colors is obvious. What Tweedy appears to be saying with his instrument is almost always as evident in silences and hoarse passages as it is in the *sung* melodies. Here it seems obvious that the manifest content of the instrument is not the true or entire content. And yet neither is a specific subtextual undercurrent being conveyed. What is being conveyed in Tweedy's voice, and perhaps in the sprawling and ambitious song cycle known as *Being There*, is discontinuity: between surface and subtextual intention, an intention, even on its own, that is very difficult to articulate.

"Misunderstood" is a popular song on the second album recorded by Wilco, entitled *Being There*. It's sort of an *anthem*, in fact, and "Misunderstood" would seem to be the correct song to write about in order to understand the evolutionary movement of the band called Wilco. Because "Misunderstood" happens to be *about* rock and roll in some ways. It also seems to be about the success of *A.M.* and the kind of expectations that an audience might have for the compositions of the album that follows. Remember that this album is named for a novel by Jerzy Kosinski about a learning-disabled gardener called

Chance, who inadvertently becomes a great politician by blurting out homely lines about trees and shrubs. Remember that the album also quotes from a song by Peter Laughner, he of the early demise from liver damage, he of the famous Rocket From the Tombs.

Thus there are interesting spots here where an interpreter might gain purchase. As when a climber ascends sheer rock face. We have the fine punk rock wailing at beginning and end of "Misunderstood," which is played well in concert, in footage I have seen, etc. I admit the importance of the line "You look honest when you're telling a lie," which is in the category of paradoxical statements that are multiply reproducible (see, e.g., *Yankee Hotel Foxtrot*, for more discussion of same) in the ongoing Wilco project. Similarly, here we have the accusatory second person that is really a first person (used to fine effect by Elvis Costello). All these reasons are exactly why I am *not* going to write about "Misunderstood." Because "Misunderstood" is trying harder than it needs to. Its anthemic quality is premeditated, which is in some respects true of the whole of the sprawling and ambitious album known as *Being There*, which could potentially be a candidate for my music-writing brethren who like to whittle two-albums sets down to *one* compact disc ("Sunken Treasure," "Someone Else's Song," "Kingpin," "Dreamer in My Dreams," "Misunderstood," "Outtasite [Outta Mind]," "What's the World Got in Store," "Monday," "Say You Miss Me," a single CD package that would top out at about forty-two minutes, the length of a perfect LP in the old days).

Instead, I am going to offer the hypothesis that *Being There* is about more than being misunderstood, although it does pass through that *topos*. It is about *not* being *here*, actually, it is about being in part absent from the creative process in one fundamental way, it is about recognizing that beneath what is *here* is a completely different address, a wormhole, a trembling ocean of *formlessness* and *ceaseless movement*, viz., the unconscious, erupting at all places and at all times, in "Dreamer in My Dreams," for example, and in "(Was I) In Your Dreams" and "Outtasite (Outta Mind)," all of them, to some extent, about the pressure of unseen worries and unseen registers of consciousness on a *love relationship*, about this recognition that things are going on beyond the perceptual capabilities of the ordinary senses. It's everywhere on this record, *Being There*, the desperation to figure out how to deal with *crisis*, the crisis of success, perhaps, but also some more chronic discomfort, some chthonic discomfort, this discomfort best summed up in the beautiful and obsessive "Sunken Treasure," a song that does exactly what it claims it's *not* going to do.

"Sunken Treasure" contains the line "There is no sunken treasure," as if attempting to deny the existence of the subliminal layers of composition, as if to strike a blow for a materialist reading of human experience. And it then goes on to chart much of its course in ambiguous figures of speech, e.g., "If I had a boat...I'd probably roll over," plunging in the process into the sea, a terrifying occurrence, as any seafarer will tell you, whereupon this seafarer will need to *turtle* the craft, in the *formlessness* and *ceaseless trembling* of the ocean; remember, for example, Pip, in *Moby-Dick*, who jumps out of the longboat, is left for several hours, and, when plucked from the sea, has lost his wits. The immensity of what's under the surface of the sea is what is terrifying; as J. E. Cirlot remarks, "A vast expanse dreaming its own dreams and asleep in its own reality, yet containing within itself the seeds of its antitheses." Oceanic anxiety, chthonic anxiety, also apparent in the "rows and rows of houses" in the first verse of "Sunken Treasure," with their television lamps running "parallel to you," the listener. Into which lurches this *noise* of sunken treasure, the sound of timpani, multiple electric guitars, much piano banging, all of it overtaking the lovely simple melody of the verses, just as in "Misunderstood," which opens the other disc. Here with a more terrifying intention is music attempting to convey what can't be spoken (see "Outtasite": "I know we don't talk much..."), attempting to summon the unspeakable, and when Tweedy gets to the chorus on "Sunken Treasure," it is less to say that he *resents the audience* or is conflicted about his place in the business of rock and roll than to say that the popular song has written its history *on* him and *in* him: "I was maimed by rock and roll / I was tamed by rock and roll / I got my name from rock and roll." As in orthodox Catholic theology, Tweedy is *with* his idiom, and he is *in* his idiom, and he is *through* his idiom, and it has inscribed itself on him, in this sprawling and ambitious album, which takes the estrangement of "Dash 7" and blows its ambiguity up into a nearly symphonic scale. Breaking with the safety of *A.M.* while observing the principle of discontinuity.

3.

One of the oldest English-language jokes, according to a teacher I had in college, is one we learn in the first phase of language development. *Q: When is a door not a door? A: When it's ajar.* What does it mean for a door to be ajar? It means that the ability to contain information and systems of meaning is in a state of eclipse; *ajar* stands for *threshold*, *ajar* stands for the fact that in churches the doorway is always farthest from the altar, and thus the door is the antithesis of the system of meaning contained in the altar, and that makes perfect sense on the way to discussing the moody and disingenuous album called *Summerteeth*, whose apparently tuneful first song nonetheless contains the lines "No love's as random as God's love / I can't stand it /...Your prayers will never be answered again," while Jay Bennett's electric piano solo tinkles merrily in the background. *Door* goes back to Middle English, *door* goes back to Old High German, goes back to Latin and Greek, goes back to Sanskrit, which means it is among the oldest of words, as *church* is likewise, deriving from the Sanskrit *sura*, which brings us to *ajar*, which comes from the Old Norse *kjarr*, which brings us, on this moody and disingenuous album, *Summerteeth*, to the song entitled "She's a Jar." It's impossible not to come to this song, as one comes to this album as a whole, with a sort of stunned feeling about the lyrics. I am not, of course, saying that the lyrics were not plenty good on the first two Wilco releases. They were good for rock and roll. They were unassuming and charming and frequently funny. And yet on the moody and ambiguous album *Summerteeth*, it's like the lyrics *want to get somewhere*, and the somewhere is really anguished and really ambitious and really beautiful.

It's my assumption that domestic life at some point becomes a factor in the Wilco biography, as with all rock-and-roll bands. The practitioners of rock and roll begin to age, and in the process of aging, they begin to run afoul of some of the hallmarks of the rock-and-roll life: traveling, fickle attentions of fans, etc. One can assume that in Wilco more permanent attachments, such as marriage and children, begin to intrude. This is evident, e.g., in the film about Wilco, *I Am Trying to Break Your Heart*, which does depict Jeff Tweedy with wife and children, in completely tender moments.

The advent of this domestic arrangement begins to intrude on the lyrics of the band; the responsibilities of family, as opposed to just *being in a love relationship*, are here on the moody and ambiguous album called *Summerteeth*. "I'm worried / I'm always in love," is the *matrix sentence* for the album, as the semioticians might have put it. Or what about: "I dreamed about killing you again last night / And it felt all right to me." Far from repudiating or explaining this line, Tweedy, newly ambitious lyricist, has volunteered to attest to the intensity of this observation. Self-evidently, it is the lyric of a conflicted participant in the domestic process, and since we are talking about dreams, as we have been above, let me point out that last night I myself dreamed of Wilco. Like this: I was invited to watch the band play in Chicago, and they were playing at some bar, as they apparently had been for weeks, and first I sat down with Tweedy and we did some Q&A, and Tweedy claimed the reason he didn't want to play the *conventional popular song* anymore was that it had *too many whole notes* in it. To prove the point Tweedy actually wrote out, on a napkin, several measures of a popular song. Other members of the band joined the discussion, and yet soon they were instead accusing someone, not anyone actually *in* the band called Wilco, of diluting the power of the music by *fucking groupies*.

This stranger was fired on the spot by bass player John Stirratt.

Yes, the song from the moody and ambiguous album called *Summerteeth* to which I want to draw your attention is "She's a Jar," which is a woebegone and beautiful ballad, such as one might not have been surprised to hear on the early Wilco albums, except for the orchestral palette that now includes synthesizer, or is it chamberlin or mellotron? Similarly ornamented is a really big bridge and chorus—yes, a soaring chorus—in which the narrator floats above the people underneath him. This being more evidence of the anxious apartness of *Summerteeth:* "Please beware of the quiet front yard," or "When I forget how to talk, I sing," or "My face gets sick, stuck / Like a question unposed." These lines admixed with fervent affections like: "She's a jar / With heavy lid / My pop quiz kid." A feeling of isolation *should* be alleviated when the domestic question is resolved, and yet somehow this disparity is *not* resolved on the moody and ambiguous album called *Summerteeth.* The interrogatives pile up violently here. The lyrics are just as unsettled as the arrangements on this calliope album, the first without pedal steel and violin, the first with Brill Building passing chords. It's an album that wants to get somewhere and which doesn't mind if it sacrifices some *No Depression* music fans in the process. *Summerteeth* says *Yes, Depression!* The somewhere it wants to get is perhaps into the terrain of Alex Chilton during the period when Alex was falling apart, viz., *Sister Lovers*, or perhaps the terrain of the early Velvet Underground, as in the end of "She's a Jar," wherein the protagonist says, of his lover, "You know she begs me not to hit her," which of course recalls the Velvets line "You better hit her" (from "There She Goes Again").

Whereas one might actually believe in Lou Reed hitting someone, or at least one believes in Lou's ability to observe someone who might hit his or her girlfriend, one feels considerable doubt about Jeff Tweedy, sensitive guy, panic attack sufferer, hitting anyone, but that is what you get on the moody and ambiguous album called *Summerteeth*, you get sweet melodies twinned with fierce and rather troubling lyrics. Which is what you should get on a transitional album. Which is to say that *Summerteeth* is the album that precedes the unearthly *Yankee Hotel Foxtrot*, and as such, at first glance, it seems inexplicable. I remember finding it inexplicable when I first heard it. I remember thinking, *What is it with this record?*, loving it and not understanding in equal measure. Because where was the pedal steel, but also, what to make of these lyrics? Because these are not lyrics that trust in the confessional, unless what is being confessed is doubt about the efficacy of confession. *Summerteeth* feels like the door to the refuge has gone ajar, and you can see in long focus into the church interior, and you know how long a sprint that's going to be, when you try to make the dash for the spotlight.

4.

Yankee Hotel Foxtrot, album of Chicago. Chicago is the place it was made, the place it was *filmed*, and Chicago is the musical environment in which its profound perfume of failure begins to smell like success. *Yankee Hotel Foxtrot* is lead made into gold. Drummer got laid off, lead guitarist got laid off, label rejected the record, another label repurchased it, album went to number thirteen, etc. We have heard these kinds of stories, and these kinds of stories are very satisfying. But is there a way to get beneath the surface of the publicist's breathless excitement, to what is going on below? Because *Yankee Hotel Foxtrot* is the triumph that does not give away its secrets immediately.

Chicago. As symbolized by the lopsided photograph of the Marina Towers on the front cover. I remember seeing the Marina Towers the first time I was in the Windy City. There's some great architecture in downtown Chicago, some of the best architecture in the country. The Marina Towers are not examples of this great architecture. The Merchandise Mart, e.g., just a few blocks away, is much more beautiful. The Marina Towers are an early example, I believe, of cast concrete, from a period in which there was a vogue for putting residential, commercial, and parking space all in one site. In Chicago they had the wisdom to site this complex in the center of town, rather than consigning it to the outskirts, as in the case of Co-op City, Bronx. Rumor has it that the Marina apartments are wedge shaped, which implies that they are *hard to decorate*. What do you put at the point of the apartment? The Marina Towers are not attractive, from a classical standpoint, but they are American, like vinyl tablecloths or corncob holders, which is actually sort of what the Marina Towers look like: corncob holders. While management denies it, local residents believe that the towers really *are* tilting. Thus, the lopsided photo on the cover of *Yankee Hotel Foxtrot* looks genuine, not stylized.

This is not the Chicago of Wicker Park, where Liz Phair lived. This is not the Chicago of tastemakers but the Chicago of Americana, where America happens, and yet this Americana is given a bizarre twist on the cerebral and affectionate album called *Yankee Hotel Foxtrot*, and you can tell this right from the beginning, because "I Am Trying to Break Your Heart" opens with a droning onslaught of noise, synthesizers, xylophone, autoharp, guitar feedback, and then abecedary lyrics. Lyrics that are at first *about* the letter *a* and the things that might be done with this letter, followed by some alliteration involving *b* and *c*, etc.: "I am an American aquarium drinker / I assassin down the avenue / I'm hiding out in the big city blinking / What was I thinking when I let go of you." What does this mean exactly? Unfortunately, *Yankee Hotel Foxtrot* does not encourage questions like *What does this mean?* Perhaps even the purveyors of *Yankee Hotel Foxtrot* know not what these lyrics *mean*, which indicates, in fact, that we are working in a context of automatic meanings or chance procedures: "I want to hold you in the bible black predawn / You're a quiet domino, bury me now." As a lyrical approach, of course, this certainly is miles from "Casino Queen," "Passenger Side," and other early Wilco songs. As an approach, it doesn't sound that far from the stuff happening in Chicago, if by Chicago we mean the Drag City / Thrill Jockey aesthetics of Jim O'Rourke, David Grubbs, Tortoise, the Sea and Cake, et al. Even the songs that are more conventionally structured, like "Kamera" and "Heavy Metal Drummer," where the progressions are not completely unknown to the rock-and-roll hordes, even in these songs we find hints of a kind of experimental ringing and droning.

On the relatively summery melodies, there are lyrical allusions to darkness and disorder, "Phone my family, tell them I'm lost on the / Sidewalk," or "There is something wrong with me," or "How can I convince you it's me I don't like?" Love songs, if that's what they are, that are all about doubt, including an entire song about having reservations about the idea of love. And there are the epistemological obsessions we found on the prior two albums ("All my lies are always wishes" and "It's beautiful to lie"). What to say about *Yankee Hotel Foxtrot*, but that it is deeply disturbed and masterful. So faultlessly produced that it makes indie rock, whatever that once was, sound like a symphony, makes post-rock sing, makes *roots music* sound like electronica, and does so while, in my view, perfectly describing a migraine.

Indeed, Jeff Tweedy's lifelong struggle with migraine seems to be *the* generator of themes on *Yankee Hotel Foxtrot*. You can see the spots where the auras begin their blossoming everywhere: "My mind is filled with silvery stuff," and "You could be my demon / Moving forward through flaming doors," and "You were right about the stars / Each one is a setting sun," and "All I can see / Is black and white / And white and pink / With blades of blue / That lay between," and also the massive amounts of pain and illness and disquiet that are the inevitable wasteland of consciousness after the migraine commences, so that Tweedy's apparently *noncommercial gambit* is actually a rather faithful and organic attempt to diagram what a lifetime of suffering feels like. And what it entails, this suffering, is the obliteration of all that linear stuff you favor so much, where part A of the song moves into a chorus that is part B, with a perfectly crafted little bridge and then some more of part A and part B. All of that goes into the compactor, and what remains is the huge implacable monolith of *pain*. Admittedly, sometimes Wilco *tries* to work the love song stuff in around the migraines.

There are any number of songs that indicate the purity of this cerebral and affectionate album. I was, initially, completely infatuated with "Radio Cure," which is morbid and almost clinically depressed until it gets to the B section, when it sounds chipper and upbeat while repeating over and over the line "Distance has no way of making love / Understandable." But in fact, "Radio Cure," with its migrainous observations, "There is something wrong with me / My mind is filled with radio cures / Electronic surgical words," is too simple as an emblem for *Yankee Hotel Foxtrot*.

No, the irrefutable masterpiece on this album of masterpieces is actually "Ashes of American Flags." Therefore, it's best to concentrate our attentions here. The title alone requires exegesis. Of course, *ashes* are what the alchemists had as their end-stage by-product, and *Yankee Hotel Foxtrot* is not without imagery of conflagration elsewhere. There is also, in these ashes, an evocation of the prehistory of contemporary Chicago, a city that has so much good architecture in part because it was burned to the ground. This was in 1871, and they'd had twenty fires the previous week. That's how dry it was. The fire jumped the Chicago River at one point, burned down the opera house, city hall, etc. It's as if an earlier idea of Wilco actually needed to be *incinerated* in order to get to this recording.

Another layer of the title clearly alludes to the perennial time-waster of congressional Republicans, the flag-burning amendment to the United States Constitution. The last major legislative push in this direction was in 2000, notwithstanding failures in 1989 and 1990 and 1995. Although it's fair to say that the lyricist of *Yankee Hotel Foxtrot*, roiling in his migrainous anguish, is unlikely to write a song *about* the flag-burning amendment, he certainly has an afterimage from the 2000 senatorial debate close at hand, as he also seems to hear Mrs. O'Leary's cow lowing sweetly.

"Ashes of American Flags" commences with its own little chamber music drone, and then we have the one four five, and we have the singer and his reification of contemporary Chicago, built on the ashes of the old: cash machines, Coca-Cola, and cigarettes. This leads him into a brief invocation of the meaning of poetry, then his usual epistemological anxieties about lying. At which point the rhythm section drops out, and there is the droning of electronic effects, echo-laden electric guitar, and from there we are at the summit of this heartbreaking song: "I'm down on my hands and knees / Every time the doorbell rings." Reminding this listener of the famous description of Nathaniel Hawthorne, that he was given to fleeing into the woods when in danger of passing anyone on the road. Not a bad gloss for a narrator who ends his ditty thus: "I would like to salute / The ashes of American flags / And all the falling leaves / Filling up shopping bags." The conjunction being between the material of everyday life in Chicago (ATMs and cigarettes) and the residue implicit in ash and dead leaves. Tweedy, that is, salutes residue, whatever is left over.

The course of the album and the progress of the band follow the alchemical model implicit in this song. *Yankee Hotel Foxtrot*, that is, is a record of what must be incinerated to be perfected, namely all popular music, so that the cerebral part, the heroic-investigation part, the troubadour part, may flourish. This process of incineration gets to why this is the perfect Wilco record, so far, and why it is not the album with the most *hits*. Whatever those are. The album recognizes explicitly what was implicit on *Summerteeth*, namely that there is animus lurking under the domestic fulfillment of the popular song, there is disgust, there is despair, there is suffering, and in the grip of this animus, there is desire again, always the recirculation between the two, disaffiliation and desire, the yearning for the happily-ever-after popular song. The thing and its obverse. *Yankee Hotel Foxtrot*, with its wall of noise, recognizes this paradox and takes what has been implicit in the earlier Wilco albums, just offstage, and brings it into the spotlight, brings it, in fact, into the mix, where complexity becomes self-evident, as a style, as a methodology, as a sound.

5.

The resource that is required for the just assessment of popular music is *adequate time*. Or: the mistake of criticism in this attention-deficit-disordered age is twofold: lack of space and lack of time. Never enough space is devoted to criticism and never enough time is given to the premeditation of this analysis. Nevertheless, this introduction, in attempting to both conclude and remain timely as to the evolution of the band called Wilco, now attempts a hasty response to *new* work by the band called Wilco, which is the recently issued recording entitled *A Ghost Is Born*, and yet this introduction does so with the idea that evolution at the instant of its transformation always looks more like mutation. Still, let it be said that *A Ghost Is Born*, in haste, is *post-historical*, in that it means to follow an album that was the end of all possible albums, as Arthur Danto has said of Andy Warhol's soup cans. What sort of art do we make after the internal imperatives of a form have been exhausted? The answer being: *anything we want*. After history is liberty. And so we have *A Ghost Is Born*, with its fluxion of styles and ambitions, some Brill Building, some stuff that sounds like gospel, some long-lost tracks from *Music from Big Pink*, some punk rock, some post-rock, and so forth. *Post-historical* and *liberated*. Free from the burden of which Stephen Dedalus spoke: "History is a nightmare from which I am trying to awake."

Certain tendencies may in this instant appear to be features of post-historical endeavor. Simplification may appear to be a feature. For *A Ghost Is Born* seems to want to repeal some of the sonic palette of *Yankee Hotel Foxtrot*; it wants less electronica, less digital flourishing, less Pro Tools, less synthesis, less lead guitar playing (of the traditional sort). It wants more analogue, more ensemble playing, more spontaneity, more raw discovery. It wants more ache in the singer's voice. As *Yankee Hotel Foxtrot* toyed with drones, *A Ghost Is Born* toys with silences. Mostly here the drones are live instruments playing, not digital signals. Post-historical endeavor also continues to favor song structure that is looser and more arbitrary, part A of the song glued to part C, with part D attached for a middle eight and then never repeated. No part B at all. Yes, that *liberated* aspect of *Yankee Hotel Foxtrot* is expanded and enhanced. Yes, many of these songs, fresh from the oven, as I have heard them, feature beautiful sonic transitions, sudden violent meta-morphoses from one section to another, because they *can*, because that's what one does with one's liberty.

The perceiving intelligence that sings out in this post-historical and liberated album has some things in common with the narrator described above, in songs one through four. In each case there is discomfort, melancholy, a kneeling posture ("I got up off my hands and knees / To thank my lucky stars you're not me," e.g.). But *A Ghost Is Born* adds new leitmotifs to the oeuvre, viz., the *infernal latitudes*, common to two of the really beautiful ballads on this recording, "Hell Is Chrome" and "Wishful Thinking." "When the devil came / He was not red / He was chrome and he said / Come with me." Likewise in "Wishful Thinking," we find "The turntable sizzles / The casting of spells / The pressure devices / Hell in a nutshell / Is any song worth singing / If it doesn't help." Hell, in a nutshell, is *all around* on *A Ghost Is Born*. The original title, *Decibels per Minute*, even internally rhymed with *hell*. And any attempt to plot an optimistic and loving course out of the infernal regions here feels sweet and ambitious and doomed.

Another fact on *A Ghost Is Born* is the insectile perspective. By the insectile perspective, I refer to the perspective that Richard Feynman described when trying to metaphorize about what a universe with more than four dimensions might feel like. Imagine, Feynman proposed, that you're a water bug on the surface of a lake, born here on the surface, destined to die on the surface. Your perspective, from here, is confined to the two dimensions of lake on which you survive, for you are never going to be beneath the surface, where the fish are busy, nor are you going to be soaring among the birds high above. How do you, water skimmer, react when a rock is thrown into the lake in front of you, and in the ensuing explosion you are cast up off the surface of the lake for the very first time, and you begin to see, as never before, that there is a whole way of thinking about the surface of the lake that you never before understood? This is the insectile perspective of *A Ghost Is Born*, the bug made aware of his predicament, the citizen of four dimensions beginning to understand for a fleeting instant the possibility of *more*.

And perhaps it goes without saying that the time of *A Ghost Is Born* was also a time of national crisis, hitherto unexamined by Wilco by reason of the fact that *Yankee Hotel Foxtrot* was finished before the World Trade Center attack, etc. The bugs, the insects, of *A Ghost Is Born* are yearning for what is next, for what is possible now, for a way of seeing after disaster (as Tom Verlaine wrote, "I love disaster, and I love what comes after") and a way of being in which the cataclysm of the rock falling into the lake and the disturbance of two-dimensionality is now a part of experience. "Hell Is Chrome," with its depiction of hell as a place of cleanliness, a place both "precise and towering," is a depiction of the time *after* the Twin Towers, and this hell as described is a place that exists outside of place and time as we normally understand them. It is a place that simplifies your options, reduces them down to the *certainties*, so that the "Come with me" of the chorus, repeated at length, is the woeful politics of hell, and this hell is about as mournful and beautiful and sad as anything that Wilco has ever recorded. This is the thing about the time after history. It is full of seductions ("Come with me"), the allure of certainty, and if you turn aside the Mephistophelian pact, well, then everything is possible for you, *everything is possible,* and you are destined to be uncertain, sad, and scared. *A Ghost Is Born,* at first blush, is like this liberty: vast, terrifying, intoxicating, true.

So these are the five songs with which to reckon. "Dash 7," "Sunken Treasure," "She's a Jar," "Ashes of American Flags," and "Hell Is Chrome." What do the songs tell us about how people mature, how songwriters grow up? What do the five songs tell us about evolution? Evolution always seems impossible, obscure. No wonder the creationists are confused. Do you ever *see* evolution take place? Can you watch natural selection in its flourishing? Can you watch a virus mutate? The same with artists and musicians. From a distance, the changes in an artist's life look violent. How does Picasso get from the Blue Period to high Cubism? What about Aaron Copland? There was all that Americana, and then later some rather strident serial stylings. In the popular song, there are the radical mutations in the work of a David Bowie or a Neil Young.

From the air, Wilco looks like a band that has metamorphosed at a great velocity, engulfing experimental impulses with each album, incorporating them swiftly, confidently, and intuitively. And yet upon close inspection, it seems to me, the five songs here wrenched from their settings have quite a bit in common, beyond Jeff Tweedy's voice and a certain way of playing the acoustic guitar. The five songs have in common a way of looking at *meaning.* In the main, the popular song is a nugget of resolution, of encapsulation. Its material is amber. "California Girls" is about girls from California. "Let It Be" is about letting it be. Love songs explicate love, bring love's inexplicabilities in close, where they can be *resisted.* But the five songs here aren't resolute at all. The five songs, in each case and taken as a whole, celebrate ambiguity and complexity and uncertainty without sacrificing deep feeling. They articulate the passions, but they don't simplify them. The five songs allow feelings to stay insoluble, as they are in life. Perceptible but insoluble. The five songs focus the lens on their narrators only briefly, after which these narrators are subdivided or combined with other narrators, other perceptions, other contexts. And in this way the Wilco project, as shadowed forth here, seems more about *possibility* than about any other subject. The five songs are about the lust for possibility. Just as evolution itself ever celebrates possibility and change.

Guilty Pleasures

1.

The Brooklyn Record Club meets quarterly and consists of twelve or so patient individuals, a good portion of them employed in various arts-related capacities. There are a few actual musicians, at least one painter of great cultural significance, two or three writers. There are a couple of corporate professionals, some freelancers. One government employee who is also a decorative-arts historian. We have been meeting since 2000, which seems like a long time, although my mother's book club has been meeting for thirty years.

I've been a participant in a couple of book clubs, and I've always found them uncomfortable. Maybe because books are my job. I got the idea to convene the Brooklyn Record Club from attending a similar group in Manhattan.* They had a lot more rules over there in Manhattan. They met every month,

---

* See also the essay on the Danielson Famile, pp. 89–105.

on a particular Friday. No bootlegs allowed. Each song needed to be commercially available. The Brooklyn Record Club, on the other hand, is permissive. Every participant brings two songs in whatever format he or she favors. Playing cards are then dealt at random, and the order of programming follows from the cards, aces being low. After everyone has spun his or her first tune, there's a break, which is normally the dessert break (ours is a dinner-oriented record club), and then the second round proceeds.

At the conclusion of each evening, a CD-R anthology of the Brooklyn Record Club is designed and constructed by whoever is feeling guilty about not having done it lately, and this anthology is handed out at the next meeting.

Two trends can be inferred from the five years of the Brooklyn Record Club. First, obscurity is highly prized. Second, humor is also popular. My wife, among others, disdains the first trend and, in a way, the second. My wife hews close to the spirit of the Manhattan Record Club, which suggests that one should bring songs that one *feels exceedingly passionate about*. I suppose obscurity and comic value don't necessarily preclude strong feelings, but, as a practical matter, if one of your selections is a young Japanese woman singing along with the Walkman playback of *Jesus Christ Superstar*, or perhaps a heavy-metal orthodox Jew who declaims his Talmudic scholarship to death-metal riffing (actual recent Brooklyn Record Club selections!), then it is fair to say that these songs are not in your top ten of all time. You wouldn't want them played at your wedding or your funeral.

There have been a couple of Brooklyn Record Club special events. In January 2003, we decided to hold a meeting to which everyone was encouraged to bring their musical favorites from the calendar year 2002, reissues deemed acceptable. This requirement engendered, despite the possibility of reissues, much grumbling from certain participants who claimed that they had not purchased a single recording, new or reissued, in 2002. On another occasion, the Brooklyn Record Club took advantage of the photo studio business owned by one of our members to stage a Brooklyn Record Club *dance event.* The room was pretty empty, since there were only twelve of us, but it was fun nonetheless. The selections lurched somewhat disjunctively from funk to punk and back again.

Neither of these special events, however, could prepare us for the night that became known as Guilty Pleasures. The way I remember it, the innocent suggestion was my own. A painter friend, whom I'll call FT (I'm using initials for everyone, to protect them from the inevitable calumnies), saw the potential in such a thing right away, and in fact there was initial common assent on a Guilty Pleasures evening. Still, almost immediately doubts set in. In fact, an e-mail bonanza followed, featuring much soul-searching. And because I like stuff like this—times when ordinary people are called upon to weigh in on the big philosophical questions—I saved the e-mail messages. Here's a sampling:

> Dear Record Club friends, I'm assuming that the consensus for a "Guilty Pleasures" theme for the next meeting meets with general approval. The idea would be to bring two songs that you are somewhat ashamed to like. I have so many the only problem will be limiting them to two.
>
> —RM

i like the 'concept' record club thing, and guilty pleasures is a great idea. i'm immediately thinking of a really
great disco 12" I have that I borrowed and never returned
to its rightful owner, for instance, and can't listen to without a sickly twinge. (I am no longer on speaking terms with
its owner, adding to the fun.)

—KH

I know that it's now hip to love Neil Diamond (Losers
Lounge et al) but I never realized he was bad. In fact I
learned 'Cracklin' Rosie' from one of my father's many fake
books (he has a wedding band—still active and performing 'Wonderwall' and 'Don't Know Why' amongst other
top tunes nightly) where they changed the words of the
song from "store-bought woman" to "starboard woman"
because obviously the real words were a bit much for us
Scottish Calvinists. My dad also does a live karaoke, all part
of the complete wedding embarrassment package.

Top Wedding Karaoke Songs from his band:

Wonderwall (obviously)
I Will Always Love You (hmm)
Ob-la-Di-Oh Blah Dah) (bride/groom)
One Day at a Time Sweet Jesus (mother of the groom)
10 Guitars (father of the groom)
My Way (mother of the bride)
I Walk the Line (father of the bride)
I Drove All Night (ex-boyfriend)

—KB

shout out to the Brooklyn Record Club, from the beautiful Castro district in beautiful, free lovin' San Francisco, California. While you all were listening to songs about gay bars, I was actually availing myself of the "co-ed" lavatory at "San Francisco's Badlands" bar, the door of which had a nice big window in the middle so people could watch me pee, though I'm fairly certain no one there was interested. It's good to be back. Guilty Pleasures is a thrilling concept. But I think the one caveat is that they should be things you REALLY are ASHAMED to like, not things that are "so bad they're good." I've had many fights about this. There was a window in the seventies when The Monkees REALLY were UNCOOL, entirely uncool. It was truly embarrassing to admit you liked them. But then sometime in or around 1982, something changed.

David Byrne is an interesting example of this phenomenon. He is obviously a genius, but at some point in the early 90's his work became unbearable for most people to listen to. I decided I'd keep a watch and see how long it took for his stuff to turn the other corner. It may be happening, only now, among folks in their early to mid twenties. George Michael, on the other hand, has always been secretly cool to like, even if he appears uncool to like, and is therefore an unacceptable choice as a guilty pleasure, as far as I'm concerned. I wanna see real embarrassment. Counting Crows. Lisa Loeb. Jewel. Third Eye Blind. Ace of Bass. Annie Lennox. The Gin Blossoms. Not that I MYSELF am a big fan of any of those artists.

—HM

totally agree with HM about the real not bogus shame. songs produced by jeff lynne or don was please.

—JLl

I completely agree, though what constitutes "so bad they're good" is highly subjective and subject to revision, as you say. In fact there's an aspect to declaring something a guilty pleasure that immediately sets it up as a candidate for ultra square hipness, thereby removing the shame. Which leaves things that are so recently anointed and beloved that most people are not yet at the point of disliking them. You could go mad thinking about it.

—JL2

Most of the hypothetical possibilities raised so far fall into a couple categories: stuff you developed an affection for when you were young, which would otherwise seem tacky, or stuff that's mainstream and slightly dated. maybe it's about music that has something unmistakably wrong with it, but is undeniably appealing as well. You know, like Al Jolson singing 'Mammy.'

—KH

Right on HM. I lived in Britain until I was 30. This is in itself a guilty pleasure. I noticed that sometimes, things cultural became sprinkled with magic stars n' stripes/union jack fairy dust on their ways across the Atlantic. Therefore I am unsure whether The Style Council are unhip/guilty for you, but . . . . . . There may be more of this phenomenon featuring in my selections. Also, I'm not guilty or ashamed of going to the

Wham farewell concert at Wembley Stadium, it's just the sparkly teacloth I tied around my head that gives me pause.

—KB

Well HM, it seems you have opened up the philosophical floodgates around the definition of guilty pleasure. As many of you have pointed out, it seems that one of the criteria for a musical guilty pleasure is a song's recent obsolescence. Songs are generally more hated closer past their expiration date but magically freshen up the longer they molder in the trash heap. It's all about timing. This is known as "the first law of disco rehabilitation," which was named after a famous incident in the mid eighties. Then there is the "Starship Paradox." In my opinion, "We Built This City on Rock 'n Roll" can never be rehabilitated. It will always be an abomination. This song fulfills the first criteria of Guilty Pleasures because I would feel very guilty for liking it or subjecting my friends to it. However, I find no pleasure in it and could not play it at record club.

The one potential pitfall of this theme of Guilty Pleasures is that our music could become an instrument for our mutual torture. But maybe that's a good thing? I promise to play music I really, really like but that embarrasses me somehow. If it's so bad it's good, so be it. If you are tortured, forgive me — I didn't mean to. Just please, don't make me buy Starship just so I can torture you all. THAT would be really, really embarrassing.

PS. I forgot to mention the "law of inexplicable and horrid future hipsters." This phenomena just may put Starship back on top causing me to be annoyed like an old person by our culture's degeneracy. (It's probably already cool and I'm just too uncool to know.) This law is similar to "the law of disco rehabilitation" but takes into account Starship's mutant molecular structure.

—FT

It is a tangled web we weave. I remember performing "we built this city" on WFMU in the mid eighties. Everyone was smiling broadly and there was a general vibe that it was the best part of the evening. Some kind of negative thrill of transgression but also genuine appreciation. We used to play songs like "Say you, say me" by Lionel Richie to the same effect. As awful as the songs were, connecting with them and experiencing them deeply produced intense happiness, like exercising our first amendment rights. We made other people take pleasure in these officially unacceptable songs. All the bands did it, and in some cases they created much more subtle definitions of "so bad it's good" by playing songs that were not universally acknowledged as bad, like Gang Green's cover of Til Tuesday's "Voices Carry." The Replacements had an especially earnest approach to the 'bad is good' material.

And you may recall that at some point Faith No More's straightfaced cover of "I'm Easy" by the Commodores started getting played on commercial, nonironic radio stations and they had their biggest ever hit. From that point on they had to play it at every show to a gigantic crowds who were oblivious to or unconcerned by the cover's rhetorical mode.

—JL2

I find myself soul-sick at the hope of outthinking or outracing the hipster-reclaiming-the-unspeakable game— that is to say, 'guilty pleasures' according to externally measurable criteria. I propose the following (at least for myself, but I'm going to make you all read it): to renew the 'guilty pleasure' as a subjective and self-ratified index. For me, the record which survived vast record-collection purges of similar dubious early or temporary loves, loves which had proven useless, embarrassing, uncomfortable. I know I've pushed a lot of uncomfortable music out of the house over the years. I *flay* my collection of that kind of material. Yet somehow certain items stick, survive multiple purges. I don't even likely play them often, I definitely don't think I get points of any kind for owning them (often they're not famous enough, or famously bad enough a la Starship to be even notable in any ironic way) but they stick. I'm thinking, of course, of Shakespeare's Sister.

—JLI

Record Gang—

Sorry to have come late to the discussion. But what a treat to read it all at once. The proposed theme really is mind-bending. It seems to have captured the tricky essence of "I'll show you mine if you show me yours" that is inherent in the record club. But I think it's the comparisons of the locker room rather than of early sexual exploration, since we all have basically the same equipment (ears?).

In some ways selecting the right disc should be easy since I'm sure we've all had selections in the 'possibles' pile and pulled them at the last minute fearing that the other kids would think less of us if they knew. It should be simple to dredge them up again but that's not quite it since we now want to isolate a particularly pure form of that feeling. There's really two record club meetings being discussed — one properly called 'guilty pleasures' and another lurking just under the surface that should be called "shameful pleasures." Guilt is probably something we can do on our own, but shame requires a record club.

I also particularly like the way that everyone seems to float an artist or two at the end of their note to test the waters and see whether anyone starts to howl. (Although HM, I'm sad that you've tipped my hand with your Ace of Base reference.)

—MB

I remember going to a Replacements show in the early 80's that featured a set composed entirely of Kiss covers. I can't say it made me into a Kiss believer but it opened me up to some of their questionable charms. There is a delicious frisson in hearing a band you love covering a song you hate. This can sometimes act as a gateway drug to a full, unironic love of formerly despised music. I'm sure that the Sex Pistols cover of "Stepping Stone" had more than a little to do with the revival of The Monkees. If you love the Monkees, you're a short step from loving Neil Diamond... and madness. I love Neil Diamond...

—FT

GUILTY PLEASURES

I've been trying to stay out of the fray, because, like LM, I'm having more trouble with the "guilty" part than the "pleasure" part. I'm sure I can dig up some guilt, with enough advance warning, though. I used to choreograph extensive ballets to my mother's Neil Diamond albums. So there.

—AO

Clearly, this upcoming record club is going to take our comradeship to a whole new level of revelation. For maximum soul-drenching, perhaps we should consider borrowing some tactics from a Catholic Lib retreat I once attended in high school:

1. Lock all doors and force ourselves (gently but firmly) to REALLY COMMUNICATE WITH EACH OTHER for forty-eight hours.
2. Decorate room lavishly with Sister Corita Kent posters. (War is NOT healthy for children and other living things. Really, it's not.)
3. Partner up randomly and stare intently into each others' eyes for twenty minutes at a time without moving or speaking. (Twitching and blinking allowed. Use sparingly.)
4. Share bread (or pizza, falafel, whatever)— frequently and lovingly. Hand feeding encouraged!
5. Sit in a circle and pass a simple, rustic musical instrument (guitar nice; spoons better). Know each participant by the song they sing. (Leonard Cohen always appropriate.)

6. Pass the Kleenex—frequently and lovingly. ALL SECRETS THUS SHARED REMAIN LOCKED IN OUR HEARTS FOREVER!
7. Unleash!
8. Go deep!
9. Forgive yourself: for Gloria Gaynor, Rufus, Roger Miller, Tony Orlando and Dawn (especially Dawn), Midnight at the Oasis, Average White Band, 101 Strings play the Theme from Exodus, Rock Me Baby, Cheap Trick, Claudine Longet, late model Rod Stewart, all singers with belly button rings, that aria used in every French and German art film and financial services commercial, the music from Mondo Cane, and Jennifer Warnes.
10. Forgive others: for The Melvins.

Hope these guidelines are helpful. Remember: what doesn't kill you makes you that much more irritated...

—LM

2.

Thus, after a fair amount of yammering about it (I have actually cut a fair amount of the yammering), we held the event in question* at FT and LM's place (they're married and have a

---

* For the track list for the Guilty Pleasures event, see the appendix at the conclusion of these remarks.

son, who sometimes interrupts Brooklyn Record Club events for a dance processional), and it was, well, kind of hard. The truth seems to be that some of what other people like but feel guilty about is, actually, rather difficult to tolerate. I hated the Style Council back then, and when KB played it, I realized that I still do hate them. Ditto the show tunes. Both of the Amys brought show tunes, and, as I've said elsewhere, I dislike show music more than any other music. For me, there's no pleasure associated with it *at all*, even in the case of *Hair*, an ostensibly tolerable musical.

There *were* a couple things I heard that I liked much more than I thought I would, namely an early Bee Gees number (from the album right before they put disco on the map) and a ditty from one of the Jefferson Airplane splinter releases, viz., Grace Slick and Paul Kantner, selected by KH, who usually brings either (1) house music, or (2) French chanson. It was utterly predictable in a West Coast hippie way, this song, but it still felt moving and innocent somehow.

However, I'm just putting off the inevitable here, which is to describe why I brought what I brought to the Guilty Pleasures meeting of the Brooklyn Record Club. That's what I want to try to get down here, what a guilty pleasure genuinely feels like. And how time plays a part in this sensation.

Of course, Record Club can be a little embarrassing under even the best of circumstances. When I first visited the Manhattan contingent, I brought a Meredith Monk tune, from one of her early albums, and a middle-period Captain Beefheart song called "Floppy Boot Stomp." The Beefheart debuted first, and I was red with embarrassment and anxiety, my head actually in my hands throughout its performance. There were some kindly words after, but I felt with this recording (likewise the Monk piece) that I was not at all certain that my taste was translating particularly well.

The Brooklyn Guilty Pleasures event, at least for me, aggravated this discomfort. Playing really *awful* stuff in front of very accomplished persons, many of whom I not only like personally but also admire, was difficult. Nevertheless, I'd searched my heart and my CD rack for something that I not only liked as a kid but *still* liked—for what is guiltier than the passions of youth?—and I was determined to press on. Maybe in this way I would stop apologizing for this particular period of my early teens, the period that could bring down upon me so much withering disregard from those who were lucky enough, when young, to have loved James Brown or Funkadelic or the MC5. What I mean is that I was going to admit to my youthful fondness for "progressive" rock.*

So: first I brought to the Guilty Pleasures event a Frank Zappa instrumental called "Regyptian Strut." I am of the opinion that Frank Zappa does not need unlimited apology, except perhaps for the tiresome guitar solo albums of his later work or his dubious racial reasoning on *Thing-Fish*. Early Mothers of Invention is still refreshing (as is the first Zappa solo album, *Lumpy Gravy*), and it's clear that Zappa had vision and the ability to bring dissonance, jazz, and tricky time signatures to the kids. This work helped me later on when I was

---

* And by "progressive" or "prog" what I imagine I mean is pop music that is reliant on some of European classical or serious music for its effects.

learning to like Stockhausen, Xenakis, Cage, Cecil Taylor, Ornette Coleman, etc. I don't get too embarrassed about Frank Zappa. In fact, he often fills me with an unrestrained kind of joy.

It's my other Record Club selection that's hard to write about without feeling desperate. Because my other selection was a song by Jethro Tull.

Many, many people have called them the worst band of all time. Even the staid *New York Times*, on the occasion of the rerelease of the Stones' *Rock and Roll Circus* DVD—which includes a great John Lennon solo performance and maybe the definitive live Who performance ("A Quick One, While He's Away")—remarked in the course of a review that Jethro Tull was really one of the most embarrassing bands ever. And *Rock and Roll Circus* features an *early* Tull performance! Not one of the later ones from when singer Ian Anderson wore the codpiece!

I liked them without reservation for a relatively brief period. From 1975, when I belatedly discovered *Aqualung*, until *Heavy Horses* came out in 1978. By 1978 it was abundantly clear that they were in decline. And yet in the period when I liked them, I *really* liked them. I think I had just about every record they released in those years, and that would include *War Child*, *Minstrel in the Gallery*, *Songs from the Wood*, *Heavy Horses*, and the so-dreadful-even-I-knew-it *Too Old to Rock 'n' Roll: Too Young to Die!* I bought the first *Best of* volume for the one unreleased track. I even managed to shell out for the better part of the back catalogue: *Living in the Past*, *A Passion Play*, *This Was*, *Benefit*, and so forth. Diehards had the collector's version of *Thick as a Brick*, where the gatefold included an entire newspaper ostensibly written by Anderson's collaborator on the project, one Gerald "Little Milton" Bostock. I was not that much of a diehard, but my friends were. I had, in fact, *read* the gatefold newspaper.

What was it I imagined that Jethro Tull delivered? Like most teenagers, I was looking for ways not to feel constantly, boundlessly uncomfortable. I was looking for ways not to feel desperate. That was the plan. Two kinds of music seemed to aid me in the accomplishment of this goal. One sort of music had rhythmic complexity. Stuff that wasn't in common time and didn't feature the inevitable cowbell favored by the guys on the football team and their friends. I liked music where the drumming was full of fills and odd accents. (Regrettably, this often seemed to require gigantic drum kits.) The other sort of music I liked was music with *tenderness* in it. I don't know any other way to say it. While I was aware, in addition to songs featuring the cowbell, that boys my age were chiefly interested in *the guitar solo*, in the ambling of Jerry Garcia through another half-hour recording of "Dark Star," or maybe some of those feedback-drenched Carlos Santana solos, or some slide from Duane Allman, I was never entirely preoccupied with the guitar solo. Nor was I preoccupied with what was most loud. I kind of dug Deep Purple in that brief moment when a lot of people did, but I didn't get stuck there. What I loved about the Who was not that they were loud, but that they were ugly, drunken, and often unhappy. They were also incredibly tender, as on "Blue, Red and Grey," "The Kids Are Alright," "Squeeze Box," and "Behind Blue Eyes."

Jethro Tull fulfilled both requirements. On the one hand,

there were plodding off-kilter band exercises, like "Aqualung," where it was really hard to figure out the time signature. Then, on the other hand, there were these tunes that were mostly about acoustic guitar and flute. There was a little love song on *Aqualung* called "Wond'ring Aloud," for example. It was just a description of Ian Anderson's lover bringing him breakfast in bed. I played it so much that it got a scratch in it. I was much more interested in these two brief minutes than in the entirety of the heinous "Locomotive Breath," the meaning of which I could never figure out anyway.

Another track that I found particularly genuine and sweet when I was fifteen was "Skating Away on the Thin Ice of a New Day," which begins with the singer sipping from a teacup and scatting a bit of the melody. Again, as if the song were a sort of domestic event. What's *prog* about this number is the show-offy use of expensive rental instruments—celeste, tablas, xylophone, accordion—likewise the rather ambitious lyrics, which don't shy away from the occasional polysyllabic pronouncement, like: "A million generations removed from expectations / Of being who you really want to be," or "As you cross the wilderness, spinning in your emptiness / You feel you have to pray." Well, there's also Ian Anderson's singing, which, with its reliance on melismatics, can definitely get a little pyrotechnical. Never mind all of that. This is a beautiful, simple melody featuring one of those catchy choruses that almost anyone could like, and the centrality of the acoustic guitar here, for me, keeps the tone closer to a folksy, or a folkie, *tenderness.*

Tenderness, like when Dock Boggs sings about killing someone and manages to do it in such a way that he sounds vulnerable and lost. Or when Skip James sings "Hard Time Killing Floor Blues" and also manages to convey something of the woe that must, it's fair to say, follow upon the act for the murderer. Tenderness like in the beginning of "Across the Universe." Tenderness like in the beginning of *A Love Supreme.* Tenderness like in some of Gillian Welch's songs. Tenderness like in some of Neil Young's ("Ambulance Blues" or "For the Turnstiles"), tenderness like you are a human easily bruised, and music is the only way to expiate this difficult feeling.

I know it's hard to believe (even harder to admit), but I still think these Tull songs are moving. Like "Witch's Promise" from *Living in the Past.* No rhythm section for about half its course. Up front again are the acoustic guitar and a beautiful piano part by John Evans. The lyrics have a rustic weirdness: "Lend me your ear while I call you a fool / You were kissed by a witch one night in the wood / And later insisted your feelings were true / The witch's promise was coming / Leaving he listened while laughing you flew." Anderson manages the vocal urgency that characterized the early Jethro Tull albums, when, notwithstanding the whimsy, the songs still seemed to be about growing up and hanging around the neighborhood.

There's a joy about the early part of a rock-and-roll career that dries up in the presence of prolonged success. Success in the long run is about keeping something, instead of wanting something. Jethro Tull were better when they wanted something. To put it another way: what was unspeakable about *prog* was over-rehearsed jazz-rock maestros who were only interested in the virtuosity and the credibility of high culture, which they would never actually have. When Emerson, Lake and Palmer (whom I also liked) started titling albums *Works* and packaging them like they were Deutsch Grammophon releases, the end was near. If I didn't understand immediately that this was pretentious twaddle, a single event nonetheless converted me.

I worked at the radio station when I was in boarding school. I may even have been the program director of the school radio station. At some point, we decided to have an album of the week. No one listened to us anyway (we weren't playing enough Grateful Dead, Dan Fogelberg, or Earth, Wind and Fire), so why not have an album of the week? When it was my turn to host, I allowed myself to be talked into playing an album I knew nothing about: *Armed Forces*, by Elvis Costello and the Attractions.

I had not been entirely oblivious to punk rock, because I liked glam, for example, the great period of David Bowie that stretched from *Ziggy Stardust* to *"Heroes."* I liked *Lust for Life* and *Transformer.* It wasn't far from there to the Sex Pistols. But I had somehow kept Elvis Costello at bay. Nevertheless, I took the LP in question up to the station and played it through, from "Accidents Will Happen" to the Nick Lowe cover at the end. And at the moment at which I finished playing the album, I sort of hated it. All of it, that is, except for the song called "Green Shirt."

"Green Shirt" had neither rhythmical complexity nor tenderness. In fact, it seemed to be about paranoia and, as Elvis called it, "emotional fascism." "Better send a begging letter to the big investigation / Who put these fingerprints on my imagination?" There was a brutal, ominous quality to the composition, though brutality in such a quiet, tuneful song was unusual. Brutality was different from what I'd liked before. Maybe you just didn't get to adulthood without a little of it. Anyway, the geeky guy pictured on the sleeve was a clever wordsmith, I recognized; he was a smart guy, not a lout, and he was clearly angry about something. "Green Shirt" was like nothing I'd ever heard. You could sing along with it! Plus, the organ and synthesizer had a little bit of *prog* weirdness.

The evacuation of all Jethro Tull from my record collection, along with all Yes; all Emerson, Lake and Palmer; all Genesis; all Gentle Giant, all Synergy, all Kraftwerk, all Moody Blues, all Utopia, began with this Elvis Costello experience, which was soon followed by a Talking Heads experience, a Devo experience, a Blondie experience, a Ramones experience, and so on. Devo had synthesizers, and I didn't care if they could play them well. And Devo were rhythmically perverse. Like where was the backbeat on that cover of "Satisfaction"? Where was the hi-hat? Soon I started throwing out all the old records. Or hiding them. By the time I matriculated at college, most of the *prog* albums had been left behind, to be picked over by my younger brothers.

When I was first living in Brooklyn, in the early nineties, Donald Antrim and I used to spook each other by calling if a particularly bad *prog* number was playing on the radio somewhere. Something from *Physical Graffiti*, by Led Zeppelin. Or *The Lamb Lies Down on Broadway*, by Genesis. I'm pretty sure Donald left the music of Jethro Tull on my answering machine a couple of times. This was a sport of great hilarity.

Not much later, in 1995, when my sister died, I managed to

spirit away from her estate a few of her CDs. Those of her CDs that had some sentimental value. For some reason my sister had always been a proponent of the Jethro Tull live album called *Bursting Out*. This was from the *last* acceptable period of Tull, the period of John Evans, David Palmer, and Barriemore Barlow. It was before Anderson's egomaniacal qualities got the best of him. I'd never much liked *Bursting Out* back when it was released, but when it was my late sister's album, it suddenly seemed worth another listen.

From there, I found I wanted to hear the earlier Tull albums again. The same process was taking place with some other things I'd jettisoned long ago, like *Foxtrot* by Genesis; *Wish You Were Here*, by Pink Floyd; and *Fragile*, by Yes. Even some ELP. They were all beginning to seem as though they weren't quite as moronic or pretentious as I had thought. Or maybe they were just lovably moronic. It helped that I didn't have any of my punk rock friends from college looking over my shoulder, telling me this record was going to affect my credibility.

The music of the past *does* give us renewed access to our earlier sense perceptions and feelings, and so there is, arguably, an inherently nostalgic aspect to the guilty pleasure (although I feel that the word *nostalgia* is inadequate here—it's like saying that all of Proust is nostalgia about a cookie). But if music is about articulating feelings that are otherwise inarticulable, then is this not enough of a reason for its being valid and important? I can't ignore the fact that like many teenagers I often felt worthless and cloddish, and I can't ignore the fact that playing some of the songs that I liked when I was feeling worthless and cloddish now smoothes the ache of my past and enables me to feel a little compassion for my younger self, a compassion I didn't feel then.

There's more to say about this period in the middle nineties when I began the tragicomic process of accepting my *prog* teens. There was something happening in contemporary music, too, some kind of historical imperative, something I date to the release of *Millions Now Living Will Never Die*, by Tortoise. For a long time any indie release that had anything *prog* about it was considered suspect. *Prog* could never pass the *cool* test. Even Sonic Youth were pushing the envelope when they had a medley on *Daydream Nation*. Slint were challenging the kids with those meditative passages on *Spiderland*. The Minutemen had a little classical guitar piece on *Double Nickels on the Dime*, horror of horrors. And *Candy Apple Grey*, by Hüsker Dü, even had synthesizers on it.

Then the Tortoise album came out. It was all instrumentals. Excepting *The Process of Weeding Out*, by Black Flag, I couldn't really remember a significant album of the indie period that was entirely instrumental. *Millions Now Living* even had a track on it that was, more or less, the compact-disc equivalent of *an entire album side*. Twenty minutes long or thereabouts. The guys in Tortoise could play their instruments well too. John McEntire, the drummer, has to be one of the really great contemporary drummers. (He did some time in the music department at Oberlin!) Later on, Tortoise even added a *jazz* guitarist to fill out the top end of the sound. And many of the Tortoise compositions, I have been assured by someone in the know, were arrived at through the time-honored technique of group improvisation.

In short, by any number of relevant criteria, Tortoise was a *prog* band.

What about Godspeed You! Black Emperor? From Montreal. They have a permanent on-staff violinist, they have two drummers, and they compose big cinematic suites with lots of bombastic crescendos. I know they espouse a radical leftist political platform; I know that they were once arrested at a gas station for resembling terrorists. But, in truth, what makes them that much different from Can or from Amon Düül II? Or Ash Ra Tempel? This is true of many similar indie bands of the late nineties and the early twenty-first century. Many of these bands, despite their bona fides, are not entirely dissimilar from a *prog* model. Trans Am. Labradford. Stars of the Lid. Do Make Say Think. A lot of this is music I would have liked back when I was an anomie-afflicted *prog* teenager.

And while I'm making comparisons, what about the whole *tenderness* thing? What about the *new* tenderness? The new quiet? What about Devendra Banhart? What about Sufjan Stevens? Iron and Wine? Will Oldham? And just about anything by Mark Kozelek, songwriter and singer on all the Red House Painters albums. Kozelek covered "Long Distance Runaround" by Yes and has often admitted to liking Genesis. In fact, he likes Genesis *after* Peter Gabriel, where even I fear to tread. Lou Barlow sounds more like Dan Fogelberg with each release. Iron and Wine is a lot like Cat Stevens.

Now that punk rock has been thoroughly and totally brought into the multinational corporate fold (the Offspring, Kelly Osbourne, Good Charlotte), along with that variety of metal that is best performed by guys with goatees and large biceps who are really angry about *that girl*, whoever she is, there is nowhere to go but out on the fringe—toward stuff that is both more rhythmically unusual, on the one hand, and, on the other, a little bit more emotionally accessible, a little more tender, a little more human, without, hopefully, becoming *too* sentimental.

All of which is not to say that history has freed me from some of my embarrassment about music of the past. Well, not entirely. In fact, these days I'm really embarrassed by the eighties—by U2, the Human League, Simple Minds, the Cure, etc.

It occurs to me that I haven't actually described the Tull song I played at the Brooklyn Record Club, and maybe I should. It's called "For Michael Collins, Jeffrey and Me," and it's from *Benefit*, one of the early Jethro Tull albums. It's another tune constructed around acoustic guitar and piano, and its bittersweet aspect, I imagine, is the result of its serving (arguably) as elegy to the passing away of a friend: "Watery eyes of the last sighing seconds / Blue reflections mute and dim." When the song arrives at its rather giddy chorus, it kind of lifts off, with a nice bit of lead guitar filling in around the singer as he catches a breath. "I'm with you boys / So please employ just a little extra care / It's on my mind I'm left behind / When I should have been there / Walking with you." There are a few bad lines, to be sure, lines that don't appeal to the forty-three-year-old the way they did to the fifteen-year-old, but in general it's a plangent and agreeably earnest song. Who are the protagonists of the title? Jeffrey turns up in a number of early Jethro Tull songs, and he is probably the bass player, Jeffrey Hammond-Hammond, who was a childhood pal of Ian Anderson's. With little information to go on, I imagine that Michael Collins is the friend being apotheosized here,* and I imagine that mortality and apotheosis are part of the reason that the song seems moving to me, now that there are so many more *lost things* to enumerate in life than there were back when I first liked it.

I felt awful before playing the Tull song at the Brooklyn Record Club, and I fretted after. But I really can't feel awful about it anymore. This is not an easy thing to overcome, the judgment of the vulnerabilities of the past, and I don't think I can do it by arguing that the music is not *that bad,* nor by proving that the music is not unlike what is happening these days on the fringes of what is estimable. Finally, forgiveness requires a more courageous effort.

My broken, lost, somewhat hopeless, drug-addled younger self wanted to feel that there was more to life than being overlooked or oppressed by the fortunate and graceful striding past him in and out of school, and this is how he did it: he learned everything there was to learn about these reviled pieces of culture with their bombast and their excess and even, yes, with their occasional bits of genuine feeling, and he hung around with the other misfits who made this indefensible

---

* An astute and informed friend has pointed out the possibility that the Michael Collins referred to here is none other than the great Irish patriot (1890–1922) who served as a captain in the 1916 Easter Rising and was later commander in chief of the Irish Free State Army. If this theory is true, it would make "For Michael Collins, Jeffrey and Me" one of a very few overtly political songs in the entire Jethro Tull songbook. Another possibility would be that the Michael Collins of the title is the *Apollo 11* pilot, the one who didn't get a chance to actually walk on the moon. I confess that I actually attempted e-mailing Ian Anderson to try to get the man himself to resolve the controversy for me, without success.

nonsense their thing. Then he waited for the winds to change. I sort of love him for it.

Brooklyn Record Club, September 2003, "Guilty Pleasures"

CD1		Artist	Album	Member
1.	"Informer"	Snow	*12 Inches of Snow*	MB
2.	"Cariño"	Jennifer Lopez	*J. Lo*	AB
3.	"My Town"	Slade	*Sladest*	FT
4.	"Odessa"	The Bee Gees	*Odessa*	JLI
5.	"North Star"	Robert Fripp / Daryl Hall	*Exposure*	LM
6–8.	"Intro / As a Child I Walked / Lost"	Jewel	*A Night Without Armor*	HM
9.	"Tomorrow Belongs to Me"	Original Cast	*Cabaret*	AO
10.	"For Michael Collins, Jeffrey and Me"	Jethro Tull	*Benefit*	RM
11.	"Million"	Paul Kantner / Grace Slick	*Sunfighter*	KH
12.	"Amor Amor"	Esquivel	*The Genius of Esquivel*	JA
13.	"Rockin' Retard"	Big Poo Generator	(unreleased)	JL2
14.	"Inverness Gathering: The Drunken Piper, 79th Farewell to Gibraltar, Earl of Mansfield"	Edinburgh City Police Pipe Band	*Scottish Bagpipes & Drums*	KB

CD2		Artist	Album	Member
1.	"Long Hot Summer"	The Style Council	*The Singular Adventures of the Style Council*	KB
2.	"Opportunity for Two"	Van Dyke Parks	*Jump!*	KH
3.	"Harley Davidson"	Brigitte Bardot	*Brigitte Bardot Show*	JA
4.	"Dulcinea"	Original Cast	*Man of La Mancha*	AB
5.	"Black Boys"	Original Cast	*Hair*	AO
6.	"White Boys"			
7.	"Regyptian Strut"	Frank Zappa	*Sleep Dirt*	RM
8.	"Stay"	Shakespeare's Sister	*Hormonally Yours*	JL1
9.	"Desperado"	Johnny Cash	*American IV: The Man Comes Around*	HM
10.	"April Fools (He Had the Change Done at the Shop)"	The Frogs	*My Daughter the Broad*	FT
11.	"Rock and Roll Love Letter"	The Bay City Rollers	*Greatest Hits*	MB
12.	"I've Never Been to Me"	Charlene	*I've Never Been to Me*	JL2
13.	"Soul Kiss"	Olivia Newton-John	*Soul Kiss*	LM

Some Propositions Concerning the Lounge Lizards

Preface: The problem with being a music listener of the relatively engaged sort is that it's unscientific. Unlike being, e.g., a deranged baseball fan, or a hard-core weather person, or a day trader, or a wine fanatic. Those pursuits have their elective affinities, but they also depend on rigorous templates of factual material. The deployment of these facts becomes an important part of the obsessive lifestyle of the cathected individual. In the case of popular music, however, this absence of statistical abstracts gives rise to annoying compilations of top-ten lists, desert island discs, accounts of various shows. Concerts especially. It's one of those *High Fidelity*–style games, talking about the gigs you've been to. Guys do it a lot. Apparently, going to concerts involves a masculine manipulation of worldly impediments. You have to wait in long lines, you have to exercise Machiavellian crowd control instincts, or you have to exhibit first-rate scalping prowess. ("I just waltzed up to that black dude and got two third-row tickets off him five minutes before the show, only fifteen bucks!") You camp out. You wait until the lights go down, and then you somehow connive your way down to the row where the industry suits repose. In these pages, I attempt to replace the *High Fidelity*–style obsession with a more serious apparatus, one that ideally gives the concert to which I address myself a stately, serious treatment. Please see below.

First proposition, *that the best concert I ever saw in my life was a gig by the Lounge Lizards, on April 12, 1992, at the Merkin Concert Hall, on the Upper West Side.* This concert was part of the New Sounds Live Concert Series, svengali'd by one John Schaefer, the host of the radio program of the same name, broadcast each night at 11:00 PM on WNYC, public radio affiliate in my fair city. I started listening to the *New Sounds* radio program when I was in graduate school on the Upper West Side—in the mid-eighties. Soon I moved to Hoboken, and at that juncture I became passionately addicted to this program, would stay up late especially to listen to *New Sounds*, often recording bits and pieces that interested me and then searching them out in record stores that specialized in obscurities. I first heard Arvo Pärt on *New Sounds*, I first heard Górecki's third symphony, I first heard David Hykes and La Monte Young and Ingram Marshall, and a lot of other stuff, on *New Sounds*. Some of this music has probably been lost to history, alas (viz., A. Leroi's placid and hilarious "Home Sweet Home"), especially now that you can no longer listen to archives of the really *old* espisodes.

Second proposition, *that a certain period of music by the Lounge Lizards amounted to some of the most transportative music ever* *recorded.* See, somewhere in the midst of my enchantment with the *New Sounds* show, in the late eighties, I heard this saxophone solo playing over the airwaves. It was late one night in Hoboken, and I was barely awake. My delusional semi-sleep was a recombinant mixture of hypnagogic voices and *New Sounds,* and I heard this saxophone playing. Sort of the most beautiful thing I had ever heard in my life. It was what I imagined music could do. I couldn't really fathom how both melancholy and enthusiastic this piece of music was. It did just what I wanted music to do, when I thought about these things in the abstract. Started out with one saxophone, and then there was a second answering horn performing these sort of arpeggio-like runs. Just when I was kind of getting used to the saxophone, a really fractured guitar came in, a downtown-ish guitar, the kind of guitar that would be used to repel gentrifiers on the Lower East Side, then some percussion, then the guitar just broke out into some massive cacophony, like a pallet of submachine guns toppling over onto the floor, drowning out the saxes for an interval. This *was* exactly what I wanted music to do, to ennoble and articulate and unsettle, but in an unpretentious way, in an affecting way. Sort of jazz-like, but too anarchic to be jazz in the *old* sense, without the requisite batch of tritones and augmented chords—instead luminous and peaceful and screechy, not ridiculous and embarrassing, like some of that supposedly peaceful, gentle music that you sometimes heard on *New Sounds.* Anyway, the piece ended with this childlike drum section, a rather meditative drum pattern. Then a little more solo sax. I woke completely, I waited, I stayed awake, just so I could hear John Schaefer announce what the hell it was.

Third proposition, *that the early Lounge Lizards dressed exqui-sitely.* Well, when John Schaefer announced the band, announced the name of the song (and what a great name: "A Paper Bag and the Sun"), I was a little stunned, because I had heard the Lounge Lizards back in college when their first recording was released. My keenest recollection of that album was that they dressed well on the cover. The cover had them all wearing shirts and ties, as if they were a simulacrum of a genuine jazz band, in which spirit John Lurie, whose band it was, had once described them as "fake jazz." This turned out to be something he ought never have said, as for a time it made it difficult to take them as seriously as they deserved. That first lineup had Arto Lindsay in it, who was a great downtown guitarist, though in my view not as good as Marc Ribot, who later filled the same chair (on, e.g., "A Paper Bag and the Sun"). Originally, they also had Anton Fier on drums, who not long after convened the excellent Golden Palominos, includ-ing a configuration with Syd Straw and Jody Harris that I liked a lot. Still, I just didn't *get* the first Lounge Liz-ards album, exactly. Seemed a little mannered to me, seemed like it was more about establishing mastery of a genre than about memorable writing. Even the producer, Teo Macero—he was the guy who had produced Miles Davis's first elec-tric period—was a little too pedigreed. Upon hearing "A Paper Bag and the Sun," however, I was in a fever; I was con-vinced that something amazing had happened to the Lounge Lizards and that I had been wrong to consign them to the file of things given incomplete attention, and so I went in search.

Fourth proposition, *that it was also occasionally important to go to the movies.* John Lurie of the Lounge Lizards had appeared in a number of movies in the middle eighties, and I saw these movies, and I thought he was great, a natural actor, but movies just didn't matter to me in the same way that music mattered. I liked Roberto Benigni's rabbit soliloquy in *Down by Law*, in which John appeared. I thought Eszter Balint was really pretty in *Stranger Than Paradise*. And I thought John Lurie's television program, *Fishing with John*, was one of the best uses ever of the medium. John had an offhanded and relaxed charisma on the screen, whether large or small, but this did not command my more careful interest. It took John Schaefer and *New Sounds* to do that.

Fifth proposition, *that the New Sounds Live Concert Series, which took place for a half-dozen Sundays each year, was almost as good as the radio show.* I think it was in 1991 or 1992 that I started going to the *New Sounds* concerts, at Merkin Concert Hall, in the Lincoln Center area, and these were often amazing events. Sometime in 1992, e.g., I saw a full-length recital of La Monte Young's *The Melodic Version of The Second Dream of The High-Tension Line Stepdown Transformer from The Four Dreams of China*, scored for brass octet in just intonation. The instruments were situated throughout the hall. Since the piece was scored in this unusual tuning system — unusual at least for western ears — the players obviously had to listen to each other *really carefully*, so as to avoid slipping back into well-tempered mode. The piece did generate waves of overtones, as advertised, and was mesmerizing and singular and strange. And that was just one show. I was always among rather eccentric-looking types when in the company of subscribers to the New Sounds Live series. They included homely downtown kids with big glasses, and old hippie guys with unconventional hygiene regimens. In fact, I kind of liked going to concerts with these sorts of people, because they were the people who really thought about music and really cared about it. Music wasn't something that played in the background while they tried to pick up somebody. Anyway, in the midst of this regular diet of concertgoing, I learned that the Lounge Lizards were going to play. And by then I was already deeply in love with *Voice of Chunk*, the 1989 album that had "A Paper Bag and the Sun" on it.

Sixth proposition, *that the phrase "the best concert I ever saw in my life" does have something fatuous about it.* Despite misgivings, it is perhaps worth mentioning that I've been to my share of interesting concerts (let's see, a Jones Beach show by Van Morrison where he sang "Sweet Thing" from *Astral Weeks* while lightning was flashing over the stage; Todd Rundgren and Ian Hunter — at a John Anderson for president rally in Providence in 1980; Red Krayola at the Knitting Factory, 2005; the dB's, Lupo's, Providence, circa 1982, opening for Tom Verlaine; R.E.M., *Document* tour; Talking Heads, *Remain in Light* tour; George Clinton / P-Funk All Stars, Brooklyn Academy of Music, 2005; the Young Fresh Fellows / John Wesley Harding in Albany, 2002); but I'm just not one of those persons who hoard their old ticket stubs and speak reverently of their one hundred Dylan shows or their two hundred Dead shows. I am glad I never saw the Doors play, and seeing U2 on the tour for the first album is not something I think about often. More often it's the strange stuff that happened at whichever concert that I remember. Like this: my very first concert was Frank Zappa and the Mothers of Invention, Halloween 1976 at the Palladium, to which I took my prep school roommate Andy, and at which Andy, after getting high with the unknown doper to his left, puked on his shoes during the encore. That I remember. Along with the banner that Zappa had strung across the stage: *Warner Brothers Record Company Sucks*.

Seventh proposition, *that it is the rare band that is actually better live than they are on their recordings.* I saw Guided by Voices once, and they were certainly better live, but that is because their recordings were deliberately low fidelity at that point. Music that is about dancing, as in the case of the B-52s, never came alive for me until I saw it performed. I liked Bow Wow Wow live, and I thought their songs were actually kind of bad; ditto, from the opposite end of the spectrum, Nine Inch Nails. In the case of the Lounge Lizards, I thought that *Voice of Chunk* was more than well recorded, and so it didn't occur to me that they could possibly be *better* than the recording. But wait, I guess I'm getting ahead of myself. Let me describe the event! The first half of the *New Sounds* concert that afternoon, yes, afternoon, 2:00 PM, was the Mikel Rouse Broken Consort. Apparently, this portion of the bill was meant to be the Kronos Quartet half (I have since seen them play a couple of times), but they rescheduled. I don't remember much about Mikel

Rouse, except that he had synthesizers. I wasn't engrossed. Then there was intermission.

Eighth proposition, *that your memory of the best concert in your life is not to be trusted*, but that doesn't make this memory less important. Your memory is not to be trusted in any case. And yet what I have learned from hoarding my erroneous memories is idealism of a kind. So: my recollection was that after the intermission on April 12, 1992, some portion of the Lounge Lizards came out onstage, after which John was meant to go over and talk to John Schaefer at a little interviewing station that Schaefer had at each gig. Schaefer was meant to ask Lurie some polite, diverting, softball questions, as he did with his radio guests. I was looking forward to this part, because I thought John Lurie was really *cool*,* and it was going to be interesting to hear what he had to say. And yet from the second he sat down, the two drummers, who had already made their way onstage, began playing, and Lurie kind of looked at Schaefer, and then he kind of looked at the audience and threw up his hands, *What am I supposed to do?*, and fled from the chair beside John Schaefer back downstage. Before it was clear what was happening, he had already picked up his horn. Whereupon he began to wail. At about the time of this show, Lurie was also playing some gigs with a much smaller ensemble (this evolved in part because it was easier than moving around the numerous Lounge Lizards) called the John Lurie National Orchestra. This ensemble involved the two drummers, who were

---

* Or, perhaps, *fraught.*

named Calvin Weston (he can be found on a number of Lurie-related recordings) and Billy Martin, who went on to be in Medeski Martin and Wood. That day, the opening number featured this trio. They just went for it. Of which more below. They were as far from the Mikel Rouse Broken Consort as you could get. Meanwhile, it's possible, of course, that the nonconversation I've just described with John Schaefer never happened at all. Before I got a copy of the set list* in order to write this piece, I was sure that the intermission had happened in the *middle* of the Lounge Lizards' performance.

Ninth proposition, *that spontaneity is highly to be prized in the concert setting.* For example, one of the most excellent concerts I ever saw was not a concert at all. It was the regular Sunday service at Al Green's church in Memphis. I went with my friend Darcey, on a break from a literary festival we were attending in Oxford, Mississippi. I guess Al talked a little bit, but what he mainly did at his service was sing. And how he sang was in a really improvised way, where he would just tease out phrases and ideas until he felt that he was done with them. This process often took a while. It was musical ministry in the best sense of the term, and we stayed for two hours or so. The service was still just getting going when we had to leave. That kind of spontaneity, where you just open your mouth and sing, was genuinely inspiring to me. And the opening section of "Lawn for People," the first song that the Lounge Lizards

---

* "Lawn for People," "Red and Gold Carpet," "Happy Old Yoy," "Uncle Jerry," "Sex with Monster, Volume Two."

played, trafficked in this very sort of spontaneity. Look, I recognize that Lurie composes a fair amount. He can write the notes on the staffs. He is not a jazz composer the way that Miles was, a purist, where there's just a little phrase, maybe a lead sheet, and once you play the phrase, everybody heads off into the wilderness. But Lurie still manages to invert, subvert, and remodel melody lines on his sax until he feels he has said what he needs to say. With just the two drummers, he was filling Merkin Concert Hall, all the way to the back wall, and he was doing this with great self-assurance. And the best part was that he hadn't even really got going, because the rest of the band came in piece by piece, somewhere toward the end of the solo, and the band consisted of (or this is my informed guess from this recollective vantage point) Mickey Navazio on guitar, Dave Tronzo on slide guitar, Michael Blake on tenor sax, Steve Bernstein on trumpet, and Jane Scarpantoni on cello, and once they were all playing, it was even louder, and even more ecstatic. And this went on for twenty minutes, this song, before they even broke for a rest.

Tenth proposition, *that call-and-response is the essence of spontaneity,* and call-and-response connects music back to some ancient impulses, its role in the formation of community, to African music, although I suppose there was call-and-response in some madrigal singing too. It is well represented in African music, however, this impulse, in Fela Kuti, in King Sunny Adé, in the music of the Pygmies, in almost any African music, and African music has influenced Lurie, at least the way I see it. You can hear West African time signatures, e.g., in the Lounge

Lizards and in his pseudonymous Marvin Pontiac CD. The relationship between the saxophones in the Lounge Lizards, it's all about call-and-response, all about the movement between players, which makes Lurie's musical ideas more forceful, legitimizes them. Though I had expected to hear the Lounge Lizards play songs from *Voice of Chunk*, and would have claimed, had I not seen the playlist, that they *did* play more than just the one tune from that album, "Uncle Jerry," I didn't care, because the principles were the same in all of these songs (most of which apparently went unreleased, in the long period of Lounge Lizards–related difficulties between *Voice of Chunk* and their last official release, *Queen of All Ears*). The audience was aware that it was hearing something amazing, something greatly celebratory, and so even though it was the *afternoon*, which is a pretty ridiculous time for a concert, there was some palpable energy that was getting fed back and forth, some vibe, and it was apparent in the relationships among the ensemble ("They have to love each other," Lurie said once), in the way ideas got transported from one player to another, and in the communication between ensemble and audience. Lurie, a rather flamboyant, even overpowering, character, was none-theless a *part* of the ensemble. It became very much a *group*, and that was part of the hard-core genius of the later Lounge Lizards, but especially of the Lounge Lizards *live*, that they just hit the groove, like an African drumming ensemble or an old Dixieland jazz band, and though Lurie wrote the material and his own solos, when these solos happened, they weren't egomaniacal or pyrotechnical or overly florid. The solos were just new ways of thinking about whatever phrase was about to be introduced into the circuit. It was ecstatic music, it was confident, it was relaxed, it was never self-satisfied, and while the music of the Lounge Lizards may have been indebted to older jazz forms, the band never *sounded* indebted. They sounded like nothing else on earth, except the Lounge Lizards (*strange and beautiful*, as Lurie's label name has it). Oh, and I haven't even said anything about dynamics, which is how the really great performing bands always think. They think about soft, loud, and then soft again, and then *really* loud.

Eleventh proposition, *that you don't need a big encore and all of that stylized nonsense in order to mount a memorable show.* On April 12, 1992, the Lounge Lizards played only five songs. They scarcely made it over the forty-five-minute mark. And only two of the songs were ever released, one of them long after this particular concert. Who cares? It was an afternoon gig. It was being recorded live for radio broadcast. I assume the Lounge Lizards were encouraged not to go on endlessly, so as to be reasonably edited into the broadcast. Knowing a little about Lurie's life and habits as a young man, I figure he might have been up late the night before too; he might not have wanted to do some afternoon gig on the Upper West Side for the Lincoln Center crowd. Maybe this was nobody's favorite gig, least of all John Lurie's, but it was *mine*, and that's the way it goes. Sometimes the really great gig is the one you had no idea would be so good, and it's not about how many people were in the audience (I saw an outrageously good Wedding Present show in Tucson last week before about twenty-five people), or whether the sound system was good, or whether the band had hangovers, or anything else. It just happens sometimes. Like the famous story about Big Star, that they did their best and worst shows on the same night, and that the really good gig was the one with fewer people. The Lounge Lizards happened to be flawless the day I saw them. I assume they were just as great other times (I saw them play on television once, and they were stunning there too). But that day I really learned something about music. There was an awful lot of disconsolate music circulating in those days (grunge!), and the only music that attempted to remediate this misery was the jam-band baby food of ersatz hippiedom. But the Lounge Lizards operated outside of this opposition. They were joyful, but never in a dim-witted way or in a way that was somehow approving of the deranged world. *Joyful* because joyful advertises what music can do, and what ensemble playing can do, *joyful* in a way that makes notions of genre and taxonomy pointless, joyful where you just pick up the horn and blow.

Twelfth proposition, *that all things must pass.* John Lurie has been ill for a few years now, and he has trouble playing his horn these days, so much so that the Lounge Lizards are probably on indefinite hiatus. It therefore now seems that the amazing last two albums, *Voice of Chunk* and *Queen of All Ears,* are the end points of an astonishing and perennially underrated musical career, a musical career that at least for me was an influential thing, a career that has made me a better writer, in a way, because of how it has reminded me to stay loose, to allow language and inspiration to flourish without getting precious or exercising too much control. That said, I want to append one last morsel of story. A couple of years ago, in the course of speaking in public about how much I love the Lounge Lizards, I got to know Lurie a little bit, and one night we did a reading together, on the Lower East Side. As part of this reading series (Happy Endings), each reader was meant to try something that he had *never done* in public before. This was hard work for Lurie, because he has done a lot of things in public, and probably reading from his memoir-in-progress *was* the thing he had never done in public before. But after he read from his memoir, which was enthusiastically admired by the crowd, he got out his harmonica. Harmonica was among John's first instruments, and he's an extremely good harmonica player, and for a couple of minutes, despite his not great physical condition, he played one of the most heartrending and beautiful harmonica solos I've ever heard, after which he stumbled out of the room and literally collapsed in the hall. He said to me later that it might have been the last time he ever plays music in public. A respectful silence is probably the only way to greet this news. It's sad, for sure, very sad. Still, I feel lucky to have been there. By its nature, live music has only its immediate duration. After that comes the respectful silence. With Lurie and the Lounge Lizards, the music is in the province of memory now, and that's where it's kept alive. A real shame for those who won't get to see them play. Memory is faulty, full of mistakes, full of longing, but still interacts with music in a flexible way; memory is kind of like music itself; like jazz, it's unpredictable, and memory gives musicians something to work toward, as it also gives writers something to write about.

Thirteenth proposition, *that the artist should have equal time, should perhaps have the opportunity to respond, in his own voice,* to lines written about him by his fans:*

I remember that show. It makes me sad what you wrote. What I remember is when Calvin would start in with that groove that was the opening for "Lawn for People." I can see him sitting back there playing and just yelling with a rage that was somehow also joy. Billy Martin would come in, playing odd time against Calvin. Then I would play over them. That way, I would really get a chance to play, because the rest of the time I was having to lead the whole band. Then the band would come in, one at a time, behind me. Then the main theme came in, with Michael Blake on tenor and Dave Tronzo on slide. It was like an anthem to a small, insane country that had just gained its independence, that thing, *ba da doo ba, bo de da.* Tronzo could really nail that line. It was, I think, the only major melody that I ever wrote.

There was so much love and strength. It was something that, while we were playing, could absolutely not be denied. Of course, in the light of day, in offices in tall buildings all over Manhattan and Los Angeles, by neurotic women in suits with tight lips and short hair, white men with exceptionally small genitalia, it was

---

* Lurie responded to my request to append remarks by phone in early March of 2006. He was skeptical but willing.

denied constantly, without exception. But while we were playing, there was a mounting ecstasy and power that could not be stopped. And what you saw was a shortened, forty-five-minute version of the set; we normally played for three hours.

It was macho in a way, but macho like your baby's first steps.

So it's sad because it was beautiful, sad in a nice way, but also it's sad because of the enormous sense of loss. And also, somehow I feel like I failed. Not that many people, especially in America, ever saw that band. The recordings capture something in moments but not the whole thing. And from what I can tell, not a ton of people own those recordings anyway, and there were enormous gaps, sometimes five or six years, where I could not afford to bring us into the studio. So as great as the music was, I did fail in a way, because it never really got out there.

If we are playing, no matter how great it is, and there is no one there to hear it, then what good is it? How does that do anything for the world? I used to say in interviews, "I am wiser, stronger, kinder, and way more handsome than George Bush; I should have more effect on the world." But of course I didn't.

I remember that I did talk to John Schaefer for a minute before going on, but it was awkward. Mostly because it is odd to switch gears like that, to go from being interviewed to playing. I remember telling Schaefer that the title of the piece was "Lawn for

People," and he made an odd face and I thought he was going to ask me what it meant, but I was rescued because the guys started playing and I didn't have to answer. And I remember because it was only one of three or four times we played in the afternoon. I'd just come back from Thailand from shooting *Fishing with John* with Dennis Hopper. I'd written "Lawn for People" there after the shoot, along with another one of the songs we did that day. It was good, and it was new material, and I remember thinking, "Good, we really got this down." And then, as excited as I was to listen to the recording, I was equally disappointed to hear the tape. It's not really fair to blame the engineer if the engineer doesn't know the music. The entrances are missed. There's all this chaos going on, but the cello's supposed to be out front. If the cello is not out front, it's just a rumbling mess. But it's not the engineer's fault, because he didn't know this.

I kind of have to agree with you about the early band. We postured really hard because we were shy. At least, I was shy. So in the beginning we hid behind humor and a sort of sneering — like, we are cooler than you. When we started out, we didn't have the courage to be beautiful. But also it took years to figure out how to make the music sound like it was supposed to sound. When it was funny and campy, everybody loved it, and then later when it got really good, evolved and became elegant, nobody liked it anymore, except you, I guess. And so now I realize that there were some people out there who were actually feeling what we were doing. I think that because of the early stance of the band and then because I was so known for the movies, that some music types decided that the Lounge Lizards were somehow disingenuous, when nothing could be further from the truth.

The Pete Townshend
Fragments

In January 2003, the British police turned up, on a list of visitors to a website devoted to child pornography, a name belonging to a certain significant "rock star." This was in the course of Operation Ore, an FBI-initiated undertaking, one that had swept into the international criminal justice system a great number of persons both eminent and unknown, all over the world, many of them involved in activities that were not going to turn out felicitously for them.

I read the item first in a gossip column. It was one of those blind squibs in which it's not clear immediately who the unlucky individual is, but it soon will be. Indeed, the identity of the "rock star," as the tabs would have it, was quickly revealed by the *Daily Mail*, and this celebrity surrendered thereafter to Scotland Yard. The musician in question was Pete Townshend. Townshend is best known, of course, as the principal songwriter and the guitar player in the British rock-and-roll band called the Who. Much horrible publicity ensued, of the sort that regular citizens like you and me can't begin to imagine. The British tabloids make the American tabloids look timid in their zeal to bait and torture, and in this matter they performed according to type. No doubt Pete was miserable leaving the house for a while. It's fair to say his career was in some doubt.

Pete's explanation, as much of it as he has given over the years, makes clear that he did in fact give his credit card number to the website in question.* And yet having investigated Pete and his claims, the authorities proffered no charges, and Townshend was free to go about his business.

The fact that Pete was not prosecuted is reassuring, insofar as I need to be reassured. The matter was closed. It probably *ought* to have been closed. Except that Pete, in his Pete Townshend way, suggested in the course of defending himself that anyone who was uncertain about the degree to which he was preoccupied with the abuse of children should look into the *work*. To my knowledge, no one has given the work the requisite sustained look, and so I have undertaken to do so myself.

Why bother with the Who now? Their best work is long behind them. They are perhaps the quintessence of classic-rock dinosaurs. Pete hasn't been a terribly convincing

---

* "From the very beginning, I acknowledged that I did access this site....I accessed the site because of my concern at the shocking material readily available to children as well as adults, and as part of my research toward the campaign I had been putting together since 1995 to counter damage done by all kinds of pornography on the Internet, but especially any involving child abuse....The police have unconditionally accepted that these were my motives in looking at this site and that there was no other nefarious purpose, and as a result they have decided not to charge me. I accept that I was wrong to access this site, and that by doing so, I broke the law, and I have accepted the caution that the police have given me."

rock personality since, well, "Eminence Front" on the mostly dismal *It's Hard* album (1982). Since then he has released some inconsistent solo work and dabbled in musical theater.

And yet: for me the reason to bother is that the Who were the first rock-and-roll band with which I was completely obsessed, beginning at about age thirteen, when the film of *Tommy* came out. I knew a little bit about the band before that. I remember hearing "I Can See for Miles" on the radio in the late sixties. At that point, I didn't really pay much attention. In fact, the route to the Who for me was through teenybopper pop. The catalyst was none other than Elton John. Before the Who I was primarily interested in Elton John, of whose catalogue I had purchased a couple of albums. I had therefore heard the recording of "Pinball Wizard" that Elton had made for the *Tommy* soundtrack.

Tommy, the film, didn't venture near to New Canaan, Connecticut. Or that's how I reconstruct it. But since I was unable to see the film, I made do with the *Tommy* soundtrack album. Among true aficionados, the Who's own recording is considered far superior, but I loved the film soundtrack. This is how it goes sometimes. You find your way to the inferior work first. The updated arrangements on the soundtrack recording, with all the synthesizer parts, sounded strange and novel to me. And trying to imagine what the film would look like just from hearing the songs, this was an activity that filled the better part of a couple years.

About the same time, *The Who by Numbers* was released. I suppose I got the *Tommy* soundtrack at the end of eighth grade. And not so long after, I purchased *The Who by Numbers* on one of my weekly record-buying excursions. This is a highly improbable album with which to enter into the story. For one thing, it has almost none of the keyboard razzle-dazzle that Pete made use of on the *Tommy* soundtrack. Also, unlike *Tommy* and its sibling, *Quadrophenia* (which had immediately preceded the *Tommy* film), the recording in question has no conceptual apparatus. It's just an album of songs. In particular, very, very bleak confessional songs. Most of the arrangements are rather simple. It's the Who as they sounded best, a little bit acoustic, a little bit electric. Roger Daltrey wasn't yelling a lot; he was *singing*. And despite the abundant melancholy, there is a little bit of whimsy around the edges too. In short, *The Who by Numbers* is an agitated, British-invasion version of a singer-songwriter album.

Something about the record rang true. I was away at school by then, and I wasn't having an easy time. It was my first year in private school, after a lifetime in the public schools in the suburbs. Many of my classmates at boarding school had been through the various "country day" academies of Connecticut or the private-school system of New York City. They seemed to know one another well. They had social skills I didn't have. They all dressed alike. They all summered in the same locales. In this rather difficult social environment, I became besotted with rock and roll, as boys do, and the songs on *The Who by Numbers*, like "Slip Kid" and "How Many Friends," songs about the difficulty of living a happy, contented, and self-assured life, were exactly the kind of soundtrack I required.

I suppose the quality I was responding to when I was a fervent believer in the Who was Pete Townshend's honesty. It was abundant on *The Who by Numbers*. The rumor I heard was that when Keith Moon, the drummer, first heard the demos for *The Who by Numbers*, he wept. It's a record that seems as though it could easily inspire this passionate response. True, there is the country throwaway, "Squeeze Box" ("Mama's got a squeeze box / She wears on her chest / And when Daddy comes home / He never gets no rest"), which is delightful, full of double entendres, and cheerful the way the Who were during the fertile interval of the mid-sixties when they recorded "Substitute," "Pictures of Lily," "Tattoo," etc. I always thought this whimsical part of what they did was moving and indisputably great, and I still do. Nevertheless, when I was lonely and woebegone, the remainder of *The Who by Numbers*, with its surfeit of misery, inspired allegiance in me, and because I felt great allegiance, I bought everything I could get my hands on. I was an adherent, as regards the Who. By the next year, I had *Who's Next*, *Quadrophenia*, *The Who Sell Out*, a couple of Roger Daltrey and John Entwistle solo albums, and of course Pete's neglected masterpiece, *Who Came First*, his album of devotional songs.

Do any of these songs have anything to do with child abuse? Did I understand the Who songs this way? What is the vision of familial care and socialization that we find in the early Who songs? Well, there is "I'm a Boy," whose first verse runs: "One girl was called Jean Marie / Another little girl was called Felicity / Another little girl was Sally Joy / The other was me and I'm a boy." In the chorus, the unhappy narrator of these aforementioned lines has it even *worse*, apparently, since his "ma won't admit" that he's a boy, he's a boy, he's a boy. From the same early period there is "Pictures of Lily," about onanistic pursuits, in which a young man is fixated upon pinup images given to him by his paterfamilias: "Pictures of Lily made my life so wonderful / Pictures of Lily helped me sleep at night / Pictures of Lily solved my childhood problems / Pictures of Lily helped me feel alright." Taken as a pair, these eccentric pop gems give a much different view of male psychology from the sort you might have found on Stones or Beatles releases. In fact, even the minor Who songs from the mid-sixties have their share of dark forebodings. We have the cheerful divorce anthem "A Legal Matter." We have the childhood beatings administered in "Tattoo": "My dad beat me 'cause mine said 'Mother' / But my mother naturally liked it and beat my brother / 'Cause his tattoo was of a lady in the nude / And my mother thought that was extremely rude." And so forth.

The family as construed on *Meaty Beaty Big and Bouncy*, their album of early singles, would seem to be a rather dysfunctional landscape, even if the Who songs are understood as occasionally comic, with their French horn solos, their three-part harmonies and childlike melodies. And I'm not even scratching the surface of "Substitute," the song obsessed with fraudulence. Or "I Can't Explain," in which skepticism about romantic language makes it impossible for love to take root. Nor am I lingering over the dark lyrics of Who bassist John Entwistle, author of, e.g., "Boris the Spider" and "Heaven and Hell."

If there is not outright child abuse in the abusive and dysfunctional psychic environment of the early singles by Pete Townshend and the Who, we have only to wait for *Tommy*. In that album, we find exhibits A and B of the child abuse theme, "Fiddle About" and "Cousin Kevin," two excerpts from Act I, more or less, of the infamous *rock opera*.

Cousin Kevin, according to the story, is mainly given to torturing the young protagonist, Tommy Walker. In the film, at least, he's quite glam, quite sexually ambiguous, and the torture does seem to have a patently sexual cast to it. "Fiddle About," which follows, is even darker and more psychosexual: "I'm your wicked uncle Ernie / I'm glad you won't see or hear me / As I fiddle about." "Fiddle About" is the more transparent of the two tunes that deal with the subject under consideration here, and in the film Keith Moon plays Uncle Ernie with a manic depravity that genuinely disturbed me the first time I beheld it. These songs *are* unequivocally about abuse, and they are about abuse in a way that does, it seems to me, have the ring of conviction, perhaps more so when one considers that they were written in a period rather more permissive and freewheeling than the present.* Only problem is: Pete Townshend didn't write either of them! John Entwistle, the bass player, wrote both "Cousin Kevin" and "Fiddle About" in his mock-horror style, also on display, e.g., in "Boris the Spider." It is perhaps interesting to note, however, that Entwistle's parents, like Pete Townshend's, divorced when he was still a very young child. He too was raised by his grandparents.

Tommy Walker, according to the well-known if thin narrative, is a war baby, like the members of the Who themselves.

---

* Townshend in *Mojo*, February 2006: "Roger had always expressed an absolute disgust of somebody that would sleep with an underage girl. And I'd often say to him, 'Well, how do we know if we've slept with underage girls? You started having sex with girls when you were sixteen, so how do you know?' So it's very difficult to be absolutely black and white and cut and dried about it."

He's born during or just before the Blitz,* and the story depicts the period from that military assault unto the social upheavals of the late sixties. It's as though the entire span, including the counterculture, were one gigantic cultural sham, in which even the most lofty attempt (Tommy's) to try to convert the broken and misguided is doomed to backfire.

In this light, it's sort of amazing that *Tommy* was considered a wide-eyed document of the *haute* psychedelic period, since, like one of the Who's best-known songs, "Won't Get Fooled Again," it's arguably just as skeptical as it is faithful. (There's an opera-within-the-opera, too, "Sally Simpson," which has an even more dire narrative about the perils of rock messianic fervor.) Unless of course the thing that rescues, the thing that promises escape, is the music itself. *Not* the lyrics but the music. The principal claim for the greatness of *Tommy* is its structure, actually, is the way an entire story is stretched out of the four sides of the LP, including an overture and instrumental portions, including reprises and leitmotifs. Music is the thing that enables Tommy's story to offer some kind of transcendence. It's not what the Who *say*, but *how* they say it.

Still, is it possible that *Tommy* is a crypto-autobiographical document about Pete's own abuse and the way in which he was rescued through the sonic liberation of rock and roll? You could make the case. It may be why, as a narrative, it's a mess — because the author was concealing and revealing at the same time. It would be hard, even impossible, to think of *Tommy*

---

* Ken Russell's film features a moment that lingers over the cages that some residents of London slept in during the war, and it's one of many overpowering images in the film.

as conclusive about this autobiographical interpretation. If it works at all,* it's by reason of clever pop songwriting and great playing by a band that was nearly at its peak as an ensemble. They could have been singing about traffic in central London and the results would have sounded just as overpowering.

I don't actually like *Tommy* that much myself, or less so than I once did. As far as I'm concerned, it created more problems than it solved. Pete is free to do whatever he likes, of course. The more free he is, the more I admire him. Yet the conceptual baggage hanging around his neck from *Tommy* was considerable. After *Tommy*, Pete, whether he wanted to be or not, was an Artist. This is evident not only on the windy and out-of-control *Quadrophenia*, whose story never gets off the ground at all, but even more transparently on such solo suites as *White City* and *Psychoderelict*. Pete's a *brilliant* writer of pop songs, as good as they get, but after *Tommy* he doesn't much *want* to be a writer of pop songs anymore. That's where the trouble starts. He made a name for himself in this band, possibly one of the ugliest, most acrimonious bands ever, a band where everyone involved seemed to dislike one another, where the drummer was so drunken and depressive that they had a hard time keeping him alive. The lead singer resented the guitar player, and Pete, who was by no means blameless, responded by exerting more control rather than less, and they all resented

---

* And not everyone thinks it works. It recently turned up on a well-publicized list of the worst albums ever made.

him for it, and in the interpretation I'm formulating here he disliked himself too. He made his name in this band, but that didn't mean he couldn't outgrow it.

Tommy might point at some explanations for the Townshend kiddie porn debacle, but I just don't think it's a complete diagram for Townshend's character, not as I'm constructing him. Though perhaps one earlier song is, namely the track called "A Quick One, While He's Away." It's a rash assertion, but I happen to think "A Quick One" is one of the best rock-and-roll songs ever written. I like few pieces of music on earth as well as I like this song. It's ridiculous, hilarious, clever, and then, in the last three minutes, transportative, generous, even numinous.

"A Quick One," the way the lore is told, was written after an assignment by Kit Lambert, who managed the Who at the time. Lambert, a fan of opera, had been challenging Pete to write a longer piece of music. It took Kit's birthday party to bring about the right circumstances. They dashed off the suite for the celebration, but short of material for the *Happy Jack* album, they also committed it to tape.

The studio recording is not bad. But you would never get to the heart of the song if you only listened to the studio recording. There are at least two superior renditions of it floating around.* The first is on *The Rolling Stones Rock and Roll Circus*, which, according to legend, is the reason that the Stones later refused to release that particular television broadcast. The Who were *too good*. However, as Pete points out on the

---

* Actually, now there's a third, a live version on *BBC Sessions*.

DVD release of *Rock and Roll Circus* (he is as engaging and garrulous as ever on the *extras* portion of the disc), a more likely interpretation is to be found in the fact that Brian Jones was on the point of leaving the band. In fact, *Rock and Roll Circus* was the last performance of Brian Jones with the Rolling Stones. There's something ghostly and heartbreaking about Brian wherever he turns up in the footage, and this would be reason enough to suppress it.

The Who play "A Quick One" in the released version of *Rock and Roll Circus* and nothing else, not one other song, and it's an amazing performance, justifiably renowned. They are completely at ease, confident to the point of cocksure, and they hurtle to the last three minutes like no one on earth could touch them.

Yes, a good version, to be sure—in front of Stones fans, no less—but it's not the rendition you should listen to. The one you should listen to is the recording of "A Quick One" from the expanded edition of *Live at Leeds*.

But wait, before I talk about that, I have to tell you about taking my mother to see *The Kids Are Alright* back when I was in high school. This, in fact, was when I first saw live footage of "A Quick One." I was home for some vacation, Christmas probably. I think my mother and my brother and I, unencumbered by other family, decided to go to the movies, and somehow my mother agreed to see this documentary about the Who. It was playing at the mall in New Rochelle. How horrible. I can only think of moments like this with shame. Why on earth did I try to persuade my mother to listen to the music

I liked? For example, I remember sitting her down one day, when I was in tenth grade, saying, in effect, *Look, if you want to know something about how I live, you're going to have to hear some of the music I listen to.* For example, I remember playing her "Heroes," by David Bowie, and I remember playing her some Roxy Music, and I can remember when, at the tolling of a telephone, she rushed from the sofa to get away from me and my apparently endless capacity for reminding her to listen *really carefully* to the guitar solo. I wish, now, that I had *not* taken my mother to see *The Kids Are Alright*. She didn't like it, and the mall in New Rochelle was always a deadening place.

And yet what I remember my mother saying about *The Kids Are Alright*, in her attempt to say something favorable, was that the sections about Keith Moon were moving to her. And this is an interesting thing to say. In my recollection we saw *The Kids Are Alright* just after Keith Moon died, and that was why Keith seemed spectral in the film, like the prankster counterpart to Brian Jones. Because he was not long for the world. In *The Kids Are Alright*, whenever the camera is on Keith, he can't stop himself. He tears off Pete's shirt in one television interview, he starts taking off his own clothes, he won't stop unless the camera cuts away. In one sequence, Keith is being interviewed while at the same time being whipped by a bemused and scantily clad dominatrix. There are also scenes in which Moon is interviewed by Ringo Starr. Ringo asks him about the other members of the band, and though Keith attempts the class-clown responses, there's a desperately sad quality to how hard he works the game. This is a guy who, at thirty-one years old, is about to overdose on a medication designed to keep him from drinking.

Many people in my mother's family had drinking problems. My grandmother, for example, died of cirrhosis. My uncle had a drinking problem. My grandfather was no slouch. I have a drinking problem. My sister drank too much. And so forth. I imagine that my mother had and has a particular sensitivity to this issue, and I imagine that even though she hated the music in *The Kids Are Alright*, maybe she saw the spectral, ghostly Keith Moon, halfway to his eternal resting place, and recognized a sad predilection she had observed close up.

Of course, Keith isn't the only doomed character in the film. John Entwistle, for example, died a couple of years before the writing of this essay, of a cocaine overdose. He was in a hotel in Las Vegas. He had a stripper with him. John says very little in *The Kids Are Alright*, though there is a funny passage in which he tries skeet shooting on the grounds of his estate, using gold records as targets. He can't seem to hit anything until he uses a machine gun of some kind. And apparently Entwistle used actual gold records for this sequence.

If John isn't enough, there is Pete in the film. In particular, I find it sort of harrowing to watch the footage of the band from Shepperton Studios. The production notes indicate that there wasn't much good footage of the Who playing "Baba O'Riley" or "Won't Get Fooled Again," two of their best-known tracks. As a teenager, I felt no hesitation in liking "Baba O'Riley," even though the "teenage wasteland" sing-along chorus of the tune would seem to be full of venom for the very thing the song does, which is to constitute community through the *anthemic*. I loved the song. And I probably still would, had I not heard it a hundred and ten thousand times. Anyway, the Shepperton gig was convened to film these songs before five hundred or so invited guests, and the performances are loose limbed and fun, if a little bit jaundiced. Pete, in particular, does some kind of deranged Sufi dance during the parts of "Baba O'Riley" in which he does not play, and when the camera closes in on him for his portion of the bridge, "Don't cry / Don't raise your eye," he sort of botches the lines at first. His own eyes are red and he seems, well, to me he seems a little fucked up, or heartbroken, or something. He's half in the song and half out of it, even though it's kind of an easy song. There's something unsettling about the whole thing, like he doesn't want to do *this* anymore. And apparently he did not. These days, Townshend says that the creative period of the Who ended with *Quadrophenia*, and that was four or five years before the Shepperton gig.

The Kids Are Alright introduced me to "A Quick One" live, and this was later supplemented by the stunning *Live at Leeds* rendition, which I first heard in Wes Anderson's film *Rushmore*. The original release of *Live at Leeds*, in 1970, mostly had chestnuts on it like "Substitute" and "Summertime Blues." It did not, until it got expanded in 1995, feature "A Quick One." In *Rushmore*, the big last three minutes of the suite are used to galvanizing effect during one of Max Fischer's innumerable bad spots. I bought the *Rushmore* soundtrack (mainly to get hold of the Faces tune at the end, "Ooh La La"), and it was then that I first heard the *Live at Leeds* recording in all its glory.

The story of "A Quick One," such as it is, concerns a

woman whose husband goes off to war (like Tommy's dad), and who then takes up with another man (just as Ann-Margret did with the creepy Oliver Reed in the film version of *Tommy*), in this case a man called by the epithet Ivor the Engine Driver. The entirety of "A Quick One" is subdivided into vignettes, e.g., an *a cappella* section in close harmony that makes clear that "her man's been gone," a B section in which the band gets involved and during which the heroine is revealed to be bereft, grief stricken, and, apparently, quite comely (since she comes from a town "famous for the little girl"). The B section is followed by a C section sung together by Roger, John, and Pete, in which the town seems to suggest that it can comfort the heroine in her time of sorrow. In the *D* section, which forgoes the peeling rock tones of B and C, Ivor the Engine Driver is introduced, via some amazing drumming by Moon and a country-and-western bass part. John, who plays Ivor, sings: "He told me he loved you / He ain't no liar and I ain't either / So let's have a smile for an old engine driver." From here we cut away to the missing paramour in E, who will soon, soon, soon be home. Throughout, in the *Leeds* recording, the Who are trying to amuse one another with interruptions about the characters in the story (Keith yells, "Dirty old sod!" when Ivor the Engine Driver is first introduced; and Pete says, deadpan, "Come on, old horse," during the C&W section, etc.). Their collective ease and joy about the material is manifest. The whole proceeding may seem like a joke, of course, since the music is occasionally parodistic, and the characters' names are ridiculous, and Pete plays the girl's role (or so he says during the introduction in Leeds), but suddenly, toward its close, "A Quick One" *is* about some variety of sexual abuse. The heartsick heroine is seduced by the much older engine driver, thinking her "man" is gone for good. Only to find, as in *Tommy*, that he who may have been lost is "only late." To put it more succinctly, the F section brings back the chiming guitars, and we get the girl's tearful confession to her man, now returned to her: "Am I back in your arms? / Away from all harm?"

And this prompts the part of the song that is germane to these investigations:* "I missed you and I must admit," the little Girl Guide sings, "I kissed a few and once did sit / On Ivor the Engine Driver's lap / And later with him had a nap." Now the band locks into a classic one-four-five chord progression, with Roger, Pete, and John all singing—John in falsetto descant—and the lyrics of reply from the man consist only of the words "You are forgiven!"

In all honesty, it's hard for me to listen to this section of "A Quick One" without weeping. And I listen to it pretty often. My feeling, and I admit it is a lofty feeling, is that Pete, in *this* moment, has somehow managed to channel something like a God's-eye view of absolution. Here is the ineffable something or other that *Tommy* rarely manages. Pete has figured out how to render compassion for the easily tempted of the world, if just for a split second, has looked down on them and has seen how flawed his fellows are, how broken, how innocent, how careless, and has announced, as the song does, that we are all absolved. In fact, Pete even says so, at the end, to the audience: "We're *all* forgiven!" And I always believe him.

---

* Let me not overlook to include here the passage where all three singers sing the word *cello* over and over again for a while. Apparently, the band was eager to have genuine cellos in this spot but were told that there wasn't money in the production budget.

*   *   *

Is this big ending (actually, it's *two* endings, because the song ends once and then everyone comes in a second time with the refrain) the work of a guy who was sexually abused as a child? And who is preoccupied or even obsessed with issues of sexual abuse? Or is it the work of a pedophile himself? Maybe Pete had or has no access to the memories of his childhood abuse. Or maybe he is experiencing so-called recovered memory syndrome. Except that recovered memory syndrome is somewhat discredited these days. Actually, it's a little hard for me, personally, to believe that Pete has the syndrome so designated. I incline toward the view of Frederick Crews (as articulated in an article in the *New York Review of Books*, March 11, 2004), that if it is so easy to forget trauma, why is it that the vast majority of survivors of the Holocaust, e.g., do not seem to have forgotten any of it at all? Crews writes, in reviewing Richard McNally's treatise on the subject, *Remembering Trauma:*

> It makes no sense...to count forgetfulness for some "aspect of the trauma" within the definition of post-traumatic stress disorder, because normal people as well as PTSD sufferers get disoriented by shocking incidents and fail to memorize everything about the event, even while knowing for the rest of their lives *that it occurred.* Likewise, it has never been established, and it seems quite unbelievable, that people can be haunted by memories that were never cognitively registered as such [italics mine].

On the basis of the big ending of "A Quick One," it's easier for me to understand Pete as someone who has equanimity for both victims and, well, perpetrators. The victims, though they may treat themselves horribly later on, do not need to be forgiven for much. We do have boundless compassion for them and for their problems. Therefore, the repetitions of "You are forgiven" are not designed exclusively for the victims. The Girl Guide is forgiven for her willing participation in the abuse/betrayal, as is the engine driver. In fact, we are *all* forgiven.

There's another way to look at these questions. The victims of trauma sometimes do have Stockholm syndrome; they sometimes do identify with the perps. Accordingly, it's possible that Pete, even in this incredibly triumphant moment, is somehow working out his identification both with those who inflict sexual abuse *and* with those who, for whatever tragic reason, cooperate with it, as the little Girl Guide does. The issue is complicated.

Recently, I read an interview Pete did with *Rolling Stone*,* from the period when the Who were touring again. Pete said some inexplicable things. For example, he said that he was only doing the tour for Roger Daltrey ("I agreed with Roger that, in order to keep him amused this year, we should go back to New York and play a couple of shows"); he said that he didn't care what the audience thought about licensing Who songs to corporate advertisements ("Who fans will often think, 'This is my song, it belongs to me, it reminds me of the first time that I kissed Susie, and you can't sell it.' And the fact is that I can and I will and I have. I don't give a fuck about the first time you

---

* *Rolling Stone*, #902, July 2002.

kissed Susie"). And he said some stuff about bisexuality when confronted by the reporter. Pete, in his Pete Townshend way, seemed to feel as if he had to try to answer all the questions put to him. But really what was the point? According to the interviewer, Danny Fields (former manager of the Doors) had on occasion referred to Townshend as his "on-and-off boyfriend." At this revelation, Pete became singularly combative, said over and over that he couldn't remember, said he might have been drugged, said it was the sixties and, as such, it was a time of great social and sexual experimentation. And finally he went wild with rage, or this is my characterization:

> To actually say that we were boyfriend and girlfriend! Boyfriend and boyfriend. I don't know what he's fucking talking about. [*Louder*] And this is it. This is the fucking thing that stinks about this whole fucking thing of doing a fucking interview with fucking *Rolling Stone* magazine in the first place when I don't need to!...The tour is sold-out. I don't want to talk about my work, I don't want to talk about The Who, I don't want to talk about any of this shit....I just don't know what Danny is talking about. I know that I spent a night in his house. I don't remember much else about it. You know, I did not go out with him. He is not my type.

This is the Pete Townshend that I really loved and admired in the seventies. Completely unpredictable, completely impulsive, but totally human and sympathetic. Because what he's saying is, well, he's being contemptuous of *Rolling Stone*, and this is a credit to him. *Rolling Stone*, even in the seventies, was contemptible, and when you compare its fiery rhetoric back in the sixties with its devotion these days to Cristal-swilling celebutantes, you can only conclude that it has fallen far. Actually, it has never met a corporate trend to which it wouldn't genuflect immediately. When Pete admits that he doesn't give a shit about discussing his work, when he's dismissive about the Who, when he says how much he loves John and Roger, you totally believe that he does love John and Roger *and* that he doesn't give a shit about the Who. It's the mix of registers that feels most honest. He's evasive about the bisexuality issue, tries every circumlocution he can come up with, and then he says that Danny Fields was "not [his] type." So what's the truth exactly? Did he sleep with Danny Fields? I don't really care whether he did or he didn't. In fact, I wish he *had*, since protestations of heterosexuality are so unsatisfying. My recommendation is that no one should ever again protest or attest as to their fixed sexuality. However, Pete doesn't exactly create a climate of reliability, on the child pornography issue later, when he says: "I'm fifty-seven, I've got a young girlfriend, I'm not gay. I'm not interested in men. I don't think I ever really have been. I've had a high sex drive all my life, which has actually been difficult sometimes to reconcile with some of my spiritual aspirations."

Similar provocations grace the pages of *Mojo*, the British music magazine, in an issue from 2006 devoted to the Who. There was, for example, the following from Townshend, about Bob Dylan:

> There was a richness around us which was totally and
> purely and entirely our own and you have to look at

Scorsese's Dylan movie to see how lost some of those older rockers were. Dylan's rock and roll was silly rock and roll, he couldn't play rock and roll, he's never been able to play rock and roll. Not only that, but the band he hired to play rock and roll was Ronnie Hawkins's old fucking backing band! He was dead meat, he was gone....We were working with something new and pure and refined.

Wow! Bob Dylan was dead meat! We should all be so badly decomposed! And the Band is "Ronnie Hawkins's old fucking band"? Nicely outrageous, these observations, but he couldn't really believe them, and when he mounted an apology on his website, it was apparent he didn't.* Later, in the same issue of *Mojo*—and despite having written at least one song lionizing Keith Moon (rightly so)—Pete took a few shots at Keith, saying, e.g., that "he was a giant of a man in so many respects, but in other respects he was a fucking tick on the back of The Who. No one's got the guts to say it...but it's true."

Townshend also touched upon the pedophilia charges† as well as his own childhood abuse. As in other published remarks,

---

* "I was trying to show how over here in the UK in the early sixties we looked at the old guard of 'white' rock 'n' roll (even Elvis) as being almost 'washed up.' I know it sounds crazy now. We still worshipped the old guard: Eddie Cochran, Elvis, Buddy Holly, The Everly Brothers, Ricky Nelson, all of them. But people like me believed R&B artists (and only the black ones like Chuck Berry, John Lee Hooker, Bo Diddley and Jimmy Reed) were the ones we needed to emulate. It seemed to me...Dylan was groping in the dark....Dylan doesn't need my puffs, but neither should he or The Band be subject to slurs I didn't intend to make."

† *Mojo*, p. 72.

he managed to be both oblique and elsewhere forthright about his experiences. For example:

> A lot of the people I was talking to when I was writing this book [his autobiographical account of his abuse], and people that I was helping to deal with recovery, had suffered when they were evacuated during the war. And the idea emerged that about a year or two before the war had ended, this message went out that we were going to lose. And there were all these people that had the possession of all these beautiful young children, and they started to abuse them. Because they thought the end of the world was coming, and nobody would give a fuck.

This outline of wartime history certainly seems a bit precarious. Beyond anecdotal accounts, I'm not sure there's voluminous support for Pete's historical suppositions, and this is a frequent trope of Townshend the interview subject. Acquaintances are adduced as evidence of this or that assertion.

Later, when Townshend placed himself within the confines of his sketch of wartime history, he seemed to do so with more emphasis on poor parenting than outright abuse: "Then I'm born right at the end of the war, May 19, 1945, the week Albert Speer is arrested. It's just bizarre, the idea that they [his parents] then have to go on and live their lives....To be a child at that time, you're saying to your parents, I need mummy and daddy, and they're going, 'Fuck off!,' because they're traumatized. So many of my generation experienced that kind of neglect."

Further on, he didn't mince words at all. In fact, in *Mojo* I came upon the one spot where Pete Townshend has been absolutely clear about his understanding of his childhood: "When I talk about abuse [after the war] I'm not talking about sexual abuse, *which I experienced*, I'm talking about postwar neglect.... I'm talking about the fact of the matter. My dad, after the war, chose to go and play Germany for a year. He stayed with the band, The Squadronaires, and as a result I never saw him" (italics mine).

This is moving and sad. And as someone also separated from his father for several months (in 1970) because of legal wrangling, I can sympathize with the kind of loss that Pete is trying to get at. Still, the logic feels muddled to me. It may be that the logic is muddled because the editors of *Mojo* have muddled it themselves. But part of the confusion also comes from the fact that the revelation of Townshend's sexual abuse is tucked into some rather passionate ranting about the war and its aftermath. Because of the way the sexual abuse is left unexamined, the remark has the effect of suggesting that it is the wartime history that has made the indelible mark on Pete Townshend. He is forthright about having been sexually abused, yes, but he is much more forthright about the neglect he suffered from parents, and the scars of the war itself.

Maybe it is simply that Townshend as an interview subject is just extremely unfocused. He has trouble with taxonomies of abuse because he has trouble prioritizing in general (earlier in the interview, e.g., he says of Roger Daltrey, "He respects my lack of boundaries and lack of ability to live in reality"). *Abuse*, the word, seems to stand here for varieties of experience, and Pete doesn't always make clear which way he's using it. Having been absolutely clear, above, he then backs away from the subject.

It's unsettling to think about Townshend's life in the aftermath of the abuse charges: "I thought, it's going to be impossible for me to live—do I have to think of some way to kill myself." It would take enormous confidence for someone who was in his position, as an alleged pedophile, not to feel devastated by the press. To the point of paralysis. However, I'm just as interested in the *end* of his further remarks,* which is broadly indicative of the way Townshend communicates to the press, and in public generally: "I was frightened, and I think it's the first time I've felt that kind of fear and panic. I did an interview with *The Guardian*, and I said that if I'd had a gun I would have shot myself. It was pulled out as a headline, and I don't think it's true."

If he *did* say to *The Guardian* that he would have shot himself, how can it not be *true?* And yet at the end of the quotation he says just this, that it was *not* true that if he had a gun he would have shot himself. These two perceptions are mutually contradictory. But this is how Pete seems to use the interviews he gives, and how he uses writing in general. He doesn't think ahead. He thinks intuitively. When he contradicts himself, he contradicts himself. He will apologize later, if need be, or he will allow the contradictions to stand. Townshend lacks, perhaps entirely, an editorial function where his mouth is concerned, and this allows for great, expansive answers to questions, but it also allows for answers that are tangled, paradoxical, or contradictory.

I sort of want to know more about Pete's grandmother, about the period of his real or imagined child abuse. This is a

---

* *Mojo.*

fascinating autobiographical subplot for those who are interested in such things. I will sketch out what is in the record. His parents were both living. They were separated, as indicated above, only to reconcile later. During the separation, Pete was sent to live with his grandma Denny, and here's his account of it (from 1995):

> I was a postwar kid. I grew up with parents who came out of the end of the war with a great resilience, excitement, and big ideas, and I got left behind for a while. My parents split when I was very young, and I was sent to live with my grandmother, who had just been dumped by a very wealthy lover. She was in midlife crisis. She was my age today, and I identify very much with this woman who had to look after me. She ran naked in the streets and stuff like that. She was completely nuts. She was a very strict woman and I hated her....I had two years with her before my parents realized that they'd left me with someone who was insane.*

Pete relocated to his grandmother's house when he was four, and by all accounts he was not exaggerating about her mental state. I've read descriptions that feature *word salad* (the verbal gibberish of psychotic people), as well as pointless street searches for lost objects, etc. His grandmother also left him alone a lot. When she wasn't leaving him alone, she was berating him.

---

* Quoted in *Behind Blue Eyes: The Life of Pete Townshend*, by Geoffrey Giuliano (Cooper Square Press, 2002).

The particulars of the unstable grandmother are among the things Pete has forgotten over the years, and in his words it was only when his mother was writing *her* autobiography that he inquired about the gaps between ages four and six. His mother, Betty, was also unconventional in the area of familial relations: "She was very, very seductive....Mum was always surrounded by crowds of men. She had plenty of money, was on her own a lot." The stories of Betty Townshend don't improve later on. For example, here she is commenting on Pete after his father's death in the 1980s: "At Cliff's funeral, we all got steaming drunk, and Peter and I made a pact to go on the wagon. I was doing great for two years and didn't touch a drop, and then a very dear friend of mine died. I went to pieces and hit the bottle again. But Peter has managed to keep off it. He is a very strong person and just has the occasional glass of champagne."*

Wouldn't this situation with his biological mother also amount to a kind of abuse? But what kind of abuse are we talking about? Most often, when he has described the trouble with his grandmother, and one finds this especially in the aftermath of the child pornography investigation, Townshend uses qualifiers to describe the nature of the abuse. He says he "believes" he was sexually abused by his grandmother, or otherwise backs away from factual accounts. "I cannot remember clearly what happened, but my creative work tends to throw up nasty shadows—particularly in *Tommy*." And yet interpreting inductively from nasty shadows can be risky. I have a friend who was repeatedly abused as a child. She had one *very clear memory* of

---

* *Behind Blue Eyes.*

the sexual abuse, and only later did the most damaging memories of several years' worth of abuse surface in her recollection, landing her pretty quickly in a psychiatric hospital. Should we take Townshend at his word and accept that something grave and soul-slaughtering took place with his grandmother, despite his lack of clarity?

If so, if he was abused, the music was compensatory, was redemptive, so I don't want to overlook some technical analysis of Townshend the musician in this anatomy of his life. For example, it's worth talking about how Pete plays or played the guitar and about his singing, as these relate to his biography and character.

Townshend thinks he's a *bad* guitar player, and that may be true, if by playing badly you mean he doesn't play like Eric Claption or Jeff Beck. And it's true he is not a phenomenally melodic guitar player. One interesting feature of his guitar playing is the strumming, the open chords. There is also the volume. Pete is all about the open chord played through the original Marshall stack. I gather that the Who were among the first to use actual Marshall stacks and that Pete and John Entwistle helped design these Marshall stacks, in order to facilitate, among other things, the way Pete manipulated feedback on his guitar. This is especially satisfying on early songs like "My Generation" and "Anyway, Anyhow, Anywhere." The big open chord, with lots of feedback, is a thing of violence, a force of nature, and perhaps an engine of *forgetting*, and it is a recognizable aspect of the Who, so much so that when Pete was really trying to escape from the Who, one exit strategy involved building the songs around keyboards (as he frequently does on *All the Best Cowboys Have Chinese Eyes*) or to confine himself to playing the acoustic guitar (which he did in the late eighties because of his hearing problems).

There is also the visual part of Pete's guitar playing, the windmilling, the jumping up and down with the power chords. I have seen the Who play live only one time, to my shame, and it was late in their career. Pete was only jumping up and down *now and then*, in this particular show. Compared with the guitar playing of others, with, e.g., a Keith Richards or an Eric Clapton, this is an anarchic way of playing, and we can observe this even without lingering over the habitual smashing of guitars, which may have been, at a certain point, a Vegas move, a bit of ritual destruction that was giving the people what they wanted, but which *began* as an earnest and heartfelt enactment of rage and frustration. The destruction suggests to me nothing so much as the anthropologically chronicled destruction of the Kwakiutl natives of Alaska: whichever clan managed to destroy more of their *own* property won the war.

How does the guitar playing of Pete Townshend serve as evidence of or lack thereof with respect to the allegations about Pete and the pedophilia, etc.? It doesn't serve at all. It serves as an engine of forgetting. Or suppressing. Playing guitar is the place where all the controversy about Pete Townshend, all the provocative nonsense that he has said on occasion, is completely set aside, and the perfect, primitive value of whatever rock and roll once was is apparent to anyone within range. Pete Townshend, no matter his condition, was not a god, was not anything but a *man* when he played guitar, but even so, yes, he was the best that man had to offer, strumming thirty-second notes faster than almost anyone else could do it, and using his thumb on the low E string so that he always had a big fat bass note on the bottom of the chord, using amplification so that he righteously fucked up his hearing ever after, bobbing up and down in the air like he was trying to get himself to coast on the sound waves coming out of the amplifiers—a great guitar player, who did as much if not more than the better practitioners of guitar craft in terms of advancing the instrument. Playing guitar is about surviving, playing guitar is about overcoming, playing guitar is about distracting, in great waves of distortion and feedback, from the problems out there in the world, or playing guitar is about distracting the player from his past.

The Smothers Brothers show is a good visual example of this transformative aspect of the guitar. The Who's appearance on *The Smothers Brothers Comedy Hour* took place in September 1967, a couple of months after they played the Monterey Pop Festival. I guess I was too young to stay up to see it, which is why I saw it instead as part of *The Kids Are Alright.* This is the footage that opens that film.

The Smothers Brothers program was a true example of late-sixties television. Which is to say: it was manifestly political but was still a television show. The script called for the Who to thrash around to backing tracks of "My Generation" (the vocals were cut live), at the conclusion of which they would smash up a bunch of equipment, and *fast*, because you only had so much time on television. Then Pete was going to smash Tommy Smothers's acoustic guitar. Normally, when they were doing it onstage, in live performance, the band took their time about the destruction of property. But you couldn't spend ten minutes busting shit up with the Smothers Brothers. The sponsors wouldn't go for that.

"My Generation" is absolute anarchic brilliance. It's one of the greatest of rock songs because of the big ending, the squalling of guitar feedback. Well, also the drum fills. Toward the end of the Smothers Brothers tape, it's quite lovely to see Pete start jabbing the neck of his guitar into the amplifier, after which, casually, as if he's done it every day, he begins destroying his guitar. What could be better? But that's still not the interesting part; the interesting part has to do with the drummer, Keith Moon, who is busy executing his rolls until the smashing-things-up portion of the song. Now, it's said that Moon put a bunch of pyrotechnics in his bass drum and somehow the prank didn't quite work as it was supposed to, because it wasn't until after the song that the explosion detonated. It's a violent song anyway, and with Pete rushing through javelining his amp and smashing his guitar, there's plenty of entertainment, but suddenly a *bang* and then lots of smoke and shit goes flying everywhere, and nobody does anything! It's like nothing at all has happened, and that's when Pete smashes up Tommy's acoustic guitar, and there's this shot of him standing in profile next to Tommy, and the look on his face is sort of arresting. It's the look of the lion that has just devoured its prey, the look of the felon caught in his felony. I remember someone describing to me the look on Bill Clinton's face when he first had to address Congress after the Lewinsky affair came to light, and I suppose I somehow associate that look with this look, the look of pure power and remorselessness. The even more amazing part is that Pete, later on, dated the beginning of his hearing loss to *this moment*. So in spite of the fact that he was twenty-two, skinny, and beautiful in a feline way, he was, at the moment, completely deaf from a drum kit explosion gone awry. Here he was, at the peak of his powers, celebrating mayhem, menace, destruction, and yet, at the same time, he was really beginning to be consumed by rock and roll but good.

Having described the brilliance and animus of Townshend the guitar player, I think it's important to try to talk about Townshend the singer a little bit too. Because this was a crucial aspect of the Who sound, and it's sort of why I still like them a lot. If Roger Daltrey's voice, the baritone, drawing heavily from blues singers and R&B/Motown, was all about the masculine hubris of the Who ("They're all WASTED!"), Townshend's voice, especially in the earlier days, was exactly the opposite. Roger is "I'm Free," "Won't Get Fooled Again," "The Real Me," the signature songs of the Who. Pete is "Sunrise," from *The Who Sell Out*, "Blue, Red and Grey," from *The Who by Numbers*, or "I'm One," from *Quadrophenia*. Pete is a high tenor, a white Smokey Robinson, with a nice, controlled vibrato. No pitch problems. He could have been a great country-and-western singer.

This is a reductive model, of course. There have been moments in the Who when they effectively exploited reversing Roger and Pete (as I've said, Roger's winsome side is even more persuasive because of his machismo elsewhere). But I think the general principle is sound: the quality best expressed with

Townshend's instrument is *vulnerability*. "I'm One" is a good example. It's one of the rare fingerpicking numbers in the later Who output, and as such it's perhaps reliant on "Behind Blue Eyes" as a forerunner, though not to its detriment. It's also got a big helping of the bruising self-criticism that Townshend saved for the songs he sang himself: "Ill-fitting clothes / And I blend in the crowd / Fingers so clumsy / Voice too loud." The band sections, where Townshend's lead guitar comes in to muddy up the pristine surface, conceal the vulnerability beneath a roar, but it doesn't quite do the job; he's still twisting in the breeze, which is part of why the song has lasted.

"Blue, Red and Grey" is possibly the best example of this vulnerability I'm describing, and Townshend, who rarely plays this song, has said uncharitable things about it. True, the refrain, "I like every minute of the day," *does* sound like a man trying to talk himself out of a really dark spot, and yet in the third chorus, when he moves to the top end of his range, there's a great restraint and understatement evoked that actually makes the song do *more*, ache more, than most of the rock-oriented compositions on the album.

The same compelling vulnerability is much in evidence on Townshend's first solo album, *Who Came First*. Townshend originally released the collection in order to preempt bootlegs of the songs, which had appeared on three limited-edition devotional albums for followers of guru Meher Baba. Although the motive may have been professional, the songs are anything but careerist. The album includes a couple of nakedly arranged standards, "Content" and "There's a Heartache Following Me," which have a remarkable power considering how uncharacteristic they are for the writer of "My Generation" and "Won't Get Fooled Again." Townshend, on these pieces, sounds like a torch singer, like the rock-and-roll alter ego of Nina Simone or Dolly Parton. Then there are two leftovers from the aborted *Lifehouse* film, which appear here in their demo versions. And, most memorably, there are two stunning and limpid ballads, "Sheraton Gibson," a folksy piece written under the influence of Bob Dylan about Pete's touring miseries, and his setting of one of Meher Baba's prayers, "Pavardigar." The singing on these latter pieces is so full of soul and, in the case of "Pavardigar," spiritual awe that it's impossible to think of this work in the same way you would think of the unpredictable and menacing band in which the author more often plied his trade. When I was fourteen and first purchased *Who Came First*, I knew nothing about gurus and very little about spirituality. I wasn't even baptized yet. But the record still moved me.

Which is to say what exactly? About his singing? It's to say that if the guitar playing of Pete Townshend somehow operates as the infernal engine that transports its player, its practitioner, above and beyond a difficult childhood and its traumas, his voice is the part of the operation that expiates the crimes and excesses of his guitar playing. If you only heard Pete Townshend singing, if that was your only opportunity to encounter him, you would think he was an incredibly gentle and sweet guy.

And yet in just the way that Brian Wilson at a certain point apparently felt that singing the falsetto part in the Beach Boys was somehow undignified, Pete seems lately to feel that this high part of his range, his lonesome vulnerability, is too easy. You can see how primal this perception might be, given what we know about his biography. The falsetto and the high tenor are just not *masculine* voices. For example, Pete, in rationalizing a new song theoretically to be included on the upcoming album he's going to make with Roger Daltrey,* has repeatedly observed that an artist in his sixties should sing with the voice of a *man*. But I suspect the issue is not where, in what clef, a man should sing. Pavarotti, also a tenor, has never been accused of being a sissy of a singer. Maybe the issue is more properly *at what cost so vulnerable?* What's it like to feel so close to permeability, as open to the whims of the world as the Pete Townshend of *Who Came First?* Like a twig in the breeze, or like a cork in the ocean, as Wilson sang in one of his later Beach Boys compositions.

Is the lonesome, vulnerable tenor of Pete Townshend the voice of a guy evoking the traumatic episodes of his past? And how to square this with fits of rage that you encounter in any précis of Townshend and his work (like at Woodstock when he says, "Fuck off my fucking stage" to Abbie Hoffman, or Long Beach Arena, 1971, when he says to the audience, "I'll tell you fuckers something! All right, now listen! Just fucking listen, and *shut up*, right. Either sit down, or stand up, or lay down, or do something, but *shut up*; this is a fucking *rock-and-roll con-cert*, not a fucking tea party"), the outbursts of violence (as when he punched out Ronnie Lane, already ill with multiple

---

* *Endless Wire*, released in 2006, of which I'll say a few words at the close of this essay.

sclerosis, in the studio during *Rough Mix*, as when he hit Keith in the face with a guitar for being late to a gig). And what about the hideous, condescending liner notes to *Maximum R&B*, the Who box set, in which he's practically giddy about how much he dislikes the band and he seems contemptuous of anyone who shelled out for the box set? How to square this with a voice of such gentleness and vulnerability?

I have so far omitted the most defensible part of the output of the Who, the album known as *Who's Next*. Let me redress the omission briefly. That album cemented their status as rock gods, and later, dinosaurs, and spawned some quite good automobile advertisements. At one time, I loved *Who's Next* so much that I had the liner notes memorized. Everything. The engineering credits. The record label information. Memorized. I would spit out the entirety of the back of the album cover whenever it came up.

Some description of the origin of *Who's Next* is therefore an obligation. It's an album of songs, which, as I have said, is what the Who did best, and what Pete is best at, despite what he may feel these days. And yet the album began as a *concept*, after the rather grand impact of *Tommy*. In specific, the concept was called *Lifehouse*, and it had to do with the Who occupying some kind of film studio set and allowing themselves to interact with fans directly. The conceptual apparatus of *Lifehouse* has always been on the hazy side, notwithstanding the fact that it spawned a raft of excellent songs, most of which either ended up on *Who's Next* ("Baba O'Riley," "Won't Get Fooled Again") or on Pete's solo album *Who Came First* ("Let's

See Action" and "Pure and Easy"). These are *all* great songs, that's indisputable, but what are they about, really? One biography of Townshend describes *Lifehouse* as a "full-length film-script about life in a programmed totalitarian society on the verge of collapse, where people wear 'experimental suits' and are fed through test tubes."* This description is enough, yes, to engender mixed feelings about the fact that *Lifehouse* never came to fruition. At one point, there was a million dollars in seed money from Universal Pictures, but perhaps Universal was a little wary of the climax, wherein a "guru figure" demonstrates how rock music will enable the masses to achieve spiritual bliss.

And skepticism about the *Lifehouse* project is undiminished by Pete's insistence, recently, that *Lifehouse* predicted the Internet. This was a theme in Pete's recent online journal, this long-ago prediction, and he mentioned it from the stage of the Royal Albert Hall in 2003. Of course, it's largely irrelevant who, if anyone, "created" or "predicted" the Internet. In contrast, what is of interest is art. The *Lifehouse* concept involved the band playing live on their film set for two weeks solid, with the audience free to come and go throughout. Now, *that* is art of a particularly meaningful kind. It's the sort of art, the sort of concord between audience and artist, that made "The Who Cares" such an appropriate and oft-deployed slogan later on. Yet this preliminary stratagem was overburdened with *ideas*, about totalitarianism, about everyone playing one note together (see "Pure and Easy") until a glorious cacophony would ensue, which would culminate in "nirvana."

---

* *Behind Blue Eyes*, p. 93.

One wonders what the other members of the band thought of this. Roger Daltrey was wont to refer to Townshend's guru, Meher Baba, as "Ali Baba" on occasion. And Keith Moon was pretty clear about getting bored playing *Tommy* during the years when the band toured relentlessly in support of that album. If the rest of the band was skeptical initially, the first rehearsals didn't help. Finally, throwing open the doors and inviting in anyone who passed by apparently resulted in audiences composed mainly of the intoxicated and indifferent. In one memorable rehearsal, Townshend roughed up a guy who charged the stage.

A consequence of the resultant collapse of the *Lifehouse* project was Pete's "nervous breakdown." I have no idea what this phrase means. And I say this as someone who is not unacquainted with mental health professionals. I have no idea what "nervous breakdown" means. It is not a genuine clinical diagnosis. I don't know if it's Townshend himself who uses the term or if doctors of the time inclined toward this quaint and old-fashioned pettifoggery. "Nervous breakdown" does, and ought to, refer to a psychotic break on occasion. The features of a psychotic break are obvious. Visual and/or auditory hallucinations, inability to distinguish reality from hallucination, and so forth. And according to the *Mojo* article about *Quadrophenia*, this *is* what happened: "Pete suffered a massive anxiety attack of such intensity the people in the room morphed into 'frogs or some strange creatures.' Later, he was told he'd tried to jump out of the window, but was restrained. What really hurt him, Pete said later, was the fact that his friend and mentor [Kit Lambert] had ostensibly referred to him out of earshot as 'Townshend, instead of Pete.'"*

"Nervous breakdown" can also refer to nervous collapse, or exhaustion, which should be plausible and is a time-honored explanation for strange turns of events in the lives of rock-and-roll musicians. It's not hard to imagine that Pete was exhausted from the relentless touring and high-profile performances that came the band's way in the wake of *Tommy*, and the *Mojo* article seems to support this interpretation.

Still another interpretation of "nervous breakdown" might be the cycle of alcohol abuse and withdrawal. And given the period under scrutiny, late sixties/early seventies, it's not hard to presume that there was some of that going on, though Pete did not embark on harder drugs until much later. Whichever way you parse the term "nervous breakdown," however, the collapse of *Lifehouse* brought about the *Who's Next* sessions, and perhaps the loudest and most unbridled music the band ever made. People adore this album, I imagine, not just because the sound is great and the keyboards are used in really inventive ways, but partly because it emerges from the despair of losing control of *Lifehouse*, because it comes out of giving up on the late sixties, giving up on idealism, on unworkable or impracticable idealism. That's why "Won't Get Fooled Again" is at the end, and why the last line on the album is "Meet the new boss / Same as the old boss."

To put it another way: even though Pete, by the time of *Who's Next*, had come to the end of his youthful ability to bear up

---

* *Mojo.*

under the worst circumstances, and even though the fissures were beginning to show in the band, the Who did take this opportunity, this failure, and make great art from it. Unlike, e.g., *Smile*, the lost Beach Boys album whose tracks, when scattered around on later albums, felt orphaned and curiously diffident, *Lifehouse* seems better, at least to this listener, when sundered from its apparatus. Townshend's self-release, not long ago, of a six-volume edition of the pieces from the project, as well as a "greatest hits" single-disc volume called *Lifehouse Elements*, feels like rationalization ex post facto. It did not improve the reputation of the lost masterpiece. Ditto his attempt to write a novel that deals with similar material. The action of this self-published novella, *The Boy Who Heard Music*, seems to mix autobiographical musings with more quasi-futuristic stuff about computers and the Internet and music, to no great effect.

Yet this does offer me a brief moment, despite not caring whether Pete predicted the Internet, to praise the way the man uses technology. Part of what makes me still kind of adore Pete Townshend is the variety and simplicity and diffusion of his interests. On the web, for example, you could until recently find his blog, and his self-composed profile. He listed his age and his interests, and his industry ("arts"), his taste in fiction (anything by Paul Auster or Siri Hustvedt, as well as Michael Chabon), and video footage of him doing almost anything around the house. This same tenderness, the aforementioned vulnerability, is barely concealed beneath his occasional outbursts of egomania ("What is well known is that I am a rock star"). It's a complicated stew to be found there, but it's a human one.

Quadrophenia, the somewhat misbegotten album that succeeded *Who's Next*, ornate in its production and overblown as to its conceptual armature, just isn't going to come in for much attention here. I think the story of *Quadrophenia* is rather hard to follow, if in fact there is a story at all. Mostly it seems to be about mods and taking speed, or mods taking speed, or mods and rockers clashing while taking speed. The big production number at the end, "Love Reign O'er Me," is cloying for me, and the songs that Pete devotes to the other members of the band (with the exception of "Bell Boy," Keith's song) feel as though he wasn't up to dealing with tensions in the group directly. There are rather lovely and astonishing moments on *Quadrophenia*, but I still don't listen to it very much.

After *Quadrophenia* came *The Who by Numbers*, which I have mentioned, and that was in turn followed by *Who Are You*, which is mainly noteworthy for being the album the band made right before Keith Moon died. It had a good photograph on the cover, and for a brief period, I personally tried to *dress* like the Pete Townshend in this photograph. It didn't work. Meanwhile, just as I was getting acclimated to this rather lackluster album, Keith Moon passed away. At which point the Who, as a useful entity, as a band of four distinct personalities balanced the way certain chemical compounds are balanced, collapsed, never to be made in the same way again.

It's fair to say that there were a lot of other problems, besides the band, besides Keith: Pete's own drinking, his hearing loss, his refusal to tour, the creative corner they had painted themselves into, etc. It wasn't just that Keith died.

And yet for my part I started to get impatient with the Who. Everything about the next album, *Face Dances*, seemed ill-advised to me. The name was ill-advised. The new drummer, Kenney Jones, who seemed fine when he was with the Faces, became metronomic and dull when attempting to fill in for Keith. I kind of like the pop throwaway that became the hit from the record, "You Better You Bet." But the rest of it? Forget it.

In the case of *It's Hard*, their last studio album, I don't think I've ever heard it all the way through. I tried a couple of times, but except for "Eminence Front," there just didn't seem to be a reason. The material feels desperate to me, uncertain. Was it uncertain because of the people involved? Or uncertain because of history? How can you be ambitious enough to make their early masterpiece *The Who Sell Out* and then careless enough to make *It's Hard*? I bought a vinyl copy of *It's Hard* on eBay a couple of years ago, when I had a turntable again, and even then, in a nostalgic moment, I was impervious to its charms.

Pete's solo recording career was, at the time of *Face Dances*, beginning to take off. Everything changed for him thereafter, and rather quickly. Even Pete's *singing* changed dramatically on the solo albums. He became a better singer. There were vast improvements in the area of basic pop craft. And the solo albums were more tolerant of the balladry in the Pete Townshend output. He didn't need to play as much electric guitar. He wasn't so hell-bent on the rock posturing that had hemmed in the Who in the late seventies, the cock rock chapter of their collective biography. And some of the parts of his character that didn't seem to win over many converts in the band were given full flower when there was no antagonist for him.

Maybe it was because he had fewer antagonists, therefore, that in this period he made some rather infamous and ill-interpreted remarks in an interview. He declared that "inside he was a woman."* Moreover, he refused to say that he wasn't a transvestite, and refused to repudiate the rumors about his gay experimentation. No doubt the mooks of Madison Square Garden and other arenas across America—that is to say: Who fans—would have misunderstood these remarks, had they paid much attention, unless they had learned by now to con-sign his more outlandish quotables to the file marked "Pete Shooting Off Mouth."

Still, the process of individuation encourages things to the surface. The longer one is busy about the game of creativity, the more twists and turns assert themselves, and that's why on the first of the somewhat inconsistent solo albums, namely *Empty Glass*, you get a song like "And I Moved." Perhaps because of the remarks above, this tune, and one other song on *Empty Glass*, really set some rather gossipy tongues wagging.

Pete notes that "And I Moved" was first written for Bette Midler. Why Pete would be writing a song for Bette Midler, who got her start in the bathhouses and who was very gay-identified, is unclear. But this is what he says. Because it was composed for a woman, it needed to have a first-person narra-tor who was engaged in a sexual encounter with a man, and thus the feminine imagery: "And I moved / And his hands felt like ice exciting / As he laid me back just like an empty dress / And I moved / But a minute after he was weeping / His tears his only truth / And I moved / But I moved toward him."

---

* Quoted in, among other places, *Behind Blue Eyes*.

It never occurred to me that this song narrated a gay sexual encounter until very recently. I thought of the song as frankly spiritual. The song does appear on *Empty Glass*, after all, and the title song on that album quotes from Ecclesiastes, and the chorus ("My life's a mess / I wait for you to pass / I stand here at the bar / I hold an empty glass") uses thirst as a metaphor for spiritual longing. Moreover, this Pete Townshend was an alcoholic, even kind of *looked* like one on the album jacket, and so it's fair to say that the empty glass of the title might be thought of as some kind of allusion to addiction and alcoholism, and the ways in which, as I have often heard said, "alcoholism is a low-level search for God." So when I thought about "And I Moved," a song I loved and felt was a big improvement over the music he was making with the Who at the same time, I thought it was about being ravished by a spiritual master.

What about "Rough Boys," then? It was the hit from *Empty Glass*. There was even a rather primitive video of it. It seemed to have something to do, like "Who Are You" before it, with an old rock star type of a guy encountering the young turks of the music scene. It is dedicated to the Sex Pistols (as well as to Pete's daughters). But it does have the lines "Rough boys / Don't walk away / I very nearly missed you / Tough boys / Come over here / I wanna bite and kiss you." And the subsequent verses would not exactly reassure the portion of the audience looking to rock and roll to affirm traditional notions of heterosexuality.

Pete, of course, says the two songs are not about homosexual longing, and then elsewhere he kind of says maybe they are. He is not conclusive on the subject, as, in fact, he is inconclusive about many things. Is memory even a useful tool in talking about the songs? Because, as Pete has observed, after a point the listeners begin to seize control of the songs and assert their own interpretations, and once the songs belong to the listeners, he is no longer able to control the way in which they are understood. Thus, though Pete says that he was not rooting around on child pornography websites with any prurient purpose in mind, and though Roger Daltrey has himself said he doesn't believe it, and though we know it's a huge mistake to assume that just because someone is bisexual or omnisexual or whatever it is that Pete is that he's a pedophile, it doesn't mean that it's not possible to believe that Pete is, at the very least, a little sexually reckless. And willing to climb into a bear cage.

In the midst of his solo career, Pete also became, for a time, an editor at the venerable British publisher Faber & Faber. He became, that is, kind of bookish. What publishing house could have been *more* bookish than T. S. Eliot's onetime employer? Moreoever, in the midst of this bookishness, Townshend (in 1985) published a book himself, entitled *Horse's Neck*. It's a collection of short stories, some of them patently autobiographical, some of them more veiled. Quite a number have a lot to do with the problem of being very well-known and lionized in the bizarre milieu of rock and roll.

There is some lean, muscular, and completely effective prose writing on display in Townshend's collection. He sometimes reads mysteries, I have heard, and I find faint traces of Chandler in his unadorned but self-assured sentences. Furthermore, he doesn't shrink from disturbing or unsettling material in the book. Men are creeps in *Horse's Neck*, and they are creeps with a lot of desire.

One of the stories goes even further than this, however, and deals very explicitly with the sexual abuse of children. It's called "Tonight's the Night," after the rather dreadful song by Rod Stewart. "Tonight's the Night" is written in the third person, largely from the point of view of a person named Pete. Let me try to summarize the story briefly.

The Pete *character* in the story is staying in California with someone called "the Baron," apparently a Kit Lambert stand-in. The Baron and Pete, at the outset, are shooting the breeze with a "pretty, spicey girl." In fact, the Baron is holding forth to the others about his rather precocious sexuality, which, according to his recollection, was fully operational from age three.

Pete and the "spicey" girl hit it off, and much discussion between the two ensues. She expatiates upon her favorite song by Rod Stewart: "Here's where she gets it! He sings about her spreading her wings—you know what that means?" Not long after, Pete effects his seduction of the woman in question. Next morning, after he drops her at her hotel, he and the Baron revisit the previous night's delights, with Pete recounting at length the woman's story: "At eleven years old she had a promising bosom and early periods. Her father, a dentist, ran off with his assistant nurse. Her mother moved her own lover in, a crazy stud of twenty-five who worked as an occasional logger in the hills."

Soon enough, the young heroine, in this story within the story, is visited in her room by the "crazy stud." The consummation is not instantaneous, or Rod Stewart–style, owing to the fact that the stud, among other things, is "very big." Further uncomfortable details are included in the conversation between Pete and the Baron. After much precoital fumbling around over the course of weeks, the stud-logger kidnaps the spicey girl *for three years*, making her his sexual slave.

When the girl returns to her mother after three years in captivity, no one makes any kind of "fuss" about her kidnapping. In fact, it goes undiscussed: "The logger never touched her again and none of them ever mentioned it."

Five years later. The Pete character is in the middle of a bad spell with his drinking when the girl suddenly reappears. She speaks: "I met this guy in L.A. He had a kind of ashram. I joined it." However, her guru has abdicated his position and only keeps in touch with followers *telepathically.* In fact, the telepathic guru somehow keeps the girl imprisoned. Pete asks how he can imprison her if he's far away, in Houston, to which she replies, "He comes in the guise of a little boy from down the street." Just as Pete is about to intervene, she rings off.

Next day, the Baron brings news that the woman has been "accused of kidnapping some twelve-year-old boy. She's been doing bad things to the kid."

"Tonight's the Night" then appends an odd postscriptus, which I need to include in its entirety:

> Pete finally got himself straight about a year later. He quit the booze, quit the casinos, and the Baron went home to England. Pete decided to close the Nob Hill apartment and put it up for sale. Clearing it up he came across a magazine full of naked people. He was about to throw it into the trash when he recognized her face.

She was with a very big man. She was holding him in one hand, and her little Cindy doll in the other. The photograph had been taken in a dentist's chair.

There's so much that's disturbing about "Tonight's the Night" that it's hard to find a preliminary handhold. The use of the third person is disturbing, for example, because it means to remove the author Pete Townshend from the character Pete, at the same time as it confuses the issue.

Similarly, the relationship between Pete and the Baron is fuzzy. Pete is said to be a "singer" and the Baron his "manager," but their relationship is a lot closer than that, and their conversation verges on the sexually ambiguous throughout. This is further confused in the fact of the triangle among the Baron, Pete, and the girl. The girl is a piece of currency that is exchanged between Pete and the Baron in the course of the story. She doesn't even get to have a name.

The story-within-the-story of the life of the "strawberry blonde," as she is also known, is a grueling tale of sexual abuse of children. It's not some episodic story where a drunken parent appears in the bedroom; it's systematic, ongoing violation, for three years of this girl's life. Even in a more permissive social environment (the rock-and-roll underworld of the seventies and eighties), it's a shocking story. Certainly, it would be difficult to write such a scene, a scene that accords this violation its proper weight and seriousness. Townshend is not a sophisticated fiction writer, and it shows. We have *none* of the girl's misery in the story. Moreover, the girl's story is recounted to the Baron *after* Pete heard it from the girl, which suggests the possibility that she told him about the abuse and yet he nonetheless managed to make love with her without significant feelings of complicity.

The traditional therapeutic equation, that sexually abused children abuse others in turn, is given an affecting treatment in the person of the little boy (her "guru") with whom the "strawberry blonde" carries on at the end of "Tonight's the Night." It occurs to me, with respect to this therapeutic equation, to ask, however, if Pete (the author) is identifying with the "strawberry blonde" or with the Pete character. The "strawberry blonde" is sexually abused, as Pete sometimes says he was, and she abuses the boy in turn, as Pete was believed to have done, briefly, by the authorities. Is he that kind of abuser? Or is he the Pete *character*, who, in a period of alcoholism and rather dubious morality, sleeps with an obviously disturbed woman and even seems to fall in love with her *after* she tells him the story of her shattering abuse? Is he the codependent trying to rescue the broken child? Or the broken child himself? And is either of these people, savior and victim, free from the inclination to abuse in turn?

All of this becomes even more unsettling in light of the postscriptus at the end of the story. Obviously, it seems to suggest that the "spicey girl" was sexually abused by her father (a dentist) as well as by her mother's lover, and the presence of the doll in the shot, in a magazine "full of naked people," further suggests some kind of ongoing sexual abuse of children to which she was party, perhaps over the course of many years.

This systematic abuse is intrinsic, is central to the story, and it implies one last question to be asked of "Tonight's the Night," and that is the question of the ownership of the magazine in which this nude photograph of the "strawberry blonde" appears. Pete the character is closing up the apartment in Nob Hill, in order to sell it. Is it then not his apartment? Is not his responsibility for its sale an indicator that he is responsible for its contents too? And does he not then own the magazine in question? Is the magazine not manifestly devoted to child pornography or, at least, to simulations of child pornography? If Pete has finally got himself straight, are we meant to understand that this child pornography, or simulated child pornography, is a legacy of his active alcoholism? If it is *not* Pete's magazine, then to whom does this magazine belong? And if the magazine doesn't belong to Pete the character, well, is it not possible that it belongs to Pete the author? Is it not possible that the author Pete is attempting to get the character Pete to throw the magazine away *for him?*

One song that I revere completely, despite its being from the inconsistent solo period of Pete Townshend's career, appeared on the album after *Empty Glass* entitled *All the Best Cowboys Have Chinese Eyes.* There are a number of moving songs to be found on that album, in fact, including "Slit Skirts" and "Stardom in Acton." But the song I mean to pursue here is "The Sea Refuses No River," which title, according to my researches, derives from an early-seventeenth-century English proverb.

I'd been kind of indifferent to *All the Best Cowboys* when it first came out, for the reasons I've already enumerated. Despite its sterling moments, the record *is* uneven. But when I got out of the psychiatric hospital in 1987, when I was suddenly in bad circumstances myself, I wanted to hear *All the Best Cowboys* again. Because, I remembered, Pete had been trying to put an end to his own period of excess. In my recollection, the songs had that self-critical quality that I needed, that I sought out in other albums during my rehabilitation, like *Astral Weeks* by Van Morrison. I liked Warren Zevon then too. Warren Zevon had done his time in the detox mansion.

Above all, one particular song on *All the Best Cowboys* went into heavy rotation, and that song was "The Sea Refuses No River."

It starts with electric guitar, harmonica, and some glockenspiel (he nicked the idea, I think, from Bruce Springsteen), and it starts right in with the litany of Pete's crimes: "I remember being richer than a king / The minutes of the day were golden / I recall that when the joint passed round / My body felt a little colder." Soon, the melody rises into the refrain, according to the "gospel in the choruses" strategy that Springsteen sometimes employs: "The sea refuses no river / And right now this river's banks are blown / The sea refuses no river / Whether stinking and rank / Or red from the tank," etc.

You can imagine, against a backdrop of domestic difficulty, with Pete's wife having already tossed him out and taken him back, that the earnest wish of the chorus was not simulated. Furthermore, there's a spot in the song when Pete truly *keens*, "The sea refuses no river / Remember that when the beggar buys a round." It still makes me shudder with awe, or recognition, no matter how many times I hear it, and here's why: because nobody, no addict, is *deserving* of another chance, another length of rope. We're more undeserving than almost anyone. And yet every now and then an addict or criminal does get redeemed, despite his or her lack of merit. This "The Sea

Refuses No River" captures as few songs have: "We're polluted now but in our hearts still clean," or, at its close: "The sea refuses no river / And the river is where I am."

It ends with a recognition of failure and desperation, and it ends big, and when it ends, with some incredibly generous acceptance of the *damned*, it's hard for me to believe that Pete Townshend, who knows himself here as he has rarely known himself (since, perhaps, *The Who by Numbers*), is the sort of guy who would, for example, launch a single-handed vigilante operation to entrap users of child pornography. He just doesn't seem like a crusader for justice. On the basis of the song, he might have compassion for perp and victim alike. And yet: he knows better how to feel isolated, alienated, alone, broken, spiritually impoverished, and compulsive than he knows how to be upright and morally correct.

When I was finished listening to *All the Best Cowboys*, I was finished with Pete Townshend for a good long spell. Ten years maybe. I heard a couple of songs from *White City*, but no one could make me listen to *The Iron Man*, and when I saw a video of a staged version of *Psychoderelict*, his last solo album of new material, I felt an inability to relate happily to the work of the guy I'd looked up to so much in my teens. And I can scarcely bring myself to touch on the Broadway theatrical known as *Tommy*. I saw it once, and I went to it, I think, out of respect for the period when *Tommy* mattered, not out of faith that this was going to be a memorable experience.

Long about 1999, the three surviving members of the Who got together to do something that Pete had done himself a couple of years prior. They played one of the Neil Young Bridge

School Benefit Concerts. The Bridge concerts take place in the San Francisco Bay Area, and they're benefit events for a school that serves the needs of children with autism and related disabilities. The Bridge concerts are usually acoustic and they are often freewheeling and star-studded, for lack of a better term. For some reason, I was eager to hear the three surviving members of the band play live together, which they had done irregularly in recent years, and eager to hear them play some old material. I actually watched the gig on the Internet, which was harder back then. I was on dial-up, so it was kind of stop-and-go. Still, there was something so unpretentious and graceful about the performance that suddenly all the slick nonsense that had disappointed me about the Who in the eighties was forgotten.

Chief among the successes of that particular gig was a new version of an old familiar Who tune, "The Kids Are Alright." The Who have done a lot of really great charitable work for teenagers (they donated a million pounds to a London clinic for teenagers with cancer), and this may have prompted them to turn up at the Bridge concert in the first place. When they sang "The Kids Are Alright," in addition to incorporating Roger on the guitar (almost unimaginable), they also added a big improvised section toward the close where Roger and Pete traded recollections of their childhoods. At this gig, the ad-libbed portion felt genuinely spontaneous, and patently directed at the Bridge School students themselves. The strange, ominous repetition that Pete favors in the extended section of the song, "I know the kids are alright, my kids are alright, your kids are alright," seemed awkwardly sincere in its early iterations.

In the years since, and especially in the aftermath of the child pornography charges, the *new* version of "The Kids Are Alright" has become predictive of Pete Townshend's problems, in a way that *does* make the charges against him look suspect. Only, that is, if you had some good reason to feel that it was possible for children to be unsafe, and that this was tragic, this abuse of children, would you go on at such length extolling the virtues of *safe children*. Either he has a reason to feel strongly about it or he's a bald sentimentalist. I'm just not willing to go that far yet. Townshend is only sentimental when he feels deeply. And he feels most deeply about the things he knows from personal experience.

The ultimate irony in the Townshend pedophilia case became apparent in August of this past year, when a former expert witness in the Operate Ore prosecutions wrote a lengthy demurral in the *Sunday Times* (of London) alleging significant prosecutorial mistakes in the course of the pedophilia investigations.* The allegations are of mistakes so systemic and so thoughtless that they certainly do undermine the supposed accomplishments of the operation:

> In information given to Interpol and in sworn statements submitted to British courts in 2002, Dallas detective Steven Nelson and US postal inspector Michael Mead claimed that everyone who went to Landslide [the website where the illegal material was said to be available] always saw a front page screen button offering

---

* A reprint of the article can be found on the Computer Crime Research Center site, http://www.crime-research.org/analytics/1453/.

"Click Here (for) Child Porn."...But what passed almost
unnoticed eight months later was that after British police
and computer investigators had finally examined American files, they found that the "child porn" button was not
on the front page of Landslide at all, but was an advertisement for another site appearing elsewhere....The
real front page of Landslide was an innocuous image of
a mountain, carrying no link to child porn.

In fact, according to at least one expert cited in this article, it
was actually rather difficult to get from the relevant website to
a child porn archive: "There was 'no way' a visitor to Landslide
could link from there to child porn sites, according to Sam
Type, a British forensic computer consultant." The bulk of
Landslide-related sites were for ordinary adult-type sexual
material, and in some cases the sites were not sex-related at all.
The website shut in 1999, as well, so by the time the arrests
took place for, in some cases, inadvertent or fraudulent use
of the supposed child porn sites, the offenses were so outdated
that it's possible that alleged pedophiles could not remember
the events they were being charged with.

Other celebrities were caught up in this investigation, like
Robert Del Naja of Massive Attack, who, like Townshend, had
his charges dropped after a month. The commander of British
forces in Gibraltar, David White, was accused in the course of
it, and he committed suicide, like thirty-three others, rather
than face the trial proceedings. Names were routinely leaked
to the press (as in Del Naja's case), so that the cases could
play out in the court of public opinion before the trials, thus

making it extremely difficult for the innocent, of whom there were clearly a number, to get a fair hearing.

If, under these circumstances, Pete Townshend really did manage to access child pornography, as he was compelled to *admit* doing, he must have worked diligently to do so. His statement on the subject admits to visiting the site, that is, but it's more than possible that the public statement was arranged with the investigators in order to assure that charges would be dropped. If, under these circumstances, Townshend did enter the site *for research*, as he further claims, one can only wonder at the poor decision-making involved in his efforts. It was a really bad idea. And why use your credit card to do it? Pete?

In the end, it is impossible to *know* whether Townshend is a pedophile or not. It's impossible to know, unless you are Pete Townshend himself. If the dark tones of child abuse are shadowed forth in his work, which is undeniable, it is impossible from these shadows to tease apart the experience of having suffered childhood sexual abuse from the guilt and remorse about having committed some of it. In art, the two are close. As to what we ought to think of his work in light of the investigation, the answer to that question is obvious: his work is what it is. It is either bad or good or outrageously great, entirely apart from his sexual peccadilloes or the lack thereof. If we hounded every rock-and-roll musician who had a tendency to morally dubious excesses, we would have no rock-and-roll musicians. I might recognize being disappointed in the person of Pete Townshend should it ever come out that he did what he was accused of doing, but I make a distinction between this and the work. His personal life is secondary when compared to "My Generation" or "A Quick One," "Blue, Red and Grey" or "I'm One." I care only about his voice, his guitar, and his songwriting talents. What if it turns out that, yes, he was falsely accused? In that instance, the work more than survives; it glitters with the sheen of triumph over adversity.

If we can never know about that moment when Pete was logged on to the offending web portal, we can know quite a bit about him besides. For example, we know, I think, that Pete Townshend is a mass of contradictory material. Pete Townshend is a rather electrifying guitar player who likes to write Broadway show tunes; Pete Townshend has a gentle high-tenor voice that he often uses to sing very masculine, even occasionally aggressive songs; Pete Townshend is a person of great garrulousness who emulated an Indian guru who never spoke; Pete Townshend is an ardent heterosexual who has had any number of homosexual experiences; Pete Townshend is a committed family man who is involved with a woman twenty-five years younger than he is; Pete Townshend is a person of keen humility and significant arrogance; Pete Townshend is a person who has written pop songs of great tenderness and who has purposefully hit fans and friends and band members with his guitar; Pete Townshend is almost always in the public eye and has been for over forty years, and yet he writes best about loneliness; Pete Townshend is both physically alluring and homely; Pete Townshend is both spiritually thirsty and breathtakingly cynical; Pete Townshend is deeply romantic and has written very few genuine love songs; Pete Townshend is deeply serious, but the most effective period of his work was his most humorous period; Pete Townshend is incredibly complicated, hard to figure out, evasive, and yet he's also completely open and one of the most accessible popular musicians in the world. Pete Townshend was raised in a jazz-playing family but helped invent British-invasion rock and roll. Pete Townshend has claimed to be a socialist, but he cooperated with Margaret Thatcher's antidrug crusade. Pete Townshend wrote his best songs about being young and is now, at this writing, sixty-three years old. Pete Townshend may have done some horrible things and he may not have. Pete Townshend may have been charged with certain horrible crimes he did not commit. Pete Townshend may have committed other crimes we know nothing about. He loved his wife and wrote memorably about her, and they divorced anyway. He wrote great songs and flat, uninspired songs. He tried a lot of new things, and many of them did not work at all. A mass of contradictions! An exasperating and erratic person! Changeable! Mercurial! Impossible! Despite this, or perhaps because of it, Pete Townshend does *not* seem different from most people you might meet, in terms of his irreducible complexity and his finicky moods. He's obvious, deep, human, impenetrable, sometimes dull. Despite everything that's happened, he's a representative man.

Which is why we loved his songs once and will again. Because he's just like us.*

---

* If I were going to rewrite this essay, now, in 2010, there would be a lot to add to it. A lot of threads to chase down. None of these threads, especially those that have directly to do with the dropped charges against Pete Townshend, would make the facts any more indisputable or any more transparent. I might, however, and without going on at any length, make a couple of observations. First: the judgment of history would seem to be that Townshend is forgiven (we are all forgiven!), whether he needs it or not, in that a

reformed band called the Who has continued to tour in recent years, even playing in the Super Bowl in 2010, where questions about the Townshend case were raised fleetingly during the promotional run-up to the game and quickly forgotten. That history has now largely overlooked this unsavory moment in Townshend's life seems to me humane and right, especially since it releases Pete Townshend to do what he does best: make music. Second: there is, since I wrote this essay, a *new album* by the Who! I don't feel, in the end, that *Endless Wire* has much within it that breaks ground on the issues addressed in these pages, although it does contain one song about priestly molestation, "The Man in the Purple Dress." More important, though, and despite the fact that the album is wildly uneven, it has a few great songs. A few shining moments. The very best of these are acoustic, oddly enough, and played largely by Townshend himself, which has inspired a few comparisons to *Who Came First*, excepting that there are elegiac moments on *Endless Wire* that manifestly include Daltrey *and* Townshend. The best of these is the slightly miraculous "Tea & Theatre," which is frankly preoccupied with looking back on some of Daltrey and Townshend's shared past. Daltrey's reading is so moving, and his voice so undiminished, that it's almost hard to fathom. "Tea & Theatre" is a beautiful song, a mature song, and one that actually adds to the band's legacy. On the basis of this song, and a few others—"We Got a Hit," the title song, "The Man in the Purple Dress"—it's fair to say that *Endless Wire* is not *just* a reunion album. It's genuinely moving, and for those of us who really cared about this band and this composer, it's a reason to be happy. Since then, from very lengthy touring, Pete's tinnitus is back, and he has said publicly that unless he can find a way to treat the symptoms thereof, the live shows are over for him. It would be sad if this was the very end of the story, since there has been so much reconciliation here recently. But with principals as unpredictable as Townshend and Daltrey, you just never know.

Two Weeks at Music Camp

Music Omi, an international musicians' residency program, was founded by Judy Willows in 1989 as part of the Omi International Arts Center in the Hudson Valley of New York. Initially, the program was intended as a vehicle for jazz musicians "as widely defined as possible." Soon, however, under the gentle hand of current director Jeffrey Lependorf, the applicant pool began to expand to include a wider range of musical styles and interests, while shifting its focus from a conventional retreat to a "collaborative music-making experience." Music Omi runs about two weeks, and at its conclusion the residents, who number between twelve and sixteen, give two concerts, one on site and one in New York City. Jeffrey invited me to participate after he heard my band, the Wingdale Community Singers, play at a benefit in 2006. The idea was that I might document the Music Omi experience while participating as a player. My notes follow.

August 2, 2007

It's about two in the afternoon on the day that I'm due at Music Omi, but instead of pulling into the driveway, I'm thirty miles away at the Blandford Plaza rest area. Killing time. It's 94 degrees Fahrenheit according to the car thermometer, and I'm watching the travelers of the interstate come and go in search of doughnuts. I'm doing this for the simple reason that I'm anxious about music camp. I'm more than anxious. It's like the first day of school. I'm going to be forty-six soon, and I have a mortgage to pay and a novel to write, but instead of attending to these responsibilities, I'm going to music camp. Back when I was a kid, I went to the sort of camp where you played soccer and tennis. I sang a little bit on the side. Probably I always wanted to go to music camp, but I just wasn't musical enough.

I'm still not. My assumption is that at Music Omi I will be by far the worst musician. I have put no shortage of effort into being a musician — it's my fervent hobby. But this has been an inconsistent effort, amounting to three years of piano lessons, a couple of years of voice (in my teens), and a couple of years of violin lessons after I turned forty. Despite the modesty of my musical education, I have played furiously, devotedly, especially the guitar (at which I've had no lessons at all).* Guitar has been my constant companion for a good eighteen or twenty years. In the past four or five, the locus of this guitar playing has been my band.

---

* Actually, I have now had a few.

The other musicians coming to Music Omi, however, have impressive résumés. They compose for orchestras, or they play jazz in combos (just the word *jazz* makes me uncomfortable, as does *combo*), or they are expert on Central Asian instruments that I don't know anything about. What I can bring to this group, besides being a guy who observes—like George Plimpton sitting in with the orchestra and plinking a triangle—I have no idea. That's why I'm in the Blandford Plaza rest area. A group of girls wearing athletic medals ambles past. They are fresh-faced, pretty, somewhat feral looking. They would mow down any and all competition. Is this what the musicians will be like?

August 3

My room is a duplex! Even though I'm not doing anything with the loft-bed part of it besides stowing my guitar cases, there is something gratifying about being able to *say* I inhabit a duplex. Otherwise, save for the absence of air-conditioning, my room at Omi is pretty great. Nice desk, bed, WiFi, phone. There's even cell coverage, despite the fact that I am surrounded by the rolling farmlands of the Hudson Valley. The Omi complex also features a pool, which, upon arriving, came in handy.

I spent the afternoon unloading and waiting around for the others, many of them coming by train from New York City. I met a couple of drummers, a bass player, a keyboardist-composer (there are a couple of these in residence), as well as a woman from South Africa, Cobi, who maintains that her instrument is "the world." This seemed to me a refreshingly evasive answer to the getting-to-know-you questions. I waved at Jeffrey Lependorf, as he hustled past, and chatted with Adam Simmons, our resident player-manager (official title: "guest mentor"), both of whom are virtuosi on the shakuhachi, the very difficult Japanese bamboo flute. The aforementioned German double bass player is called Sebastian, and he lives beneath me in the dorm. Upon settling in, he began tuning up and bowing in a way that was, even overheard, luminously beautiful. Soon there were drums coming from somewhere too.

Just before dinner, my friend and Wingdales bandmate Nina Katchadourian turned up. She's here with her Balinese gamelans, as well as various other instruments. The two of us made our way down to one of the silos on the Art Omi property. Grain silos are resonant, as you can imagine, and so they are exciting places to sing. They're also full of pigeon droppings, pigeons, bats, and assorted other wildlife, so the music is punctuated occasionally by a mad flapping of wings. You have to get your entrances and exits exactly right or the reverb muddles the whole experience, but it's still incredibly fun. (For some reason, right from the beginning, we sang a lot of rounds in the silos.) Meanwhile, it's good to have a close friend here. Will it inhibit my ability to get to know other people? I always *avoid* getting to know people — the legacy of having been a shy kid. I hope I will do better.

There were two tables at the first dinner. At the other table, Chris Chalfant, one of the pianist-composers, discoursed on La Monte Young, Pandit Pran Nath, and the tuning standard known as just intonation. These are subjects about which I have passionate feelings. At my table, Jeffrey Lependorf recounted the specifics of his former career as a professional *mingler* in Tokyo. In Tokyo, perhaps this profession is not so far-fetched. Among us was a Japanese composer, Sumiko, who sat patiently through the story without defending her homeland. Was she just being generous?

In the dwindling light after dessert, Nina and I went to look at the sculpture park. Omi is well-known for its sculpture park, the Fields, which amounts to a generous several hundred acres. Some of the pieces are owned, and the rest are on consignment. They stay here for a while, then move on to some other collection. A number of the big minimalist pieces on display are stunningly good. Jeffrey and others, however, have expressed grave reservations about the giant *heads* that abut the county road, and Nina and I wanted to form opinions. It was coming on night, though. I was banging on all the sculptures, which I was later told not to do. I was trying to see how they *sounded*.

August 4

What I did yesterday—instead of getting to know people—was go to a memorial service. My stepmother's mother died some weeks ago. A woman of dry wit and solidity, a woman who'd been frank about the fact that she'd lived longer than she needed to. There was lots of sorrow at the funeral, naturally. But not much of it was of the openly weeping sort. My stepmother's family (which is my family, since my father and my stepmother have been together more than thirty years) felt subdued. Or maybe it's I who feel subdued, far from the lives of my stepcousins, who are enthusiastic and good-natured and busy. I felt as I always feel at funerals: that what life does is grind you down, stealing grace and enthusiasm bit by bit, until what is left of you is somewhat desperate. No affable Presbyterian minister could convince me otherwise.

On the way down, I listened to a brace of folk music CDs. Traditional Irish stuff. Woody Guthrie. Johnny Cash's recording of hymns from his mother's hymnbook. The Byrds' *Sweetheart of the Rodeo*. I ended up playing the Byrds' cover of the Louvin Brothers song "The Christian Life" about fifteen times. Because I am a negligent and skeptical Christian? Well, it's an incredibly *uncool* song, notwithstanding having been sung by Gram Parsons on the record in question, but it's a beautiful song anyhow, with great potential for harmonies, and I am bent on teaching it to some people at Music Omi, despite its limpid folkiness.

When I got back, it was time for people to begin presenting their work. A name was picked from a hat, and that musician played two or three compositions, after which there was discussion. A timer went off at the twenty-minute mark to indicate that this presentation was now complete. The featured musician then picked the next name out of the hat. And so forth. We did five of these presentations last night. My friend Nina went first, followed by Jeffrey Lependorf, David Freeman, Nuala Kennedy, and Nadje Noordhuis. What was fascinating was the range of styles and interests. Nina comes out of visual and sound art. She played pieces from some of her sound installations, and one song (she's a gifted songwriter).

David, who is a jazz drummer and student of the tabla and all-around nice guy, played some lovely improvised "orchestral" pieces for strings, sitar, piano, and percussion. Nuala is a virtuoso of tin whistle and flute, and operates mainly in a traditionally Irish idiom. And Nadje is, on the basis of what she played last night, a jazz trumpeter (and flugelhorn player) who is possessed of spectacular tone. Her compositions varied from some ECM-style pieces to something that sounded more like New Orleans.

August 5

I guess I have deep insecurity around jazz players. Jazz really *is* the new classical, in that its practitioners (of whom there are four or five here) are technically superlative and not unaware of this. It's intimidating. I find myself comfortable enough and consonant with the people who are working out of the traditions of minimalism and experimental new music, but I guess because I can't play jazz, am simply not good enough, jazz players are a tough crowd for me. Jeffrey, when charging us with our mission last night, said something about how important it was for everyone to work *outside* of the styles to which they are accustomed. But the jazz players seem happiest with one another.

This jazz anxiety persisted as we sat through some more presentations. A number of them were particularly impressive, like Sebastian Gramss's meta-jazz compositions that, e.g., mimicked the sound of a jazz CD skipping. Christian Pincock showed a video of something called Soundpainting, a gestural conducting style that involves visual cuing of improvisation. It was as much dance and theater as music, and as such it was very entertaining. I was also really taken with Jacek Kochan's electronic music–jazz hybrid, at the forefront of which was his incredibly beautiful and skittery drumming. He's like Keith Moon if Moon had done some time in the loft music movement. In fact, there was little that I *didn't* like from the presentations. Everybody had some quirky, creative aspect to what he or she was doing.

I had a stubborn sense, though, that I was illegitimate. This illegitimacy persisted into the moment when I had to do my own presentation, which involved excerpts from spoken-word things I have made over the years, and then one new recording by my band. I had assumed that the serious players would look down on the homely folk musician origins of what I do as a songwriter. But they were reasonably supportive. In fact, I was a little surprised at how supportive they were.

Meanwhile, there are deer on the grounds. A mother and two fawns, among others. Last night, the mother seemed to be limping.

August 7

Yesterday: we served as an orchestra for Christian Pincock, who practices the forementioned conducting style, Soundpainting, invented by one Walter Thompson. Soundpainting amounts to a series of gestures designed to allow musicians to understand musical directions in the absence of score with a minimum of fuss. We served in this capacity for more than three hours yesterday, going through some of the elemental gestures—about forty of the eight hundred possible signs. What the other seven hundred and sixty do I can't imagine. As to instrumentation: percussion, some winds, and a string section consisting of myself (on guitar) and Sebastian on stand-up bass. Then there were a whole lot of vocalists, including Philippe Guidat, the awesome flamenco guitarist who for some reason didn't want to play his instrument. It was a genuine honor to work next to Sebastian. He's such a beautiful player—so versatile, with such remarkable melodic sense. He makes everyone else sound good. I was also really interested in Christian's choices in directing the players. The bench is deep, as they say. Adam, Nadje, Philippe, Jeffrey, Sumiko, Nuala, they're all great improvisers. Christian can use one player for a wild solo—Adam on sax, e.g.—and move on to another soloist who is just as inventive.

We were all really tired out by Soundpainting, though. It requires an enormous reserve of attention. There was some resistance to the discipline, some grumbling, and I understand the feeling. People want to *play*. They don't want instructions. It's worth pointing out, though, that Soundpainting was optional. No one was required to sit in. I expect attendance will be less universal going forward. And I may have to move from the guitar seat and work as a vocalist. I've been resisting that, notwithstanding the presence of a flamenco genius, because I'm trying to stretch, as per our instructions.

After dinner, we all went for a walk on the roads around the property, in the darkest dark. There was an immensity of stars. And grandly singing bullfrogs.

August 8

Yoga class at eleven. There are studies on the efficacy of yoga and meditation for composers. I can also recommend yoga for shutting down the music-on-the-brain phenomenon that afflicts here. Songs and fragments of music are caroming in my brain all the time now, to the point that this inhibits my sleep. I have also experienced something like *piano satiation*, an illness characterized by a total aversion to hearing a piano in the distance after playing music for six or eight hours a day. Sometimes, you know, no sound is its own kind of music. Others are reporting similar phenomena. Yoga seems to help.

After lunch, Jacek, the drummer; Nina; Sumiko, the pianist; Sebastian, the bass player; and I all went into the nearby town of Chatham to pick up Sebastian's repaired bass. I needed guitar supplies as well. (Soundpainting is destroying all my picks.) Chatham is the next town over, and there's not much there there. A few bars and a couple of antique stores of the variety that seem endemic to the Hudson Valley. The music store owners were friendly and let us play expensive guitars and mandolins. Sebastian, it seems, is playing a very substandard rented bass, and despite the fact that it sounds great through the floorboards, he has already been twice to have it repaired. That he can make anything good come out of it is a testament to his skills.

In general, smaller ensembles have broken out in the larger pool of Omi musicians. I am not in any of the more virtuosic groups. This is perhaps a feeling that many of the others are dealing with as well. And whatever else I might be thinking, Nina and I have been working on songs every day and have amassed a generous helping of songs very quickly. We worked out an easy one that is simply a list of *dental diseases*. It is not full of pathos, but it amuses. And last night, after dinner, the two of us finally managed to lure the Irish music maven Nuala Kennedy into playing with us for a bit. We worked out "Death Is Only a Dream," a Carter Family song that the Wingdales cover, and "The Christian Life," which did, as I hoped, successfully make the journey back with me from the funeral in Connecticut. And then Nuala taught us "The Parting Glass," a devastating lost-love ballad that the Clancy Brothers (among many others) once recorded, and which has the totally inconsolable quality that I associate with Irish music. We got a nice three-part arrangement down. Then Philippe sat in and contributed some guitar parts.

Earlier, we also had an ear-training workshop offered by a German jazz vibraphonist, Karl Berger. Karl and his partner, Ingrid Sertso, had us clapping in sevens and singing African-inflected melodies over the top, that we might better explore some of the elements common to *all* styles of music. That was the concept. They were earthy, parental figures, unworried about contemporary trends or musical idioms, and this was winning. Karl and Ingrid used to run a music conference, Creative Music Studio, in nearby Woodstock, which involved residencies by jazz composers like Anthony Braxton, Don Cherry, and Ornette Coleman. Their musical exercises evolved from that experience. Among Karl's choice bits of wisdom: "If you find yourself, while improvising, believing you know what you're going to do next, *don't play that*." I'm a captive audience for anyone who insists that the sixties were especially creative, so I enjoyed Karl's easygoing countercultural spiel. And playing in sevens is good for any musician. Even the drummers in the room fucked up once or twice.

August 9

It's coming on a week since we got here, and maybe the bloom is being sundered from the rose. We're nearly halfway to our public concerts and we're therefore trying to organize ourselves into legitimate performing entities. With limited success, in some cases. Maybe we've just grown tired of one another. I had a day of just total poverty of imagination about music. I helped Nina work on a good new song, and I sang a bit more Irish folk music with Nuala Kennedy in the evening, but other than that I sulked.

In the morning we worked in another conducting style, as articulated by Adam Simmons. This technique is called Conduction, and it's quite a bit less performative than Soundpainting. I think the composer Butch Morris is the avatar of the style. Unlike Soundpainting, Conduction makes use of an actual baton. Players are told simply to *play*, and others are told to attempt to follow them, and that's pretty much it. This performance was far looser, which felt nice. And there's an interesting gesture in Conduction: the conductor makes a sort of squiggly sine wave with the baton. You're meant just to try to follow, instrumentally, the twists and turns, the particularities of the gesture. This seemed emblematic of the whole. Some colleagues dropped out of this particular exercise—tired of direction, I suppose, or because they had other pieces to work on. Those who remained were really into attempting to make something of the group sound. Adam directed me to attempt a guitar solo over some beautiful bass playing by Sebastian Gramss. This felt challenging, to say the least. And yet perhaps I did not totally humiliate myself. Later, there was a satisfying portion of things wherein Sebastian came up with a sort of death metal bass line and various instrumental voices were cued to attempt to follow. There's a memory function in Conduction (as with Soundpainting), so Adam kept leading us out of death metal, giving us a few bars of something else, and then starting anew with Metallica. What could be better?

August 10

I woke with a genuine musical idea. Or this is how it seemed to me. The backstory is: Sebastian, in his role as composer, had asked if I had an E-bow with me here. An E-bow, for the non-specialist, is a sort of electronic magnet that you can use on your guitar to enable it to play long tones, such as a violin or a cello might. Most acoustic players are not terribly cozy with the E-bow. I don't have one with me and rarely do. However, I *am* in possession, here at Omi, of a genuine violin, the one that I have been attempting to learn for five years. The idea that I woke up with was that it would be fun to try to bow my acoustic guitar. Jimmy Page–style. Thus, before breakfast, I got the guitar out of the case, likewise the bow, and I started trying to make the two work together. My violin lessons have given me enough bow dexterity to come up with something. I was excited to tell Sebastian about the discovery.

This I did at lunch. Sebastian was reasonably enthusiastic about the possibility of bowed acoustic guitar at his rehearsal. And that night I also had a promising conversation with Adam Simmons about what to do for the upcoming Music Omi concert. As of this day, it seemed, we had all stopped jamming and had begun worrying about playing live before audiences, which we are to do very soon. I'd been thinking I wanted to use the entire ensemble for some kind of spoken-word extravaganza. I even imagined music cued to certain words, so that people would have to *freak out*, or engage in *pointillism*, as Christian Pincock says (when engaged in Soundpainting). Adam and Jacek Kochan had some good ideas about how this might be carried out, and Christian was there, too, trying to encourage live electronic sampling of vocals. I was inspired by the conversation, even though there were more ideas contained in it than I could likely fit into my allotted six minutes of concert time. At the end of the conversation, Jacek invited me to try to do a duet piece with him: voice, drums/electronics.

Then: some more singing with Nuala Kennedy and a ringer, a former Music Omi resident who'd come back for a visit. With this ensemble, we got to some fine harmonies. After which I went down to Christian's music studio, where he and the other digital-music aficionado, Cobi van Tonder, have made a sort of electronic-music lair. In the big barn at the edge of the Omi property. Bats and mildew! Cables everywhere! Alas, Christian's computer had crashed.

August 11

It poured. A heaviness to everyone's energy levels. Still, we had a really great morning rehearsal with Sebastian for his concert piece. With eyes closed, we were directed to play so slowly and in such a spare way as to be able to hear every other player. Since we number fourteen when we're all here, this is a lot to listen to, but eventually I felt like we were getting there. Even sounds that were being played very subtly, like my acoustic guitar and Cobi's gentle washes of electronics, eventually became audible. Of special interest to me, though, was Sebastian's comment that there's a moment in a construction like this when the ear suddenly wants *more*. That's the point that you have to start playing *with* the other musicians. After we pursued this meditative approach, we attempted a further exercise, in a circle, in which each musician was meant to play an unpitched note as quickly as feasible after the person to his or her left. It was great how this fell into a time signature (in fourteens). There were spots that were faster and spots that were slower, almost predictably so. And surges in dynamics. You really had to listen.

After Sebastian's rehearsal (and some bowed acoustic guitar playing), I went to write some words for the collaboration with Jacek. He is a very gracious man from Kraków, who has flawless English and who has spent time in the jazz and funk demimondes of nearly every western city where there is such a thing. He's a very placid, *cool* guy, but is also supportive and funny. It's thrilling to see him get excited, which he does occasionally, like when we sang Beatles songs around the piano last night. What he and I did today was sit in his little pigeon coop down by the barn and work on this instantaneous lyric of mine, a bunch of sentences completely organized around how they *sound*. The grim, rainy day was perfectly calibrated for Jacek's accompaniment, as it was evolving, which featured a lot of dark, enveloping electronic noise.

The rain was also good for a trip to the Book Barn of Hillsdale, which is just what you'd expect: a two-story upstate barn filled to the rafters with used books, some of them quite good. On the way, I'm pretty sure I went past the farm where my father used to go hunting when I was a kid. It was in the midst of one of those hunting trips that, on Route 22, I first gazed upon the sinister exterior of the Harlem Valley Psychiatric Center, a.k.a. Wingdale. Thus, the name of my band.

August 12

After yoga, we ambled down to the barn to be conducted by Chris Chalfant, who is from Akron, Ohio, but who wafts with a counterculture-inspired perfume. She might have stepped freshly out of the ashram. I think she was trying to counterpose her meditation-inspired approach to group playing with the more demanding structure of Christian's Soundpainting. So we played long, open notes for some twenty minutes before she introduced a melodic element. It was so meditative, in fact, that a couple of the jazz guys fell asleep. Chris remarked that this was now *part of the piece*. After we droned on at length, she at last introduced a couple of chords—among which was B-flat, not the most natural chord for a folk player. We did this two-chord vamp for easily half an hour, and I'm not sure everyone saw the virtue in it. I'm not sure I saw the virtue in it. And yet it was good to get a different perspective and, for me, to play guitar in the band while keeping my mouth *shut.*

Later, Nina and I worked on songs out by the pond. Sebastian sat in. It's true: compositions are improved when played by someone who is faultless on his instrument. Admittedly, Nina has written a very beautiful new song ("Sore Loser"), which sounds a little like Simon and Garfunkel. The raw material was great. But the addition of the bass improved it substantially. Our harmonies are strong at the moment— from singing together so much. Then, after working with Nina, I headed to Vermont for a party where I would get to see my wife for the first time in a week. I was looking forward to seeing her, as well as our friends up there. I was feeling that I was really getting something out of Music Omi, something I was eager to share with my wife and friends. I guess what I was wanting to share was *confidence.* I was also feeling that my sense of direction, normally very serviceable, was enough that I didn't actually *need* the directions to the party. Big mistake.

August 13

I got back the next morning just in time for Soundpainting. The Soundpainting ensemble has now dwindled down to six (two guitars, percussion, accordion, saxophone, and trumpet). But as a result we have become ridiculously splashy. Christian seems to take great pleasure in the versatility, the turn-on-a-dime capabilities of the ensemble. Nina, who is playing accordion, had the idea that everyone would bring to rehearsal (without disclosing) a degraded popular song, which he or she could be cued to perform by Christian. I was singing "What a Fool Believes," e.g., and Jacek, the drummer, was playing, or so he said, "Smoke on the Water." This exercise introduced a goofy, tonal aspect into the largely noisy, free-jazz feel of Soundpainting (and it eventually resulted in a group obsession with a truly dreadful Japanese pop song called "Gandhara").

Later, I worked on singing harmonies on Chris Chalfant's songs. I don't have any interest in her lyrics, but there's a sort of folk-gospel-spiritual simplicity to the melodies that is undeniable. I begin to see how being a session musician might be fun. Nina and I applied the same principles by inviting the trumpeter Nadje Noordhuis to play on some of the rough Wingdales recordings we'd been working on. Nadje is such an inventive and tasteful player that she makes it look easy. You say: "Play something big and moving here." And then she does. That's what sheer talent sounds like. In two takes, she recorded some lines that made our song exciting all over again. Emboldened, we've decided to get Jacek to record some percussion as well.

The afternoon featured a pool party. It's a shallow pool. So shallow you can't dive. More like a wading pool. People were wearing plastic visors and other dollar-store items that had been procured for the express purposes of mutual assured ridicule.

In the evening, Jeffrey Lependorf, fearless leader, performed for us the world premiere of his one-person chamber opera. It's the musical setting of a podcast about the television program *Project Runway*. The piece was about an hour long and was very, very witty. I loved it. The singer, John Schenkel, was great despite the fact that he'd only rehearsed the composition once. That afternoon.

August 14

It would be unsympathetic and moralistic of me to chide the couple who are rather publicly romancing, but let me try to talk about it without being unjust. In this case, one of the two, the fellow, is an ebullient and hilarious class-clown of a guy. It seems obvious, at least in retrospect, that he would have found a kindred spirit in one of the most effervescent of the women among us. During the period when they were getting to know each other we were all their beneficiaries. People who are falling in love have so much energy to give away, as if it's a requirement of falling in love that it be *witnessed*. However, after a particular moment, and I guess which moment this is is obvious, the observable part of the romance is withdrawn. There are fewer and fewer hours in the day for any orbiting bystanders, because the lovers are busy refining and eliminating extraneous interests.

When there are only the fourteen of us here, when the experience of being here is about collaboration, a full-on affair, despite magnanimous intentions, is to the detriment of the whole. People start not showing up for things, or they show up sleepless or badly hungover, etc. In fact, there are a number of musicians here who are not infrequently hungover. I have sympathy with hangovers, with the excess merriment that engenders them, but I resist the *celebration* of the hangover. As I resist allowing romance to get in the way of work.

That said, we did more Soundpainting stuff today, and then I spent more time trying to count impossible rests in Jacek's group piece, which sounds like "Fanfare for the Common Man" on Ecstasy. Nina and I then went to fetch ingredients for *s'mores* (which were not made until our last night upstate), as well as the ingredients for the rocketry experiments that can be undertaken with Mentos and Diet Coke. After dinner, there was more singing, this time Australian folk songs, led by Adam. And maybe this is the point to note that in contrast to the intensity of the playing during the day, which is often about chops and talent, the playing we did in the evening was canted in the direction of Nina and me, toward, that is, informality and traditional music. The Australian songs were a good example. All of them seemed to be about sheep shearing or drinking. Or they were popularized by this Australian country singer Adam loves, a guy with — in the photographs — the worst teeth I have ever seen. Everyone sang with gusto, as they did every night. When it wasn't Adam teaching us songs, it was Sumiko, or Chris, or Nina, or Nuala. We learned songs in Japanese, Finnish, Afrikaans, and Irish in the course of our evenings, as well as the proper fingering for a tin whistle. In the evening we were all the same kind of musician, we were generalists, and I think it really helped the group cohere better during its more official daylight mission.

August 15

Sebastian Gramss has been attempting, for much of Music Omi, to get me to speak German, a language of which I know not one word. This seems to date from the moment when I failed, at dinner, to pronounce correctly *Einstürzende Neubauten*. To further the cause, he suggested that he try to *play along* as I read aloud from a book in German—about diet and health. Despite the great potential for humiliation, I gave it a shot. Sebastian always has something beautiful to say with his double bass no matter the environment. We worked in the library, which is lovely. I hadn't been in the room before, and it's lined with some fine books. When I was done fumbling in German, we set one of these oblique lyrical constructions I've been making in the last year or so, entitled "Whatever."

After that, more Soundpainting. Today I spontaneously broke out a Britney Spears song in an attempt to try to disarm my peers. And in the afternoon Nina and I went back to working on a long-dormant project, a cycle of extended-vocal-technique compositions in which multiple singers attempt to imitate the electronic loops from a little plastic device known as the Buddha Machine. We drafted just about everyone we could get into this project, whether they were singers or not, pressing them into service with headphones and microphone. There was something really intimate about seeing David Freeman, the tabla virtuoso, eyes squeezed shut, attempting to mimic the burblings of the Buddha Machine with nothing but his voice.

August 16

We got schedules for the concerts today. And schedules for rehearsals. The next few days look very busy, especially for Adam and Nadje and Sebastian, who are playing on virtually every piece. Now that I'm faced with the end of my time here, I am feeling apprehension about going back to my normal life. Sitting around talking about music and being fed by someone else for two weeks is excellent, and though I have missed my wife and my garden and my cats, I am having a very good time. For example, I am having a good time even when, in a rehearsal of Cobi van Tonder's song "Blow," Philippe, flamenco genius, gets up *during the song* and walks over to tell me how to play the barre chords better. I guess I can feel inept and happy at the same time.

Sebastian's group composition is a bitch, and he has now persuaded me to open and close the composition with little sections of this lyric, "Whatever," that I used with him the other day. I'm not doing that well at it yet because I am having trouble integrating myself into our duet passage while all these amazing musicians are sitting around waiting for their entrances. I trust I will get better. The piece is enormously complicated *after* our duet, before the coda, featuring all kinds of electronic interventions and two drummers and a big groove. Sort of like Miles Davis in the *Live-Evil* period. I don't want to botch it.

In the evening, in recognition of the fact that we are going to be playing nonstop for the next few days, we all took the night off and went into Chatham to see the new John Travolta film, *Hairspray*, based on the musical (which is in turn based on the movie by John Waters). As is the case in all such deracinations, with each generation of remove from the source material, the story has become less compelling. The film, in fact, bugged me. I hated it. I felt as if Travolta, the Scientologist, was mugging, and that whereas Divine, in the original, celebrated her body, Travolta behaved with the same contempt that has animated recent Eddie

Murphy and Martin Lawrence investigations of similar drag characters. In the company of a lot of Europeans, I felt that the film made America look bad. And I was right about this. The heavy-drinking contingent from Omi bolted about a half hour into the film and descended on the bar next door.

August 17

I had some stomach-related problem overnight. I was awake with cramps and related miseries. That was bad enough. But then I got up early to check e-mail (which I have been avoiding), and I came upon a note of the sort that one wishes never to get. It was from a writer friend: *Call as soon as you get this*. My heart sank. With good reason. What I learned in the course of the telephone call was that my boss at the writing program at Bennington College, the institution where I have taught officially and unofficially for quite a long time, had taken his own life. It was nearly impossible to comprehend this news, the suddenness of it, the violence of it. And what to do with my feelings of aggrieved sympathy for his wife and daughter? Liam, my boss, was a dark, hilarious guy who was always fighting off his demons. While his death was a total shock, it's also *not*. Afterward, I found the concerns of music camp—whether Cobi's song is improving, whether Nuala was going to need lyrics for hers—suddenly irrelevant.

I tried to keep busy. At Cobi's rehearsal, I felt I could have accepted being demoted from guitar if I didn't think the words of her composition less pungent than they might have been. It's a Brit pop song, a Cure song, a New Order song, which should have been easy to play and is for me. Not so much for some of the others. The lyrics go: "Blow-ow-ow-ow-ow-ow me a kiss, blow me a kiss, before you go," and so forth. Though there was the risk of hurting her feelings, of seeming impertinent, I offered to make some lyrical suggestions.

Cobi was followed by a very good Soundpainting rehearsal, and then by another rehearsal of Sebastian's piece, which I'm still fretting about. I'm just not feeling great. I have no appetite. I managed to improve my spoken-word performance a bit by lunch, and I managed to get through Jacek's rehearsal. After that, I slept and chased down news about Liam.

Over dinner, Nina and I whipped out a new set of lyrics for Cobi's song. About Lyme disease. Of the old lyrics, Cobi said, in her enthusiastic and hilarious way, "Once I translated them out of Afrikaans, I realized they were really dumb!" I think we managed to help a little bit.

August 18

I earned considerable enmity from Nuala by impugning her ability to count rests during Jacek's rehearsal. The melody line on this bright, stirring piece is just very difficult to play, and everyone was having trouble counting it, myself most of all. But Nuala was playing the melody *first*, in tandem with Sebastian on bass. I made the mistake of suggesting to Jacek that maybe he wanted to think of having one of the stronger soloists — like Christian or Adam, both faultless sight readers — do the first iteration of the melody. Nuala looked at me as if she wanted to run me through with her flute. I apologized vigorously. But I still feel like an asshole. What the hell do I know? I've played gigs in public maybe thirty times in my entire life, and Nuala, in particular, may have played music in public three hundred times. Or three thousand. She opened for the Pogues once. Shane MacGowan told her he needed a new tin whistle player in his band.

It's not that I'm feeling so nervous about the performances. I used to feel very nervous about any Public Display of Music. The night I performed with Syd Straw at Fez, almost ten years ago, the night that inaugurated my adult attempts to play seriously, now that *was* terrifying. But if I have learned anything here at Music Omi—besides where to chop a wave form on Pro Tools, or how to count sevens and nines—it's that I shouldn't be quite so self-conscious about singing. I will never be Otis Redding, but if I sing with confidence I don't have to be ashamed. You only get one singing voice, and one span of decades in which to use it. I don't want to wake up years from now regretting that I couldn't bring myself to sing.

August 19

Slept like shit, and I'm still kind of torn up about Liam Rector's suicide. I was therefore up early enough to help lift and carry equipment to the tent where we were going to perform. I hate carrying equipment. This is one of the reasons I play in a band without a rhythm section. And yet: laziness is tedious. So we carried equipment for a while, and then when the piano tuner showed up we scattered until lunch.

This was a brief interval of inactivity, lunch, and yet in the available moments I managed to find another opportunity for despair. The upper layer of my misery adhered to the fact that everyone likes Nina Katchadourian so much and recognizes what a true musical talent she is. More than once in the past couple of days, people have leaned across me at meals to ask her to sing on gigs in New York. Well, here's another problem: my piece with Jacek always gets short shrift at sound check and at rehearsals, because Jacek and I don't *complain*. The result is that we just haven't really worked the piece out. These are both selfish issues, but somehow they were enough for me to chew on. I felt a bit better by show time.

And then the audience arrived, congregating under a hastily erected tent. And so we began, and I was swept into the theater of performance. In this way, I finally got to hear everyone's pieces, some of which had been rehearsed apart from the larger group of us. There were a few noodly, solo-heavy numbers that didn't mean that much to me. On the other hand, even with warts, a couple of the ensemble pieces were quite magnificent, for example Jacek's "Arukoo." And Cobi's big finale of the first half, the song now called "Broad," came out fine. Nina sang two of her own songs. (I sang harmony on one.) The first, especially, a duet for voice and double bass, was incredibly lovely. And my later appearances, on the spoken intro to Sebastian's ensemble piece and then during my piece with Jacek, were a lot of fun. Sebastian's piece was especially great. Splendid, I thought, full of menace and virtuosity. I hope it goes as well on Monday for the second show.

After dinner, which followed the gig, everyone got sentimental. Nuala performed her "Parting Glass" song again, the old Irish standard that Nina and I sang with her a week or so ago, which, at the advent of parting, was indeed incredibly sad. Philippe was nearly weeping during it, and he then gave a moving speech, in French, about how this has been one of the great experiences of his life. I said a few words later myself. What I tried to say was this: when I came to Music Omi, I had a particular idea about musicality, and that idea was that if you could play your instrument quickly and did a lot of practicing of scales, then you were a legitimate musician. Of course, I didn't measure up to that standard. But what I found, through the gracious acceptance by the musicians at Music Omi, the acceptance of traditional music idioms, the acceptance of spoken word as a practice, was that in fact there are many ways of being musical, and that *commitment* is the main quality that is required for music making. Adam Simmons, really an incredibly gentle and smart guy, replied that in fact Nina and I had done something to help break the ice at Music Omi, by keeping everyone rooted in old forms. I was especially moved by this. Adam and I were followed by nearly everyone else in the ensemble speechifying in some form. Sebastian hated the whole thing and kept telling people to shut up. I think in Germany this kind of thing passes for sentimentality.

Then we went outside to prove that Mentos and Diet Coke really can create spontaneous explosions.

I don't want to go back to my regular life.

August 20

Breakfast with Nina and the curators of the Fields, the Omi sculpture park. As with many such things, the more I knew about how the Fields were curated the less I wanted to know. There's something about a naive apprehension of art that makes it that much nobler to me. I don't really *want* to know what Donald Judd was like, or that Dan Flavin did nothing but watch television in his later years. I care about the work. And there really was some great work out there, like Jeff Talman's sound piece, in which speakers broadcast an ambient soundscape in and around a chortling stream that runs through the Omi acreage, as well as the piece there that involves *live sheep*. I'm not interested in who made this work. Not really.

Or maybe I was sad about leaving. But before I had time to feel sad about it I was gone. I made it home to Fishers Island in just over two and a half hours. And not long after pulling into the driveway, I was playing tennis with my dad. Which is a good thing to do when your heart is heavy. It wasn't until nightfall that I felt the ache of music camp past, the ache of knowing that I had a lot of other things to do in the fall, a novel, a bunch of writing assignments, anxieties of every kind.

It was the first day in almost three weeks that I didn't play my guitar.

August 21

During my sentimental drive into NYC for the final Omi show, I liked everyone from Omi, and all the recollections were good. Then I tried to find somewhere to park off Canal Street and had one of those unpleasant transactions with a Russian parking-lot guy.

At sound check, people mumbled hello as if they'd already

seen enough of me. Everyone treated everyone this way. Like it was *just another gig*. Play and go. Maybe this is how you get after a while. Roulette, where we were to perform, is a small space, and we probably didn't need many microphones, but even so there weren't enough to go around. What mics there were kept feeding back. And the electronics were way too loud. And the drums were too loud. The whole atmosphere was petulant and grim. One piece got the lion's share of rehearsal time, though its conductor seemed a little more interested in how people *looked* as they were playing than in the fact that the players were missing their entrances and exits.

On the other hand, sound checks are always awful. Sound check is no predictor of the show. This was the point Jacek made, and he has played a lot of shows. He idles low through it all. At times I have wanted to shake him and say, But isn't this *nice?* But during a bad sound check he is really graceful. What matters, he argues, is what happens the moment *after* the first piece gets counted in.

Jacek, Nadje, Nina, and I all went to Gourmet Garage for dinner before the show and sat outside watching the models of Soho coming and going. Soho is a neighborhood whose affluence I find garish. I remember its art ghetto days. While we were finishing dinner, on a bench, Nina ran across the street into some shop and tried on an overcoat in the doorway, modeling it for us. Price tag: $800. She was going to wait for the sale.

The crowd was good at Roulette. I thought the first couple of pieces were not bad, the jazz fusion monster from Christian, and Philippe's world music suite. We did better on Jacek's "Arukoo" than we'd done upstate. Nina sang her songs without difficulty, and they were quite beautiful. Then we finished the first half on a bum note, with the somewhat sloppy pop song by Cobi van Tonder. Well, it *felt* sloppy, but when I listened to the recording of this gig, "Broad" didn't sound bad at all—in fact, it had a loose-limbed enthusiasm that I enjoyed.

My wife turned up for the show, having missed the first few pieces, and her remark at the intermission was that we really *did* sound like band camp. She'd had a number of creative metaphors for what I'd been doing those two weeks; band camp was one. The other was Harry Potter. To her, Music Omi sounded like Hogwarts, Harry Potter's academy. But without the British class system.

Then the second half of the show went very well. Sebastian's piece, in which I was featured, was strong, and Jacek and I took the time to let our duet really happen, without feeling rushed. It began to reveal the requisite spookiness. Chris Chalfant operated at something close to the six minutes that she had available to her, making her piece sound much stronger than it had upstate (when it was less concise), and Nadje was predictably understated but moving in her elegant quartet. The finale, the Soundpainting demo, was funny and spirited, including repeated excerpts from the Japanese pop song "Gandhara." We finished the show almost half an hour shorter than on Saturday, and we were better for it.

Then we broke down the set. People hustled things into vans, folded up music stands and mic booms, stowed their guitars or their horns. All at once, Music Omi was genuinely over. Like it had never happened. We were out on the streets of Soho, heading for Fanelli's. I forgot, for a moment, that I can't stand bars, and that I particularly hate *that* bar, in which I drank once upon a time. I turned back before joining the after party, therefore, and missed all the farewells.

The next day I listened to a lot of pieces I'd worked on while at Music Omi. And I even tried playing one of the songs I'd written there. My conclusion? That I am not good enough. Still, a couple of nights ago Nadje, the trumpeter, remarked that it was time for me to stop using the word *sometime* before the word *musician* in my descriptions of what I do. It was a generous thing for her to say. After these two weeks I feel I ought to consider the suggestion.

On Celestial Music

1. Otis Redding as Purveyor of Celestial Music

Music has soul. We operate as though it does nearly all the time. In fact, music is one of the few areas of human endeavor where the word *soul*, even among secular types, is liable to go unchallenged. All kinds of music are occasionally imputed to have soul. Even music that doesn't have anything but volume or a tiresome double-kick drum sound will sometimes be described as having soul. Ray Conniff, to a listener some- where, has soul. Michael Bolton has soul. Who am I to say otherwise? Soul in these cases perhaps indicates earnestness, rhetorical force, and/or vocal polyps. Nevertheless, there are persuasive indications that the word *soul* does indeed manifest itself in music, and it's perhaps useful at the outset to point to one such recording in order to make plain the fact that music belongs in a discussion of the celestial. Before getting fur- ther into my account, I will therefore adduce one example from the genre nominally referred to as *soul music*, namely, a live recording by Otis Redding entitled "Try a Little Tenderness."*

First, there's the lyric of the composition, which begins as an exhortation to do better at peeling away the layers of defensiveness in a lover, a woman who is not only *weary* in the general sense, but also weary of the traditional role of woman, whose only job at the song's opening is selflessness. This condition is well indicated, for example, in the limpid perception "I know she's waiting / Just anticipating / The thing that she'll never possess." What to make of this? What exactly is "the thing she'll never possess"? Is it love? Is it justice, in the prejudicial landscape of the USA in the middle and late sixties? Or, as with the weariness in the first line, is some more general dissatisfaction implied herewith? I'd like to submit that what Otis Redding intends, in his role as purveyor of celestial music, is to make us conscious of our human frailty (cf., as well, "[Sittin' on] The Dock of the Bay"), our lack, our incompleteness. And he does so with perfect phrasing and with the kind of deceptive vulnerability that is all but absent from music in these troubled times.

Still, this is to avoid mention of the dynamically satisfying *freak-out* at the end of the song. The big ending! If celestial music is the music of the spheres, in which heaven was once alleged to repose, then the big ending of "Try a Little Tenderness" proves that music here on earth can also be tuned to the interstellar realms, especially when the rhythm section kicks in, and the horns start, and Otis begins his passionate exhorta-

---

* From, e.g., *The Stax/Volt Revue, Vol. 2: Live in Paris*, Atlantic Records, 1991.

tion as to how, exactly, tenderness is meant to be practiced (holding, squeezing, never leaving), and the horns work their way up the scale, likewise the rhythm guitar, chromatically, while Redding commences his soul shouting, and the crowd goes wild, hoping that he'll play through the chorus just one more time! Yes, *try a little tenderness!* How could we resist! We have not tried sufficiently! So many areas of our lives remain unexplored! So many virtues lie dormant in us! So much is failure and halfheartedness! Tenderness as opposed to oppressing the poor and disenfranchised, tenderness as opposed to military intervention in foreign countries, tenderness as opposed to fear of other ideologies and ways of negotiating the world! Tenderness as opposed to the amassing of money, power, and real estate!

This live performance of Otis Redding (especially) *enacts* the attempt at tenderness he describes (and let me not forget to address the alliterative strategy of the title of the song, as though the repetition of *t*'s were also close to God, euphony being an aspect of the beautiful that is present in all possible heavens), and thus the song *proves* itself, proves the validity of *soul* in music, by persuading in a very abbreviated space, not through empirical means but by *exercising* the soul, and if you are not convinced by my recitation of these facts, get the *Monterey Pop* DVD and watch it, because, I swear, just as you can be absolved of your malfeasances by watching the pope on television, you can be made a better person by watching Otis Redding deliver this song; you will go into the next room, and you will look at your husband, or your wife, or your child, you will look at the people whom you have treated less well than you might have, and you will kneel in front of these people and you will beg for the chance to try a little harder and to make their burdens a little less burdensome. And if those five minutes of grace are not an example of what lies out there, beyond what we daily understand, if those five minutes are not like unto a candle that glimmers in the face of the unending darkness of life on earth, then I have no idea what paradise is.

2. Heaven and Premium Stereo Equipment

Music is of God, that is, and music is with God, and music is how God expresses Him-, or Herself, and music is everywhere, and music is a crafty art and is completed in places inside us, in the impossible-to-locate precincts wherein there is access to feelings that we might otherwise ignore. Or: the abstraction of music is how God conceals His or Her complicated plan. Or: the abstraction of music, its connection to deep feeling, has all the traces of the Holy Ghost, so it seems to me, and if I didn't understand this logically as a kid, I at least understood how moving music was, when I was first going to church in the suburbs.

Back then, I wanted to lay eyes on things. Because when you're a kid you're open to all kinds of things, but you trust what's in front of your face. I remember feeling that the praying part of the religious service was deeply suspect. People would get this expression on their faces, something near to earnest self-regard. I was supposed to overlook this earnest face-pulling, and I was meant to know intuitively the precise organi-zation of hands for prayer, and then I was supposed to know what to murmur and to whom. And then there was the posturing *after* church. Forget about it! That was not what I associated with God, heaven, the sublime, the celestial. There was some talk, during Sunday school, about heaven, and it was always of the-place-where-the-old-guy-with-beard-lived variety, and I never believed any of that. I had a bullshit detector where ideology was concerned. I resisted what I was told, even if it was good for me, even if it made the world a better place.

What moved me was the music. Music filled me with this intense feeling about the state of things, from my earliest recollections. Not only the organ music before and after services. The organ music was sublime, even when I didn't know anything about harmony and counterpoint. Organ music scared me and demanded something of me, by virtue of its grandiosity. (This would perhaps be the moment to say the obvious, that if earthly music is played in heaven, then J. S. Bach really must be the *capellmeister*.) There was also the choir singing during church service. My mom was known to sing in the choir (later on I did a bit of it myself), and there was a lot of singing going on around my house generally. The human voice, raised in song, was important, was routine, was unearthly, gave access to the numinous. And obviously there are indications of this across the centuries of recorded time, almost wherever you look. In David's psalms, e.g.: "Sing unto the Lord a new song, and his praise in the congregation of saints."* I

---

* And especially in Psalm 150: "Praise him with the sound of the trumpet; praise him with the psaltery and the harp. Praise him with timbrel and dance; praise him with stringed instruments and organs. Praise him upon the loud cymbals; praise him upon the high-sounding cymbals. Let everything that hath breath praise the Lord. Alleluia."

wouldn't have had any idea what this meant back when I was first in church. But I knew I liked the singing.

At about the same time, my mother became highly partisan about the popular recording artists known as Simon and Garfunkel. We had a lot of their LPs. In fact, we had all of them. I could make a good argument about the sublime and the song known as "The Sounds of Silence," electric version, which would then lead to a discussion of John Cage and the theological importance of silence, but I'm putting that off for another time. Instead, I want to talk about a mostly forgotten Simon and Garfunkel tune on the album *Wednesday Morning, 3 A.M.*, entitled "Sparrow." This song, in the folk genre that characterized early Simon and Garfunkel recordings, unfolds as a series of sympathetic questions about a sparrow, addressed to the other preoccupied living things of the world: Who will love a little sparrow? Who will speak to it a kindly word? A swan is posed this question, a field of wheat, an oak tree, and yet all of these eminences decline the opportunity to become stewards of the common sparrow, herself adrift on the callousness of the world, where it is the fate of tenderness to be squandered. Then in the last verse the *earth* steps in, having been asked the same question. The earth responds with a forceful affirmative, in regards to the sparrow, quoting from scripture, "From dust were ye made and dust ye shall be."

This little song shook my earthly foundations, back in Connecticut, where my early music-appreciation lessons were taking place. Not only because it had that mysterious, unearthly quality that English folk music had about it. Not only because of the harmonies, which were always pretty extraordinary in the Simon and Garfunkel corpus. Above all, the song moved me because it depicted so much loss and so much weariness, and because the sparrow, it seemed to me, *had to die.* These days, "Sparrow" might sound a bit quaint to the average listener, owing to its self-evident allegorical scaffolding. But this is also what makes folk songs profound, that they are simple, unadorned, and eager to confront religious, philosophical, and political questions. They are modal, polysemous, difficult to pin down; they are fairy tales with melodies. This makes folk music ideal for a kid who's six or seven. I didn't have any defense against the emotional freight of the song, and it shook me. What was "Sparrow" about for me? "Sparrow" was about loving the forgotten, the marginalized, the sick, homely, and despised, and it was about how everything has to die, and if heaven is a locale wherein the injustice of earthly mortality is repaired, uh, for *eternity,* then "Sparrow," in its radical acceptance of the spurned little bird, points in the direction of heavenly music, what it might do, how it might make the case for paradise.

I guess I'm covering up if I'm not saying that I admired this particular song at a troubling time, the time when my parents were divorcing. I suppose it's obvious that I was identifying with the sparrow, feeling, like her, as though refuge from heartache was hard to come by. In this way, many of the songs I liked then seemed kind of sad. For example: another song I cherished was "Golden Slumbers" by the Beatles. It's the lullaby on a very complex, protean album, *Abbey Road.* Let me explain where I listened to it. My parents had this new stereo system, in a big wooden cabinet in the living room. It was a *hi-fi,* in the classic sense of the term, and it was maybe the expensive hi-fi that they bought to convince themselves, through amplification, that they were more allied and resilient than they were. My father, who never seemed to be home, was not there while we were making dinner, and so he probably wouldn't remember my mother putting on *Abbey Road*, whereupon we would dance around to the rock numbers, like "Mean Mr. Mustard" and "Come Together." Nor was he there when we sang along with "Golden Slumbers" and "Here Comes the Sun."

Eventually, an evening came to pass that I understood as the moment during which my parents were discussing how to tell us they were separating. They were enclosed in that family room with the expensive hi-fi. The louvered doors were closed. There was an unsettling silence in the house. We (my sister, brother, and I) looked at these closed doors, from up the staircase, between the balusters supporting the banister. Something lasting and sad was taking place. It was obvious. And soon my mother came to break the news to us. Ever after when I imagined this scene, I heard in my head, chief among other songs, "Golden Slumbers." Once, as the song suggests, there *was* a way to get back home. In the past tense. The song still calls forth that loss in me, that time after certainty. Does this melancholy reside in the lyrics, because the relationship between the singer of the song (Paul McCartney) and the children to whom he sings is, arguably, not dissimilar to the relationship between the divine (from some perch in heaven) and His beloved flock here on earth?

Actually, I probably liked "Golden Slumbers" because no one much sang lullabies to me as a kid. I had no idea about *agape* and *caritas*. I had no idea about heaven. I was skeptical. Even a lullaby, from my point of view, would have been like a happy ending in a movie. Happy endings were for people who believed any nonsense that came along. So I liked "Golden Slumbers," from the newly released *Abbey Road*, because I secretly wanted somebody to sing a lullaby to me. Admitting such a thing makes me uncomfortable. And yet it was from unfulfilled longing that I formulated some ideas of that *elsewhere* of paradise, the place where no longing goes unfulfilled.

3. The Heavenly Jukebox

So far it sounds like I'm making a playlist for a heavenly jukebox. What would be the selections on such a jukebox? Is this jukebox any good? From an earthly point of view, I imagine that if there is music in heaven, it should celebrate virtues and ideals. Does the heavenly jukebox therefore contain only songs by Pat Boone and Deborah Gibson? Does God, whatever He, She, It is, have some amazing celestial version of iTunes where you can hear the songs you like all day long as long as you have, as a virtuous individual, gained admission to the celestial realms? Could I, for example, hear "The Spirit of Radio," by Rush, in heaven (assuming I'm virtuous), even though I won't allow myself to listen to it on earth because it is simply too embarrassing? What if hearing Rush would (arguably) make me happy for all eternity? Do people in this kingdom of the worthy get to play Whitesnake around the clock, just because they are good and deserving? Or have they transcended Whitesnake, having passed beyond the earthly realms? Do they allow Metallica in heaven? What about that Finnish band where the lead singer wears satanic horns? Maybe he's a really good, hardworking guy, despite wearing the horns, and is just trying to provide for his Finnish wife and child. Will he be admitted into heaven and be able there to play a big gig with Jimi Hendrix sitting in?

Does God allow celestial broadcasts of Led Zeppelin's "Stairway to Heaven"? Or "Heaven Is a Place on Earth," by Belinda Carlisle? Or "Just Like Heaven," by the Cure? Or "Heaven," by Talking Heads, or "Pennies from Heaven," or the oft-covered "Knockin' on Heaven's Door"? These songs all have *heaven* in the title, but I don't think they are good songs, except maybe the Dylan composition, and they don't teach me anything about what kind of music exists in heaven.

And what kind of musical instruments *do* they have in heaven? In the old days, they had trumpets and lutes. Many accounts substantiate this point. Are we to believe that heavenly instrumental groups stopped innovating a thousand years ago? Unlikely! So are there, in fact, electric guitars in heaven, or things that sound like electric guitars? Are there didgeridoos in heaven? What about synthesizers or digital samplers? Do they have the latest plug-ins for computer-based music in heaven? Does one have to clear his or her samples in heaven (because stealing is a venal sin), or can you go ahead and pilfer copyrighted music to your heart's content? What about all those exotic world music instruments? Tibetan bowls? Mouth harps? Are these instruments available to all who need them for the sake of expression?

Well, it's a real stretch to posit a jukebox in heaven, and I don't think God is a jukebox, and you cannot take your iPod with you when you are gone, and there is no digital sampler and no mixing board to connect it to. Music in heaven probably would not have lightweight lyrics, or even unimpeachably useful lyrics like "All You Need Is Love," and since it's unlikely that we will reach heaven in our corporeal forms, we may not have ears with which to listen to music, nor voices with which to sing it.

4. The Groove in Heaven

Common time is said to be the time signature that closely resembles the human heartbeat, and 4/4 is also the time signature with the best opportunity for the *groove*. If in my early life I might perhaps have advanced the notion that the music in heaven would be noteworthy for lyrical exegesis on subjects like compassion and love, in my teens I would have thought it was all about the groove. Bass and drums, those were the things that made music heavenly, as when you are a teenager or a young adult, and you like the endless groove, for example, in "Sister Ray," by the Velvet Underground, and you are willing to hear that groove go around and around, and you do not exactly care what the lyrics say, if indeed you are able to decipher them. The view from rock club floors and dance clubs and mosh pits is that music is ecstatic, that the groove is ecstatic, and if music is ecstatic, then heavenly music should be the acme of this ecstasy. It should be all about union and the sense of community, things that are self-evident at concerts and clubs. When I am in the groove, the groove is good. Thus, the teenage version of myself imagined that heaven, or paradise, was where there was always a good groove, and all kinds of people could dance around to it together, for light-years at a time. When I was in the groove, wallowing in the one-four chord progression, let's say, or during a song by Funkadelic, then it was all about how many people you could get playing at one time, and the entire audience was on its feet and chanting along with some line like "Get up for the down stroke! / Everybody get up!" even if many listeners were not exactly sure what the downstroke was nor why they should get up for it. At one time, I would have said that if heaven could not deliver on these things, on the promise of community, and on a music that had a good groove to it, then I didn't think heaven was heavenly.

Meanwhile, it would be logical and easy to make the argument that the groove has a sexual cast about it, and that people respond to the groove because it is suggestive of the pace and rhythm of sexuality. If this were the case, then again we might have to disqualify this music from heaven, on the basis that there is no corporeal resurrection, in my view, and thus no need for music that appeals to the carnal (or procreative) ecstasy of the flesh. Perhaps for similar reasons, Cotton Mather frowned upon dancing: "Their Children dance, and They go down the Grave into Hell."

In the vicinity of this notion of the sexual cast of the groove, for me, would be the related notion of intoxication in heaven generally. There is no need for intoxication in heaven. I suppose this is kind of obvious. Why would you need to be intoxicated there? Up there, you have not fallen short, you are not in a condition of wanting, you are theoretically happy, and so you are not looking for music or drugs or spirits to intoxicate you in any way. You don't need to be bludgeoned by the music in heaven, you don't need to dance until you are exhausted, you don't need one more rousing chorus, because you don't need to be roused, and you are not going to get banged up in the mosh pit, nor are you going to suffer hearing loss, and no one is going to cough during the most beautiful part of the aria, and no one is going to climb over you to get to their seat during the opening measures of the second movement of the symphony.

5. Music for Canyons

I bring up this fact of intoxication because of how quitting drinking improved and defined my own spiritual life. I didn't have any genuine conviction about heaven, or God, or spirituality, or an afterlife, or anything else, really, between the ages of fifteen and twenty-six, when I was often busy doing other things, most of them not very good for me. This came to an end in 1987,* after which it occurred to me to go back to church, out of gratitude for my reprieve and for the remission of the considerable pain I'd been living with.

Music also came back into my life in a number of ways. First, I started dabbling in it again. I'd taught myself guitar as a teenager, and so I bought a guitar anew and began practicing it, and I began writing songs, which I had also done when young. I also started listening to things in a new way. I can chart the subsequent metamorphosis in my musical taste with a number of recordings I first heard on a local new music program that was broadcast each night in New York City.

---

* Committed to psychiatric hospital, got sober, etc.

First among the discoveries of that time was the music of Arvo Pärt. Although I can't remember exactly which piece I first heard by Pärt, I can remember the first album I bought, which was the ECM release called *Tabula Rasa*. On this recording, both the piece called "Cantus in Memory of Benjamin Britten" and the cello piece "Fratres" genuinely moved me in ways that "serious" music rarely had. These pieces, which are said to have been composed as a way out of the dead end of serial music and academic atonality, are frankly spiritual and completely tonal, using elements of early music, like plainsong, for their raw material. Elsewhere, Pärt set liturgical texts. For these reasons, and because the pieces are *so* simple, there is some grumbling in classical music circles about Pärt's work. He's not serious, he's conservative, etc.

I didn't care about any of this when I first heard these recordings, and I still don't. Pärt's compositions split me open like I was an oyster, and the way they did it was by exploiting the simple harmonies of ancient western music, the kind of dignity and stateliness that I associated with the music of the church as I first heard it. I can't fully explain what it is about this simplicity and tonality that was so moving to me. And I'm not sure I want to. *Tintinnabuli* is the term that Pärt has in the past used to describe these pieces, meaning that they sound like bells or have the uncomplicated grace of bells.

Pärt led me to other things. Not just spiritually inclined classical music, but to kinds of music that were organized along similar principles, where there was simplicity and elemental harmonics, and where the devotion was to serenity and austerity and to the notion of music itself. That is, I wasn't as interested in the noise that was very moving to me as a young person, nor was I interested in virtuosity for its own sake. Rather, I was after a rather baroque idea that tonality *was* spiritual, and even divine. I was therefore moved by minimalism, by La Monte Young, by Meredith Monk, by chamber music like the Penguin Cafe Orchestra, by early music, by Hildegard von Bingen, William Byrd, Purcell. It also seemed as if anything contemporary that I liked, anything that had a lot of echo in it, as if it had been made in canyons, was somehow better than music that was made anywhere else. Music that celebrated or was illustrative of sound and nature, and the physicality of things.*

Maybe in this way I'm beginning to answer the question about *why music in heaven at all?* One thing that everybody always talks about in heaven is the *light*. Dante talks a lot about the light in *Paradiso*. Such a pleasing light! When other chroniclers have made it up there and reported back, there's always ecstatic light in their description. No paintings, no sculptures, no epic poems. No one in heaven is busy making installations or performing performance art. But there *is* music.

This goes all the way back, I imagine, to when there was music to the planets themselves, the heavenly bodies. It's an old perception, the music of the spheres; you find it as far back as Cicero (in *De re publica*), and if he was writing it down, he probably wasn't the first to have remarked on the subject: "This music is produced by the impulse and the motion of these spheres themselves. The unequal intervals between them

---

* I am not, however, a partisan of the music known as *New Age*. I do not endorse bland sheets of wallpaper over a machined bed of "exotic" percussion, even if I am in a spa or a yoga studio.

are arranged according to a strict proportion, and so the high notes blend agreeably with the low, and thus various sweet harmonies are produced." Music, according to this view, is an essential quality of creation, and we might mention especially the sublimity of harmony. And, as Cicero further observes, along with the ubiquity of heavenly music goes the tendency of men to want to imitate it: "Skillful men reproducing this celestial music on stringed instruments have thus opened the way for their own return to this heavenly region, as other men of outstanding genius have done by spending their lives on Earth in the study of things divine."

Why music, then? Because when we sing it and play it, we are not only imitating the things that are, but we are praising them, praising the things that are, and praising is good, and you find it, too, in almost any account of heaven. The angels sing their praises, and when we sing, according to, among others, the Levites, we are imitating the angels.

6. Heaven and Nonbeing

Still, in the end, any discussion of heaven hinges on the injustice of nonbeing, and whether you are worried about this injustice. This seems to me the weakest link in the argument about heaven. That there must be some reward for living through this life in the first world, living through war and greed and hypocrisy and selfishness. Maybe there *is* no reward, really, but having done a good job here! That is its own reward! The reward for living in a dignified way in the first world is dignified life in and of itself. Who isn't full of longing for a place better than this place? Who, driving through Elizabeth, New Jersey, or Omaha, Nebraska, or Indianapolis, Indiana, wouldn't long for an idealized heaven? And if the longing is good and human, what need for heaven? Longing, and compassion, and tenderness *are* heavenly, and they make you better than you otherwise were.

If the whole belief in heaven depends on a fear of nonbeing, then it's no more realistic than the notion of naked people sitting around on clouds playing lutes. Myself, I have little fear of nonbeing. I fear mortal pain, which so often seems to precede nonbeing, but otherwise I don't fear the end of the author of these particular sentences, and I don't need, for his sake, everlasting life. There's enough hassle involved with the temporary life. Everlasting life would be closer to hell, for me, than any fiery lake clogged with politicians. Because what would one *do* with eternity?

Unless, for the sake of argument, we are simply talking about energy. Unless we are talking about the little spark calved off the big creative first cause. Maybe we are simply talking about our ability to unite with that first cause. Maybe we are talking about a union that might take place, in which I can be, ideally, some little spark, some match light in the mostly dark and empty universe, the thirteen dimensions of it, and my eternal match light would not necessarily require consciousness or lutes. And along with being this spark, I can imagine that I have a tone, and if I were going to pick one, I would pick something high, in the treble clef, something I couldn't reach when I was a baritone pretending to be a tenor. As this note, or some other note, I can imagine a heaven where I get to play this tone, and to collide with other notes, as if I were a constituent in a John

Cage piece, and here there are no entrances and exits, and I don't have to have perfect rhythm, nor do I have to know my scales, because I am all scales. Therefore I have no responsibilities, as a note, I just am, because I can't be entirely eliminated, because that doesn't happen—energy gets reused—and in this piece of music you can come in anywhere, and you can be a part of it, or not a part of it, and this composition has a long duration, an eternal duration, but you don't have to worry about this, because you are no longer a perceiving entity, you are just the note and the note is a good thing to be, in this composition, which has all the characteristics that good things have, namely it causes no harm, and believes only in its iteration as goodness, which is harmony and sublimity, and all kinds of other music are apparent in this music, even though they are lost, all possible music is contained in this infinite music, so Otis Redding is in there, and Simon and Garfunkel, and Funkadelic, and Arvo Pärt, maybe even Rush, because everything is in there, and in this way I am gone and gone is good, but I am also a very excellent musician and no one is any better, except the artful arranger of all sounds.

The Problem of Impairment

The manifest layer of this essay concerns the Pogues show I saw in March of 2007 at the Roseland Ballroom in New York City. Or, to be more precise, the manifest layer of this essay concerns the Pogues show I *intended* to see on March 15 of 2007. My cohorts in this *excursus*, doomed from the start, were my bandmates (in the Wingdale Community Singers) Hannah Marcus and Nina Katchadourian, as well as novelist Fiona Maazel. Hannah and I met in midtown west, excited at the prospect of the event, however doomed. We made our way toward the venue. Fiona and Nina were there already (having come from the southerly direction). Their telephone call from the vicinity of Roseland, however, contained the bad news that was in some way expected. The Pogues show was rescheduled, owing to an injury suffered by lead singer Shane MacGowan. The show was too good to be true, it seemed—the Pogues near upon St. Patrick's Day—and now things had unraveled, as things do. We landed at Roseland, aggrieved, and there the reports became more complete. Shane MacGowan had slipped and sprained his ankle, it was said. Tickets would be honored the following night, it was said. And yet even the official security guys out front of Roseland were in on the ironies of that moment: "Shane MacGowan has injured himself! Read between the lines!"

Which is to say: Shane was too ill to perform. Shane was, in all likelihood, too drunk, too incoherent, too semiconscious. He may well have injured himself (he had, in fact, as you shall see), but the injury probably had much to do with the advanced stages of alcoholism with which the singer was afflicted. We all scattered in the direction of home, wondering if there would be a show the next night or not.

Now to the backstory. The Pogues were the most important and most original band of the hard-to-love 1980s, on either side of the Atlantic. However, I resisted them at first. At least, I resisted their first great album, *Rum Sodomy & the Lash*. I was drinking then myself, and I liked anything that had a self-destructive aspect (the Replacements, for example, or the New York Dolls). And yet I also believed I had an intellectual obligation to support music that was loud, dark, and challenging: Sonic Youth, Hüsker Dü, Pere Ubu, the Minutemen, Black Flag, and so forth. Upon my release from the psychiatric hospital in July 1987, on the occasion of my first sober days, I had a sort of an epiphany. It occurred to me that maybe it was okay to like whatever I liked, regardless of whether it cohered with the requirements of artistic credibility or doctrines of cool. It was about this time that someone gave me a copy of *If I Should Fall From Grace With God*, the Pogues album that succeeded *Rum Sodomy & the Lash*.

What I had found folksy before, I found, nearly all at

once, complex, mature, proud, sad, and very, very catchy. Indisputably, this album was one of the indelible masterpieces of postpunk rock and roll! There wasn't a bad song on it! Naturally, I soon saw the video for "Fairytale of New York," the album's best-known composition, and I marveled at the dark, forbidding dissipation of the lead singer. Even at this early stage, he didn't look terribly upstanding. The song was (manifestly) concerned with drunkenness, and so a simulation of intoxication was to be expected. But this was more than that. This was both filmic simulation and the thing itself. Distracting from the darker themes, however, was the fact that the composition was masterful. The melody, the piano line, the dueling put-downs of MacGowan and guest chanteuse Kirsty MacColl, the sublime string arrangements, the Christmas imagery in the lyric, the drumming (you just can't talk about the originality of the Pogues without talking about Andrew Ranken's drumming). I can think of only a few songs in my life, and I really mean this, that I have loved as passionately right from the first notes and from which I have never once turned away. I still can't hear "Fairytale in New York" without crying. In fact, I watched the video today—in order to write these lines—and I cried again.

I could have been someone... Well, so could anyone...

And the rest of the album is just as remarkable. It holds up today. Twenty years later. It triumphs. It sounds as wild, passionate, out of control, and heartbreaking as it did back then. Whereas so much other work from the period has dated—the Cocteau Twins, New Order, the Cure—the Pogues sound just as energized in the present. They're timeless and indomitable.

From the first song on *If I Should Fall From Grace With God*, the Irish-music-at-punk-rock-tempos of the title track, to the last song, the genuinely stirring "Broad Majestic Shannon" ("Take my hand and dry your tears, babe / Take my hand, forget your fears, babe"), the album veers from punky, drunken screeds like "Bottle of Smoke" to world-inflected workouts like "Turkish Song of the Damned" and "Fiesta," where the folk instrumentation of the Pogues—acoustic guitar, tin whistle, banjo, accordion—suddenly enables them to sound like klezmer band or Arabic ensemble or jazz combo. They're jaundiced and romantic, incisive and undependable, wise beyond their years, startlingly adolescent. They'd been a punk band with Irish music leanings before *If I Should Fall From Grace With God*, one that didn't have a reputation for instrumental prowess, but suddenly they could play anything, at any tempo, and make it sound furious and moving without sounding shallow or sentimental—the way Madness always did, among their contemporaries.

Above the racket, Shane MacGowan bellowed, exhorted, ranted—who could tell if he was tenor or baritone—spitting out syllables that couldn't possibly be spit out that quickly, rushing the beat, his tuneless but expressive voice perfectly suited to the tempos and careening disorderliness of the compositions. The others in the band could sing, true, and did when Shane was forced out in the nineties, but MacGowan had some kind of fervent *vision*, some mad need to discourse, and so the Pogues just couldn't be the same, and weren't, without him. Even when his lyrics were tossed off, as they often seemed to be, scatological, irritable, provocative, there was something in them that was continuous with the heartache and sublimity of the Irish folk tradition. The Pogues made Irish music contemporary again, but without diluting its convoluted pathos, rescuing it from the banality of musical tourism while striking a blow against what was, at the moment of their ascendancy, a virulent and popular strain of British anti-Irish racism.

I couldn't stop playing *If I Should Fall From Grace With God* for a long while. Long enough that I was just feeling I was thoroughly schooled in it when *Peace and Love* came out. The successor album. *Peace and Love* had, it seemed, many of the same concerns as *If I Should Fall From Grace With God*, and it was just as carefully arranged and produced, just as worldly. But there was also something less focused about this album, as if the cracks in the edifice were beginning to show. Shane was still in charge, still writing about dog racing or Christy Brown (paralyzed Irish scribe), but the songs were slighter, as if they were being carefully arranged to conceal a less generous supply of genius. The other Pogues were filling in between Mac-Gowan compositions or cowriting more copiously, with less felicitous results ("Blue Heaven," e.g., a mere Brit pop song, and not a very good one). That said, *Peace and Love* remains a strong album, for "Misty Morning, Albert Bridge," "London You're a Lady," "Cotton Fields," and the tragicomic "Boat Train," the last of these recounting a ferry ride across the Irish Sea, an Irish protagonist bound for London, the cultural uncertainty thereof. There was so much music coming out of the Pogues, even at three-quarter strength, that there was something arresting on any album they released.

An EP followed *Peace and Love*, and it prominently featured a pop song called "Yeah Yeah Yeah Yeah Yeah" (two more *yeah*s than the Beatles), and it was also great. It included one of the few good Stones covers ever: Spider Stacy, the tin whistle player, singing "Honky Tonk Women." This abbreviated release amounted to an unalloyed gem of instant pop, but it was followed in turn by the *last* Pogues album, *Hell's Ditch*, produced by the eminent Joe Strummer of the Clash. Abruptly, to even the casual listener, it was clear exactly what was happening. Shane's voice was beginning to fail, and in the process the material had apparently become fragmentary, dissolute, recorded in a way as if to try to force the record to cohere even though it couldn't or wouldn't. *Hell's Ditch* was unable to conceal the fact that the singer now had trouble enunciating, whether by reason of inebriation or missing teeth, and his intonation was little better. If they'd had an Auto-Tune plug-in back then, they could have cleaned him up, but they did not. Shane remained Shane, unexpurgated, while the music around him filled in, characterized by a general anxiety. The production feels forced, full of instrumental geegaws like unto the less effective and cannabis-enhanced portions of the Clash's *Sandinista!* album. Strummer must have tried to mobilize the troops, only to find that there was no lieutenant competent enough to halt this retreat.

Here the story ended for a long while. There are many versions of the did-he-quit-or-was-he-fired variety. You can imagine how hard it must have been. By all accounts the band toured relentlessly, and Shane MacGowan was probably trying to balance, on the road, the amount he needed to drink in order to avoid withdrawal with the amount that would render him unable to perform. This is how alcoholism goes. Other members of the band straightened up in the meantime, as if trying to shake off their legacy. Perhaps the most drunken rock-and-roll group in Europe was, it turned out, less chaotic than its reputation. The choice for the remaining members of the Pogues seemed to be: watch the singer kill himself, since he was unwilling to act on his own behalf, or break up a collaboration that had become phenomenally successful. They tried for a while to find a third way.

Thereafter, Shane (who claims to have been fired) went off and formed his band the Popes, a roadhouse outfit with Irish inflections that never amounted to anything much. The remainder of the Pogues carried on for two albums, the second of which, *Pogue Mahone*, sounds like the Faces, in a good way, full of bluster and barrelhouse, but for all its competence could never be the Pogues, not as we once knew them, a band with historical vision, imagination, cultural longing, and very human passions and failings.

I lived on the Pogues for the first four or five years of my own sobriety, despite their besottedness, their dwindling into ignominy. There was no one else I liked as well, although I also investigated Van Morrison and, to some degree, Warren Zevon and Tom Waits. I failed to accept that Shane wouldn't do what he needed to do to continue making the astringent and luminous music he'd made earlier in his life. Perhaps because I'd done what I imagined he needed to do—get sober—and it didn't seem so impossible or even disagreeable. True, I had a few ideas about alcoholism and recognized that the sufferer didn't always have a choice. Relapse, as has often been said, is the order of the day. But I'd managed to claw my way to uncertain sobriety, and I thought Shane ought to have been up to it, and I was disappointed when he wasn't.

Why wasn't he? It *is* important to remember that Mac-Gowan, while born of Irish parents, was raised mainly in London, and his cherished construction of Irishness, the Irishness that's at the center of the Pogues oeuvre, the identity politics of the Pogues (if you will), is the *diaspora* version of Irish culture. A number of Pogues have said as much publicly. The Pogues, in re-creating Irish music in London, with Englishmen among them, were re-creating a lost thing, a compendium of Irish music for expatriates and second-generation Celts. What's the relationship between this diaspora and alcoholism, you ask? Well, alcoholism, in my view, is an *illness*, or at the very least alcoholism behaves like one, and though there is a significant likelihood that it is either genetic or that some disposition to its rigors is genetic, there's also the melancholy of diaspora, the loss implicit in expatriation. There is the nearly sacramental notion about drinking that is so central to this re-created Irish identity. Diaspora doesn't cause Irish alcoholism, but it certainly doesn't help. Irish civil conflict and terrorism—the Troubles—don't cause alcoholism, but they don't help. Viewed through the prism of these difficulties, the alcohol problem in the Pogues is more poignant (in addition to being an *illness*); it's about losing a culture, wanting to preserve it against great odds, and accepting self-destruction as a reasonable price to pay. This is the kind of Irishness that I sometimes feel in myself, the Irish American melancholy of my mother's side, the Flynn side.

When I've been in Ireland over the years (and I guess I have been a half-dozen times now), I've had the Pogues playing on my iPod like a soundtrack, as though they were the only way to articulate this sensation of returning to greensward and barren mountaintops, stone walls, sheep wandering everywhere. I always go scouring the local record stores looking for other Irish bands that offer this suspect, romantic essence of the Irish folk tradition that the Pogues convey, whether they want to or not. Back to the Clancy Brothers, or the Dubliners, for example, or Christy Moore, or even the Horslips or the Boomtown Rats. None of these bands has ever, for me, been quite as moving and reckless and incendiary. Not like the Pogues. As an Irish American (one with a lot of British and Scottish DNA in him too), I always feel like I can't put my finger on the soul of Eire, can't participate in it, can't be part of it. To my Irish acquaintances and friends, I'm always just another American coming over for holiday and buying a tin whistle to take back to New York.

On one such trip to Ireland, I happened to watch a documentary about Shane MacGowan, *If I Should Fall From Grace*. It was actually available on the flight over. This is noteworthy. Because Shane MacGowan, as depicted in the film, is a haunted, immobilized, all-but-incoherent husk of a man whose claim to fame seems tenuous, long past, and who, if the documentary is accurate, lives in a hovel with a long-suffering girlfriend and doesn't do that much besides, well, servicing his addiction. That Aer Lingus should consider this biography a legitimate promotional tool for Irish tourism is surprising, and yet in the end is this not what Irish culture is like, at least on occasion? Irish culture is full of paradoxes. For all its vestigial Catholic (or Protestant) conservatism, Ireland is ravaged by its unstoppable excesses. It's full of bitterness, mood disorders, self-slaughter. It tolerates more alcohol abuse than anyplace I have ever been on earth. And yet never does Ireland shrink from the acknowledgment of its shortcomings.

Shane, in *If I Should Fall From Grace*, the documentary, looks like he could weep bloody rivers at any moment, like he won't lift a nicotine-stained finger to prevent his next indignity, and just when you think you can't possibly feel any greater compassion for the man, he offers the kind of stinging vengefulness and offhanded arrogance that you would associate with an artist well aware of his gifts, or at least the gifts he once had. Shane is hopeless, vindictive, but very perceptive. He drinks continuously. That he is still alive, on the basis of the film, seems difficult to fathom. He's fifty-one, as I write these lines, but he looks fifteen or twenty years older, and he totters around stages like he could fall over at any moment. Which apparently he does.

Knowing all of this, knowing what I knew about the Pogues, having heard recordings of him in the latter days, mediocre recordings in which he can barely get through the lyrics and is incomprehensible during stage banter, I nonetheless greeted with enthusiasm the news that the Pogues had begun playing reunion gigs. Why? Because when you revere a band, when you have that fervent connection with a band, you always believe the romance can be renewed. As with absent lovers. There have been other rock-and-roll bands for me wherein the inevitable loss and heartbreak of being a fan has long been delayed. The Who, whom I saw play as recently as the last tour before John Entwistle's death. R.E.M., whom I kept expecting to be vivid and uncanny in the nineties and who just were not. Big Star, whose recent reunion album is one of the great disappointments among such efforts. With these experiences in mind, I had few illusions about the Pogues. I thought Shane would probably be awful. But the Pogues still seem to stand for something, not only for an idea of music, but for a culture. The Pogues are alien to what rock and roll is now, to something airbrushed, stylized, corporate.

So: on March 16, 2007, the four of us who had convened the night before got back in the line at Roseland to try *again* to see the Pogues play. Could the gig possibly come off as planned? We had our doubts. Still, upon our arrival, fashionably late, the opening band was to be heard in the distance, some indie rock aspirants whom we immediately recognized, in fact, from our own shows the prior fall. In The Hague. These guys had played there too. Nina Katchadourian had been forced to sit in front of these whippersnappers on the plane home, all of them unshaven, unwashed, none older than twenty-eight or -nine. Really strange to see these guys up on the stage before the Pogues, in a packed house, a house with the kind of great antic-ipatory nervousness that I don't often find at shows anymore.

And then the lights went down. Out the Pogues came. It was the whole band, understand, the band from its peak, all eight of them. Spider Stacy was the first to seize the micro-phone and to venture an overdue apology: "Sorry about last night. Shit happens." A mocking simulacrum, I suppose, of the rock-and-roll entrance. Then the band ventured into a couple of numbers to warm up the crowd, and the band was as tight as a band can be, full of cocksure vitality. Then, when the players were situated, exercised, and the crowd was ready, they *wheeled out* Shane. Yes, they wheeled him out in his *wheelchair.* There was a handler, a Shane handler, an old biker sort of a guy who seemed as though he wouldn't have been out of place at a Hawkwind reunion, and he was wheeling out the injured Shane MacGowan, as if Shane were some kind of gerontological specimen who could only be witnessed under controlled circumstances: *You see, ladies and gentlemen, there is no reason this man should be breathing.*

We'd managed to get close to the stage, stealthily, during the opening act. I'm not sure how we managed to accomplish this exactly, since the median age in our posse was probably forty-two and there were many other eager Pogues fans, kids from Bay Ridge and Bensonhurst, who'd probably come to the Pogues via the Dropkick Murphys, and they were more eager. Still, somehow we managed to get near, and the only problem was that once near you could see Shane's waxy gray pallor and his matted hair. Everybody else in the band looked pretty good. Older, to be sure, sporting a few extra pounds, but stylish and mean. Then there was Shane. When he tried to talk between songs, it's true, you couldn't understand one word of it. I don't know how the man chews. And there is a weird, ghostly cackle that issues forth from him when he's mumbled some one-liner that he finds particularly compelling. Something between a snicker and a seizure.

Very sad. Very hard to watch. Excruciating in some ways. But you know what? It was also an amazing show. Probably one of the best gigs I've seen in a few years. In fact, a number of nostalgic "reunion" gigs I've witnessed in the past three or four years were compelling: Rocket From the Tombs (featuring members of Pere Ubu and the Dead Boys, and Richard

Lloyd from Television), Red Krayola (in which David Grubbs, another member of my band, occasionally serves), even Aerosmith at Madison Square Garden a few years back. Fleetwood Mac at a big stadium event in Washington, DC. But the Pogues were better than all of these.

They played every song you would want them to play. Without remorse. All of the best stuff from *Rum Sodomy* and *If I Should Fall From Grace With God*. They played at their usual breakneck tempos. And the band were obviously having a great time, enjoying themselves, because they all got to take turns singing lead in order to permit Shane his frequent breaks. The audience knew every word and sang along ceaselessly. And, best of all, there was a churning, writhing mosh pit in front of the stage throughout. I don't know if people *mosh* to the Pogues in England, Ireland, Scotland, and Wales, but they do in New York City. The strategic decision for the older members of the audience was: *do we participate?*

Though I sound perhaps like an obsolete appliance in saying so, I did like to get into the pit when I was younger. Once upon a time. Moshing, pogoing, generally causing trouble. But the last show at which I really tried to mosh was a Ramones gig in the early nineties. Do people mosh at a show by the Animal Collective or Arcade Fire? The Ramones played by the numbers. I was wearing eyeglasses in those days, and I got worried about someone knocking my glasses off, and I moshed for a few songs and then I decided that I was too old for moshing.

Despite the fact that I am in my later forties, I somehow felt, on this memorable occasion, that I wanted to dip my toe into the maelstrom, just as, independently, my friends were being borne away into that undulating mass of Irish

Americans. Even Hannah Marcus, who doesn't have a punk rock past and who is Eastern European by extraction (in fact, our group consisted of two Jews, an Armenian, and an Irish American — a who's who of *diaspora*), drifted off into quarters where I couldn't see her any longer, except during the ballads.

I found, as I hadn't since my twenties, that the mosh pit is a caring and loving community. If someone falls, he is picked up. No pushing is more than affectionate, and when you are pushed you are invited, or even compelled, to push back. No one's ass gets grabbed nonconsensually, and when a song stops, so does the madness. From "A Pair of Brown Eyes" to "Thousands Are Sailing" to "Rainy Night in Soho," the Pogues played everything, and everyone got sweaty and covered in beer, even if they didn't drink, and they danced.

So why this horrible feeling the next day? What was this hangover feeling after the Pogues, when I hadn't drunk at all and had got to bed at a reasonable hour? Thus do we come to the subliminal layer of this essay, which is perhaps no longer subliminal at all.

Remember the common witticism about Eric Clapton, that he *played better high?* People have been saying this for a long time, that Clapton *played better high*, that the best Clapton shows were the ones in Cream when he was probably smacked out and drifting in some psychedelic blues-rock ether. Later, when he got clean, the theory goes, Clapton started recording the horrible pop songs like "Wonderful Tonight" and "Tears in Heaven." Personally, I don't like much Eric Clapton either way, no matter his cleanliness, or lack thereof, but whatever your feeling about him, the witticism is *inhumane.* Thoughtless.

Rude. Unfeeling. Historically shortsighted. Dim-witted, even. And it's not only Eric Clapton whose mythology is thus inscribed. How many great rock-and-roll personalities have been encouraged in their ability to self-immolate before the audience? Lots and lots. Certainly any number of punk rock icons: Sid Vicious, Iggy Pop, Stiv Bators, Johnny Thunders, Richard Hell, Kurt Cobain, Bob Stinson. Plenty of classic rock types: Jerry Garcia, Brian Jones, Keith Moon, Jim Morrison, Syd Barrett, Sandy Denny. I'm leaving out the cartoon players in their hair metal bands who all seemed to thrive only with needles in their arms. Nikki Sixx, e.g. Not to mention the jazz world: Miles Davis, John Coltrane, Billie Holiday. Did they all *play better high?* Did Miles Davis *play better high?* Is it possible to utter a sentence like that without being shamed by the perception?

The same conundrum presents itself in literature, where the examples are legion too. William Faulkner, F. Scott Fitzgerald, Ernest Hemingway, Dorothy Parker, John Berryman, John Cheever, Anne Sexton, Frederick Exley, Jack Kerouac, William S. Burroughs. Many, many others.

The problem with impairment, the problem it raises for the discerning enthusiast is: can you love the artist despite what he or she has become? Or must you love them in the process of unbecoming? Can you bear witness to impairment without participating in it? Is it possible to love the drunk and hate the drink? Recognizing the infirmity, can you love an artist nonetheless?

The problem of impairment gets more reflexive, and paradoxical, when you attempt to consider whether the work itself somehow *depends* on the intoxication. In the documentary *If I Should Fall From Grace*, Shane MacGowan's girlfriend, Victoria, says, "Maybe he was put here on earth to write about the experience of drinking." In just the way that Frederick Exley, in *A Fan's Notes*, has the one purpose only, the purpose of delineation and articulation of drink, and having discharged it magnificently, he was all but blocked from that point on. If Shane MacGowan is drunken precisely so that he can give the best rock-and-roll account of blackouts and cirrhosis and dementia, then have we a right to complain about his investigations? To lament them? Imagination would suffice, you'd think. Shane might have written "Boat Train," e.g., or "The Sunnyside of the Street," in which he boasts that he will never reform ("I will not be reconstructed / Just wanna stay right here / On the sunnyside of the street"), without having to destroy himself, his voice, his livelihood. But in this case, for reasons I cannot articulate, imagination did not, does not, will not suffice.

I met John Perry Barlow, lyricist for the Grateful Dead, once at a party, and I remember asking him about the band, because the band was still trudging along at that point, and I remember a cloud passing over his face. Someone told me later that evening that "everyone was worried about Jerry." What to do about Jerry? Jerry Garcia stayed on the road until he died of it, just as John Entwistle, who went into cardiac arrest in Las Vegas in the company of a stripper, died on the road, died from being an artist, died of the inability to do other than he had always done. The other members of the Grateful Dead couldn't do anything to stop Jerry, just as they hadn't been able to do anything to stop keyboardist and vocalist Pigpen McKernan, who predeceased him.

And if the extended Pogues family can do nothing about

Shane, we can rest assured that the casual fan, or even the extremely partisan fan, can do nothing either. But it makes the experience of watching the Pogues perform a bittersweet thing. I, for one, don't think anyone ever, at any time, has made their best work high. I think people have made great work *despite* their shortcomings. I think most artists make their best work when they are sober, well-rested, and able to take in the complications and crosscurrents of the world around them. And these artists will make more of the work we revere them for if they aren't poisoning themselves day after day.

Impairment, in the end, knows best the drama of itself. The truth about Shane MacGowan's lyrics is that by the end they stopped conveying the Irish heartbreak they had in the earlier records. They became mannered, silly, occasionally even embarrassing. As in all cases of impairment, what I hear after a point is the *illness* talking, and what the illness says is that it has seized control of the organism, and the organism henceforth will not have volition as regards its wishes, its ambitions. And now when you hear the organism speak, not to mention when the organism makes its art, you will hear this other voice, and therefore the organism has these *two voices*, and the two voices are the voices of the organism and of the *illness*, and the *illness* may be forced, where its needs are not being met, to cause the organism to dissemble, to act contrary to itself, to berate loved ones, to neglect itself, to confuse things deliberately; the *illness* may even cause the organism to *fail*, generally speaking, because the *illness* requires that the organism first attend to the requirements of the *illness*, and only when there is time left over (and there is less and less time left over), can the organism concern itself with the facts of its daily life. What is this thing that inhabits me but is not myself? Which is somehow inimical to myself? Let's not romanticize the travails of the organism, yes, but neither should we shrink from an honest appraisal of the organism's impaired state. It is not that we want to *watch*, nor that in watching we are complicit, but that sublimity is such a rare thing that we ought to honor it even when the artificer is unable to do so himself.

The New York Underground, 1965–1988

1. The Dream Syndicate

What's so "underground" about the underground? What is it about the word that makes it so attractive and so inadequate, especially in the arts, especially with respect to music in particular? The term, as we use it now, has its origins in politics, in, for example, the German resistance;* but we also have the Underground Railroad, the network that sheltered runaway slaves, the nomenclature of which dates back to the middle of the nineteenth century or even earlier. There's a Latinate version of the same concept in the word *subterranean*, which appears in English at about 1600, roughly contemporaneous with the Anglo-Saxon usage conjoining *under* and *ground*, about 1571. It would seem, therefore, that the concept of the *underground* dates back nearly as far as the notion of people

---

* See, e.g., http://www.etymonline.com/index.php?search=underground&searchmode=none, etc.

standing on the earth's surface, in the light, among a confraternity. It would seem that though there is life and community happening here in the world as we know it, there's always, too, a sense of things happening *beneath* the civilized surface. The underground, that is, is *counternarrative*, or *counterculture*, constituting itself in a different history, an alternative genealogy, a worldview that is other. And when you think about "underground" this way, you have to think about it as a philosophical or even psychological concept as well, as a relief from the constraints and the preoccupations of the arts as they are more superficially understood.

And so: New York City has always operated both as a hub for rock and roll and as an outpost in the resistance movement to its constraints. That's part of what makes it attractive for musicians: it's for *and* against. And it's this way, as we'll see, because New York City has always featured a thriving civic multiculturalism, not only in the political sense, through its waves of immigration and in its international feel, but also in the way in which the city lives with and in "high" art, with and in the avant-garde and the experimental. Rock and roll in New York City, therefore, has always been responsive to all this, to politics and art and indigenous forms of music (whether local or from abroad), and as a result it has never been very good at the kind of world-class meat-and-potatoes rock and roll that characterizes, say, Los Angeles or Detroit. This despite the fact that a lot of the record business has been located there. New York City, I mean, by reason of its diverse cultures and interests, its unusual stew of influences, would be unlikely to produce Van Halen. Or the Eagles. It's not a predictable-enough place. My constructed lineage of New York underground music probably begins right at the beginning of rock and roll itself, right at the moment of the birth of the form, so that the resistance to rock and roll is coincident with the instant of its inception. If not *before*—because from the moment when rock and roll was getting up its head of steam, New York City was operating as one of the citadels of the folk music revival. Bob Dylan played in Greenwich Village (in 1961 to 1962), for example, in a scene well established with acts like the Clancy Brothers, Dave Van Ronk, Mimi and Richard Fariña, and Joan Baez. The folk scene eventually succumbed to its internal contradictions, its ahistorical paradoxes,* swallowed up by more adulterated forms, by folk rock and then by rock and roll. True, for a while there was a "pure" version of folk, which involved some kind of devotion to the music examples of Appalachia, to the Mississippi Delta, conceived in opposition to mainstream music acts. This oppositional approach had one foot in New York City (on West 4th Street, and Bleecker Street, where the clubs were), through the folk exegetes Pete Seeger, Alan Lomax, Harry Smith, etc., as well as in the voices of the Beat period (who knew their jazz *and* their old time), who celebrated what was old and intuitive, and when this folk music transmuted itself into something like folk rock or "psychedelic" music in the mid- and later sixties,

---

* Since it couldn't be the *original* folk music, in the same way that the Italian Renaissance couldn't be identical with the Greek classical period, at some point it was doomed to be played on electric guitars and recorded in multiple tracks at fancy studios. And thus Dylan's Newport Folk Festival appearance of 1965.

some of its great progenitors also hailed from here, from New York (I'm thinking, for example, of the Fugs and the Holy Modal Rounders).

Rock and roll would seem, that is, to have one foot in folk and blues, in the devotion to the traditional, and, paradoxically, it got some portion of this traditional material from New York. Who would have thought, though, that another point of origin for underground NYC rock and roll of the late sixties would have been not a folk icon, nor a jazz great, nor even a doo-wop singer, of which New York had many in abundance, but a serious music composer called La Monte Young? Young was born (in 1935) into a Mormon family in Bern, Idaho, and he was trained in composition at UCLA and UC Berkeley—though he also did a stint under the tutelage of German composer Karlheinz Stockhausen. He corresponded at some length with John Cage, whose advice bore upon a number of Young compositions involving *indeterminacy* during the first part of the Fluxus movement. Then, in the early sixties, La Monte Young heard his calling and began experimenting with frequency and pitch duration (among the compositions of this period is the fancifully titled *The Tortoise Recalling the Drone of the Holy Numbers as They Were Revealed in the Dreams of the Whirlwind and the Obsidian Gong and Illuminated by the Sawmill, the Green Sawtooth Ocelot and the High-Tension Line Stepdown Transformer*). Here extremely *long* durations were the norm. Some of the compositions are even meant to be continuous—as in never ceasing. Many of these pieces, by reputation, became early classics of the so-called minimalist movement in classical music.

It all sounds very serious, and it is. Should you ever have

occasion to read Young's composition notes, which are often novella length and have much reference to the numerological and the obscure, you will grasp the extent of his ambition. And yet coterminous with this seriousness, in the mid-sixties, Young began playing in (and composing for, according to the composer)* an ensemble consisting of himself; his partner, Marian Zazeela (vocalist); Tony Conrad; and John Cale (violin and viola, respectively). Many of the pieces that resulted were in *just intonation*, a tuning standard that emphasizes exact harmonic intervals between notes instead of the fudged intervals of western tunings. For this reason, because of this tuning system, the pieces involved a level of technical sophistication (i.e., one had to be able to sing a perfect harmonic interval, or play one on a violin, and, therefore, one had to be able to *hear* it, despite being accustomed to western tuning from a lifetime of concerts and recordings), but they also offered a stunning and immediate result: overtones. The overtone sequences that result from just intonation are that much more audible and that much more beautiful than we normally expect from our conventional tuning standard.

The underground-rock-and-roll part of the story begins here with John Cale, violist, in the aforementioned ensemble, variously known as The Theatre of Eternal Music and The

---

* The facts here are a matter of great debate between Young, on the one hand, and John Cale and Tony Conrad on the other. It is hard to imagine how a composition of *one note* is still a composition, although Young does claim to have chosen the note. Cale and Conrad say that the music in their ensemble amounted to group improvisation. There's much to read about this controversy for interested parties. And for an example of the music, try *Inside the Dream Syndicate* (Table of the Elements, 2005).

Dream Syndicate (depending on whom you believe). John Cale, in Young's ensemble, got very good at a certain style of playing; he got good at a provocative attitude with respect to volume and the audience. Cale had been studying serious classical music, it should be said, and had even won an Aaron Copland fellowship to Tanglewood in the mid-sixties, though he didn't get along with that master of Americana very well—according to legend, Copland wouldn't allow Cale's compositions to be played because he worried about his piano being damaged. Cale, that is, was well schooled in the rigors of classical music. And yet just as he was learning the avant-garde drone in La Monte Young's ensemble, he was getting to know Lou Reed, a young songwriter and aspiring poet who had been educated at Syracuse University and who was writing rock-and-roll songs that droned in a way not at all dissimilar.

In fact, Cale sat in on one of Reed's first recordings, a composition called "The Ostrich," at which Reed allegedly tuned all his guitar strings to *one note*.* Cale no doubt recognized a kindred spirit. One of the collaborators in The Theater of Eternal Music was a percussionist called Angus MacLise. MacLise made compositions for shortwave static and echo and other electronic effects. Soon he too was drafted into the nascent lineup of the band composed of Reed and Cale, as was Sterling Morrison, a friend of Lou Reed's from Syracuse. This early edition of the Velvet Underground, therefore, was half

---

* See, for example, http://wapedia.mobi/en/Lou_Reed/ and http://en.wikipedia.org/wiki/Lou_Reed.

about the classical and experimental musical investigation and half about the rock-and-roll primitivism.

As to the lyrics: Lou Reed had been studying writing at Syracuse with the great poet and short-story writer Delmore Schwartz. Schwartz himself was near the end of an illustrious career, and apparently his principal relevance to Reed was in encouraging him to use his colloquial narratorial voice. Reed's attachment to the underground literary sources was along similar lines: Nelson Algren's *The Man with the Golden Arm*, Leopold von Sacher-Masoch, the Marquis de Sade, William S. Burroughs, and so on. These inflammatory interests are manifest in the lyrical approach to the songs by the early Velvet Underground, all of them in a very American tongue. Heroin and masochism were atypical subject matter for rock and roll, which more often dealt with girls and cars. These lyrics were dark. When Angus MacLise was passed over for the drumming seat and the Velvets instead drafted in non-drummer Maureen Tucker, the younger sister of a friend of Sterling Morrison's, the sound began to duplicate the bluntness of the lyrics. It was propulsive, uncompromising, and overwhelming.

There's still another *underground* part of this story, and that concerns Andy Warhol's influence on the band's early development. According to most accounts, the Velvets had played a very few gigs, during which they had mainly confused and repelled audiences (in 1964 to 1965), before Warhol happened upon them at a club. Perhaps he had heard something of the group, since Billy Name, Warhol Factory acolyte, was also known to play occasionally in The Theatre of Eternal Music. Whatever the cause for the first encounter, once Warhol saw the Velvets, he immediately enlisted them into the "happenings" with which he was touring the country in 1966, the Exploding Plastic Inevitable.

Happenings? They were performance art before there was performance art; they were light shows and projections and dancers. Warhol was restless about genre and had been making paintings and films, and (later) books and magazines, and there was nothing that he was unwilling to try. It was natural that he should work synergistically with live performance, with a band. In this case, he would persuade the band to use a European model as their lead singer (thus the Velvet Underground and Nico) and to write some songs that this model might sing. The early reviews of the Exploding Plastic Inevitable were uncomprehending, somewhat malicious, but the Velvet Underground made the most of their touring experience and honed songs like "Heroin," "I'm Waiting for the Man," and "The Black Angel's Death Song," in which Cale's avant-garde viola and Reed's very simple Buddy Holly–oriented song structures merged into one dark, unrelenting vision of life in the city. Whether New York returned the love, initially, is another matter. But on the first album, *The Velvet Underground & Nico*, everything came together, the disparate creative intentions, the high and low, the artful and the musical, the literary and the quotidian—and the only surprise was that no one had thought to merge these base metals before.

As Brian Eno has famously noted, *The Velvet Underground & Nico* didn't sell well, but nearly everyone who bought it started a band. How would rock and roll sound now if this record had never been recorded? There were the Mothers of Invention in 1966, and there were the Byrds, and there were the aforementioned Fugs, and there was the poet from Minnesota called Zimmerman, who was just getting friendly with his electric guitar, but none of these artists balanced such a catholic range of influences in the same way, with the same dynamism and the same brutality.

It's probably a fact of creativity that this sort of ingenuity can't last. Lou Reed has always been restless, as even a brief look at his solo output will make clear. In the forty years since the Velvets broke up, he has gone from pop to white funk* to minimalism to glam to punk to jazz to chanson to straight-ahead rock and roll, with nothing much connecting the projects except the instantaneity of the lyrics and the refusal to compromise. The Velvets, in a similar way, were not exactly consistent, and by the time they were finishing the second album, Nico and Warhol were gone and John Cale was about to be furloughed as well, at the urging of the Velvets' manager. Like some short-lived radioactive element, the Velvets did what they needed to do very quickly, and although Sterling Morrison once remarked that the friction between Reed and Cale was somewhat overstated, it's hard to see Cale, the Welsh-born (and, originally, Welsh-speaking) classicist and Reed, the Brooklyn-born rock-and-roll primitive, seeing eye to eye for very long.

White Light/White Heat, the second album, set aside the gentle moments of *The Velvet Underground & Nico* and went straight for the noise, even dispensing with song structure in the process, the main result being "Sister Ray," which at seventeen minutes (and edited down, according to various sources)

---

* His own idea thereof, on *The Bells* and on the electric side of *Street Hassle*.

was a harbinger of a later notion—the album-oriented composition—whose time had not yet come. One groove, one riff, lyrics probably improvised or composed on the road during the process of repetition, and with a theme devoted to the excesses of a particular high ("I'm searching for my mainline"), "Sister Ray" toyed with audiences, toyed with what might have been expected from a rock-and-roll album, and in the process all but thumbed its nose at mainstream success.

Underground, indeed. The Doors got more credit for this sort of approach (in "The End," e.g.), and there's no reason to talk down the Doors. When the dust had settled and Jim Morrison was dead, the Doors appeared to be a very unsettling and interesting band. But "The End" is positively middle-of-the-road compared to the *underground* qualities of "Sister Ray." Let's consider the lyrics, for example, such as they are. Is it about a nun? A transvestite? A sibling? And how does the opiated part figure into it? Is it just about the *sound* of certain words? Eventually, the lyrics are swept aside by the unyielding immediacy of the groove, as convected by Maureen Tucker and Sterling Morrison. There's something intensely sexual about the song, as though it's as much about the groove as a funk song from the late sixties might have been, some kind of experimental refraction of James Brown—but mainly the thing just keeps going, flattening preconceptions, and it has to keep going; at thirty minutes it would have made more sense, been more conceptually rigorous, but there was no real precedent for seventeen minutes on the long-playing format, let alone thirty or forty.

And yet the working conditions were too brutal! Reed and Cale parted ways, and Reed drafted into the band a young player named Doug Yule. There was nothing unconvincing about Doug Yule. He was a very professional musician, with a nice voice. And since Lou couldn't go on singing the way he did every night, someone had to sing some of the prettier songs, and prettier songs there were in abundance on the third album, *The Velvet Underground*, which contained the germinating seeds for much of the indie-rock revolution of the eighties and nineties on songs like "Pale Blue Eyes" and "Candy Says." This was a very different band. There were some similarities, but this was a more accessible band, a band with less at stake. The lyrics still demonstrated an inability to mince words, and when compared with what was happening elsewhere in the American popular song, the Velvets still seemed like they were adorned with the grime and attitude of New York City. Nevertheless, what was *underground* about the band was beginning to feel less so, and this would be even more the case on their final studio album, *Loaded*.

Loaded is a rock-and-roll album at the behest of a record label,* and at the advent of its release toward the end of 1970, Lou Reed himself was on the verge of leaving, having nonetheless written and recorded "Sweet Jane" and "Rock & Roll," two of the best rock songs ever written in New York City or recorded by a New York City band. The album was indeed *loaded with hits*, but perhaps somewhat to the detriment of

---

* Atlantic, being the label that signed them at the end but without supporting them much beyond lobbying for hits. Here's Doug Yule on the subject: "On *Loaded* there was a big push to produce a hit single, there was that mentality."

what made the Velvet Underground underground in the first place.*

They came from the demimonde, from the drugs and sexual license of the Factory crowd, from the otherworldly drones of serious experimental music. But maybe what is most *underground* about the *underground* is the way in which, in the end, its boundaries are in dispute, so that what's above and what's below are always up for debate. Nirvana is a punk band one year, and the next year Nirvana is the most popular band in the world. Could they really be both things? The Velvets didn't become popular in their creative lifetime (the crowds at their reunion gigs in the early nineties were a lot bigger than the crowds that first saw them perform), but they were *influential*. Arguably, they were as influential as any band performing in the late sixties.

Sterling Morrison went on to teach at the University of Texas, Maureen Tucker became a mom, John Cale produced, became an A&R guy, and made at least one absolutely perfect solo album (*Paris 1919*) that had nothing at all in common with the Velvets, and Lou Reed became synonymous with New York rock and roll: unpredictable, impolite, cynical, ambitious, artful, relentless. He promoted the idea, on occasion, that the Velvets were nothing but his backup band, proof enough that he had long since traveled out of the underground.

---

* I'm not the only one to feel this apparent contradiction, that it's a great rock-and-roll album but in a way, not a perfect Velvet Underground album. Here's Lenny Kaye, future Patti Smith Group member, writing in *Rolling Stone* in 1970: "Yet as good as *Loaded* is (and as far as I'm concerned, it's easily one of the best albums to show up this or any year), there are some minor problems which tend to take away from its overall achievement. Namely, and whether it's the fault of the mix or the production is hard to say, it feels as if many of the harder songs on the album lack punch."

There was, as I've said, a brief Velvets reunion in the early 1990s, in the midst of which Cale sent Reed a nine-page fax, detailing a great number of complaints, on behalf of himself and the others, and that, apparently, was the end of the rapprochement.* Which is to say: light and dark, simple and complex, sacred and profane, full of conflict at all times and in all places, and frequently reviled at the time of their most indelible accomplishment, the Velvet Underground are where underground New York begins, and begins, in fact, in almost total neglect. Nothing that any of the members have done since, and they have done a great deal, exceeds the influence of these early underground releases.

2. Personality Crisis

We've neglected the *name* of the Velvet Underground. Where did it come from? And what did the Velvets think they meant by it? Apparently, the title came from a book given to the band by Tony Conrad, violinist in La Monte Young's Theatre of Eternal Music. *The Velvet Underground*, by Michael Leigh, is a pulpy account of the concealed sexuality beneath the pristine surfaces of the suburbs, and the band long trafficked in the associations that came with this volume and its title. If the

---

* Cale, from his autobiography *What's Welsh for Zen* (Bloomsbury, 2000): "Although we realized that the work was being damaged by the fury of the moment, we had not reached a sufficiently enlightened state of consciousness to see the error of our ways. There were many blow-ups. I'm sure there will be many more. The fax machine should really be taken away from Lou and me" (p. 253).

Velvets weren't quite as preoccupied with sexual transgression after *White Light/White Heat* (not as preoccupied, for example, as Reed was himself on *Transformer* and *Coney Island Baby*), their legions of imitators took much from the implications of the name, and from the reputation for sexual frankness of the band that wrote "Venus in Furs" and "Sister Ray."

By the time the Velvet Underground played at Max's Kansas City in August 1970, after mostly avoiding their hometown for some years (by reason of a perceived lack of loyalty), they were legendary among their small but vital fan base, in part because of the sex and drugs of their more *underground* work. With Doug Yule on bass and Billy Yule on drums (Maureen Tucker was on pregnancy leave), the late-period Max's show featured only Lou Reed and Sterling Morrison from the original Velvets. They demonstrated their beautiful guitar interplay, but they lacked the dramatic contrast of the band's early lineup. Max's had its share of celebrities in attendance, and it was Brigid Polk, from Warhol's Factory, who taped the show, using some handheld recording device that was nearly as effective at picking up the crowd sounds as it was at picking up the music. Sterling Morrison has commented that the people talking on the live recording of this show are as interesting as the music—among these, allegedly, Jim Carroll, talking about scoring drugs.

Max's, then, even if it wasn't a great place to hear the Velvets anymore, *was* a great place to hear music, and was known as a "glam" rock hangout, which means that David Bowie went there, as Lou did, as Iggy Pop occasionally did. Among the cognoscenti of Max's, the venue went downhill after they opened the "disco" upstairs. The *back room*, where everyone wanted to have sex with everyone (see Legs McNeil and Gillian McCain's *Please Kill Me* for more refreshing terminology), lost some of its cachet. Even one of the least glam of all rock-and-roll acts of the early seventies played Max's in 1972, namely the young Bruce Springsteen. To put it another way, a more democratic way: once the *discotheque* part of Max's Kansas City was open, there was an opportunity for kids from the outer boroughs and from New Jersey and Long Island to experience the artier and more esoteric, in short, the more *underground*, part of the underground, and so Debbie Harry, who worked at Max's, was getting ready to become Debbie Harry, the singer of Blondie, and David Johansen and Johnny Thunders of the New York Dolls were also, on occasion, in the audience.

This latter pair was part of a gang of overdressed rock-and-roll miscreants from Queens and the Bronx. Their band, the New York Dolls, was originally convened by Thunders and Billy Murcia, the drummer who died during the band's first tour in England. Thunders and Murcia added Arthur Kane on bass and Syl Sylvain on rhythm guitar, and, when Thunders no longer wanted to be the front man, David Johansen as singer. The Dolls, according to their own version of the story, got their name from a business situated across the street from the general-merchandise store where Sylvain and Murcia worked as teenagers, viz., the New York Doll Hospital.

Max's Kansas City was one point of origin for a rock-and-roll band that found it entirely reasonable to dress like transvestites, or women of the oldest profession, while playing in a style hitherto more noteworthy for protestations of masculinity. But there were other influences. There were the post-Velvets bands, like the MC5 and, above all, the Stooges. And there was also, arguably, a relationship between the flamboyant culture of Max's Kansas City and the Stonewall riots of 1969, in which gays and lesbians in Greenwich Village began to fight back against selective persecution and entrapment by the New York City Police Department. The rights of the gay underground in the city were in the process of being secured, and with this came a great liberalization in the matter of art and culture and sexual expression, with less fear of persecution. This liberalization, slower to take hold in the outer boroughs, attracted to Manhattan upstarts and outcasts of every type. Manhattan was more forgiving. This liberalization, this tolerance, was perhaps under way before Stonewall but found its culmination in that moment, and the effect was felt far and wide in the culture of the city, in, for example, the early collages of Robert Mapplethorpe, in the Continental Baths of the Ansonia Hotel (which opened in 1968), where Bette Midler got her start, in the gay pride marches that followed Stonewall annually, and in the Greenwich Village Halloween Parade, which began in earnest in 1973.

There was also the avant-garde theater movement in the village, a movement that often burlesqued and celebrated the vitality of gay culture. John Vaccaro and Charles Ludlam were two playwrights associated, early on, with Warhol, but who later went on to found the Theatre of the Ridiculous and offshoots thereof. For their subject matter, these downtown plays depended on chewing up and spitting out popular culture, particularly the more melodramatic and excessive aspects of pop culture, and they included, as a matter of course, lots of cross-dressing and transgender imagery. Indeed, in Charles Ludlam's case, that was an essential part of the project, as in plays like *When Queens Collide* and *Camille*. John Vaccaro had a slightly more pantheistic or polyglot quality to his outrageousness, as Leee Childers remarked (in *Please Kill Me*):

> John Vaccaro was dangerous. John Vaccaro could be very embarrassing on many levels. He used thalidomide babies and Siamese triplets joined together at the asshole. One actor had this huge papier-mâché prop of a big cock coming out of his shorts, down to his knees. He also couldn't control his bowel movements, so shit was dripping down his legs the whole time and everyone loved it. People loved this kind of visually confrontational theater.

David Johansen, among others,* appeared in one of these plays, as a "spear carrier," though he wasn't given a leading role because he was straight. Or so the story goes.

The Dolls imported a generous helping of this downtown theatrical excess into their performances, if without altering the surface of rock and roll to do so. In fact, the Dolls were given to covering rock-and-roll chestnuts like "(There's Gonna Be A) Showdown," and "Don't Start Me Talking," all in their seat-of-the-pants style. In the end, there was not terribly much that was new about the *music*. They played the changes. Johnny

---

* Patti Smith being among the others. She appeared downtown in a play by Jackie Curtis entitled *Femme Fatale*.

Thunders recycled Chuck Berry riffs, if in a way that sounded as though he knew that the first take was the best take. The rhythm section was by the book. Still, in part because of the unpredictability of Thunders, and because of Johansen's incredible energy, not to mention the sturdy rhythm playing of Syl Sylvain, the band operated as a gleeful demolition machine for everything that was pompous and stiff. Remember: *New York Dolls*, the first of their two albums, came out at about the same time as Elton John's most well-known hits, or the high period of Emerson, Lake and Palmer. These recording artists sounded totally laughable after a few minutes spent with "Trash" or "Babylon" or, of course, "Personality Crisis," one of the undisputed classics of early New York underground music. The lyrics of "Personality Crisis," to the extent that the Dolls' lyrics are decipherable, seem to have to do with drugs and celebrity and sexual uncertainty, and, one supposes, the way in which the *parents* of various Dolls worried as to how their kids, dressed in this particular way, were going to make out professionally. Amazingly, there's even a little piano on the track, a sloppily played barrelhouse part, presumably added by the producer of the album, Todd Rundgren, who insisted, in retrospect, that he just *turned on the tape machine*. All this mayhem in pursuit of the one-four-five chord progression, many, many repetitions thereof. By dwelling on the song's structure I fail to celebrate its magnificence, and it is magnificent and I should celebrate it. There are, for example, Johansen's double-tracked vocals, so memorable on lines like "All those times you butterflied about (you was *butterflyin'*)." And there are Thunders's sloppy squeals of lead guitar. Not terribly complicated, and yet full of joy and impossible to duplicate—though many have tried.

Soon, however, despite their legitimate and indisputable energy and their instinct for transgression, the Dolls lost the edge they had, and by the time that Malcolm McLaren (future manager of the Sex Pistols) came from London to oversee an ersatz *communist* period of the Dolls (they performed in front of flags featuring the hammer and sickle), they were already well on their way to falling apart. The last straw seemed to involve the difficulty in procuring heroin for Johnny Thunders and Jerry Nolan (drummer in the band after Billy Murcia) while on tour in the American South. And so the band splintered in 1975, whereupon Sylvain and Johansen went in one direction and Thunders and Nolan in another. Arthur Kane, the alcohol-afflicted bass player, ultimately sobered up and became a Mormon (and for a very tender evocation of this story, see *New York Doll*, a film about Kane's trip to play with a reconstituted version of the New York Dolls in 2004), after which he passed away suddenly of leukemia.

One last piece of the story is worth noting, and that is the piece in which we observe that both Sylvain and Murcia, founding members of the Dolls, were recent American immigrants. Sylvain's family were Egyptian Jews, from which part of the world Sylvain emigrated as a very young person, coming in past the Statue of Liberty. Murcia's family, meanwhile, came from Colombia. Though the New York Dolls seemed anything but political, even in their communist days, that layer of geopolitics hovered beneath the fabulous artifice of this legitimately beloved New York band. Syl Sylvain's family was persecuted in the Middle East, and they came to New York City, according to some American dream, where their son learned to wear makeup and play some of the most spirited rock and roll of the seventies. (And we should note that he's playing in the twenty-first century, too, because as of this writing he and Johansen have been playing with a revived version of the Dolls for four years.)

The recipe here, of flamboyant and unrepentant rock and roll that didn't break with tradition as regards the song structures but which lyrically still managed to provoke and charm, became an important formula for some of the music that followed the New York Dolls, one example being not at all as well known as it ought, namely, the Dictators, the protopunk band that would in turn influence legions of others (the Misfits, the Queers, Flipper, and so on). Another example would be Kiss, who stole all of the makeup from the Dolls and then some, recycled the guitar riffs of the Dictators and the Dolls, and made something that was about as crass and *not* underground as you could get. Kiss, who at one time legendarily shared a rehearsal room with the Dolls (when Gene Simmons et al. played *country and western*), created a multinational merchandising juggernaut! The Dictators, on the other hand, remained underground, mostly local, and carved out their reputation on records like *Go Girl Crazy!* They were (and are, as they still play the occasional reunion gig) decidedly masculine in a way the Dolls couldn't and wouldn't be, with their reliance on a very simple roster of chords and some blustery but charming early-seventies lead guitar stylings. While the Dictators' lyrics were often very funny, meanwhile (and the interested listener is encouraged to check out "Back to Africa" or "Teengenerate"), the Dictators had genuine chops of the garage rock sort, and some pop instincts besides. (They covered "I Got You Babe.") For all that, their tour bus still said *The Bronx* on its mudflaps.

3. The Municipal Assistance Corporation

In 1975, New York City was teetering on the precipice of bankruptcy. It's important to remember that whatever "punk" refers to, if it refers to anything, punk was happening against this backdrop of political failure and fiscal hardship. New York City was, except in isolated cases, poor. Manhattan was not the mecca of global franchising that it is now. The East Village and the Lower East Side were neighborhoods noteworthy for privation and, in the case of the Bowery, where CBGB's was located, indigent people living in extreme circumstances. The city could not meet its bills, could barely provide city services, and if Felix Rohatyn and others had not come up with the Municipal Assistance Corporation (a.k.a. Big MAC) to issue bonds and finance the shortfalls, things could have become quite a bit worse. When friends of mine who lived through this time in the city's history speak of it in retrospect, it's always about *the trash.** The trash! It piled up so that the sidewalks were barricaded in with black plastic. A friend told me of a restaurant in the Village that, one December, had so much trash out front that they decided to outline the mounds in Christmas lights. The accounts are legion. And what about the

---

* Also the title of a great song by the New York Dolls.

subway? Mass transit? It was the beginning of subway tagging, which is another story entirely, but besides being covered in Day-Glo spray paint, the subways were un-air-conditioned, frequently malfunctioning, overcrowded, dangerous. Track fires were the rage.

The federal government, in the person of one Gerald Ford, was unwilling to step in to help (thus the famous *New York Daily News* headline of the day: "Ford to City: Drop Dead"), and so the economic struggle lingered, notwithstanding Big MAC. In the daily lives of New Yorkers, it may have seemed that this was business as usual, that the breakdown of services and widespread crime, petty and otherwise, were part of civic life. But by today's standards, the city was remarkably unstable. This was the essential backdrop for what happened in music in the mid-seventies in New York City (both in the black music revolution that was about to emerge from the projects and in the underground music of lower Manhattan). But it was not the only influence on that moment. There was also poetry.

The poetry scene in New York dates back to the Beats, really, and thus to jazz and folk and the Vietnam protests of the late sixties, to the coffeehouses that were part of that beatnik time and after. The popularity of poetry was in evidence during the folk music revival (Bob Dylan, e.g.), but during the late sixties and early seventies the emblem of poetry in New York City was the St. Mark's Church Poetry Project. The Poetry Project was founded in 1966, and Ted Berrigan and Allen Ginsberg were its original leading lights, though many other great poets have been involved (Anne Waldman, to note a very compelling example). Over the years, the church welcomed nearly any approach to words on paper, the experimental as well as the accessible. But it was the street-oriented and performance model of American poetry that most succeeded there. Ginsberg was an early progenitor not only with epic works like "Howl" but with his later more political work as well. The political and confrontational aspect of Ginsberg was essential to the church's vision of itself as a poetry institution. Many a protest started nearby and moved outward into the city. As Luc Sante noted in his history of the ferment of the East Village,* anarchism in the late nineteenth century was just as reliably located in nearby Tompkins Square Park. The Poetry Project was especially situated to drink deeply of that antiestablishment stratum of New York history. And it did.

The Poetry Project was developmentally essential for many a downtown artist, therefore, especially Patricia Lee Smith. Patti Smith grew up in Philadelphia and in southern New Jersey, in a devout household of Jehovah's Witnesses. But as soon as she was able, she made her way north to the city, where she was a regular at Max's, sometimes even *outside* when she was unable to gain admission. But as much as at Max's, Smith learned to articulate her singularly ecstatic performance style from the poetry world. Smith's early gigs, in fact, were at the St. Mark's Poetry Project, where, after a time, she began to use accompaniment alongside her readings. The accompanists were frequently Lenny Kaye, on guitar, himself a rock critic (and later the noted compiler of the *Nuggets* anthology of sixties garage rock), and Richard Sohl, a particularly lyrical

---

* *Low Life: Lures and Snares of Old New York* (Farrar, Straus & Giroux, 1990).

downtown pianist. It's worth remembering here that there was no rhythm section at first, so that Smith was borrowing a potent symbol of rock and roll (the electric guitar) and a melodic vocabulary without quite giving herself entirely to the idiom. The electric guitar must have been startling at a poetry reading (at, for example, Smith's St. Mark's reading of 1971), but it indicated that Smith was making the transition from poetry to music very carefully. The words were out front and were meant to be out front. The cacophonous part of rock and roll, the swaggering part, came later.

Smith's first songs, insofar as these compositions were songs, borrowed harmonically from the oldest rock forms, from sixties pop,* and fused these pop structures with much more arcane, and evocative, lyrical compositions, some of them improvised. The verses went on as long as they needed to go on; there was no rigid verse, verse, chorus superstructure. Of these songs, "Gloria," which begins "Jesus died for somebody's sins but not mine," has to be the most notable. With it, with this line, Smith put herself on the map. She wasn't quite yet a rock-and-roll *personality*, since she was still a poet with guitar accompaniment, as of 1974. But she was close.

Smith was romantically involved, in the early period of her performances, with Allen Lanier of Blue Öyster Cult (and may even have been considered a possibility for lead vocalist in the band). And BÖC, which had not yet given itself to the mainstream with "Don't Fear the Reaper," was an interesting lens

---

* John Rockwell, quoted in Victor Bockris and Roberta Bayley, *Patti Smith: An Unauthorized Biography* (Simon & Schuster, 1999): "All eight songs [on *Horses*] betray a loving fascination with the oldies of rock.... The music just sounds like something you might have heard before" (p. 135).

through which to see some of the rigors of band life up close. They were making gleeful parody of the excesses of rock and roll, and had Richard Meltzer, the philosopher king of rock critics,* on board as a lyricist. Perhaps it was after watching Lanier that Smith felt her ecstatic conception of performance wouldn't be complete without bass and drums.

She was also a close friend and sometime lover of photographer Robert Mapplethorpe, who took many of the early images of her, chief among them the photo that adorned *Horses*. Mapplethorpe later became a provocateur with his iconic images of gay life, and some of his capacity to provoke and create controversy found analogue in Smith's presentation. They were lovers, they were collaborators, they influenced each other. Mapplethorpe paid for the first Patti Smith single, "Hey Joe" b/w "Piss Factory," the latter of which concerned Smith's professional career prior to her incarnation as poet-artist-singer, at a toy factory. (Her father had also worked at a Honeywell factory, and, therefore, like those of so many of the musicians in this story, her working-class roots are genuine.) With this stew of influences at hand—the high art of Mapplethorpe, the working-class experience in the toy factory, the rarified poetry world of the St. Mark's Poetry Project, and the old three-chord rock and roll that she loved—the Patti Smith of *Horses* was ready to begin playing the songs live.

Among Smith's other acquaintances in the New York "underground" scene of the mid-seventies was Tom Verlaine

---

* His *Aesthetics of Rock* is maybe the single greatest book ever written about the meanings of rock and roll and trumps even Lester Bangs and Greil Marcus for sheer dogged interpretive thoroughness.

of the band Television. Where Smith, lyrically, was influenced by stealing a copy of Rimbaud's poems from a bookstore while she was working at the toy factory, Verlaine was more obsessed with Rimbaud's onetime lover, after whom he named himself, the poet Paul Verlaine. The guitarist, born Tom Miller, grew up in Delaware and came to New York as a student of poetry and music (he'd studied sax and piano as a child but traded them for guitar) with his friend Richard Meyers, who upon arrival rechristened himself Richard Hell.

Their band was originally called the Neon Boys and featured Hell on bass and Verlaine on guitar. Soon enough, the search was on for a second guitarist, and it's a measure of the intimate scale of the "street music" scene that the Neon Boys auditions included both Chris Stein (later of Blondie) *and* Dee Dee Ramone. The Neon Boys were originally conceived of as a vehicle for Verlaine and Hell, with the latter singing the compositions that later turned up on his album *Blank Generation*. But Verlaine quickly consolidated his own position in the band, subordinating the incredibly gifted second guitarist, Richard Lloyd, himself a fixture in New York music circles going back to the late sixties (Lloyd even took guitar lessons from Jimi Hendrix). While Lloyd brought a rawer and more bluesy soloing style to the band that became Television, Verlaine still arrogated to himself the majority of the solos. Subsequently, friction between Hell and Verlaine mounted, as Hell found less and less to do in the band (eventually he was allowed to sing nothing but "Blank Generation"), and soon he was forced to quit. He joined, thereafter, the rather menacing band made from the ashes of the New York Dolls—or half of them, namely Johnny Thunders's Heartbreakers—before recording on his own.

Hell and Verlaine, before parting ways, did give the New York underground one of its greatest gifts, and that was the venue called CBGB-OMFUG. In the New York City of economic turmoil, there were not a lot of places to play.* Verlaine and Hell liked the location of Hilly Kristal's club, and they weren't particular about its name, which amounted to a celebration of country, bluegrass, blues, "and other music for uplifting gourmandizers." Television managed to convince Kristal to let them play on weekends for a month, and soon Patti Smith followed, and then the Ramones, and Mink DeVille,† and so on.

---

* Like now. Like in New York City now.

† Mink DeVille is a great example of the disparate set of styles that somehow was being shoehorned (awkwardly) into "punk," or "street music." Willy DeVille, the band's only constant member, grew up in working class Stamford, Connecticut, but was playing in San Francisco when he convinced his band to move back east to New York to audition for a weekly gig at CBGB's, alongside Television and the Patti Smith Group. DeVille had little in common with those bands except that he had stripped his sound of all the excess. But he also had a decidedly urban vision, all grit and romance and drug addiction. As a lyricist, he wasn't that far from Lou Reed, and as a singer his white soul mixture of Phil Spector and Motown and the blues had something in common with David Johansen of the Dolls. It was only later, when he moved into soul and Spanish-inflected pop, that it seemed as though he had never been punk at all. And yet he certainly had the hard living in common with Dee Dee Ramone and Johnny Thunders and Richard Hell. (And his story intersected with Thunders's, too, because he was living near Thunders in New Orleans when Thunders died.) As others have noted, it *is* strange that roots-oriented artists like Southside Johnny or the Stray Cats achieved great fame in the period when DeVille recorded, when they didn't have the same commitment to the material that he did. In a way his curatorial obsession with antique sounds and recording technologies is what was "underground" about DeVille. He wasn't made for these times, and when he was singing at CBGB's, he was singing around others who weren't made for those times either. With this in mind, it's no surprise that DeVille went

Television was different from "punk"—if by punk what you mean is the Ramones, or the Dolls, or something similar. In fact, so is Patti Smith different from punk, who by the time *Radio Ethiopia* was released didn't sound punk at all, soon after which she had a top ten hit ("Because the Night," mostly written by the much more popular and very well-known Bruce Springsteen). What could be less "punk" than that? All of which is to say that the "street music," or "underground" music, of the mid-seventies didn't have anything homogenous about it. It was noteworthy for its diversity of influences. (Surf music, Phil Spector, and bubblegum in the Ramones and Blondie; jazz, folk, psychedelic, and garage in the cases of Television, Mink DeVille, and Patti Smith.) Television, after all, liked *really long guitar solos!* And not minimalist solos, as in the case of the Velvets (who went on to be a more potent influence on Patti Smith, when John Cale himself became the producer of *Horses*); Television played long, soaring guitar solos, as on "Marquee Moon," their best-known song, and their most ambitious. At about the halfway point in the composition, Verlaine begins his solo just the way a saxophonist would, building up the material bit by bit. His plangent use of tremolo and vibrato—he almost always used a Fender Telecaster on the early recordings, a guitar more often associated with country and early rockabilly than with the rock and roll of the seventies—is particularly effective and feels indebted to Miles Davis, to the way Davis used quarter tones in his solos. And

---

on to compose with Doc Pomus (who cowrote, among other classics, "A Teenager in Love") and to record with Jack Nitzsche, who was an in-house arranger and producer on many of Phil Spector's wall of sound classics.

whereas a guitar solo on a studio recording during or after the "punk" period was not meant to last more than a verse, Verlaine just keeps going, as the rhythm section, and Lloyd on second guitar, organize toward a sort of evolved march and then into a beautiful sustained crescendo. He's ecstatic. In just the way that Patti Smith believed she was being ecstatic.

Then there are the words. Verlaine, in the end, because of his frail and untutored singing, isn't always remembered for his words, but the "Marquee Moon" lyrics are just as compelling as the solos, beginning with: "I remember how the darkness doubled..." and moving into the mortally preoccupied: "I spoke to the man down at the tracks / And I asked him how he don't go mad / He said, 'Look here, junior, don't you be so happy / And for heaven's sake don't you be so sad.'" The Verlaine lyrical technique is about multiple layers, double meanings, reversals, obliquities. The closest analogue, for this listener, is the poetry and prose of the French surrealist period.

Since Patti Smith and Tom Verlaine were also briefly lovers, there was a lot of cross-pollination between the two bands. Verlaine played on and cowrote "Break It Up" on the first Patti Smith album, and Jay Dee Daugherty, drummer for Patti Smith, played on some of Verlaine's solo work later on. And, as I've said, you can feel how Verlaine was trying to do with his solos some of what Smith was trying to do on, for example, "Birdland," one of the best tracks on *Horses*. Both musicians had a *poetical* ambition, the desire to describe the spiritual, or at least the ineffable, in music without falling into oversimplifications.

As with the Velvets, for both Patti Smith and Television this level of accomplishment was unsustainable. Maybe that was part of what "street music" was—a form that burned brightly. Smith broke her neck on tour for *Radio Ethiopia*, her second album, and it was at first unclear if she would be able to walk again. Richard Lloyd, the second guitarist in Television, fell dramatically into a heroin addiction, as did virtually everyone who played in the Heartbreakers. As did Dee Dee Ramone, as did so many other players in this high-water moment of the New York City underground.

In retrospect, this period looks like one of the most aesthetically potent grassroots movements of the postwar period, wherein a group of musicians, just by virtue of pursuing what was of interest to them, managed to change the way people thought about the popular song. And the ramifications weren't confined to this country. Richard Hell, with his self-inflicted haircuts and torn clothes, became Malcolm McLaren's blueprint for the fashions and sensibility of the Sex Pistols. The ideas—against the bloat! against the pretense!—of "street music" were exported across the Atlantic, where they emphatically took root.

But the really dark influences that had hindered the Velvets reappeared to sap what was great about the mid-seventies in New York, of which heroin is only the most obvious manifestation. It seems to go with great music that the players somehow can't withstand the attention (Television's song "Glory," in part a response to Smith's "Gloria," it seems to me, is also a commentary on the "fame" that came to the players on the scene), and then the drugs are at hand, and the drugs take the players, and the players are lost. It's sobering to think of all the talent and all the resources that were kicking around the Bowery in those days, and how little music these talented people actually produced. Television reunited in the nineties and made one more great record (probably the one great comeback album of the CBGB bands), and Patti Smith, who left music after her fourth album, *Wave*, to marry and raise a family, made some records more recently, but in the period when these writers were at the height of their powers they were almost constitutionally unable to produce. Maybe part of it had to do with the amount of privation and failure taking place around them. Maybe New York loves best the sheep that goes astray. "Never the rose / Without the prick," Verlaine sings on "Guiding Light," as if the good can never come to pass without the disconsolate right alongside. Or maybe this line describes the perennial complexity of rock and roll: once *everybody* knows about a band, it just can't be underground anymore.

4. No New York

Rock and roll, in its later incarnations, was not primarily made by African Americans. Rock and roll was very heavily *influenced* by African American music; it borrowed liberally from the music of African Americans. It stands on African foundations. Occasionally, maybe even more than occasionally, as with Chuck Berry and Little Richard, or Jimi Hendrix, or the Bad Brains, it has been *best* played by African Americans. But in the seventies, when black and white radio became increasingly segregated, increasingly separate, rock and roll was— though a hybridized form—largely white, suburban music. Black musicians played soul or R&B, and these forms happened somewhere else on the radio dial, in different clubs, different neighborhoods, for different audiences. At the Apollo Theater, or at the juke joints of Mississippi, or in Detroit or Watts. Charitably put, rock and roll borrowed from this legacy, adapted it—as in Elvis Presley or, later, Marshall Mathers— and built its own traditions. But in the later seventies, this musical apartheid became obvious, and occasionally sad and grim, especially with the appearance of the genres called *disco* and *funk*.

Disco happened concurrently, more or less, with funk, which was more improvised, more raunchy, and harder to corral onto an LP, and so disco was the more streamlined presentation of black music. It was, in record company circles, phenomenally successful, especially when interpreted by three white Australian guys singing close harmony in eerie falsetto. It was especially beloved of the American immigrant working class, because it was dance music, and so, as in the film *Saturday Night Fever*, it was the music that some people who lived in the outer boroughs of New York City chose to dance to. It seemed to be the antithesis of "punk," especially as punk migrated back from England, and perhaps for this reason an anti-disco sentiment arose, which was fanned by some deejays around the country, and at times this furor had a racist feeling to it. There were disco albums dumped outdoors and burned, and "Disco Sucks" was emblazoned on bathroom walls and in the alleys. And yet there were aspects of disco that were not at all unlike what was happening in the next manifestation of the rock-and-roll underground in New York City. For example, disco was mostly free of instrumental soloing. It often made use of tried-and-true chord progressions and was thus repetitive, and it was more interested in the rhythm section than it was interested in melodic development. It didn't require astounding pyrotechnical skills, since in its musical development it was rather predictable. And this was true of a lot of underground music that was happening in New York. The relationship between disco (and funk) and the underground became very important when some of the bands that played at CBGB's began incorporating elements of African American music into what they were doing. Blondie was probably first, when their *Parallel Lines* album, released in 1978, spawned a massive dance hit with "Heart of Glass." Talking Heads, on their second album, produced by a ubiquitous presence in the New York underground in that period, the British electronic musician and theoretical ideologue Brian Eno, covered Al Green's "Take Me to the River." Not a disco song, true, more a Memphis soul song, but a covert admission of a relationship with black music that would be exploited with great abandon on the fourth album by the band, released in 1980, *Remain in Light*, in which Talking Heads fused their cool, arty minimalism with the sound of the great exemplars of funk, Parliament-Funkadelic, adding Bernie Worrell from that confraternity to the tour.

Was it funk and disco that moved these "rock" musicians? It was in part. But it was also black music in general. Certainly, James Brown (and Marvin Gaye and Diana Ross and others) exerted a certain gravitational pull on the music of New York City. But there was also jazz, and especially the free jazz of the loft jazz tradition. Loft jazz, in New York, had come to pass when there were no more venues in which to play improvised music. In this way, jazz in New York, which had, after the explosion of the free jazz genre in the mid-sixties, moved far from the mainstream, became something that people did in their apartments. Jazz was as underground as you could get in New York music, and since jazz was outsider music, it was important to founders of the "street music" period of New York. Albert Ayler, Sunny Murray, Ornette Coleman, and later exemplars took the music out of nightclubs and returned it to the people who really cared about it.

The bands that followed the first generation at CBGB's (the generation that went on to have major label deals and to move decisively out of the underground*), therefore, lived in a New York City in which racial tension, while it was part of life, was not a feature of musical experience. Many of these bands knew well their disco, funk, and jazz, and all of them knew Patti Smith and Television and, arguably, the British punk bands, and as those bands had once mined the distant fringes before moving into the center, the next generation of "underground" bands, the No Wave bands, were trying to find a way to push the envelope even further. They were even less concerned with instrumental prowess and with melody, and they liked, understood, and admired minimalism and the melodic simplicity of popular black music.

The decisive document of the period was an album curated and produced by Brian Eno called *No New York*. Eno, at the same time, was himself making what he referred to as "trance music," or "ambient music," of which the best example is his

---

* In 1979, the Ramones, for their fifth album, recorded with reclusive legend Phil Spector. You know you are no longer in the underground when you record with the man whose recent projects included Leonard Cohen and the solo work of the Beatles.

album *Music for Airports*, in which tape loops (actual tape, as opposed to the digitally prepared loops of contemporary music), and thus repetition, played a major role. This music was heavily influenced by La Monte Young and by the early minimalism of Steve Reich and Philip Glass, which, though it was considered "classical" music in some circles, was also a reference point below 14th Street, where Philip Glass actually lived. Eno picked the bands for the *No New York* compilation from what was happening around him in the clubs of lower Manhattan, when he was living and working there. There were several songs each from Teenage Jesus and the Jerks, Mars, DNA, and the Contortions—by no means a definitive sampling of the scene. And whereas Eno's other productions at the same time, the Talking Heads albums, Ultravox, Devo, etc., were studio savvy recordings, replete with synthesizers, multitracking effects, and so on, *No New York* is noteworthy for its *audio verité* approach. These bands were sloppy, inflammatory, and lively. Eno chose to leave them mostly the way he found them.

Chief among the No Wave movement, as it came to be called, was James Chance, the leader of the Contortions, also known, in his disco guise, as James White and the Blacks. The No Wave idiom as practiced by James Chance featured some totally rudimentary harmelodic saxophone, borrowed from some deranged idea of what Ornette Coleman was doing, and some funk primitivist guitar, often played by Pat Place, who went on to form the Bush Tetras, another great band from the period. There was also, usually, a loud, up-front bass part, in concert with some pretty discofied drumming. At another extreme, in No Wave, was Teenage Jesus and the Jerks, the first band to feature teenage poetess Lydia Lunch, who borrowed Patti Smith's ecstatic lyrical approach but applied it to more confessional and sometimes funnier conceits, in the process becoming a less distant narrator than Smith was. Teenage Jesus featured electric guitar, bass, and drums, the way the West Coast punk bands would soon after, but it also had the ubiquitous jazz sax of the period, so unpredictable that it sometimes sounded more like an analogue synthesizer than a saxophone.

Mars and DNA, meanwhile, sprang the songs loose from the normal time signatures, so that it wasn't always clear if the players were listening to one another at all. But DNA, at least, somehow managed to sound very musical, in part because of the presence of Arto Lindsay, who'd grown up in Brazil and whose peculiar set of influences included the classics of the Tropicália movement. Lindsay went on to be a force in almost every part of the underground music of New York City in the next decade, playing with John Zorn and Anton Fier in the first iteration of the Golden Palominos, and then in the Ambitious Lovers, a Brazilian-inflected pop group.

The Lounge Lizards, a self-identified "fake jazz" band, were also exemplary in the No Wave period. They were started by two brothers, John and Evan Lurie.* John, who wrote most of the group's compositions, got his start in the wave of underground filmmaking in the East Village. Both Luries could play better than most of the No Wave players, though, and by the time the Lounge Lizards stopped performing in the nineties,

---

* See above, pp. 158–175.

each brother had a reputation as a composer of note. The band came to be among the most respected new jazz bands in the city.

However, probably no other band in the No Wave period had the impact of the electronic duo called Suicide. They'd begun playing in 1971, when the artist Alan Vega began offering concerts of new music and jazz at his art gallery. In this context, he encountered the keyboard player Martin Reverby, and the two began collaborating. They were playing during the original wave of CBGB's punk, but their preeminent recordings came later. Suicide played minimal electronic music, all performed by Martin Rev, while Alan Vega improvised vocals in a style probably influenced by ? and the Mysterians and by underground poetry. Death and destruction were the frequent entrees on this menu, as in Suicide's masterpiece, "Frankie Teardop," about a deranged military veteran, slow to build, ominous, and without a crescendo that would release the tension at all.

Even at the time, Suicide were considered nearly unlistenable. Though Ric Ocasek of the Cars produced most of their early music, Suicide never quite acquired the smooth electronic veneer that Ocasek affected in his own work, or that some of the British synth pop of the same period would display. (Soft Cell, for example, was clearly indebted to Suicide, but with none of the gravity of Rev and Vega.) They never fell into the habit of buying whatever new high-tech appurtenance was available. As a result, they never dated. The interested listener owes it to him/herself to listen to a commercially available recording of a show Suicide played in Brussels (*23 Minutes Over Brussels*) in 1978 in which the audience's inability to understand what was happening to them is terrifying to behold. If No Wave, by virtue of its astringent qualities, never found a large audience (though members of these bands went on to considerable critical acclaim), it nonetheless influenced a great deal of what happened after. Still, on the Brussels bootleg, where the audience chants, "Elvis! Elvis! Elvis!" between fits of booing, you can understand just how provocative this music really was at the time.

No Wave made palpable, in a way that early punk had not quite, the sense that *anyone could make a band.* As it coincided with the East Village gallery movement, where anyone could, to some extent, be an artist, wherein the arts were no longer controlled by gallerists in Soho or the museums uptown, there was a feeling that what made the underground underground was *permission.* And this was true across various genres. Artists like Robert Longo played in a band, filmmaker Jim Jarmusch (who would later feature John Lurie in his early films) played in a band, and some musicians who had formerly been associated with the "serious music" of the period, like Rhys Chatham, began not only playing in bands but composing for them. Glenn Branca, one of the leading voices of the No Wave period, had (according to Branca himself) only six months of guitar lessons under his belt when he formed the Theoretical Girls. Even Jean-Michel Basquiat, the art phenomenon, had a band, Gray, that played at CBGB's and the Mudd Club. If, during the punk period, the idea was that rudimentary skills were no impediment to musical expression as long as the performance was passionate, the idea during No Wave seemed to be that inability was *better,* that it fostered new musical pathways and new ways of thinking about rock and roll. But maybe No Wave wasn't even rock. You'll notice that *glam rock* and *punk rock* still allude, in their terminology, to rock-and-roll origins, but No Wave is part of a period in which the word *rock* doesn't even get employed in the genre designation.* Was it rock and roll that was being played by these musicians? And were they even musicians?

Meanwhile, the black music that was being reconfigured in No Wave was itself in danger of becoming a thing of the past, because of some explosive developments taking place in the housing projects of Manhattan and the Bronx. Black music was galloping into its own new terrain. It started with a deejay and party promoter called Kool DJ Herc. Herc threw his parties (on Sedgwick Avenue) first indoors, and then outdoors when the parties got too large. What Herc did was to *talk* quite a bit over the albums he played. To the point where his rapping over the records became an integral part of the performance. To the point where the "rapping," even if it didn't quite have that name yet, *became* the performance.

There was a precedent for this kind of thing. Partly it was a gospel precedent. And partly it was a Caribbean precedent. Reggae had been influential in British punk (as in Bob Marley's "Punky Reggae Party"), and if it didn't yet have mainstream acceptance in American popular music, that only made it sound that much fresher to the kids in the neighborhood. Kool DJ Herc made it possible for MCs to talk over the records, until the boasts and imprecations of the deejay became as important as the records themselves.

---

* And *rock* pretty much stays dead until the "alternative rock" boom of the early nineties, which always felt more like a term dreamed up by a marketing executive than an actual description of music.

Another innovation in those heady days was the use of multiple copies of the album during the "break" or the breakdown portion of the albums. Herc made a sort of "merry-go-round" out of the breaks, extending them, because of the effect these percussive intervals had on the audiences. Thus the loops of experimental music (that propelled Terry Riley's compositions, Brian Eno's work, Robert Fripp's guitar solos in the same period) found a real-world analogue in the hands of the deejay and his two turntables. In the projects, it was hard to get bands together, hard to find rehearsal space, hard to find a way onto the playlists of radio stations that had much less historical memory for black popular music than they did for white artists. When the musicians of the Bronx discovered the turntable, they bypassed the recording studio that Eno had described as the *new instrument* of the contemporary moment, relying instead on a device that was much more accessible, much more mobile, and whose rewards were more immediate.*

From a retrospective angle, what binds together all the underground music of the late seventies and early eighties, beyond its coincidence with the great economic hardship of the period, was its resistance to melody. Both the early hip-hop albums, with their refreshing and revelatory insistence on being newsworthy to the citizenry of the projects, and the No Wave bands were particular in their resistance to the singable. That is, this was music that was taken up primarily with rhythm. Bass and drums became the most crucial instruments—when there

---

* They also discovered a very site-specific musical effect made possible by the turntable, one that became a hallmark of the developing hip-hop medium: scratching.

were instruments—and the ability to play a great guitar or sax solo, or the employment of some very expensive synthesizer, became a thing of the past. In No Wave, people played guitars and basses with missing strings, and they put cheap organs through a few stomp boxes to arrive at sonic novelties that otherwise had yet to be explored. In the Bronx, they made do with a public address system and a record player. In each case, the musical thing, the underground thing, was the commitment to the vision and to the violent break with what had come before.

Of the two forms, the more influential and more culturally relevant was hip-hop, now a multibillion-dollar industry with myriad international offshoots. No Wave, which always defended its reputation for being *against*, was probably never liable to sell out. Though its luminosity was limited, its impact was unmistakable just the same.

5. Daydream Nation

"This is the era where everyone creates," Patti Smith sang on *Wave* (1979), her last album before her lengthy retirement, borrowing an idea from William S. Burroughs. No Wave and the East Village scene exploited this notion of music and art and literature for a good fifteen years after *Horses* was recorded. Kids came to New York City (I was one of them) because of what was happening and how creative it felt and how possible it was to make a life in NYC then. If the music of the original CBGB bands was no longer of surpassing interest, and if Ronald Reagan had assumed his apotheosis, there was still the trickling down—*not* of the wealth accumulated among the very richest* but of the ideas happening in visual art and in performance and in jazz and in "serious" music.

How did this trickling down take place? It took place because the differences between high and low were so porous in New York City, where artists like Laurie Anderson and Klaus Nomi and Yoko Ono, serious artists in their own right, began making music available on widely distributed LPs, where composers like Rhys Chatham, Glenn Branca, Peter Gordon, and Arthur Russell started making albums featuring rock-and-roll instrumentation, moving these ideas uptown alongside the "classical" music of Philip Glass and Steve Reich. Chatham and Branca drafted neighborhood guitarists in order to bring about their recombinant vision. Both composers, that is, started composing "rock and roll," for lack of a better term, or at least they began *manipulating* rock and roll. These pieces, though rhythmically propulsive, didn't sound like regular rock and roll, but more like rock and roll fused with things that were happening elsewhere in serious music.

Among their players were Thurston Moore and Lee Ranaldo. Moore came to New York City from Connecticut, drawn by the sounds of No Wave, specifically Lydia Lunch and Patti Smith (his excellent book, *No Wave*, written with Byron Coley, documents him, gaunt and lanky, in the audience at these gigs). Ranaldo came from Glen Cove, Long Island, via SUNY Binghamton. The two played in Glenn Branca's ensemble about the time he was performing the work known as *Inde-*

---

* Matthew Stearns makes a similar allusion to Milton Friedman's voodoo economics in his excellent book *Daydream Nation* (Continuum Publishers, 2007).

terminate Activity of Resultant Masses, a presymphonic Branca work. A memorable controversy erupted around this piece. John Cage himself attended a performance at the New Music America festival, in Chicago. Afterward, he made some disparaging remarks about Branca in an interview,* going so far as to allude to a certain "fascist" quality to Branca's method of conducting and performing. And yet the lineage is so clear! Cage leads to La Monte Young leads to John Cale leads to Lou Reed leads to David Johansen leads to Dee Dee Ramone and to Richard Hell and to Tom Verlaine and to Patti Smith, who leads to Lydia Lunch and Arto Lindsay and James Chance and Rhys Chatham and Glenn Branca, and they in turn lead to Thurston Moore and Lee Ranaldo and Kim Gordon and Michael Gira. Cage is practically the point of origin for all this music! Cage later amended his comments about Branca, but by that time the damage had been done.

After playing with Branca, Moore and Ranaldo and Kim Gordon (who was an artist and art critic at the time she met the two guitarists) formed Sonic Youth in 1981. Gordon originally played bass.† The three worked hard at what they were doing,‡ at a kind of punk–No Wave idiom that owed as much to DC hardcore, to the Bad Brains and to Minor Threat, as it did to the strange tunings and heavy droning of Chatham and

---

* For a thorough discussion, and a recording of the Cage interview, see the CD rerelease *Indeterminate Activity of Resultant Masses* (Atavistic, 2005).

† She now often plays guitar too.

‡ Holding down, in the process, some horrible day jobs, including house painter, copy shop employee, and, in the case of Moore, Chipwich salesman.

Branca. Alongside Sonic Youth, sometimes sharing a rehearsal studio, were Swans, an even more aggressive and nihilistic ensemble featuring Michael Gira and Jarboe. The music (as practiced by both bands) was *loud* and often dissonant, and these were its noteworthy calling cards, at least for a time. The urban desperation of the Reagan years helped to bring about this *noise*, this *skronk*,* and it also spawned *hardcore*, an approach practiced in New York, but also in Boston, Minneapolis, LA, Phoenix, and elsewhere. Hardcore was practically a national style. Finally, America had an indigenous sound that answered to the British manifestation of punk. But this early incarnation of Sonic Youth, the part that temporarily emphasized *youth* as much as the *sonic* part, was not really the band as it would be at its height. That band had to wait until it got its most effective drummer, Steve Shelley, who had more versatility than those who had come before him. With *Bad Moon Rising* and *Evol* and *Sister*, three albums from the middle eighties, Sonic Youth began to articulate what was unique about them.

What made Sonic Youth arresting in this high period was the singularly inventive use of the electric guitar, the unusual tunings, the feedback, the carefully deployed effects. Lee Ranaldo has cited, among others, the influence of the great instrumental guitarist John Fahey on his playing, and Fahey was an exponent of the alternate tuning. Still, there were other guitarists in the city mining similar areas of interest, many of them in the jazz world, many of them using Ornette Coleman (and his Prime Time recordings) as a precedent. I'm thinking,

---

* Robert Christgau's word, along with the unpleasant later coinage *pigfuck*.

for example, of Sonny Sharrock, who'd been playing since the seventies but whose work in the eighties had the cross-genre flexibility that animated downtown music. Sharrock could play rock and roll with an originality unmatched by few outside of Jimi Hendrix, he could play soul, but he also could play a theme and solo structure like he'd grown up in jazz ensembles since the fifties. He understood the abstract squalls of eighties jazz too.

Ronald Shannon Jackson & the Decoding Society also borrowed from the Ornette Coleman playbook, including multiple bass players and abstract song structures. But the chief exponent of the alternative guitar tuning in the improvised music world in the eighties was James "Blood" Ulmer. Ulmer tended to tune *all* his guitar strings to various octaves of E (as Lou Reed did on his first recording), which gave him a whole lot of sympathetic strings and which, theoretically, left him in the right key for a great many blues and rock standards. Ulmer's untrained voice, much more like a blues singer's than a jazz singer's, was especially beautiful on songs like his well-known single from the period "Are You Glad to Be in America?" But he could also shred his open tunings on more solo-oriented instrumental compositions (on, for example, his best-known album, *Odyssey*). And he also worked well within unusual ensembles: guitar and string ensemble, or guitar, violin, and drums.

The early eighties were also noteworthy for the emergence of John Zorn in downtown composing and jazz circles. Zorn's early pieces are known, at this remove, as the "game pieces," *Cobra, Archery, Hockey*, etc. Zorn didn't *compose* these pieces so much as he used instructions for the players somewhat in the way that Steve Reich used instructions in *Music for 18 Musicians*, or the way that Terry Riley used instructions for the ensembles that played his masterpiece *In C*.

Zorn also played on the first album by the Golden Palominos, which featured Arto Lindsay, Anton Fier (of the Lounge Lizards), Bill Laswell (of Material, also a music producer of considerable reputation throughout the eighties), and others. The Golden Palominos, years away from their more accessible song-oriented recordings (when Syd Straw served as lead vocalist), created an important bridge between the funk-disco nihilism of No Wave and the jazz world. Having worked with the Golden Palominos, Zorn went on to form a number of ensembles that were a bit more accessible and compositionally oriented (he made an album of "covers" of Ornette Coleman and an album of Ennio Morricone compositions), culminating in one of the very greatest bands of the eighties, Naked City, which sounded a lot like a nine-year-old flipping the radio dial between stations.

Sonic Youth seemed to process all of this New York music, alongside its hardcore preoccupations. Lee Ranaldo held down the experimental-serious music chair and balanced this against the more aggressive punk–free jazz inclinations of Thurston Moore. Kim Gordon's role, at least on these middle-period compositions, was as a vocalist and theoretician and, if it's not overstating the case, *feminist*, an unusual flavor in a medium mostly dominated by masculine guitar heroics. Gordon had (and has) a slightly weary and somewhat confrontational voice somewhere between Lydia Lunch and Lucinda Williams.

A representational song for the period, for me, was the recording called "Flower," from *Bad Moon Rising*. It opens with extended-technique guitar noise, with Gordon's bass doing repetitive eighth notes, and then the lyrics begin, which are at once rhetorical and ideological: "Support the power of women / Use the power of man / Support the flower of women / Use the word *fuck!* / The word is love!" The root chord never moves for long—down a whole step, just for variety's sake, and then back—while the guitars screech along, pulsing and bending for some just-out-of-tune beating of feedback waves. Gordon repeats the lyrics a few times, third verse same as first, getting a little more insistent, and then at about the four-minute mark, the whole thing ends in a wall of feedback and hiss. A great song, a moving song, a song that gives one the chills. *Sister*, two albums later, had a couple of compositions with a similar cast, like the unnerving and fabulous "Schizophrenia," which opened the record ("I can feel it in my bones / Schizophrenia is taking me home"), and "Kotton Krown," a rare duet between Gordon and Moore. But neither of these records had the urgency the band was soon to develop.

Somehow Sonic Youth had a complete breakthrough in 1987, as they began writing and rehearsing *Daydream Nation*. A breakthrough: because they had by now toured the world, because their budget was a little more liberal (a whopping $37, 000), because they had played the songs live first, because the lineup was stable, because they were in the right place at the right time. Which means that: they managed an album that somehow catalyzed this entire lineage of underground music in New York City. But how? What enabled them? Was it just the *confidence?** Was it that Kim and Thurston had become downtown celebrities by then? Was it a commitment to melody? Because there *was* something more melodic about Sonic Youth, despite the warbly and sometimes insubstantial vocals, and the occasionally metallic din of the guitar parts. In part, what they were doing was restoring belief in melody to the underground scene, but in a way that didn't sound prissy or pandering to the kids who'd gotten comfortable with dissonance.

Still, this doesn't quite describe the sense of history, the sense of culmination in *Daydream Nation*. The Sonic Youth lineup had a lot in common with the Velvet Underground, the mix of technical expertise (in Ranaldo and Shelley) and theoretical expertise used for the sake of *expression* (Moore and Gordon), and it had managed to refine itself into a rhythmically dexterous ensemble in the way that the Velvets had on *White Light/White Heat*. It had some of the erotic decadence that the Dolls seemed to have, and though Sonic Youth has never had its *obvious* share of rock-and-roll excesses, it seemed to know all about the derangement of the senses that came with the further extremes of the "street music" scene. But with *Daydream Nation*, they suddenly had the compositions too. In fact, the weak link in a lot of underground music was the composition. Lydia Lunch could have great lyrics but music of no surpassing interest. James Chance could have provocative music but not much lyrical aptitude beyond insolent bluster. It was only in rare moments of this entire generation of music

---

* Kim Gordon, quoted in Greil Marcus's *Lipstick Traces* (Harvard University Press, 1990): "People pay to see others believe in themselves" (p. 45).

(the first Velvets album, *Marquee Moon*, some of *Horses*) that New York underground music fired on all its cylinders and cleared away the attitude so that you could appreciate the music *as* music as well as performance. *Daydream Nation* was one of those moments. The band had three writers at the time (Ranaldo later wrote and sang less), and it wasn't afraid to incline toward the *long* compositions that were more associated with the reviled prog rock seventies or with jazz rock. Even a throwaway like "Providence," a blast of amp noise and an old answering machine message, had an eerie musique concrète quality about it that lofted it above its materials.

And then there was the cover image, a painting by Gerhard Richter. A totally inspired choice. The prior album, *Sister*, had a jacket that looked indisputably No Wave. It was threatening, sexy, violent, collaged together. But the very simple Richter painting of a candle against a dark backdrop seemed to say everything that needed to be said about the album and its approach. It was in the minimalist direction, the "punk" direction, but it was also expressive, almost romantic. Light in the cultural darkness, the socioeconomic darkness, the darkness of a homogenized and soulless music business, a Republican presidential administration, etc.

After *Daydream Nation*, in the nineties, the terminology changed. The terminology with which we label movements in music is always dangerous. Mere taxonomic distinctions in music run the risk of reducing originality in order to make it understandable, and so Sonic Youth was recording *Daydream Nation* at a time that offered up terms like *hardcore* and *thrash* to describe the really aggressive and animated music that was happening in pockets all across the nation, but soon after there was *indie rock*, which was meant to suggest music that was produced by small independent labels. All of these terms were applied to Sonic Youth during or after *Daydream Nation*, but none of them seems correct now. It was underground music, true, in that it was happening in opposition to a radically homogenized music industry, in a radio environment in which music like this was likely to be played almost nowhere. But even *underground*, as a term, seems imprecise, even vague, when applied here.

As Reagan gave way to Bush (the elder), Sonic Youth managed to capitalize on what they had accomplished on *Daydream Nation*, continuing to write great songs that mixed unusual guitar technique with dark and allusive lyrics. And they even managed to sign with a major label, almost unheard of in the No Wave period. But this was also the beginning of the end for the underground, in New York City and elsewhere, occasioned in part by the rise of that guy in Seattle. And when this guy, Kurt Cobain, recorded his second album, and with it the song called "Smells Like Teen Spirit," all of the music world hiccupped, and suddenly Sonic Youth, like many other "underground" bands, found themselves in the limelight in a way they could never have predicted.

For a time thereafter, New York was no longer the underground epicenter it had been. It wouldn't be again for ten or fifteen years, by which time it was acoustic guitar, not electric, that was the weapon of choice and Brooklyn was the borough. But that story, about the changing cabaret laws and the 311 switchboard that made it easier to file noise complaints, is an essay for another day. In concluding, let's say that it's probably the vertical qualities of NYC, the ways in which we lie atop of one another and ride the same subway lines, poverty and affluence cheek by jowl, black and white, immigrant and blue blood, that have made the city's rock and roll so replete with cultural interpenetration. Everyone knows about just about everything in New York, high and low, sacred and profane, first world and third, all this admixed in the spin cycle that is city life before the automobile. And so the influences for musicians, and artists generally, are complex and dynamic. That's what made New York underground music so exciting in the generation I've described, its heterogeneity. While there's a direct lineage here, in which grit and noise always figure, the musicians are all listening to everything happening around them, really listening, in even the most neglected corners of the city. What you're hearing here is the sound of the city itself. The whole city. Not just the part with the money and power.

Europe, Forsake Your Drum Machines!

A *Genealogy*

1.

Drummers of Europe, throw off your chains! For too long now you have let the soot collect on your kits, in the garage where you once kept a car. Many have been the days when you have happened through there and seen the kit under its plastic sheet or moldy, discolored blankets. Have you not wondered what it would sound like to busy yourself on the skins? Drummers of Europe, is it ever the philosophy of your continent to say a thing is lost, and then to yield to that loss as though it were a virtue, as though nothing can be done to redress the situation? Drummers of Europe, don't go on this way! You might, anew, at first timidly, apply your sticks and your brushes to the cymbals and toms. You might, again, attempt the impossible threes against fours, you might completely blow some maniacal fill as perfected on the recordings of jazz drummers of old. You might again annoy neighbors and passersby until late in the night. Drummers of Europe, once there were jokes in profusion at your expense, that you were always the least sophisticated member of the band. Your wife, or your husband, or your partner has told you that you are not a very *good* drummer, that you have trouble keeping time, that you are unable to avoid speeding up. Drummers of Europe, these things are no obstacle to what lies before you today, the restoration of Europe to its greatness in the matter of its indigenous musics—if by indigenous music, we are understood to mean, simply, music that is primarily made by human beings in a particular place and time, all attempting to play *together*. Drummers of Europe, they will, it is true, eject you from the clubs, where they have grown decadent and somehow satisfied by the sight of a pair of guys twitching over laptops. They tolerate the predictable video projections on the JumboTron. But it is no matter if you are ejected from the raves! It is no matter if that one irritating acquaintance, the one with the really foul breath and meth teeth, attempts to make you believe that your time, drummers of Europe, is gone! Drummers of Europe, if it is necessary to be *alone*, at first, practicing on mattresses with well-worn sticks, or on rubberized practice pads, then so be it! Drummers of Europe, even if you have sold the kit, borrow a plastic paint container, or a garbage can, to serve as both kick drum and snare! So be it, drummers of Europe! Your inability is your mastery! Your enthusiasm is all that is required! Remember, drummers of Europe, the wind that blows north from the Sahara! Remember, drummers of Europe, the Gypsies that moved across your plains and mountain ranges a thousand years ago! Drummers of Europe, look at your waves of immigration and consider how you are the greatest polyglot experiment. You are at the center of the world, what with all the musical idioms that are part of your ensemble now, the polyrhythms of Africa, the drones of Asian music, the klezmer music of your missing Hebraic minority, the reggae that has been exported back to you from your former colonies! Drummers of Europe, this is all your legacy! All you have to do is take up your sticks! The day job you have, there in your contracting economy, should be no impediment! Embrace your unprofessionalism. You cannot deny it—that you never did anything in your life that has made you as deliriously happy as when you play! Those days need not be in the past, drummers of Europe! Those days may be at hand! Anew! Drummers of Europe, your time is now!

2.

The first drum machine, after a fashion, was the metronome. It was invented by Dietrich Nikolaus Winkel in 1814, and patented a year later by one Johann Mälzel.* Evidently, the device caught on, especially after Beethoven made notation in a score for the metronome setting he favored. Salieri was also a fan. Soon metronome markings were common. Ostensibly, the purpose here was to torture poor music students in order to rid them of their listing and surging rhythms. Faster when *excited*, slower when pondering the meaning of a particular passage. And yet eminent composers began complaining of "metronomic regularity" soon

---

* Winkel was Dutch, but Mälzel, a German, borrowed, perhaps in an ethically questionable way, many of his constructions and managed the first patent. He also developed a fraudulent chess machine.

enough ("I do not mean to say that it is necessary to imitate the mathematical regularity of the metronome, which would give the music thus executed an icy frigidity; I even doubt whether it would be possible to maintain this rigid uniformity for more than a few bars"—Hector Berlioz). The two feelings, even at the outset, are coincident: the feeling that rhythmical imprecision is somehow a danger to musical perfection, and the feeling that rhythmical perfection lacks humanity.

Still, the metronome, in one form or another (these days you can get electronic ones, which are really irritating—like a smoke detector on a low charge), achieved market dominance and held it for a very long time. The music students of the world attempted to find the lessons of the metronome and to write these lessons on their hearts. Often to no avail. (I can remember my own piano teacher remarking with scorn that I didn't need to *tap my feet* while I played, the proper rhythm was *in there somewhere*.) Moreover, the percussionists who would have been only too willing to serve as the metronome, perhaps with a clave or a woodblock or a tambourine, began, we assume, their quiet, private envy of the metronome, perhaps going as far as to worry about the very future of the percussionist.

True, for the purpose of a music lesson, the ticking of the metronome could be anywhere you wanted it to be in the time signature. For example, if the piece in question was a waltz, you could set the metronome for 90 and then imagine that the TICK of the metronome was in the middle of the measure—beat, TICK, beat—or at the beginning—TICK, beat, beat, which would be a rather traditional waltz—or even at the end—beat, beat, TICK. The same was true whether the piece was in threes, fours, fives, or nines, as long as its measures were evenly subdivided. This was plenty of rhythm; this was a versatile rhythm, even if unsophisticated. The metronome, that is, was great for *practice*, and for building the rhythm fascist within, but it did not offer, in the long run, a pleasing sound.

In the course of music history, when music runs into an implacable and immutable truth, such as the truth which holds that the metronome has its *limitations*, then music history has no choice but to call out for someone like Léon Theremin.

Yes, Léon Theremin, the late great inventor of the radio wave playback device known by his surname, the musical instrument that launched the *electronica revolution*, the instrument that made Clara Rockmore one of the foremost classical musical interpreters of her time (and if you have never heard her renditions of the classics on the Theremin, you owe it to yourself), Léon Theremin, erstwhile KGB agent, was also a designer of a *drum machine*, perhaps the first drum machine that was ever to have any impact.

The request for the Rhythmicon, as Theremin's percussion device was soon to be known, came in 1930, from the American composer Henry Cowell, who, according to later versions of the tale, felt that his microtonal and polyrhythmic compositions needed some kind of percussive accompaniment that was not available in this world. Which was another way of saying, as is so often the case in this story, that the drummers of the time were simply not up to the task. Theremin's Rhythmicon, of which only three were built (the one built for Cowell was rather quickly abandoned), had sixteen keys, each featuring a different rhythm based on a different note.* Two keys could, of course, be played together, so that you could get the cross-rhythmical purposes of the different rhythms, and would that later drum machines made polyrhythms so easy. After Theremin's rhythm generator failed to take off with the same renown that greeted the inventor's earlier Theremin, the drum machine, as an idea, failed to find a new champion for about fifteen years, until, that is, Harry Chamberlin invented his Rhythmate (in 1947), which used actual tape recordings of an *actual jazz drummer* (there wasn't really rock and roll yet) and made possible the playback of these recordings, up to fourteen at once. This design was somewhat along the same lines as the Mellotron (which became the orchestral tool of preference for the progressive rock bands of the middle and late sixties).

After Chamberlin's experiment, there was a sudden rush to eliminate the feckless drummers of the world, as technology made solutions easier for musical tinkerers and dreamers. It's not surprising that some of these early drum machines were packaged into the electric organ, which was *the* electronic keyboard of its time, among these the Wurlitzer, which shipped, for a while (like the Casio did later), with a rhythm generator called, in this case, a Side Man. This was in the late 1950s. As with the Rhythmicon and the Rhythmate, the Side Man played very specific rhythmical patterns, the cha-cha, the

---

* For those who are interested in hearing the device, there are a number of re-created versions of its textures available online, including one software package at a site called American Mavericks, http://musicmavericks .publicradio.org/. It's well worth a listen!

tango, the foxtrot. Apparently, nothing, in these early days, could be better than obtaining a mechanized drummer who would play a very specific dance beat (though owners of the early Casiotones will testify as to how quickly its similar beats could drive you insane).

The next inventor to get involved on the design side of the problem was none other than Raymond Scott. Scott, who in the forties was a writer of "jazz" tunes (you can sort of see the contradiction here right away: Scott "wrote" jazz tunes, which is to say he through-composed them, though jazz, theoretically, was semi- or entirely *improvised*), among these the famous "Powerhouse," which became a standby for Carl Stalling, who reused its theme again and again for the Looney Tunes soundtracks. However, by the early sixties, Scott had turned his attention elsewhere, to early electronic music, some of it produced for advertising and some for other ends more nefarious. Among the latter were his *Soothing Sounds for Baby* series of album releases from 1964. These pieces are lullabies, or ostensible lullabies, created for babies of specific ages (there were three volumes, each for a different infant demographic), and for these recordings Scott devised first his Rhythm Synthesizer and, later, the more covert Bandito the Bongo Artist (c. 1963). A good example of this sort of a sound can be found on Volume One of the *Soothing Sounds* series, on the song called "Tic Toc," a metronomic piece for unaccompanied rhythm synthesizer.

There's a problem with a piece like "Tic Toc," however. As indicated among my friends who have attempted to play "Tic Toc" and, indeed, other compositions from Scott's series for their children. The results have not been perfect.* Your baby, apparently, sometimes responds to Raymond Scott's infant music only with *resistance*. One friend, when I told her that I had purchased a volume, back upon the rerelease of these Scott compositions, was very open about the difficulty: "Kids hate that stuff."

Why do some kids hate *Soothing Sounds for Baby?* On its most superficial basis, this music isn't terribly different from the tinkling of music boxes—there *are* some things contained within Scott's baby oeuvre that sound plausibly like a music box. There is a judicious use of echo throughout. There are, on many of the compositions, melodic bits to chew on. ("Tic Toc," it should be said, has none of these virtues.) Nevertheless, I would contend that the absolute lack of variation in the rhythmic patterns can, and will, create baby *apoplexy*, because baby, like his or her parents, cannot and does not thrive when the rhythmical construction is not more organic, when it is not more *human*. And so: Scott's electronic compositions for babies *were* about twenty years ahead of their time in one feature: they had figured out how to eliminate *all the soul*.

The invention and perfection of the drum machine happen against a backdrop of other technological advances in music in the forties, fifties, and sixties, many of these having to do with technology and the way in which music interacts with technological development in history. Music is *always* interacting with technology, that much is assured. In one moment in history, *the*

---

* In fact, I defy you to listen to "Tic Toc" all the way through. Just turn it on and try to listen to it. If you cannot stand it, why should your baby?

piano itself was a newfangled technology, replacing a keyboard, the harpsichord and its family, that had no potential for dynamic variation. And it's the same with the saxophone, or with the electric guitar, which in turn enabled an instrument that was mainly good for ballads or for chording in larger ensembles to become the focal point of entire ensembles (rock-and-roll bands, that is). It would be unwise, counterproductive, faintly ludicrous, to argue against innovation in musical technology entirely, since that is to insist on a static idea of what music is.

But when the music of the middle part of the twentieth century rubbed up against technology, the result was often rhythmic experiment and, in particular, the imposition of the *pulse*. On the one hand, you have Cagean experiments like "Credo in Us," from 1942, held by some to be a repudiation of Aaron Copland's folk-inflected pieces of the same period, which include the use of radio and which are more percussive than anything else, as John Cage often was, to a nearly industrial ploddingness. Then, in later generations, you have György Ligeti's 1962 Fluxus-influenced piece for a hundred *metronomes running down*, called *Poème Symphonique*. What starts as a wall of disagreeable clacking does, in the eight or nine minutes of the piece, begin to assume a kind of delicacy, as one after another the metronomes are no longer able to perform their vaunted function. The music is in the beginning of the silence. The annoying part of the Ligeti piece is its commencement, wherein the metronomes are behaving like metronomes. Pulsing, in their unrelenting and mechanical way.

Steve Reich's early tape pieces are another example of this tendency of technologically flavored musical compositions inevitably heading for the pulse. The best of these pieces, to these ears, is "Come Out" (1966), in which Reich takes a tape loop of a young African American man from Harlem who is recounting an encounter with the police ("I had to like open the bruise up and let some of the bruise blood come out to show them," *them* meaning the NYPD) and manipulates the tape loop, in and out of phase, pushing the recognizable language of the piece until it becomes a murky sludge of pulsing, without any *civil rights content at all*. What's the point of this piece? I confess that I really love it, and I confess that it gives me chills on occasion, but is not the meaning of the piece in the way that technology vitiates the powerful first-person of the narrator, shearing him away until he is not there at all? Is this process not like the judicial process abbreviating the rights of the African American in the New York City of 1966? Or is the point simply that technology, when it encounters what is most heartfelt, most personal, most dramatic, inevitably pushes it toward a machined veneer in which the personal becomes wholly secondary? Reich perhaps sensed the tricky interpretive environment surrounding "Come Out," because he made only one other tape piece, "It's Gonna Rain" (1965), which is more about the sound of African American street preaching, and thus a little less politicized. Also the tape murk toward the end of part two of "It's Gonna Rain" is slightly more rhythmically complex than on "Come Out."

Whatever the interpretation of these pieces, the middle sixties, in the midst of this technological ferment, soon found a crowded field in the development of drum machines and rhythmical synthesis. On the whole, these rhythm generators from the sixties were analogue re-creations of drum sounds, most of them made with oscillators, the primitive version of synthesizers, which were also beginning to be employed melodically elsewhere (in Raymond Scott's work, for example, or in Wendy Carlos's *Switched-On Bach*). Because the timbre of these synthesized drums didn't sound very much like drums at all, they were, in their way, somewhat beautiful, and insofar as they have dated now, they have grown only more ephemerally lovely in their old-world homeliness. They are things of the past.

When the great period of pop music experimentation collided with the drum machine, which is to say the period between 1968 and 1974—the pre-punk period of pop music modernism—people began to do some interesting things with these technologies. It turned out there were two ends of the electronic spectrum available to the discerning listener in 1971. The synthesizer had already been used in popular music by 1971, by the Beatles (on *Abbey Road*), by the Monkees, by the Mothers of Invention, by some of the prog rock pioneers (Rick Wakeman, Keith Emerson). But the drum machine didn't really begin to get its showcase until later. There were two divergent examples, as I say. One was rather unlikely: the soul music masterpiece of Sly and the Family Stone, *There's a Riot Goin' On*. Listen, if you will, to "Family Affair." The groove is beautiful, the melody is beguiling, Sly's voice, which kind of purrs, going in and out of the baritone, is *incredibly expressive*, but what is making that rather strange percussive sound that seems to be coexisting with some live drumming? Now you know. The drum machine.*

---

* A drummer friend, by way of contrast, notes the way Andy Newmark, on Sly Stone's next album, *Fresh*, fights against the drum machine on "If You Want Me to Stay." According to my friend, the sound is "both funky and uptight sounding."

The other example from 1971 couldn't be any further afield. It's to be found on *Tago Mago*, the wild, improvised, noisy, improbable album from the German experimental music pioneers Can. The particular track to showcase the drum machine, "Peking O," is long, quixotic, glued together in that sort of Karlheinz Stockhausen way that Can favored (indeed, one of their members studied with Stockhausen), and has plenty of acoustic drumming alongside its rather wild and irregular drum machine passages. Though I am no expert, these passages sound suspiciously to me like the Rhythm Ace, which, it's my understanding, came bundled with the Hammond organ in those days. And this would follow reasonably, since Can used electronic keyboards, organs among them, to great effect.

Can also had one of the very best drummers in rock-and-roll history, Jaki Liebezeit. His style, which left room in the groove, so that the bass and rhythm guitars might find their way in and out of the beat, but which had enough jazz in it not to sound, well, metronomic (*half man and half machine*, the band called him), would seem to have been the kind that manifestly opposed all the evils of drum machine technology. And, in fact, "Peking O" managed to use the drum machine without allowing it to dominate the rhythm at all. This sophisticated application is not unlike Can's sophistication with electronic voicings in general. Can were nothing if not experimenters.

Therefore: in the early seventies, there were two ways to use a drum machine. The first way was in the context of soul music. It seems clear to me that for Sly Stone the drum machine was part of an ongoing search for the *perfect rhythm section*. In Motown, of course, black music in the United States had accomplished something like rhythmical satori. The players in the Motown orchestra, not to mention in James Brown's band, or in Parliament-Funkadelic, were capable of such inventiveness that it was, arguably, impossible to do better. Sly Stone seemed to have decided, therefore, that the only way to play any tighter than James Jamerson and Uriel Jones was to be a machine.

That was one way to think about it.

The other way was German.

3.

Let it be said that I understand the *concept* of preferring robots to humans, because who does not find this flesh *too weak?* And I admire the honesty of people who claim they prefer robots to humans, but in the long run I do not entirely believe these futurists. I don't believe a unilateral robot preference. When Kraftwerk say that they want to be robots, or that they constitute a *man-machine symbiosis*, what I really think they are saying is that they are incapable of working with drummers.

The initial Kraftwerk, the repressed Kraftwerk, the band *before* its breakthrough of monotony, "Autobahn," made three albums: *Kraftwerk, Kraftwerk 2*, and *Ralf und Florian*. These albums, which reflect the origins of the two composers of the band (Ralf Hütter and Florian Schneider) in German experimental music (Stockhausen, especially), are interesting and, in the case of *Ralf und Florian*, singular, even strange. Among the uncharacteristic features of early Kraftwerk was Florian Schneider's interest in Hawaiian steel guitar, much present on the comical and heartwarming (it's almost a lullaby) "Ananas Symphonie," which manages to transcend the preset rhythm generator that appears on it. He (Florian) also played a fair amount of flute on these recordings, which is about as twee as you can get and still be a part of the rock-and-roll orchestra.

Kraftwerk also employed, in this early period, a sequence of drummers, most notably Klaus Dinger, who, with Michael Rother, then left Kraftwerk to form NEU!, the Krautrock band that exerted a significant influence on punk. Dinger's style, the so-called *motorik* drumming style, was noted, like Jaki Liebezeit's, for its simplicity and its absence of fills. Dinger did not hold the Kraftwerk drumming chair for long, though he played like a metronome, and that goes for all the other early Kraftwerk drummers too. If one were attempting to make a comparison between *motorik* and the "metronomic regularity" of Kraftwerk's later canned and sequenced electronic rhythms, you might suggest that German popular music generally seems to favor its totally stripped-down beats, its *clean* rhythms, its manufactured and repetitive drum parts. But there is a difference between *motorik* and drum machines. The difference is that Klaus Dinger is human, and his decision to limit his expressiveness is *discipline* in a live drummer, which is what makes the clean sound even cleaner. Kraftwerk wanted the drummers to accept the limitations imposed on them, at first, and for this reason they were unpopular with percussionists, as Ralf Hütter himself admitted: "Not only were we interested in Musique Concrète but also in playing organ tone clusters and flute feedback sounds that added variety to the repeated note sequences that we recorded and mixed on tape. Then we used several acoustic drummers as we turned our attention to more rhythmic music, and soon found that amplifying drums with contact mics was desirable for us but not readily accepted by the players."* Really? Was it the contact mics that the drummers objected to? Karl Bartos, who, with Wolfgang Flür, was one of the "drummers" during the high period of Kraftwerk's music, admitted to finding the job somewhat tedious, according to Pascal Bussy's *Kraftwerk: Man, Machine and Music*: "There were no offbeats and if I played offbeats they were rather disturbed by it."

Flür, who joined on drums in 1973, in order to facilitate a television appearance by Kraftwerk, remarks in his autobiography[†] that he followed a string of drummers who didn't work out: "They [Hütter and Schneider] told me about their appearances with Thomas Lohmann, a jazz drummer who was well known at that time, and how, after him, they made an attempt to get on with Klaus Dinger. This must have been a trial for them because both drummers had strong personalities and both regarded their drums as solo instruments."

Flür's autobiography, it should also be noted, is mostly about touring and frequently about the pursuit of groupies. Kraftwerk, in his version of the story, are more like other "rock bands" (I use the term for its quaintness) than we might suspect. For example, Flür argues that "The Model," the one and only Kraftwerk song about a specific desire for a specific woman, was about a great beauty from the Düsseldorf club

---

* Quoted in Pascal Bussy's *Kraftwerk: Man, Machine and Music* (SAF Publishing, 2001).

[†] *Kraftwerk: I Was a Robot* (Sanctuary Publishing, 2003).

scene called Christa Becker. Human, all too human! His autobiography is also notable for allusions to the homoerotic in its
pages, which perfume seems to go with drum machines and
dance rhythms like barbecue goes with condiments. Perhaps
because of these revelations, when the autobiography was first
published, the remaining band members sued, claiming,
among other things, that Flür did *not* play drums on "Autobahn." Legally, they seemed to be saying that there were *no
drums* on the album at all, or that they had machines do all the
heavy lifting. And yet with minor corrections (none of them
having to do with this classic early Kraftwerk composition),
the autobiography continues on in print. In those days, Kraftwerk were young, they crisscrossed the globe, they drank
occasionally (Flür apparently had a weakness for "sweet"
drinks), and they were mobbed by fans:

> The following day, I was lying with Ralf on a sun-
> lounger by the pool and we were talking…as so often,
> about girls. We felt safe talking in German, and were
> certainly not over-scrupulous about our language,
> until suddenly an amply built, fashionable lady next to
> me protested angrily in a Bavarian accent, "You could
> talk a bit more quietly.… Don't think that you're alone
> here in Miami!" We were shocked but we had to laugh
> out loud. We'd gone too far, expressing our intimate
> desires too loudly. When you're traveling, though,
> there's no more pleasant theme than love and desire.

And yet at the same time the band had begun assuming
the depersonalized guise of *robots*. I imagine that Kraftwerk is,

in part, intended to be a comedy act, and that all Kraftwerk albums are meant, to varying degrees, to be ironic. (I believe, for example, that *Radio-Activity* is not a pronuclear-themed album but, contrarily, an album about wanting to have your music broadcast on the radio.) See, for example, "Computer Love" and similar compositions. But it is also apparent that the cyborgian theme begins to rear its head ("Showroom Dummies," on *Trans-Europe Express*) at about the same time that the drummers become *unnecessary* to the band. "We are standing here / Exposing ourselves / We are showroom dummies / We are showroom dummies." While musicologists and cultural critics may try to create an argument whereby the doggedly moronic qualities of Kraftwerk lyrics are clever and forward-thinking, a sly compositional strategy somehow related to the Ramones ("Beat on the brat / Beat on the brat / Beat on the brat with a baseball bat / Oh yeah, oh yeah, uh-oh"), I feel that it's more likely that Kraftwerk simply could do no better and that "Showroom Dummies" is the beginning of a sense of alienation from the writing/recording/touring obligations of life as a successful musical act in the late seventies.

Thus, the band made actual robots to cavort at their gigs because it was *funny*. (Flür: "We found some standard clothes for our robots, which had wooden ball-and-socket joints at their shoulders, elbows and knees to allow them to be bent into position. Wooden rungs rose from the top of the models' torsos, and our finished heads were set on these. Now all we had to do was buy red shirts, black trousers and shoes for them.")* It was showbiz. And apparently Kraftwerk felt about touring

---

* *Kraftwerk: I Was a Robot.*

the same way that Andy Warhol did: he felt that it would be nice to have a double do his live appearances. Similarly, Kraftwerk perhaps found their predicament, their fame, inexplicable and strange, and they wanted to continue to enjoy a certain anonymity. Before long, Ralf Hütter even spoke of a halcyon future in which he could have his robot do his interviews for him, saying that the robot would know all the answers. And yet a trial run along these lines didn't go so well in Paris, according to Flür: "The press had been thoroughly unimpressed, and had pulled our dummies apart over the course of the evening."

The joke went too far, beginning on *The Man-Machine* (1978). And the relevant song from that album is "The Robots": "We're functioning automatic / And we are dancing mechanic / We are the robots / We are the robots / We are the robots / We are the robots," after which the vocoder enters with a Russian-language passage: "Ja tvoi sluga (I'm your slave) / Ja tvoi Rabotnik (I'm your worker)."

The album in question also had a song at its terminus designed to summarize the concept, lest the listeners fail to understand. The track was called "The Man-Machine." There, the will-to-cybernetics lyric goes thus: "Man Machine, pseudo human being / Man Machine, super human being."

What are the distinctive features of the Kraftwerk robots, as we understand them according to these lyrical iterations? The robots seem to function like *fembots*, or like sex slaves; that is, they offer pleasure without human consequences; additionally, the robots represent both a comical reduction of humanity ("pseudo human being") and Nietzschean evolutionary triumph ("super human being"). The music on the album likewise reflects a transition, becoming less an experimental inquiry (as had been the case since *Trans-Europe Express*) and, therefore, less unpredictable. *The Man-Machine* is a pop music confection, a mechanized, sequenced, and streamlined sound in which all the unpredictability has been left out. The jacket of *The Man-Machine*, meanwhile, was controversial in that the design, which mimicked Russian Constructivist El Lissitzky, featured the four members of the band wearing identical red shirts and black ties. Hard not to find a bit of totalitarianism lurking in the imagery, and indeed, the *perfection* of German culture, even when parodistically applied, does summon such a thing. The immediate postwar generation of German young people always faced this choice, for or against a legacy of the totalitarian. One result of the struggle is what you get in W. G. Sebald, a recoiling from fascism, a constant wrestling with the legacy. The other result is to constantly play with the edge of German *perfection*. As Flür has it in *Kraftwerk: I Was a Robot:*

> We had no adult role models from whom we could learn to take pride in our own culture. How could we comfortably feel German in a country where there had been book burning, banned pictures, ruinous film criticism and "degenerate art" a short time ago? A time when many of our German poets, painters, composers, actors, and the most ingenious engineers and inventors had been driven from the country and fled into exile?

Maybe the drum machines, in this circumstance, become a necessity, or a natural outgrowth of a music that, whether or not for comic effect, refuses to engage with humanism, whether in order to make comment on native German culture or in order to call attention to the rigidities in German politics. Ralf Hütter and Florian Schneider, in the end, *wanted* to disaffect themselves completely, in the context of Kraftwerk, and to make themselves fit only for parody. As if to say something about the choices left to them in the cultural moment?

There was one more "good" album, *Computer World* (1981), true, the title of which no longer feels futuristic at all but feels more like the name of a popular technology magazine, one with a diminishing number of ad pages. I really liked this album when it came out, and I still do kind of like it. I confess, I also like *Trans-Europe Express* a lot. I confess, and it is an unavoidable confession, that Kraftwerk wrote very good melodies, and when they bothered to excel at writing melodies, they stood for something musical. It is no coincidence that they constantly refer to the Beach Boys and the Ramones as fellow travelers and influences. Both bands, though aesthetically far from the "metronomic regularity" of Krautrock, were great melody writers, great evokers of place and time. Kraftwerk, in their musical compositions, which is to say in their *melodic* composition, and their minimal chord voicings, clearly *do* have a great gift for popularizing and for writing the catchy hook. They reached their apex on *Computer World*.

"What music isn't experimental?" Hütter once reportedly asked of Brian Eno, apparently to try to rationalize their more commercial output. The level at which this question is posed is not a terribly complex level. Indeed, any time you record a track, you are trying something *new*, even if in doing so you are doing it exactly the same way you did it before. Historical repetition is not as easy as it would seem. But still. After *The Man-Machine*, Kraftwerk's output is more concerned with technological innovation than with musical innovation. The songs, after a point, sound identical, and the same is true of the lyrics, with their campy celebration of gadgetry. What changes is the synthesizer technologies and, to some extent, the timbre of the drum machines.

Which means that this music dates very, very quickly. In fact, Kraftwerk, in lieu of releasing a greatest-hits package, did release a remix package in 1991 called *The Mix*,* which tinkered with the classics of the band by attempting to update the drum sounds. By then, however, there was nothing more to say. Ralf Hütter's obsession with cycling gave the band one new track in 1983, "Tour de France," which they then tricked out with some samplers and digital geegaws for 2003's *Tour de France Soundtracks*, after seventeen years of silence.

What are these middle-aged guys doing in Düsseldorf now? Why so long between albums? Why so much silence, so much inaction? There are a couple of possibilities. Either (1) they are *afraid* of trying to live up to what they have done, or (2) they have realized that their metaphor, the will-to-robot metaphor, the hybrid or cyborgian metaphor, is played out, has no *life* left in it, is a dead end. They would probably assert, (3) that they are perfectionists, and that they have been laboring for most of the past twenty years in the studio, staying ahead of the curve (like Axl Rose) by realizing the new potential in computers, in sampling, and so on. Don't believe these rationalizations.

Which is another way of saying that staking your musical

---

* They recently released remasters of their early albums as well.

creativity on drum machines and synthesized technology means not only that you drain your work of most of its warmth, but also that you build in your own obsolescence, and that is what Kraftwerk have done. In the late seventies, they were influential, in that they spawned a great number of imitators (of which more below), but both Kraftwerk and the imitators sound, these days, hopelessly quaint. They sound as new as doo-wop or hot jazz. They sound about as futuristic as "Popcorn" by Hot Butter. Kraftwerk have *toured* recently, but what does it mean to make live music by Kraftwerk in the twenty-first century? Apparently it means that everyone in the early versions of the band is retired or forced out except Ralf Hütter (who is accompanied by some lighting designers and video designers who stand onstage manipulating prerecorded tracks with their laptops). It also means that they are not going to play anything substantial that was written after 1981, or, at the time I write these lines, twenty-eight years ago. I for one would rather stay home. Which is what Florian Schneider now does too.

4.

Something in me cannot fail to associate the German perfectionism of Kraftwerk with the broad outlines of Nietzschean thinking. There is some of Nietzsche's vigorous and slightly terrifying self-will in Kraftwerk, likewise some of Nietzsche's paradoxical approach. A German orderliness, a German mania, and a German lack of humility. And it was with this in mind that I stumbled recently on the following from Oliver Sacks's *Musicophilia* (2007):

Nietzsche was intensely interested, throughout his life, in the relationship of art, and especially music, to physiology. He spoke of its "tonic" effect — its power of arousing the nervous system in a general way, especially during states of physiological and psychological depression.... He also spoke of the "dynamic" or propulsive powers of music — its ability to elicit, to drive, and to *regulate* movement. Rhythm, he felt, could propel and articulate the stream of movement (and the stream of emotion and thought, which he saw as no less dynamic or *motoric* than the purely muscular). [Italics mine.]

Sacks goes on in a footnote:

Nietzsche, in his essay "Nietzsche contra Wagner," speaks of Wagner's late music as exemplifying "the pathological in music," marked by a "degeneration of the sense of rhythm" and a tendency to "endless melody...the polypus in music." The lack of *rhythmic organization* in late Wagner makes it almost useless for parkinsonians; this is also true of plainsong and various forms of chant. [Italics mine.]

Polypus? Is that what Nietzsche really means? Melody is a kind of octopus? And octopi are to be *avoided* for some reason? Sacks then alludes to the way similar ideas about rhythm get expanded and articulated in Nietzsche's later work, *The Will to Power*. Readers more interested in music, or neurology, would be inclined to overlook the fact that *The Will to Power* is generally, among scholars of Nietzsche's later work, completely repudiated—having been cobbled together posthumously by his sister and heavily redacted (not to say adulterated) by her in order to distort Nietzsche's work in directions that satisfied her anti-Semitic needs.

There has been some really great German electronic music made in the past twenty years. I'm thinking of Oval, Microstoria, and Mouse on Mars (the last of which eventually collaborated with former Kraftwerk "drummer" Wolfgang Flür), bands that solved the problem of "metronomic regularity" and the totalitarian stain of German rhythmic perfection by (in the case of Oval, e.g.) avoiding drums and rhythm entirely (much of Oval's music was composed by using skipping CDs) or, in the case of Mouse on Mars, by affecting a very comical warmth that depends on reggae, bossa nova, surf, tango, and other somewhat effusive musics. Mouse on Mars is a libidinous, whimsical, and hilarious band, one constantly fighting off the cool exterior of synthesized music, and it's for this reason that they get away with their technological felicities.

The first bands slavishly to follow Kraftwerk, to drink deep of their Apollonian linearity, had none of this comedy and warmth. They took not only the electronic surface from Kraftwerk, but they took, if you like, all the will-to-power imagery; they took the dehumanized thematic material of *The Man-Machine* and *Computer World* and fused it with some of the recessionary post-Christian, secular gloom that, while it can undergird German culture, never found in that country a host body as perfect as in *England*. The synthetic bands of the early eighties, the primarily British synthetic bands, missed the irony and paradox in Kraftwerk, which is like thinking that *The Will to Power* has anything to do with *Beyond Good and Evil*, and they embraced the despond and numbness of electronica as though this were *the* affect of the times. Whereas punk, played primarily on guitars, made and felt fury in order to empower politically and emotionally, synthesized postpunk—in bands like Ultravox, Visage, Orchestral Manoeuvres in the Dark, Magazine, the Human League, Heaven 17, Blancmange, Soft Cell, and so on—was about disengagement and anhedonia. Many of these bands (with some notable exceptions, Gary Numan and the later OMD) used drum machines, as if the absence of a drummer, and with it the absence of the Dionysian joy of great drumming, were somehow essential to the dehumanized and slightly sophomoric dejection sketched out in this work.*

And from out of the tortured but slightly embarrassing depths of British electropop of the early eighties came, arguably, the preeminent exemplars of the form, at least in this first incarnation, Depeche Mode. They are unlikely musical heroes, for the simple reason that they have, twice over, off-loaded the best musicians in the band along the way. And yet they have, like certain indestructible species of insects, endured. They were founded in 1980, in Basildon, which is about twenty-five miles east of London, just far enough away to be *out of town*, which is to say *parochial*, which is to say confined to the borders of the parish, and initially they were formed from the comingling of a pair of bands that featured old-fashioned guitars and

---

* Precisely sophomoric for me, as it was in sophomore year in college that I bought *Organisation* by OMD and *Tubeway Army* by Gary Numan. I thought, at the time, that the brooding, lovelorn futurism of these albums was sublime.

even *drums*. All the usual rock-and-roll stuff. Two of the members of the resulting collective, keyboardist and songwriter Vince Clarke and singer David Gahan, were poorer, were solidly working-class, and therefore more driven by need and circumstance. The other two members, Martin Gore and Andy Fletcher, had proper jobs. Gore, in fact, worked in banking. These two were considered the less gifted members, and Fletcher, in fact, played an instrument, the electric bass, that was quickly eliminated from the ensemble upon its movement into the synthetic realm.

What did it mean to go *electronic?* In part it meant that you were under the sway of Kraftwerk. It also meant that you couldn't afford a drummer or a rehearsal space, things that had probably been easier in an earlier period of rock and roll that didn't require walls of amplifiers and mixing boards and expensive electrical gadgets. Indeed, Depeche Mode, in their early rehearsals, played with headphones on, so as to avoid *bothering the neighbors.* Of the decision to eschew a drummer, Dave Gahan, ever the talkative member, said, "The tapes we've got now sound like real drums anyway. I know Orchestral Manoeuvres in the Dark were put down for using a drum machine on stage but the worst thing they ever did was to get a drummer. It was really bad after that. We don't need one anyway—*it's just another person to pay.*"* The early drum section therefore consisted of "one of those Selmer auto-rhythm drum boxes with the little pitter-patter beats that you put on top of your home organ" (p. 3).

---

* Steve Malins, *Depeche Mode: Black Celebration* (Andre Deutsch, 2007), p. 30, italics mine.

The first Depeche Mode album, *Speak & Spell*, was a huge success for a band still only in their late teens and early twenties, and the compositions, while mostly rudimentary (especially with thirty years' hindsight), have an appalling tunefulness, even a cheerfulness, notably absent from the later work. That is probably because the chief writer, Vince Clarke, soon to quit the band, wrote the songs and, though much alienated from this somewhat alienated band, he prevented goth moping, under his reign, from rising to the surface. "Just Can't Get Enough," the best-known song from the album, is cut-rate Motown fluff, as singable and as cheery, with some gospel passing chords and synths that are just duplicating what the horns would otherwise be playing. This album has nothing to do with the Kraftwerk part of this account, and that is perhaps why Vince Clarke *had to go*, and why Depeche Mode had to turn in a much different direction in order to achieve its infamy.

This different direction runs from the second album, *A Broken Frame*, released in 1982, up to *Violator*, from 1990, a span of six studio albums, and it includes some of the most popular "alternative rock" songs of the period, on the basis of which many wildly excessive epithets have been affixed to the Depeche Mode legacy. The thematic material of most of this work is somewhat superficially dark, somewhat brooding, and obsessed with sex, in particular sadomasochism, or at least a sadomasochism as imagined by a seventeen-year-old from the suburbs or, later, a twenty-five-year-old from the suburbs, and this is how the band got a reputation, despite its squeaky-clean synthesizer parts, its drum machines, and its dearth of sexiness, for being *goth*.

It's very difficult to listen to this music now without embarrassment. It was also difficult back during the period of Depeche Mode's chart success, which began with the baldly simplistic "People Are People," or perhaps with the single that preceded it (from the prior album), "Everything Counts," which at least had the virtue of being anti-capitalist, but which also managed to combine economic naïveté with music that had to be played by machines, it seemed, for the simple reason that the players themselves were not able to do otherwise (which is another important reason for the drum machine revolution: inability), this being especially evident in the case of Andy Fletcher, who has managed to remain in Depeche Mode without writing, singing, or playing anything on the recordings or during the live shows. It's as if the band insisted their accountant have a place on the stage with them.

Their determined oversimplification persisted well beyond "People Are People," in such dramas of insight as "Master and Servant," "Black Celebration," "Never Let Me Down Again," and later works. If, in the middle 1980s, you were listening to the stuff coming out of SST Records, say, or maybe, to be slightly less inflexible, the poppier material released on Coyote Records in Hoboken, as I was, there was good reason to think of Depeche Mode as the leading edge of a certain kind of mall music.

It didn't seem to make a difference what the critics and rock-and-roll enthusiasts thought, though, since by 1988 Depeche Mode was headlining in Pasadena, at the Rose Bowl, in front of seventy thousand, a feat preserved by D. A. Pennebaker in *101*, which documentary proved not only that the band had almost nothing to say backstage, but that its fans didn't either. Pennebaker apparently knew nothing about Depeche Mode before he contracted to make the documentary, but he says he wasn't really interested in Bob Dylan's work before *Don't Look Back* either. What is undeniable in the film is the absolute lack of live energy apparent during the course of the program. (If all your rhythms are preprogrammed, e.g., there is no chance that your excitement will cause the tempos to surge.) A great portion of the material is played by samplers and MIDI keyboards without undue input by the musicians, excepting Alan Wilder and Martin Gore, about the latter of whom it might be said that his diffidence is sweet but not musical. Gore just seems to stand there, and since Fletcher contributes nothing, and Wilder has to cue the machines, that leaves David Gahan, the lead singer, to do most of the work with respect to the audience, which he is not entirely capable of doing, despite a great deal of hortatory shouting—and no wonder he fell into the chasm of addiction for a good long spell in the nineties (which is why the significant period of Depeche Mode ends with *Violator*, during the tour for which Gahan apparently began his free fall and not long after which Wilder quit).

Was it the times? Did the eighties just make tinny, irritating superficiality inevitable? Along with digital reverb? Did anyone think to *avoid* putting digital reverb on their drum tracks? Could Kajagoogoo or Wang Chung have come from any other time in history? Even people who should have known better, like the members of New Order, fell prey to the allure of the drum machine and the sequencer, and the fashionable anomie of the dance-inflected fully programmable pop song. It was like a sexually transmitted virus sweeping the British Empire.

And yet my argument is that the drum machines dictated the material, not vice versa. Once you have the drum machines, the material *inevitably* tends toward "Master and Servant," or "Blue Monday," or "Tainted Love," or "Sweet Dreams (Are Made of This)," and this is in part because after Kraftwerk, and the robotics that had been brought into being through their work and fused with their drum machines, you had a *thematic tendency*, a theme that made the most out of the inflexibility, the rigidity of the beats, and that rigidity made for an unfeeling surface, which in turn led to songs about an absence of feeling. There is no moment of joy in a Depeche Mode performance when the players are swept up in Dionysian celebration, and there is no surprise in the compositions, because they are played the same way every night, and it's no wonder that Martin Gore, despite having written the songs, looks bored or depressed while playing them.

The nihilism of this approach also implies, in due course, another inevitable subject, at least in Britain, and that is European secularism. British atheism is part of a storied tradition. It's so fervent that it seems, on occasion, indistinguishable from the Church of England itself. Indeed, if you imagine that the Church of England is a particular philosophical system, if you imagine that Anglicans are "people of the book," as they are said to be, then *complete doubt* about the central tenets of Christianity seems simply to be one more interpretation among others, one that is completely consistent with total interpretive liberation, a hallmark of the national faith. Atheism, that is, is very Anglican, very Church of England, and that is perhaps why the British are so unyielding about their atheism. The relentlessness of it, the hectoring of it, the guy-in-the-pub-with-the-gin-blossoms-and-incipient-cirrhosis-who-won't-quit-bludgeoning-you-with-his-boorish-point-of-view, this relentlessness is hard to take, especially among people who used to, at one point, be noted for their fine manners. But there is nothing surprising about atheism, viewed from a historical perspective, except the fact that the British keep on insisting that it's all about *science*. You'd think that the esteem for a certain penurious bohemianism in Britain, not to mention Fabian socialism, would drive the citizenry back into the arms of faith, where at least there is ritual, seflessness, sexual license, and wonder,* but no, for the moment, in England, the British subjects would rather be miserable, correct, and condemned to Marks & Spencer and Marmite.

And thus, in England, the history of drum machines and of *rhythmic organization* is conjoined to a Nietzschean feeling of *neglect by God*, and this comes up again and again in the Depeche Mode story, since nearly every one of the original members was a churchgoing kid, and some of them even met there. Gahan "had a religious upbringing thanks to his mother's side of the family, who were involved in the Salvation Army" (*Black Celebration*, p. 6). And Martin Gore's extensive trail of comments on churchgoing includes the following: "I was going...a lot [as a child], not because I believed in it, but

---

* Of course, some people think this is true of the raves of 1988 to 1989, that they constituted an engagement with the numinous, but more on that subject in a moment.

because there was nothing else to do on a Sunday. I found the service very hard to take seriously. The whole set-up is quite handy but I'm not sure that's what God intended. Particularly a part of the service called the Prayer List, when the preacher rattles off the names of those sick and about to die. The person at the top of the list was guaranteed to die, but still everyone went right ahead thanking God for carrying out his will" (*Black Celebration*, p. 90). Andy Fletcher was also a regular church attendant, to the point of going, in childhood, "seven nights a week" (p. 2), and Vince Clarke, according to Fletcher himself, was the same: "He was a real Bible basher" (ibid.).

If much of the British synthetic pop of the eighties had Anglican atheism serving as its structuring absence, in addition to a lite version of the existentialism of Nietzsche, then why was Martin Gore so preoccupied with God later on? (As in the following from a midcareer interview: "I do believe in some sort of power even though I haven't really had any experience myself. I'm still searching. I really like the idea of belief, but I've never found anything to believe in. The only Godlike things I know are sex and love. In my eyes God is sex personified.... Therefore it's no surprise that I write about God, sex and love all the time. As far as I'm concerned they're the biggest mystery of the planet" (p. 182). Or even later: "I wake up every day and I see sunshine and I see amazing mountain views and I do feel a little more in touch with God, whatever God is" (p. 265). Thus, it appears: Depeche Mode loved their perfect beats, they loved their psychosexual darkness, but they were also preoccupied with spiritual questions.

Which is why I want to talk about a few songs in the Depeche Mode canon that seem to *violate* the Nietzschean anti-Christian tradition, asserting instead a kind of engaged spirituality that has grown more sustained over the decades. While still intellectually soft, the more middle-aged these synthetic goth avatars have become, the more mortal, the more human, they appear. They are, on the basis of these songs below, a gospel band, a gospel band pretending to be a rock-and-roll band pretending to be a synth pop band. It becomes truer with each passing year.

The first song I want to examine is "Blasphemous Rumours," from *Some Great Reward* (1984). Now, the *narrative* of "Blasphemous Rumours," such as it is, is glaringly insipid: "Girl of sixteen / Whole life ahead of her / Slashed her wrists / Bored with life / Didn't succeed / Thank the lord / For small mercies / Fighting back the tears / Mother reads the note again / Sixteen candles burn in her mind / She takes the blame / It's always the same / She goes down on her knees / And prays." That's verse one. In any accounting of the compositional shortfalls here, one has to include the "Sixteen candles burn in her mind" line, as well as the "Bored with life" formulation. But I enjoy the fact that the verses don't rhyme—it gives the whole a ripped-from-the-headlines salaciousness. Furthermore, the "Thank the lord for small mercies" passage has an irony that is winning. If the song at this point is meant to be "blasphemous," it manifests only a very gentle blasphemy, confining itself, in fact, to a sorrow that the story as described *exists*, that the girl *slashed her wrists*, that this Depeche Mode audience member, for such are the implications, *slashed her wrists;* or perhaps the blasphemy finds itself in the sorrow that the writer, viz., Martin Gore, had to bear witness; or perhaps the blasphemy is in the chorus of the song, the incredibly catchy chorus, where the song rises up from its sluggish verse, its goth verse, into the gospel affirmation of the chorus, an ostinato of a melody that feels very Beatles-ish, in which the narrator repeats, "I don't want to start / Any blasphemous rumors / But I think that God's / Got a sick sense of humor / And when I die / I expect to find Him laughing."

What's revealing in this catchy chorus is first the blunt expectation of the narrator's own death (it's always an excellent lyrical trope—in the blues, or in "My Generation," or just about anywhere—the foreknowledge of the narrator's own death), but further there is an implication in the chorus that God's omnipotence is *limited*, and just as He/She/It cannot prevent the suicide attempt in verse one, God also cannot prevent the car crash in verse two: "Girl of eighteen / Fell in love with everything / Found new life / In Jesus Christ / Hit by a car / Ended up / On a life support machine / Summer's day / As she passed away / Birds were singing / In the summer sky / Then came the rain / And once again / A tear fell / From her mother's eye." One wants to ask if this character, this second *girl*, otherwise unknown, is the same as in verse one, but let's not pursue what is avoidable, let's say instead that in verse two the girl is simply one further example of the *flock* who, according to the theology of Depeche Mode, is unable to sidestep tragedy this time, in the form of car accident, despite her faith, and this inevitable tragedy is ironic, as in verse one. After which: we get the chorus again, with multiple reiterations, and thus multiple invocations of Martin Gore's own death, or David Gahan's death (if you accept the idea that Gore writes for Gahan's point of view).

This would be the interpretation according to the

commandments of Anglican atheism, according to the rigidities of the drum machine and its ethos. People suffer, God laughs. But what if the irony is even deeper than it looks, and what is happening here is that Gore's ability to observe the hardships and tragedies of his core audience, the teens of the suburban latitudes and their aggrieved parents, *is somehow generous*, strangely generous, and that a laughing God, a sort of a Buddhist God, a noninterventionist God who perhaps laughs morosely with sorrow, is somehow the only one to expect, and that what is under scrutiny here, in the song, both lyrically in the chorus and in its sad, dirgeful verses, is *not* theology as a whole but just a slightly *moronic* theology that expects an easy parking-space God who oversees the minutiae, but that gets instead not a callous God but a noninterventionist, compassionate God who, as Tolstoy said, *sees the truth but waits*, and whose compassion is, in this case, being redoubled by the compassion of a lyrically challenged songwriter who nonetheless *feels much*, e.g., his own death, among others.

I've said little about the music, which, I'm ashamed to say, I still find rather moving, despite the dated sequencers and the leaden thud of a really plodding drum program (a Roland or a LinnDrum). But it bears mentioning that in the single edit of the song, with one minute remaining, the drum machines *give out*, and there is a sort of plangent inspiring of breath (the protagonist on the life-support machine or, perhaps, Martin Gore breathing in the implications of his own observations for a solid minute). It can't, this section, have received much *airplay* when the song was in wide circulation. But it is integral to the full spectrum of threnodic misery here. In short, "Blasphemous Rumours," despite its modest origins, rises to a level of strange, ambiguous spiritual insight, especially when the drum machines give out at the end—perhaps *because* the drum machines give out—and it affirms the unlimited *agape* of the divine space and even admits to an afterlife, in that Martin Gore's lyric implies a posthumous encounter with God, all this, even as the song preserves a sort of cynical veneer for those who do not feel invited into the greater profundities.

A second stop in any theological tour of Depeche Mode must land at "Personal Jesus," from *Violator* (1990), which, frankly, is a very good song, if you like this sort of thing—the electropop sort of thing. "Personal Jesus," at the very least, is the end point for a certain kind of Depeche Mode, for the simple reason that it's the first time the band permitted the unalloyed use of the instrument known as the *electric guitar.* They had, it is said, sampled guitars before, but they had not made the electric guitar the mainstay of a composition, as it assuredly is in "Personal Jesus," since the whole is organized around a blues riff that wouldn't have been out of place on a composition by Stevie Ray Vaughan or Eric Clapton. The synthesizers make their appearance eventually, as they must, but in the main the guitar is the thing here, and the rhythm is dumb and loud, like an infant beating on a shoe box, though the synthetic percussion tries to manage a double-time chirping (in the B section) to keep it all from getting too rhythmically Cro-Magnon. In vain. It's a rock-and-roll song, a blunt force instrument, by a band more given to "dance music." As such, it has the sacred-and-profane paradox that great rock and roll often had in the fifties.

Is it an Elvis Presley composition, therefore? Something influenced by the King? A synth band trying on *delusions of*

Vegas? In fact, Martin Gore has remarked that "Personal Jesus" is a *Priscilla* Presley song. He further describes it thus: "It's a song about being a Jesus for somebody else, someone to give you hope and care. It's about how often that happens in love relationships—how everybody's heart is like a god in some way" (p. 150). However, if this was meant therefore to be a secular composition, in which Jesus is just one aspect of the contemporary relationship, "some radio stations [nonetheless] interpreted it as a 'religious tribute.'" And no less an expert than the Man in Black, a.k.a. Johnny Cash, was willing to throw his weight behind this religious interpretation when he later covered the song (with the usual sublime touch) on *American IV: The Man Comes Around:* "That's probably the most evangelical song [I've] ever recorded. I don't know that the writer ever meant it to be that, but that's what it is. . . . It's about where you find your comfort, your counsel, your shoulder to lean on, your hand to hold on to, your personal Jesus" (p. 272).

Even more than those of "Blasphemous Rumours," the lyrics in "Personal Jesus" repel a definitive interpretation. It's clear in the song that the telephone is the operative technology for theological exchange ("Lift up the receiver / I'll make you a believer"), which gives the whole a tawdry phone sex vibe, just as the second person, in the context of the bludgeoning clumsiness of the lyric ("Feeling unknown / And you're all alone"), leads the listener far from the lexical units of the *conversion narrative,* and yet the tawdriness is so tenderly evoked (as in "Put me to the test / Things on your chest / You need to confess / I will deliver / You know I'm a forgiver") that the whole does suggest a route to the kind of absolution that one would *like* to have in a redeemer, and this even if the sex part is all mixed up with the redemption part, according to the kind of gospel tropes that we would associate more frequently with a song like Al Green's "Take Me to the River." Again and again in "Personal Jesus" the line "Reach out and touch faith" recurs; it's the hook, and while it's possible that *faith* would mostly seem abstract or even completely *delusional* (to use the Richard Dawkins word) according to Anglican atheism and to the dehumanized veneer of the drum machine, Gore affirms its *tactility*, its texture, and makes faith fleshy and unabstract.

"Personal Jesus" was a monster of a song, true; it changed the landscape for Depeche Mode entirely, it *crossed over*, it had massive global penetration, it probably played in the Casbah from the radios in the stalls of rug merchants and in the opium dens of Southeast Asia, just as it played at the recruiting stations where the American military was organizing and recruiting for the first Gulf War, and you can sort of imagine the infantry playing it in the tanks and on sand dunes and on rooftops. It was everywhere. From a careerist perspective, it enabled the longest and largest tour of the band's history, which tour enabled the flowering of David Gahan's drug problem. It also created a need for something Depeche Mode had never needed before: *a live drummer.* Alan Wilder served in that capacity occasionally, and then, when Wilder left, the role was mainly occupied by one Christian Eigner.

Live drums! True, there was a lot of programming and live drums playing along with synthesized drums, but there was also, in Depeche Mode after *Violator*, a lot of *faith*; their next album, in fact, was called *Songs of Faith and Devotion*, and it featured an out-and-out gospel number called "Condemnation," as well as another, only marginally concealed, called

"Higher Love." The tendency toward articulations of spiritual material, furthermore, was not confined to albums released during Gahan's heroin addiction, because once he was clean, the band made *Playing the Angel* (2005). *Sounds of the Universe* (2009), to bring the catalogue up to date, issued about the time I started writing about Depeche Mode, includes "Peace," a chant of the frankly spiritual sort: "I'm leaving bitterness / Behind this time / I'm cleaning out my mind," and, later, "I'm going to light up the world." Not exactly the brooding, self-absorbed, bondage-and-discipline-lite synthetic pop you associate with a band of squeaky-clean naïfs from the early 1980s. Which indicates, it seems, the limitation of the approach, the limitation of the Kraftwerk-influenced, *rhythmically organized*, drum-machine-addicted nihilism of early British electronic pop. *You can't live like that forever.* If you are lucky enough to survive living that way (which Gahan did, by surviving his heroin addiction; which Gore did, by surviving his drinking-related seizure disorder; which Fletcher did, by overcoming multiple *nervous breakdowns* during the *Violator* period), you can't help, it seems, but begin to express some gratitude. And then the music begins to reflect this gratitude, this human feeling. Which is why Nietzsche, you know, intervened to save that horse from being flogged.

5.

The historical significance of Depeche Mode was already beyond dispute by the era of *Violator*. Whether you liked them or not. The stadium shows ensured that this was the case.

Their superficial, frothy, sexually ambiguous, disconsolate, heavily machined sound was already influential, had already made its mark. The later albums, the ones made by middle-aged men, with actual drums, sold exceedingly well (still do) to auteurists, to people who are deceived by the lighter sentiments of pop songs. But the influence of the early Depeche Mode, that dank worldview, had long passed on, at one extreme to musicians who would make dirge-oriented guitar music like Linkin Park or Fear Factory, and at the other extreme to the composers who would start a very different and parallel revolution, the begetters of Detroit House.

Indeed, Derrick May and Juan Atkins and Kevin Saunderson, also known as the Belleville Three for the suburb that spawned them, Belleville, Michigan, have each cited Depeche Mode among their influences. Here's Derrick May on the subject: "They set a standard in what they do. In America they've been able to please almost everyone, from a guy like me who's a hard-core dance addict, to the stadium crowds. They're *right on time, right in sync,* and they can't even help it. They have dance in their blood" (p. 140, italics mine). The remark implies a veiled or slightly inadvertent bit of racial stereotyping, i.e., the Belleville Three are African American artists, and they come from a music tradition that is often noteworthy for rhythmical sophistication, and yet May is here bestowing upon the British band the highest sign of respect an African American can give a white European act: they are *right in sync.* Of course, the Depeche Mode at the time of the ascendancy of *Detroit House* was a Depeche Mode *in sync* with a *drum machine;* they were shackled to their devices, and so what May is approving of is just that. They were *in sync* with *machines.* And the drum machine so much beloved of the early Detroit House artists was the Roland TR-909—probably used by Depeche Mode, too, at one point or another—which had an onboard sequencer so that entire songs could be stored in it. It was both analogue and digital (could contain samples), and it has had such an impact that now, in the era of computer-triggered drumbeats, it's still being sampled, for that vintage *semi-analogue* vibe.

At one point, sensing cultural fusion, a magazine actually paid for Depeche Mode to take a trip to Detroit, in order to forge a sympathy with the emerging artists of American electronica. With mixed results, according to Depeche Mode's Alan Wilder:*

> The remit was, You lads fly over to Detroit and meet Derrick May, pretend you're old buddies and talk about Techno. Our press guy said, "Yes, OK, that's an angle." So I was like, "Who is Derrick May?" I didn't want to go halfway across the world to pretend to be buddies with this bloke but that's exactly what we did. We all went to May's flat and pretended we were part of this scene. Derrick May was horrible, I hated him. He was the most arrogant fucker I've ever met. He took us into his backroom where he had a studio and played us this track and it was fucking horrible.

Racial cross-pollination is happening here, after a fashion, and continental cross-pollination, and these are significant things, because these kinds of stylistic influences happen less

---

* Quoted in *Black Celebration*.

frequently than they ought. How did it happen? Part of the reason the Belleville Three were able to understand and appreciate the blunt, unsophisticated rhythms of European electropop has to do, I'd argue, with the automobile industry. Belleville was home to a large number of American auto workers, workers in an industry that was completely multiracial and that had raised up a great number of black families into the middle class (before, that is, the American auto industry began to *collapse*, taking the Detroit area along with it). May, Saunderson, and Atkins, therefore, went to an integrated high school in Belleville, and they were able to soak up a range of music happening around them, not only the funk and soul on the inner-city Detroit FM stations, but the corn-fed midwestern rock and roll, and even some of the new wave that was popular in the early eighties (they have cited, for example, the B-52s on the playlists of their youths).

In passing, Derrick May has referred to Detroit House as "like George Clinton and Kraftwerk caught in an elevator with only a sequencer to keep them company," and this is witty and appropriate, but he's unstating the assembly line imagery that connects Detroit to Düsseldorf, and the mechanization of automobile manufacture as it specifically relates to the *rhythmic organization* of Detroit House. This is where Kraftwerk and Detroit House really meet up, because, as already noted, "Autobahn," the first recording of the fully matured Kraftwerk, is another piece of music that depends on the aural landscape of the automobile and its manufacture.

If, by way of comparison, you take a track like "Clear," by Cybotron, one of Juan Atkins's earliest compositions in the style of Detroit House, it's clear that it's not only the drum machine, the *motorik*, that the artist is borrowing from Kraftwerk (likewise from the high period of Depeche Mode et al.). He's also borrowing the dystopian worldview from the British synthetic movement and the robotics from Kraftwerk. The lyrics, such as they are, both sped up and slowed down, are futuristic, cyborgian, and already seem to forecast a dystopian Motor City that is fallen on the hardest of times. "Clear" sounds really dated now, very skeletal, in the same way that *Computer World* by Kraftwerk sounds dated, and yet the effect it had on dance music is almost incalculable. Between the Detroit sound, with its postindustrial futurism, and the slightly more louche Chicago House sound, as characterized in, e.g., Frankie Knuckles, electronic music of the Midwest spawned an entire form, especially when the music was first licensed in the UK (about the time that Depeche Mode was making *Violator*). The UK was beginning to have a club scene, and it needed club music, as it had not much of its own, and so it turned to Detroit, where the sonic innovation was. Thus the thematic material of Detroit House, the approach and the subject matter, became the bedrock on which a lot of the British variant, *hardcore*, was later produced.

It would be bad faith to understate the fact of the racial identity here, as it relates entirely to the way the music was programmed and constructed. There was, as I have said, the tradition of groove-related excellence in African American popular music. As noted above, with Motown there were the great rhythm sections in the label's house band, and Motown came from the same city as Detroit House, and so the drum machine, to the artists of the form, must have represented an affordable way to get somewhere near to the perfection of an *ancestral sound*, a Motown sound, especially poignant in view of the fact that that label had, by the late nineties, decamped to Los Angeles. And there's that John Henry analogy here. A flawless live drummer playing a backing track for the Supremes or the Temptations is a thing of grace because he is *just a man*, with a commitment to flawlessness, a man who shall never get there; whereas a drum machine, playing the same part, can do nothing but what it is programmed to do. A machine flattens the rhythm, dumbs it down, doesn't play well because it is a sign of respect and honor to do so, but plays because it does exactly what it is told to do and nothing else. This drum machine has no commitment, it has only *engineering*.

The Belleville Three grafted the politics of the assembly line and the cyborg onto this rationale for their rhythm, and they did so with a genuine political astuteness, but they also ensured in the process that a lot of drummers would be put out of work, and that syncopation would become an endangered species, at least for a time (until subgenres like drum and bass and jungle), and, to these ears, they would inadvertently spawn one of the dullest, most plodding, and least human musical rhythmic approaches to music *ever invented*, one that barely needs the hands of a human creator to engender it. *Four to the floor*, as it is sometimes called, the thudding downbeat on the one and trebly imitation snare snap on the other three.

But before I talk briefly about how Ecstasy helped make the European response to this music even stupider, I want briefly to remind those who have forgotten that the African American music that *bucks* the drum machine trend (which now afflicts hip-hop, too, as it edges ever closer to a purely synthetic, or electronic, veneer) is almost always more fascinating, more rich, more indelible than its mechanized relations, and this is why, I would argue, *Phrenology*, by the Roots, is among the *greatest hip-hop albums ever made*, by a band that, without a doubt, is the most creative and most interesting *band* playing these days, a band, a group of like-minded people making art *together*, celebrating *together*, and when I say the Roots are the best, I mean the best band playing music of any genre or sub-genre. I mean: in terms of *band sound* and group discipline and revolutionary capabilities, the Roots are up there with, e.g., Metallica, or Tinariwen, or Ladysmith Black Mambazo, or Orchestra Baobob, or Huun Huur Tu, or Sonic Youth, or the Meredith Monk Ensemble, or even *the Rolling Stones;* in fact they are *better* than the Rolling Stones. More disciplined. Only the P-Funk All Stars for sheer understated excellence give them a run for their money. The Roots have had a rotating group of players and are currently using a tuba player (more exactly a sousaphone player) to hold down some of the bass parts, and this is evidence *exactly* of the greatness I'm attempting to describe. The sound, the *discipline* of the Roots, comes from ?uestlove, otherwise known as Ahmir Thompson, the drummer, who is, according to what I've read, a backstage kid, son of a doo-wop singer, a performer since earliest childhood, a street performer, and because he is at ease in his role, he always makes it look easy, makes drumming look easy, doesn't have some gigantic drum kit, doesn't use double kick drums, is not above using electronica as a palette, *a flavor,* but without ever sacrificing his old soul interests (the recent Al Green "comeback" album, which he coproduced, is a good example). He has eclectic tastes. He is a drummer like Elvin Jones was a drummer (which is to say a *melodic* drummer), he is a drummer like Bernard Purdie is a drummer (which is to say a drummer who has a *touch*), he is a drummer like John Bonham was a drummer (which is to say with perfect time), he is a drummer like Max Roach was a drummer (he's a bandleader), he is a drummer like Levon Helm is a drummer (he has *soul* and he stands for something), and he's a drummer like Al Jackson Jr. was a drummer, which is to say indefatigable and unimpeachably joyful.

I am aware that most hip-hop critics and aficionados seem to have decided that Black Thought, the vocalist for the Roots (at least since vocalist Malik B. mostly went into retirement), is not a *groundbreaker* among hip-hop vocalists, is perhaps too subdued, but I think this is because people always prefer the *obvious* to what takes *effort*, and they are unprepared for an MC who subordinates himself to a band instead of serving as some kind of narcissistic energy vortex; and then, additionally, there's the problem that the band comes from Philly, not noted for its *scene*; and: each album has been dramatically different from the one that preceded it—none of these issues concerns me. Furthermore, I know that the indisputable commercial success for which the Roots are best known is *Things Fall Apart* (1999), which was recorded at Electric Lady Studios at the same time as a hat trick of amazing other documents, releases by Common and Erykah Badu and D'Angelo, and so *Things Fall Apart* is about empowerment, and about a sense of community; I understand all these things. And I am aware that *Phrenology*, their fifth album, took two years and is artistically ambitious on a scale that is almost ludicrous in a form that is not generally ambitious so much as cautious and conservative; but, listen, *Phrenology* has *vision*; it has vision in its title, first of all, which is of course a caustic and critical vision of degraded science and oppression,* degraded science as the bedrock of degraded white oppression; in the two years between an album (*Things Fall Apart*) made during the Clinton presidency (at about the same time as the high-water period of the rave movement) and an album released post-9/11, during the administration of George W. Bush, this white, degraded culture must have been much more in the forefront of the cultural and political experience of the album's creators, such that the history of oppression, not the *playah* version of this story but the overwhelming historical *oppression*, the genocidal wiping out of African culture that is the ongoing background radiation of the diaspora—which arguably achieved its most violent and most unrelenting apex here in North America—must have become unavoidable during the genesis of the album; the title gets into your head, as it were, and says that the entire history of American oppression is a fit subject for an album made by African American popular musicians, and this while other hip-hop artists weren't doing much beyond their balletic gang simulations; the album, *Phrenology*, immediately advertises its aesthetic militancy and then begins in earnest by (intro aside) quoting a Queen song and sort of proving that the band can play rock and roll as well as hip-hop, even as the song, "Rock You," is perhaps the mostly heavily programmed, the most synthetic on the album, after which there is a bona fide punk rock song called "!!!!!!!," which lasts exactly twenty-five seconds, a really good punk rock song, actually, giving way in

---

* And for an astoundingly good essay on the subject, see Nathaniel Mackey's "Phrenological Whitman," which can be located online at http://www .conjunctions.com/archives/c29-nm.htm.

turn to the neo-soul vibe of "Sacrifice," and so on, unto a ten-minute opus about Philly called "Water," which has some of the history of the band secreted away in it, ten minutes about getting *over the water*, which is the Schuylkill River, or perhaps the Atlantic, and this opus contains a whole middle section of electronic drone and samples and musical illustration, all of it like a walk through Philly, hopefully without getting sucked into the drug demimondes celebrated by so many other hip-hop stars, *Ecstasy* being specifically enjoined by the song in question, and *heroin* — but none of this, understand, this uncomplaining but elegant *journalistic observation* of the Philly experience, likewise this incredibly beautiful band sound, prepares one for the revelation to come on the album, which is the track called "Something in the Way of Things (In Town)," which makes its mark initially with a beautiful double-stopped bass part that is chromatic like contemporary jazz, in some slippery time signature like 19/16, after which the vocal, which is by Amiri Baraka, who at the time of the album's release was notorious, infamous even, for some remarks about 9/11 that made him seem a somewhat reckless conspiracy theorist, according to the press, and a literary dweller on the fringes to such a degree that everything that LeRoi Jones once wrote was suddenly *effaced* from the college reading lists, and yet Baraka, on *Phrenology*, is, despite his reputation, at the top of his oratorical game, speaking to the African American experience in the violent midst of post-9/11 menace: "In town / In town / In town / Something in the way of things / Something that will quit and won't start / Something you know but can't stand / Can't know get along / Like death with / Riding on top of the car / Peering through the windshield for his cue." The whole thing rolls forward like a sermon from the cracks in your floorboards, a sermon for lost souls, like some politics of bipolar disorder, complete with hallucinations, and in which all the *isms*, all the ideologies, *collapse*, and then there's just the black American stuck in the state of permanent urban exile, trying to find a way to survive amid the Darwinism to which the power elite is so happy to consign him, and all this with a really amazing, beautiful improvisation happening in the background, mixing electronic effects with live drumming, Baraka rising up from the sound bed like he is being challenged in a way that he long resisted, after which—if in fact there can be an "after"—the album falls into two blanks, two blank tracks, a suitable silence, a sepulchral silence, a reprieve, forty seconds thereof, the silence of the beyond the grave of African American history and identity and oppression, and then there's a last song that has a big chorus: "When I say *pump that*, y'all say *shit up* / When I say *stand up*, y'all say *git up* / When I say *rise up*, y'all say *now*." A little ditty, a little throwaway to please the record company, which must have been scared shitless at the apprehension of the Baraka poem, and all the bad, evil press orbiting around Baraka, some of it perhaps self-inflicted, flowing like a red tide in Baraka's direction; still, the throwaway says, *When I say rise up, y'all say NOW.* Now. Now. Now. Now *that* is a record, now *that* is a band, now that is a point of view, and it's made by people with a history and with something to say, and it makes people *dance*, if that's all you want to do, but it also tackles history, injustice, race, capitalism, democracy, degraded science, and it gives voice to those who did not (do not) have a political voice, and it celebrates their exile and *triumphs* over it. Now that is a band, now that is something to be proud of, now that is something that would not be what it is if all the drums were played by a machine.

6.

Okay, back to rave culture, and to the apologists for its monotony. Apparently, it all started in *Ibiza*, and like all things that have the ring of the hyperbolic about them, when it was in Ibiza, it was *different*, it wasn't all the same, there were a lot of different kinds of music on the sound system, there were *all kinds of music*, it wasn't mindless drug promotion, it was a bunch of guys from London on holiday in Ibiza, *chilling out*, and the clubs were open to the *sky*, and there was coastline, and it was warm, and everyone was *in love*, at least with the idea of love, and this was an ideal thing; it was a setting aside of Margaret Thatcher and her love twin, Ronald Reagan, and their ratcheting up of Cold War rhetoric, and the guys from London, because they were mostly guys, can be forgiven for wanting to be able to *see the stars* while they listened to all these *different kinds of music*, and they loaded up on this new drug that was plentiful in Ibiza, if not in London, and they found that certain kinds of things, which is to say very repetitious things, sounded extremely good on this new drug. They were experiencing a sort of hyperacusis, and hyperacusis was good. Of course, as with all things that seem ideal, there was an attempt to repeat the success—back on the home ground. And so the raves began in London.

What was the thing that made the raves the raves? There were clubs already in London, and these were clubs where people drank. There were pubs and clubs where people drank, but at the raves they didn't drink. They drank *juice*. And instead of boozing they took the drug that the Londoners had experienced on holiday in Ibiza. The drug was methylene-dioxymethamphetamine, better known on those shores as *E*, short for Ecstasy. It was an admixture of speedy effects and mild hallucinogenic effects. And because the latter were mild, like the first hour of an LSD trip, the users apparently felt, at least initially, in the first few months of recreational use, *well-being and warmth*, feelings that people seem to have a need to overstate rather grandly, e.g., "When large numbers of people took Ecstasy together, the drug catalyzed a strange and wondrous atmosphere of *collective intimacy*, an electric sense of connection among complete strangers." And when the music started, "MDMA turned out to have a uniquely synergistic/synesthetic interaction with music, especially uptempo, repetitive, electronic dance music."* Suddenly, the drum machine, which was in danger of being phased out of British synth pop as the bands from that movement grew up, found a new foothold in a form that was *supposed to be monotonous*.

The raves caught on, as just about everyone knows, and the raves drew the kids from the suburbs, and the music followed the drug, and, where once the music of drum machines had a dark thematic tendency in the decade prior, during the *summer of love*, which was the summer of 1988, the music was rich with the idea of union, unless it was just the drugs talking, and no amount of hyperbole was enough hyperbole, and the commonplace that was trotted out to indicate the uniquity of

---

* *Generation Ecstasy* (Routledge, 1999), p. 83.

the *summer of love* was that British soccer fans of differing teams did not seem to have a need to beat the shit out of one another. E made it possible for them instead to love one another. Meanwhile, the drum machines did that thing that drum machines do, which is play the same thing over and over.

Simon Reynolds's *Generation Ecstasy: Into the World of Techno and Rave Culture* is the *ur*text here. And Reynolds is not only unwilling to speak ill of the drugs, indeed, just the opposite: "Ecstasy has been celebrated as the *flow drug* for the way it melts bodily and psychological rigidities, enabling the dancer to move with greater fluency and 'lock' into the groove" (p. 84), he is also unwilling to budge from a certain idea about the music of raves. In fact, he dislikes anything that militates for change within his genre:

> Self-proclaimed progressive initiatives usually involve a backing away from the edge, a reversion to more traditional ideas of "musicality." *Hardcore* is that nexus where a number of attitudes and energies mesh: druggy hedonism, an instinctively avant-garde surrender to the "will" of technology, a "fuck art, let's dance" DJ-oriented funktionalism [sic], and a smidgen of underclass rage. Hardcore refers to different sounds in different countries at different times, but the word generally guarantees a stance of subcultural intransigence, a refusal to be coopted or to cop out [p. 6; italics in original].

But what *intransigence* might mean, in the context of a synthetic dance form that basically involves a machine reiterating the 4/4 time signature without any variation at all, is hard to say. Is not all club music, by its very nature, *intransigent?* Does not *intransigent* refer to a refusal to budge on the mass-produced throb of the backbeat, the facelessness of the music, the same hackneyed chord progressions, the same total absence of Nietzsche's *polypus* of melody? But maybe the pitfalls of *Generation Ecstasy,* this journalistic appreciation, have most to do with its having been completed in 1998 and published the following year, which is so long ago that the final chapter concerns the greatness of Fatboy Slim. The *summer of love,* at the time of Reynolds's composition, was ten years prior, and what had not yet happened, of course, was 9/11 or 7/7. The politics of 1999 were the politics of the Internet bubble and the New Economy, and Reynolds's rhetorical flourishes often sound *a lot* like all those New Economy day traders who, in trying to *pump and dump* a certain stock, suggested that an actual product was as unnecessary as profitability.

Leaving aside the rhetoric, therefore, what happened was that the big party hit London, and soon people were paying a lot of money to get into the raves and likewise for the rather expensive drug in question (twenty dollars a dose), and the underworld elements, of course, got excited by all this cash changing hands. Eventually, the authorities recognized that thousands of kids drugged up and funneling money into the coffers of less-than-savory promoters had to stop: "Graham Bright," according to Reynolds,

> a Conservative MP, drafted a private member's bill to increase the penalties for unlicensed parties, propos-ing huge fines and six-month prison sentences. In response, Tony Colston-Hayter and his libertarian

sidekick Paul Staines attended the Conservative Party's annual conference in November (1989), where
they announced the formation of the Freedom to Party
campaign. Although all the leading rave promoters
were involved, the movement petered out after a few
sparsely attended rallies—seemingly yet more proof
of the apolitical, unmotivated character of the Ecstasy
generation [p. 79].

It seems the dance music partisans were *too high* to care if
their parties were being closed down.

Moreover, the drug began to produce some side effects. A
mild embarrassment seems to overtake Reynolds when he is
forced to address this, this way the drug turned on the adher-
ents of the cult after their first handful of nights of deliri-
ous fun:

Because the original blissed-out intensity of the early
experiences never really returns, users are tempted to
increase the dose, which only increases the speediness
and amplifies the unpleasant side effects. Serious hedo-
nists get locked in a punishing cycle of weekend excess
followed by a savage midweek crash. As well as compulsive binging on E, many get drawn into compensatory polydrug use—taking other substances to mimic
the effects originally achieved by MDMA alone.
Alongside the physical attrition wreaked by such a lifestyle (weight loss, frequent illness caused by sleep
deprivation in tandem with the virus-fostering nature
of hot, sweaty clubs), the long-term abuse of Ecstasy

can also result in psychological damage (anxiety disorders, panic attacks, paranoia, and depression) [p. 76].

And *you know* if the guy who thinks the rave scene is *the* new British religious experience says the drug can turn on you, it can turn on you. Eventually, after the British authorities put the large-scale raves out of business, a second wave of the movement came about, and this second wave included the soundtrack to *unpleasant side effects*, also known as *dark hardcore*. More exactly, though, the second wave of club music was not a wave at all but a fragmentation of what once seemed like an edifice, and so the four-to-the-floor sound migrated to Manchester, to Liverpool, back to the United States, and even to Belgium.

Belgium? In Belgium, it's true. When the Ecstasy started to get speedier, the producers responded by increasing the beats per minute, to 150 to 160 and sometimes even higher. A good example of this, a song sampled endlessly, reworked endlessly, thereby becoming among the more repetitious pieces of music *ever made*, is entitled "Mentasm," by Joey Beltram (an American, from Queens, but adopted as Belgium's own when his work was released on Belgium's R&S label). The track consists almost entirely of a braying synthesizer riff (the "Hoover sound"), the ugliness of which was apparently meant to suggest Black Sabbath. These synthesizer squawks, however, are nothing compared with the utterly doltish *drum part*, whose comings and goings are the stuff of "a speed freak's drug 'flash,'" according to Reynolds. The increased beats per minute that followed Beltram's breakthrough, on competing tracks like "Dominator" by Human Resource, also took advantage of the possibilities inherent in a dark, paranoid amphetamine buzz. A wealth of subgenres then splintered off of club music in those transitional years of the early nineties, and in general they, too, were in the direction of *darkness*. Reynolds invokes a great number of small labels, one-off projects, and producers who didn't really last in this subatomic period, many of the songs involving shrieking vocal samples, hints of violence, a general sense of "the long-term costs of sustained use of Ecstasy, marijuana, amphetamine: side effects such as depression, paranoia, dissociation, auditory hallucinations, and creepy sensations of the uncanny" (p. 206). The dance floor, apparently, "was full of dead souls, zombie-eyed, and prematurely haggard" (p. 209).*

In this way, the drum machine had again engendered material it was well suited to, the enslavement of dead souls to a rigidified *Apollonian* structure, the four to the floor, the empty-headed

---

* As with Depeche Mode, who seemed to outgrow their own sound, a number of influential composers of electronic music became, after the first phase of the raves, disenchanted with the relentless repetition of hardcore and its spawn, and Reynolds, despite disagreeing, is good about cataloguing them. Derrick May: "I don't even like to use the word 'techno' because it's been bastardized and prostituted in every form you can possibly imagine.... To me, the form and philosophy of it have nothing to do with what we originally intended." C. J. Bolland: "Most new tracks aren't tunes anymore, just a very hard kick drum and a very mad sound." Brian Eno, as redacted by Reynolds: "[Eno] complained that digital, sequenced music had merely resurrected many of the inherent limitations of classical orchestral music, with its hierarchical ranking of instruments in the mix, its rigid sense of pitch and its locked rhythms tied to the conductor/timekeeper. 'Classical music is music without Africa.'" D. J. Pierre, on leaving Acid House behind: "It's kinda soulless.... There's no emotion that goes with it apart from jumping up and down and making you want to dance." Brian Dougans, of Future Sounds of London: "I see the term 'dance' as really restrictive for us."

rhythmic organization of a form from which all melody had been removed. Everything pleasant about the communal dance, the traces of ritual that might have adhered, however artificially, to the early raves, was gone, as was all the sex. In fact, a sound that at least nominally had a lot to do with gay cruising back when it was being played in Chicago now had become, in Europe, completely desexualized. As Reynolds notes repeatedly, pacifiers were popular among ravers, as were lollipops, and a certain *homosocial* male bonding, and the author of *Generation Ecstasy*, in protesting too much, goes to great lengths to try to find a critical apparatus for all this nonsexuality:

> One of the most radically novel and arguably subversive aspects of rave culture is precisely that it's the first youth subculture that's *not* based on the notion that sex is transgressive. Rejecting all that tired sixties rhetoric of sexual liberation, and recoiling from our sex-saturated pop culture, rave locates bliss in prepubescent childhood.... For men, the drug/music interface acts to de-phallicize the body and open it up to enraptured, abandoned "effeminate" gestures. But removing the heterosexist impulse can mean that women are rendered dispensible.

This rationale is particularly ironic in view of the fact that club-oriented music is now *the* international theme music of choice for pornography. But perhaps this conjunction, between a certain idea of unsexed dance music and *hard-core* porn, is not so unlikely as it seems. In each case it's the affective intimacy that is being leached from the experience—in the raves, there's no *self* there, if you believe Reynolds. You are nobody and you *love everybody*, without regard to specifics, without regard to personhood. And so there is no *self* to express (and thus the paucity of narrative accounts of the *summer of love*) and no intimacy to share. In pornography, which is about shutting down the consciousness and the self, the better to buy into a systematized tableau of preordained consumptive gestures, the *rhythmic organization* of the drum machine, and its attendant musical clichés, helps to make depersonalization easy, and *synchronous*, so that there is no self to bother about, just orifices or zones of sensation with a hackneyed menu of needs and requirements.

The implicit misogyny in all of this, the feeling that "women are rendered dispensible," arguably reached its apex with Gabba, a Dutch variant on the faster-darker-speedier variants of techno that had been bubbling up in 1992 and 1993. From a musical standpoint, the "melodic" aspect of Gabba was not dissimilar to the braying of the Roland 303 bass synthesizer that was popular in British hardcore and the Belgian refraction thereof. But the beats were pushed up to a nearly cardiologically unsound tempo (in a form that was almost completely unsyncopated). The titles of the songs were all "Ye Shall Die," and "No Women Allowed," and the like. Which is to say, with historical hindsight: things were getting stupider at an alarming rate. (If you don't believe me, try listening to "No Women Allowed," by Sperminator.) Not surprisingly, this music appealed to the extreme right, and two Canadian deejays associated with the Detroit techno sound, who appeared in Rotterdam in this period, reported hearing a crowd chanting *Joden, Joden*, during a night of working the decks. While this *was* apparently a soccer chant of some kind, Reynolds reports, "I've heard stories of Austrian neofascists doing drill to [Gabba's] regimented rhythms, or jackbooted and swastika-adorned thugs at Italian hardcore events" [p. 286].

From here, from the dawning of a militarized sound, a misogynist subgenre, a joyless, compulsive, lifeless repetition, it would seem there was nothing more to say about the drum machine and the music it has spawned. If the philosophy of the drum machine was somehow articulated first in a spurious posthumous Nietzsche publication, compiled before the drum machine even existed, created by Nietzsche's nationalist and anti-Semitic sister, and if the first iterations of the music were about the joys of being a robot or the existentialist abyss of a godless and forsaken British Empire, the drum machine seems to have worked out a sort of Nietzschean eternal return, by recirculating back to its proto-fascist Northern European roots. Or has it?

In a way, the explosion of innovation in the mid-nineties that provides ammunition to the other side of my argument coincides with the creation of Pro Tools, the first popular and accessible music-editing program. Pro Tools was programmed *ex nihilo* in 1989, but the commercially available version appeared in 1992. What this music-editing suite made possible was sampling for anyone who could afford a laptop, and further, the ability to alter and rearrange samples, and in particular, *drum samples*. Where breakbeats, the fancy syncopated parts of hip-hop songs, had previously been achieved with the famous two turntables, upon the advent of Pro Tools it became possible to write particularly complex and astounding drum breaks on your computer. The same was true, of course, of the synthesizer parts. You didn't even need to *own* a synthesizer anymore. You could just use a commercially available sample and manipulate the wave form. But it's the drums that really changed with digital editing, and this became abundantly evident in the jungle and drum and bass subgenres of electronic music that revolutionized the genre in the middle-nineties. On the one hand, it's impossible to call what Goldie did *techno* in the same sense that Orbital is *techno*, nor is it possible to dance to it in the way you would dance to the four-to-the-floor synthetic stylings that, even at 150 beats per minute, still undergird Belgian hardcore and Gabba. And yet drum and bass is still primarily electronic or electro-acoustic music. Interestingly, it's a mostly *black* form. It borrows from black music, especially jazz, but also from American soul and hip-hop and dub reggae, and it strips these down to their minimum, exaggerates the rhythms, and allows the faintest traces of these sources to remain.

A fine example of the style is Roni Size and Reprazent and their album *New Forms*. At this late date, almost fifteen years after the album was released, it does sound a tiny bit of its time, as if certain kinds of sound effects that were surprising on Pro Tools or other editing suites are no longer as revolutionary as they were then, but in the end, *New Forms* is all about the *drums*, and the drums, unplayable by human hands, are so dizzy, so out of control, that the virtuosity of the editing suggests a human whimsy, as if writing in all those offbeats required a sensibility that could *delight* in offbeats, and whereas some early techno had been more or less unsyncopated so that *white people* could dance to it, Roni Size goes in the other direction entirely. You *could* dance to the bass or to the melodies on *New Forms*, but you would have to be very talented indeed to dance to the drums. You would have to be an artist of dance. Additionally, there are genuine lyrics and that *polypus*, melody, extruding itself, actual sung melodies, and so there's a sense that the abstraction and the collage-oriented nature of the drum and bass architecture has a point, a narrative, a trajectory. Part of the intent was making the club music endeavor creative for those who lay outside of the totalitarian strains of dark hardcore and Gabba, inviting back in the politically marginalized, and this is a noble cause. Once it was accomplished, in the late nineties, there was almost nowhere for techno to go, and so, in a way, the historically imperative techno died. There are movements descended from it, like dancehall and grime, but the ravers died, or some of them died, or got carted off to the flight deck, or they simply realized that they needed to hold down a proper job.

Furthermore: when rave culture, and the politics that spawned it, began to wane, the sounds that were integral to the raves began, as most musical composition moved onto the laptop, to get absorbed by, not to say thoroughly coopted by, the *mainstream*. A few recent examples? Try "Blah Blah Blah," by Ke$ha; "Hips Don't Lie," by Shakira; or "3," by Britney Spears; or "Poker Face," by Lady Gaga (or anything by the Backstreet Boys or 98 Degrees—the more faceless the band, the more faceless the sound), or many, many, many other Top 40 songs from the past five to ten years. Many of these tracks are unthinkable without the advances, if that is the right word, of electronica, of club music, and without the technological bedrock of the drum machine, in the guise of either an actual machine or, more reliably these days, a computer sampling an older drum sound, whether acoustic or synthesized, this sound affixed to a grid, to a click track, on a computer program that ensures that the sound will always be *in sync*. What started as a tonal color or a timbre became a thematic tendency and then, in the course of things, became an *absolute requirement*. That is, almost everything you are hearing on the radio now, at least if it's coming out of a Top 40 station or an urban station, never had a drummer present at any of the recording sessions. Lately, you may not in fact have heard a live drummer playing as you have walked through the streets, listening to songs coming from here and there, but once in a blue moon.

Unfortunately, for listeners who prefer that music suggest certain of the human passions, who recognize most in music its ability to summon up some of the bittersweet feelings of being *alive*—memories, dreams, wishes, regrets—this contemporary music is emptied of any meaningful affect. Just as a sonnet produced by a computer is an inherently boring sonnet, whether or not produced with the requisite rhyme scheme and syllabification, just as a chess match played by computers, no matter how unorthodox, is a tedious chess match, a music produced entirely by machine is a dead, emotionally flat music, with none of the ritual for which music was really intended.* I

---

* And all of Simon Reynolds's amplified prose will not convince me otherwise. A ritual has an eye on what's tragic, noble, and infinite in human experience, and it exudes compassion for the daily struggles, so that we might suffer them with more equanimity. It doesn't distract us, it instructs us, and though I have never been to a rave on Ecstasy, I have been to clubs and heard the sounds in situ, and I was left uninstructed, and without *feeling*, no matter how sweaty, well exercised, and *regulated*.

am not going to go so far as to say that all synthetic musical products are not, in fact, music, but I will say that music produced by machines is really good at getting you to *obey* the beats; it is really good at getting you to *submit*, and apparently if you are on Ecstasy it is good at getting you to feel your hair follicles. It is not, however, lasting art. Except in certain very singular cases. Electronica is good at *rhythmically organizing* you, it is fine for dispensing a certain music-like aurally packaged sound sweetmeat, and because it is good at this, you can understand how, in fact, through the action of history, synthetic music has become the corporate music par excellence. What the multinational entertainment providers earnestly require, after all, is recordable and reproducible *predictability*, and with certain minor adjustments, now all music can be recorded by a solitary producer whose sole instrument is his computer, in his apartment or in similar venues, with a few fancy plug-ins, with a few specific reverb-like effects, some stereo panning, some phase shifting, a sample of a Roland 303 bass synthesizer. If a bit of voice is required, in order to give the whole a bit of a human something-or-other, a trace of the human, a vanishing remainder of the human, then that can quickly be accomplished, and any stray hairs on the human voice can be worked out and machined—with the Auto-Tune software! The Auto-Tune software! O next step in musical factory farming! The last vestige of unmusicality, or nontraditional musicality, can be wiped out now; just as the rhythms are made completely predictable with the drum machine, or the drum sample, now the intonation can be fixed mercilessly with the Auto-Tuning module, so that everyone can have the same perfect pitch, the same synthetic high gloss, *everyone can sing*, making the robotics that much more apparent. (And this reminds me how, when I went to Italy in 1999, everywhere I went I had to hear Cher's Auto-Tuned voice singing "Believe," even in towns where no English was spoken, in landscapes where the acreage was given over to kinds of agriculture that had been practiced for hundreds of years, everywhere, in public squares, was Cher "believing," but what was it that Cher *believed* in? That the music-delivery system can be made scientific, that a reliable return on investment can be promised to shareholders everywhere? That music, in fact, must be made more predictable, in a music business environment like ours, in order to ensure a specific bottom-line-oriented result? That musicians must be sacrificed to ensure a strong price-to-earnings ratio?)

I expect this sort of thing on our shores, where bottom-line callousness and mercenary conduct are built into the economy, ratified by theocrats, supply-siders, and biblical literalists. In Europe it depresses the hell out of me. In Europe it seems to herald the beginning of the end of continental cultural difference. What is Europe, in the end, but a huge amalgam of things that are heterogenous? Europe is where you have Romany music and everything that goes with it, where you have Eastern European jazz and its experimental variants, where you have the Bulgarian Women's Choir, and klezmer, in Eastern Europe you have the birthplace of klezmer, you have European classical music, with all the ups and downs associated with it, twelve-tone composition, e.g., or Italian opera, you have Turkish music, which is frankly Arabic in so many ways, and you have Tuva, and Tuvan throat singing (if you're willing to accept the Russian Republic as a European country, and a potential member of the EU), you have fado from Portugal, you have Celtic music, about which so much *could be said* that to even bring it up is somewhat unfortunate in this context, you have the Scottish variants of Celtic music, and the folk music of England, as gathered up by Francis James Child and others, French chanson, Spanish flamenco (which may, arguably, be best interpreted by the Romany), not to mention a great many other indigenous musics of Europe, some of them not known to me (so that I have them to look forward to, if in fact they endure), from the former Yugoslavia, Albania, Greece, Crete, Lithuania, Finland, Norway, Iceland, you name it. In the pursuit of a globalized, corporate Europe, an EU,* you are going to flatten out all this difference and apply a nearly uniform sound to it, a martial, regimented sound to it, which is the sound of the drum machine? You are going to *rhythmically organize* Europe so that in its new secular guise its music is wholly explicable, without mystery, or you are going to take every immigrant music and subject it to this same spin cycle that wrings out all the differences and gives the music the same dull intention? And in the process you are going to *rid the world* of the actual music makers so that there is no one left making the music, just the ill-at-ease boys with their laptops? That's it? That's all that you can do for yourself, Europe? Were

---

* And in the realm of historical coincidences it's worth noting that the Treaty of Maastricht, which codified the European Union, was signed on February 7, 1992, just about the time of the commercial introduction of Pro Tools, and that its capital city is Brussels, the site of the influential techno label R&S, which first released, in 1991, Joey Beltram's "Mentasm," the blueprint for European hardcore. So that a unified EU (whose motto is "Unity Through Diversity") and a globalized European techno seem historically coeval.

you not once the cauldron of the arts? Are you not where all good literature comes from, not to mention Impressionism, Dada, and Surrealism, and do we not, here in North America, merely imitate you? Are you not where all the really interesting philosophy comes from, like Marxism and psychoanalysis and post-structuralism? Are you really going to *abdicate* your post and hand the entire game over to the ill-at-ease guys with their laptops? And are you going to call *that* a revolution? You are going to vacate all of this history and leave us with a computer pounding out a bass drum at some predictable number of beats per minute with some frothy, forgettable, and already-run-well-into-the-ground melody over the top that probably borrows from African American music, though no African American was ever involved in the recording? That is the best you can do? And then you're going to Auto-Tune it all?

Acknowledgments

These essays, roughly speaking, are included here in the order in which I wrote them: "Against Cool" was first excerpted in *GQ* in 1999, and then later appeared in its entirety in *The Gingko Tree Review* in 2003. It was also issued in *The Best American Essays* in 2004. "On Meredith Monk" first appeared in *Tin House* in 2002. "Thirty-One Love Songs" appeared in *The Believer* in 2003, which also published "How to Be a Christian Artist: On the Danielson Famile" in 2004 (and the latter also appeared in their anthology *Read Hard* in 2009). "Five Songs," my essay on Wilco, appeared in their 2004 publication *The Wilco Book*. "Guilty Pleasures" first appeared in *Black Clock* in 2005 under a different title. "Some Propositions Concerning the Lounge Lizards" appeared in *The Believer* in 2006. "The Pete Townshend Fragments" first appeared in *Conjunctions* in 2006. "Two Weeks at Music Camp" appeared in *The Believer* in 2007. "On Celestial Music" was commissioned for a 2007 anthology called *Heaven* by Seabury Books and appeared there slightly abridged; before that, however, it appeared in *Salmagundi;* it also appeared in *The Best American Essays 2008.* "The Problem of Impairment" is from *Conjunctions*, from Spring 2008. "The

New York Underground: 1965–1988" was commissioned by Little Steven's Rock and Roll Forever Foundation for their upcoming volume *Little Steven's Rock and Roll High School*, and I thank Steven Van Zandt for permission to reprint it, as well as Warren Zanes for invaluable editorial input here. And finally, "Europe, Forsake Your Drum Machines!" was excerpted in the 2010 music issue of *The Believer*. Everything here has been modified, retooled, remixed, sometimes significantly.

The editors who believed in this work, chief among them Heidi Julavits at *The Believer*, Bradford Morrow at *Conjunctions*, Rob Spillman at *Tin House*, Steve Erickson at *Black Clock*, and the team of Robert Boyers and Marc Woodworth at *Salmagundi*, have taken some risks in doing so, since I normally publish in a different prose medium. I am extremely grateful to them for their kindness and their trust in me, as I am to the support system at Little, Brown and Company, and at the Melanie Jackson Agency.

As always, I thank my family and friends, especially my daughter, Hazel Jane Moody, whom I hope I can interest in music, in much the way my mother must have hoped she could interest me.

Index

Abbey Road (Beatles), 271–273, 362
"Absolutely Cuckoo" (Magnetic Fields), 88
"Accidents Will Happen" (Elvis Costello and the Attractions), 149
AC/DC, 96, 110
"Acoustic Guitar" (Magnetic Fields), 83, 84
"Across the Universe" (Jethro Tull), 148
Addison, Joseph, 14, 16
advertising, 31–34, 40, 52, 55
Aesthetics of Rock (Meltzer), 29, 325n
African Americans, 96, 331–335, 339, 340, 361, 363–364, 391, 394, 395–396, 398, 399–400, 411, 417
alcohol, 188, 213, 215, 218, 223, 224, 276, 277, 284, 285, 288–290, 292, 297–300, 319, 390, 402
Allen, Woody, 50
All the Best Cowboys Have Chinese Eyes (Townshend), 203, 224–225, 226
alternative rock, 339n, 378
Ambitious Lovers, 336
"Ambulance Blues" (Young), 148
American IV: The Man Comes Around (Cash), 388
A.M. (Wilco), 107–112, 115

"Ananas Symphonie" (Kraftwerk), 365
Anderson, Ian, 145, 146, 147, 148, 151, 154, 155n
Anderson, Wes, 189
"And I Moved" (Townshend), 217–219
Ansonia Hotel, 316
Antrim, Donald, 150
"Anyway, Anyhow, Anywhere" (the Who), 202
Aqualung (Jethro Tull), 145, 147
Armed Forces (Elvis Costello and the Attractions), 149
Art of Courtly Love, The (Capellanus), 87–88
"Arukoo" (Kochan), 259, 262
"As a Wife Has a Cow: A Love Story" (Stein), 59
Ashbery, John, 45
"Ashes of American Flags" (Wilco), 123–124, 129
Astral Weeks (Morrison), 163, 225
"At the Hop" (Danny and the Juniors), 26
atheism, 381–382, 383, 386, 389
Atkins, Juan, 391, 393–394
"Autobahn" (Kraftwerk), 393
Auto-Tune software, 414–415, 417
Ayler, Albert, 334

B-52s, 164
"Baba O'Riley" (the Who), 188–189, 210
Babbs, Kenneth, 41, 42, 43
Bacharach, Burt, 85
Bach, Johann Sebastian, 8, 269
"Back to Africa" (Dictators), 320
Bad Moon Rising (Sonic Youth), 346
Baker, Chet, 21
Baker, Nicholson, 4
Balint, Eszter, 162
ballads, 81, 118
Bandito the Bongo Artist, 358
Baraka, Amiri, 399–400
Barlow, John Perry, 298
Barlow, Lou, 153
Barrett, Syd, 89, 297
Barthelme, Donald, 45
Barthes, Roland, 57
Bartos, Karl, 366
Basie, Count, 15
Basquiat, Jean-Michel, 338
Bay City Rollers, 82
Beach Boys, 208–209, 214, 371
Beatles, 8, 26–27, 28, 86, 181, 271–273, 334n, 362
Beats (Beat Generation), 17–25, 29, 30, 33, 35, 36, 40, 44, 47, 52, 303, 322
bebop style, 15, 16, 17, 33
"Because the Night" (Smith, P.), 328
Beckett, Samuel, 3
Beck, Jeff, 202
Beck, Marc, 78
Bee Gees, 143
Bee Season (Goldberg), 5
Beethoven, 6
Beghtol, LD, 79, 81, 88
"Behind Blue Eyes" (the Who), 146, 207
Being There (Wilco), 112–115
Belgium, 406
"Bell Boy" (the Who), 215
Belleville Three, 391, 392, 393, 395
Beltram, Joey, 406–407, 416n
Benefit (Jethro Tull), 154

Benigni, Roberto, 162
Bennett, Jay, 116
Berger, Karl, 244
Berlioz, Hector, 355
Bernhard, Thomas, 4
Bernstein, Leonard, 30
Bernstein, Steve, 167
Berrigan, Ted, 322
Big Star, 76, 170, 293
"Birdland" (Smith, P.), 329
Birth of the Cool (Davis), 15–16, 21
bisexuality, 194, 195, 219. *See also* homosexuality
"Black Angel's Death Song, The" (Velvet Underground), 308
Black Flag, 76, 152, 284
blacks. *See* African Americans
Black Thought (Roots vocalist), 397
Blake, Michael, 167, 172
"Blank Generation" (Richard Hell and the Voidoids), 48
Blank Generation (Hell, R.), 326
"Blasphemous Rumours" (Depeche Mode), 383–387, 388
Blondie, 86, 150, 315, 326, 328, 333
"Blow" (van Tonder), 255, 256–257
"Blue Heaven" (Pogues), 287
Blue Öyster Cult, 324
"Blue, Red and Grey" (the Who), 146, 206, 207, 231
"Boa Constrictor" (Magnetic Fields), 84
"Boat Train" (Pogues), 287, 298
Boggs, Dock, 147–148
Bolland, C. J., 407n
Bolton, Michael, 13, 265
"Book of Love, The" (Magnetic Fields), 87
"Boris the Spider" (the Who), 181, 182
"Born in the U.S.A. (Springsteen), 27
Bostock, Gerald "Little Milton," 146
"Bottle of Smoke" (Pogues), 285
Bowie, David, 27, 149, 314
Bow Wow Wow, 164

"Boys" (Moody), 67–70
Boy Who Heard Music, The
   (Townshend novella), 214
Branca, Glenn, 338, 342–343, 344
Braxton, Anthony, 244
"Break It Up" (Smith, P.), 329
Brent, John, 12, 43
Bright Lights, Big City (McInerney),
   51
Britain. *See* England
"Broad Majestic Shannon" (Pogues),
   285
"Broad" (van Tonder), 259, 263
Brooks, Gwendolyn, 25
Brown & Williamson, 32–33
Brown, James, 333, 364
Brubeck, Dave, 21
Brush, Claire, 41–42
Buddha Machine, 254
Burke, Solomon, 97
Burnham, George F., 14
Burroughs, William S., 20, 23–24, 25,
   48, 52, 341
Bursting Out (Jethro Tull), 151
"Busby Berkeley Dreams" (Magnetic
   Fields), 81, 83
Bush Tetras, 335
Bussy, Pascal, 366
Byrds, 239, 308
Byrne, David, 28, 60, 135

"Cactus Where Your Heart Should
   Be, The" (Magnetic Fields), 88
Cage, John, 110, 145, 270, 281–282,
   304, 343, 360
Cale, John, 27, 305–306, 308, 309,
   310, 312, 313, 313n, 328, 343
call-and-response, 167–168
Can (band), 363
Candy Apple Grey (Hüsker Dü), 152
"Candy Says" (Velvet Underground),
   311
"Cantus in Memory of Benjamin
   Britten" (Pärt), 278
"Can We Camp at Your Feet"
   (Danielson Famile), 103–104

Capellanus, Andreas, 87–88
Captain Beefheart, 69, 89, 143
Carlos, Wendy, 362
Carroll, Jim, 314
Carter Family, 244
Cash, Johnny, 239, 388
"Casino Queen" (Wilco), 107, 121
Casiotones, 358
Cassady, Neal, 19, 20, 21, 25, 36–37
Cather, Willa, 14
Cave, Nick, 5
CBGB-OMFUG club, 327, 327n, 331,
   333, 334, 337, 341
"Celebrated Summer" (Hüsker Dü), 8
celestial music, 265–282, 269n
Cervenka, Exene, 48–49
Chalfant, Chris, 237, 249, 251, 263
Chamberlin, Harry, 357
Chance, James, 335, 343, 348
Chapman, Mike, 86
Chatham, Rhys, 89, 338, 342, 343
Cherry, Don, 244
Chicago, 119–121, 123, 124
Chicago House, 394
"Chicken with Its Head Cut Off, A"
   (Magnetic Fields), 83
child abuse / child pornography,
   176–177, 177n, 180–182, 182n,
   183, 185, 190–193, 195, 196–203,
   219–224, 226, 227–233, 232–233n
Childers, Leee, 317
Chilton, Alex, 118
"Christian Life, The" (Byrds),
   239, 244
Christian music, 90–105
Cicero, Marcus Tullius, 279–280
Cirlot, J. E., 114–115
Clancy Brothers, 244, 291, 303
Clapton, Eric, 202, 203, 296–297, 387
Clarke, Vince, 377, 378, 383
Clash, 28, 48, 288
"Clear" (Cybotron), 393–394
Clinton, George, 163, 393
Close, Del, 12, 42, 43
Coasters, 26
Cobain, Kurt, 55, 90, 93, 297, 350

Coleman, Ornette, 145, 244, 334, 344, 345, 346
Collins, Michael, 154–155, 155n
Coltrane, John, 21, 27, 55, 297
"Come Back from San Francisco" (Magnetic Fields), 84
"Come Out" (Reich), 361
Computer World (Kraftwerk), 371, 375, 394
concerts. *See* Lounge Lizards
"Condemnation" (Depeche Mode), 389–390
Conduction, 245–246
Coney Island of the Mind, A (Ferlinghetti), 25
Conniff, Ray, 265
Conquest of Cool (Frank), 30–32
Conrad, Tony, 89, 305, 313
"Content" (Townshend), 207–208
Contortions, 335
"Cool Blues" (Parker), 16
"Cool Change" (Little River Band), 27
"Cool for Cats" (Squeeze), 27
"Cool Love" (Pablo Cruise), 27
"Cool Places" (Sparks), 27
cool (as term), 11–20, 26–27, 31–50, 52, 53, 55–56
Coolio, 53
"Coolsville" (Jones), 27
Copland, Aaron, 306, 360
"Cortez the Killer" (Young), 54
Costello, Elvis, 113, 149, 150
"Cotton Fields" (Pogues), 287
"Cousin Kevin" (the Who), 181–183
Cowell, Henry, 356
"(Crazy for You But) Not That Crazy" (Magnetic Fields), 88
"Crazy Little Thing Called Love" (Queen), 27
Creative Music Studio (Woodstock), 244
"Credo in Us" (Cage), 360
Creed (rock band), 97
Crews, Frederick, 192
criticism, 125

Crosby, David, 86
Cybotron, 393–394

Daily Mail, 176
Dalcroze eurythmics, 66
Daltrey, Roger, 179, 180, 182n, 190, 191, 193, 195, 198, 206, 212, 219, 233
dance, 57–60
Danielson Famile, 90–104
Danny and the Juniors, 26
Danto, Arthur, 126
"Dash 7" (Wilco), 109–111, 115, 129
Daugherty, Jay Dee, 329
Davis, Lydia, 3–4
Davis, Miles, 15, 16, 17, 21, 24, 27, 46, 52, 55, 161, 167, 255, 297, 328
Davol, Sam, 73, 77
Day, Doris, 16
Daydream Nation (book by Stearns), 342n
Daydream Nation (Sonic Youth), 152, 347–348, 349, 350
dB's, 163
Dean, James, 54
"Dear Prudence" (Beatles), 28
Death Comes for the Archbishop (Cather), 14
"Death Is Only a Dream" (Carter Family), 244
Dedalus, Stephen, 126
Del Naja, Robert, 229–230
Depeche Mode, 376–391, 394, 407n
Detroit House, 391–394
DeVille, Willy, 327–328n
Devo, 27, 48, 150, 335
Dharma Bums, The (Kerouac), 18–19
"Diamond Dogs" (Bowie), 27
Diamond, Neil, 134, 140, 141
Dictators, 320–321
Dictionary of Slang and Unconventional English (Partridge), 16–17
Dinger, Klaus, 365, 366
disco music, 332–333, 334, 335
DNA (band), 336

Dolmen Music (Monk), 60–63, 68, 70

"Don't Fear the Reaper" (BÖC), 324

Don't Look Back (documentary by Pennebaker), 380

Doors, the, 164, 194, 310

Double Fold (Baker), 4

Double Nickels on the Dime (Minutemen), 152

Dougans, Brian, 407n

Down by Law (film), 162

"Do You Be?" (Monk), 67

"Dreamer in My Dreams" (Wilco), 114

Dream Syndicate, The, 305–306

drugs, 25, 36, 39, 41–46, 49–51, 188, 213, 232, 276, 297, 312, 314, 319, 330, 389, 390, 399, 401–407, 413n, 414

drum machines, 354, 356–373, 362n, 376–382, 386–387, 389–397, 401–403, 406–417

Durivage, Francis Alexander, 14

Dylan, Bob, 30, 101, 164, 195–196, 196n, 208, 274, 303, 303n, 309, 322, 380

E-bows, 246

Een, Robert, 60

Eigner, Christian, 389

Einstein on the Beach (Glass), 60

Eisenstadt, Jill, 51

Electric Kool-Aid Acid Test (in Compton, California), 41–43

Electric Kool-Aid Acid Test (Wolfe), 34–35, 37–39

Electric Light Orchestra, 85

Ellis, Bret Easton, 51–52, 53

Emerson, Lake and Palmer (ELP), 148–149, 150, 151, 318

Emerson, Ralph Waldo, 24

"Eminence Front" (the Who), 178, 216

Empty Glass (Townshend), 217–218, 224

Endless Wire (the Who), 209n, 233

"End, The" (Doors), 310

England, 295, 315, 332, 375, 381–382, 416. *See also names of individual British musicians and bands;* rave culture

Eno, Brian, 60, 69, 308, 333, 334–335, 340, 371, 407n

Enormous Changes at the Last Minute (Paley), 54

Entwistle, John, 180, 181, 182, 188, 190, 191, 195, 202, 292, 298

"Epitaph for My Heart" (Magnetic Fields), 82

Eraserhead (film), 78

Eugenides, Jeff, 62

Europe, 110, 352–354, 381, 408, 415–417, 416n. *See also* Belgium; England; German music; Ireland

Evans, Gil, 15, 21

Evans, John, 148, 151

"Everything Counts" (Depeche Mode), 379

Exley, Frederick, 298

"Experimental Music Love" (Magnetic Fields), 84

Exploding Plastic Inevitable, 308

Faber & Faber (British publisher), 219

Face Dances (the Who), 215–216

Faces, 189, 216, 289

Fahey, John, 344

"Fairytale of New York" (Pogues), 285

"Family Affair" (Sly and the Family Stone), 362

Fan's Notes, A (Exley), 298

"Fat Stream" (Monk), 70

"Feeling Tank" (Danielson Famile), 102, 102n

Ferlinghetti, Lawrence, 25

Fetch the Compass Kids (Danielson Famile), 92–94, 98, 99, 101, 103–104

Feynman, Richard, 127–128

"Fiddle About" (the Who), 181, 182

"Fido, Your Leash Is Too Long" (Magnetic Fields), 80, 84

Fields, Danny, 194, 195
Fields, the (sculpture park), 238, 260–261
Fier, Anton, 161, 336, 346
"First Party at Ken Kesey's with Hell's Angels" (Kesey), 39
Fischer, Max, 189
Fishing with John (TV show), 162, 174
Fitzgerald, Ella, 60
"Flaming Cool Youth of San Francisco Poetry," 30
Flavin, Dan, 261
"Flesh Thang" (Danielson Famile), 94
Fletcher, Andy, 377, 379, 383, 390
"Floppy Boot Stomp" (Captain Beefheart), 143–144
"Flower" (Sonic Youth), 346
Flür, Wolfgang, 366–370, 375
Fogelberg, Dan, 153
folk music, 303–304, 303n, 322
"Fools Fall in Love" (Presley), 26, 27
"For Michael Collins, Jeffrey and Me" (Jethro Tull), 154–155, 155n
"For the Turnstiles" (Young), 148
Foucault, Michel, 57
Foxtrot (Genesis), 151
Fragile (Yes), 151
"Frankie Teardop" (Suicide), 337
Franklin, Aretha, 54, 96
Frank, Thomas, 30–32
Franny and Zooey (Salinger), 97–98
"Fratres" (Pärt), 278
Freeman, David, 239, 240, 254
Fresh (Sly and the Family Stone), 362n
Fripp, Robert, 76, 340
From Rockaway (Eisenstadt), 51
Fugs, 309
Funkadelic, 276, 282
funk music, 332, 333, 334, 335
Future Bible Heroes, 73

Gabba, 409, 410, 412
Gabriel, Peter, 153
Gahan, David, 377, 380, 382, 385, 389, 390
Gallop, Jane, 50

"Gandhara" (Japanese pop song), 263
Gangsta's Paradise (Coolio), 53
Garcia, Jerry, 30, 44, 146, 297, 298
Garden State (Moody), 63
Gates, David, 5
Gaye, Marvin, 30, 333
Generation Ecstasy: Into the World of Techno and Rave Culture (Reynolds), 403, 404, 408
Genesis, 150, 151, 153
Gentle Giant, 150
German music, 375–376. *See also* Kraftwerk
Ghost Is Born, A (Wilco), 125–129
Giddins, Gary, 16, 21
Gilbert and Sullivan, 81
Gillespie, Dizzy, 15
"Gimme Shelter" (Rolling Stones), 28
Ginsberg, Allen, 4, 22–23, 24, 25, 36, 39, 48, 52, 322, 323
Gira, Michael, 343, 344
Glass, Philip, 60, 335, 342
"Gloria" (Smith, P.), 324, 330
"Glory" (Television), 330
Godspeed You! Black Emperor, 93, 153
Go Girl Crazy! (Dictators), 320
Goldberg, Myla, 5
Golden Palominos, 161, 336, 346
"Golden Slumbers" (Beatles), 271–273
Gonson, Claudia, 73, 75, 76, 77, 78, 79, 82, 84, 88
Gordon, Kim, 343, 346, 347, 348, 348n
Górecki, Henryk Mikolaj, 159
Gore, Martin, 377, 380–390
"Gotham Lullaby" (Monk), 61, 70
Gothic Archies, 73
Graham, Nan, 28
Gramss, Sebastian, 237, 240, 242, 243, 246, 247, 248, 250, 253–254, 255, 257, 259, 260, 263
"Grand Canyon" (Magnetic Fields), 78, 83, 84
Grateful Dead, 19, 44, 48, 298
Gravity's Rainbow (Pynchon), 45

"Great Balls of Fire" (Lewis), 96
Green, Al, 96, 97, 166, 333, 389, 396
"Green Shirt" (Elvis Costello and the Attractions), 149–150
Greenwich Village Halloween Parade, 316
Grubbs, David, 89, 121, 295
Guaraldi, Vince, 93
Guardian, The, 199
Guidat, Philippe, 242, 244, 255, 260, 262
Guided by Voices, 164
"Guiding Light" (Verlaine), 331
Guilty Pleasures theme (of Brooklyn Record Club), 133–145, 142n, 156
Guns N' Roses, 74
Guthrie, Woody, 239

Hairspray (film), 255–256
Hammond-Hammond, Jeffrey, 154
Handler, Daniel (a.k.a. Lemony Snicket), 74, 75, 77
Happy Endings reading series, 171
Happy Jack (the Who), 185, 185n
Harding, John Wesley, 5, 163
"Hard Time Killing Floor Blues" (Jethro Tull), 148
Harper's Magazine, 16
harp singing, 64–65
Harris, Jody, 161
Harrison, Harry, 107
Harry, Debbie, 315
Harvey, PJ, 93
Hawkins, Ronnie, 196
Hawthorne, Nathaniel, 124
"Heart of Glass" (Blondie), 333
"Heaven and Hell" (the Who), 181
Heavy Horses (Jethro Tull), 145
"Heavy Metal Drummer" (Wilco), 121
"Hell Is Chrome" (Wilco), 127, 128, 129
Hell, Richard, 48, 297, 326, 327n, 330, 343
Hells Angels, 37–39
"Hells Bells" (AC/DC), 96
Hell's Ditch (Pogues), 288

Hendrix, Jimi, 72, 274, 326, 331, 345
Henley, Don, 97
Henry, John, 395
Herc, Kool DJ, 339–340
"Heroes" (Bowie), 149, 187
"Heroin" (Velvet Underground), 95, 308
"Hey Jude" (Beatles), 8, 26–27
"Hey Joe" (Smith, P.), 325
"Higher Love" (Depeche Mode), 389–390
"Highway to Hell" (AC/DC), 96
hip-hop music, 53, 64, 340, 340n, 341, 395, 396, 397, 398, 410, 411
History of England (Macaulay), 14
History of Rock 'n' Roll (Time Life), 48–49
hocket, 60
Hollies, 27
"Holy Kisser's Block Party" (Danielson Famile), 90–92
homosexuality, 20–21, 79, 101, 217–218, 231, 316, 325, 408. *See also* bisexuality
"Honky Tonk Women" (Pogues), 288
Hopper, Dennis, 174
Horse's Neck (Townshend book of short stories), 219–221
Horses (Smith, P.), 30, 48, 324n, 325, 328, 329, 341, 349
"How Fucking Romantic" (Magnetic Fields), 80
"Howl" (Ginsberg), 323
"How Many Friends" (the Who), 179
How to Speak Hip (Close and Brent), 12, 43
Human Smoke (Baker), 4
Huncke, Herbert, 18
Hunter, Ian, 163
Hüsker Dü, 8, 50, 152, 284
Hütter, Ralf, 365–366, 367, 369, 371, 372, 373
Hykes, David, 64, 159

I Am Trying to Break Your Heart (film about Wilco), 117

"I Am Trying to Break Your Heart"
(Wilco), 121
"I Can See for Miles" (the Who), 178
"I Can't Explain" (the Who), 181
Ice Storm, The (Moody), 63, 69
"I Don't Believe in the Sun"
(Magnetic Fields), 83
"I Don't Want to Get Over You"
(Magnetic Fields), 83, 84
If I Should Fall From Grace
(documentary), 291, 292, 298
If I Should Fall From Grace With God
(Pogues), 284–287, 295
"If You Don't Cry" (Magnetic Fields),
83
"If You Want Me to Stay" (Sly and
the Family Stone), 362n
"I'm a Boy" (the Who), 180
"I'm Free" (the Who), 206
"I'm One" (the Who), 206, 207, 231
"I'm Sorry I Love You" (Magnetic
Fields), 88
"I Must Be High" (Wilco), 107
"I'm Waiting for the Man" (Velvet
Underground), 308
*Indeterminate Activity of Resultant
Masses* (Branca), 342–343
indie rock, 73, 94, 152–153, 311, 350
"Indistinct Notion of Cool" (Cale),
27
Ireland, 62, 290–292
Iron and Wine, 153
Iron Man, The (Townshend), 226
"I Shatter" (Magnetic Fields), 83, 84
"I Thought I Held You" (Wilco),
108–109
"It's Gonna Rain" (Reich), 361
It's Hard (the Who), 178, 216

Jack Kerouac ROMnibus, A
(CD-ROM), 18
Jacquette, Julia, 92
Jagger, Mick, 93
Jamerson, James, 364
James, Skip, 148
Jarboe (singer/songwriter), 344

Jarmusch, Jim, 50, 338
jazz, 24, 152, 232, 234, 236, 240–241,
358, 411, 415
bebop style of, 15, 16, 17, 33
Lounge Lizards and, 160, 161, 169,
336–337
New York underground music and,
309, 322, 333–334, 342, 345–346
term "cool" in, 15–17, 19–21, 26, 29,
33, 43, 44, 52
Jefferson Airplane, 143
Jernigan (Gates), 5
"Jersey Loverboy" (Danielson
Famile), 94
Jethro Tull, 145–148, 150–155, 155n
Johansen, David, 315, 317, 318, 319,
320, 327n, 343
John, Elton, 45, 178, 318
John Lurie National Orchestra,
165–166
Johnson, J. P., 16
Jones, Brian, 186, 187, 297
Jones, James, 41
Jones, Kenney, 216
Jones, Rickie Lee, 27
Jones, Steve, 76
Jones, Tommy Lee, 52–53
Jones, Uriel, 364
Joplin, Scott, 6
Joyce, James, 4
"(Just Like) Starting Over" (Lennon),
28
"Just Can't Get Enough" (Depeche
Mode), 378
just intonation, 305

"Kamera" (Wilco), 121
Kane, Arthur, 315, 319
Kantner, Paul, 143
Katchadourian, Nina, 237, 238,
239–240, 243–244, 245, 250–251,
253, 254, 257, 259, 260, 262–263,
283, 293
Kaye, Lenny, 312n, 323
"Keep Cool, Fool" (Johnson), 16
Kemmler, William Francis, 111

Kennedy, Nuala, 239, 240, 242, 243–244, 245, 247, 253, 257–258, 259–260
Kerouac, Jack, 18–21, 22, 24–25, 27, 35, 36–37, 43, 47
Kesey, Ken, 19, 34–39, 41, 43, 44, 49, 52
Key (Monk), 67, 70
Khan, Nusrat Fateh Ali, 64
Kids Are Alright, The (documentary), 186–188, 204
"Kids Are Alright, The" (the Who), 146, 227–228
Kiss, 320
"Kiss Me Like You Mean It" (Magnetic Fields), 83
Klute, Dudley, 79, 80, 81
Knack, 86
Knuckles, Frankie, 394
Kochan, Jacek, 241, 243, 247, 248, 249, 251, 253, 257, 259, 262, 263
Kool-Aid, 34, 40–42
Kool (cigarettes), 32–34, 40, 43
Kosinski, Jerzy, 112
"Kotton Krown" (Sonic Youth), 347
Kozelek, Mark, 153
Kraft Foods, 40, 41
Kraftwerk, 150, 364–375, 377, 378, 381, 390, 393, 394
Kraftwerk: I Was a Robot (Kraftwerk), 368n, 370
Kraftwerk: Man, Machine and Music (Bussy), 366
Kramer (producer), 94
Kristal, Hilly, 327
Kronos Quartet, 164

Lambert, Kit, 185, 213, 220
Lamb Lies Down on Broadway, The (Genesis), 150
Landslide (website), 228, 229
Lane, Ronnie, 209
Lanier, Allen, 324
Laswell, Bill, 346
Laughner, Peter, 113
"Lawn for People" (Lounge Lizards), 166–167, 166n, 172, 173–174

Led Zeppelin, 150
"Legal Matter, A" (the Who), 181
Lehmann-Haupt, Sandy, 37
Lehrer, Scott, 69
Leiber, Jerry, 26
Leigh, Michael, 313
Lennon, John, 28, 145
Lependorf, Jeffrey, 234, 237, 238, 239, 240, 242, 251–252
Less Than Zero (Ellis), 51
Lethem, Jonathan, 5
"Let's Pretend We're Bunny Rabbits" (Magnetic Fields), 81
"Let's See Action" (Townshend), 210–211
Lewis, Jerry Lee, 96
Lewis, Jim, 69
Lick My Decals Off, Baby (Captain Beefheart), 89
Liebezeit, Jaki, 363, 365
Lifehouse Elements (Townshend), 214
Lifehouse (film), 208, 210–212, 213–214
Ligeti, György, 360
Lindsay, Arto, 161, 336, 343, 346
Lissitzky, El, 370
listening, 7–8, 10
literature, 3–10, 24, 79, 97–98, 101, 297, 341, 417
Little River Band, 27
Live at Leeds (the Who), 186, 189
Live/Dead (Garcia), 30
Living in the Past (Jethro Tull), 148
Living Theatre, 45
Lloyd, Richard, 294–295, 326, 330
Loaded (Velvet Underground), 311–312, 311n, 312n
"Locomotive Breath" (Jethro Tull), 147
Lohmann, Thomas, 366
"London You're a Lady" (Pogues), 287
"Long Cool Woman (In a Black Dress)" (Hollies), 27
"Long Distance Runaround" (Yes), 153
Longo, Robert, 338

Lotringer, Sylvère, 57
Lounge Lizards, 158–175, 336–337, 346
Louvin Brothers, 239
"Love Is Like a Bottle of Gin" (Magnetic Fields), 88
"Love Reign O'er Me" (the Who), 215
love songs, 85–86
Love Supreme, A (Jethro Tull), 148
Lowe, Nick, 149
Ludlam, Charles, 316, 317
Lumpy Gravy (Zappa), 144
Lunch, Lydia, 336, 342, 343, 346, 348
Lurie, Evan, 336
Lurie, John, 161, 162, 165, 167–169, 170, 171, 172n, 336, 338
Lust for Life (Bowie), 149
Lynch, David, 78

Maazel, Fiona, 283
Macaulay, Lord, 14, 16
MacColl, Kirsty, 285
Macero, Teo, 161
MacGowan, Shane, 258, 283–285, 287–295, 298, 299
MacLise, Angus, 306, 307
Magnetic Fields, 73–88
Mälzel, Johann, 354, 354n
"Man in the Purple Dress, The" (the Who), 233
Man-Machine, The (Kraftwerk), 369–370, 372, 375
Mapplethorpe, Robert, 316, 325
Marcus, Greil, 50, 325n
Marcus, Hannah, 283, 296
Marina Towers (Chicago), 120
"Marquee Moon" (Television), 328, 329
Mars (band), 336
Marshall, Ingram, 64, 159
Marshall stacks, 202
Martin, Billy, 166, 172
Massive Attack, 229
Mather, Cotton, 276
Maximum R&B (the Who), 210
Max's Kansas City, 314–316, 323

May, Derrick, 391, 392, 393, 407n
McCartney, Paul, 28, 72, 272
McEntire, John, 152
McInerney, Jay, 51
McKernan, Ronald (Pigpen), 298
McLaren, Malcom, 319, 330
McLuhan, Marshall, 53
McNally, Richard, 192
Mead, Michael, 228
Meaty Beaty Big and Bouncy (the Who), 181
Medeski Martin and Wood, 166
Meher Baba, 207, 208, 212
Mellotron, 357
Melodic Version of The Second Dream of The High-Tension Line Stepdown Transformer from The Four Dreams of China, The (Young, L.), 162–163
Meltzer, Richard, 29, 54, 325
"Mentasm" (Beltram), 406, 416n
Merkin Concert Hall, 159, 162, 167
Merritt, Stephin, 73, 74, 76–88
Merry Pranksters, 19, 35–44, 52
metronomes, 354–356, 360, 365
Mezzanine, The (Baker), 4
Michael, George, 135
Midler, Bette, 217, 316
migraines, 122–123
Mikado, The, 81
Mikel Rouse Broken Consort, 164–165, 166
Millions Now Living Will Never Die (Tortoise), 152
Mink DeVille, 327, 327n, 328
Minnelli, Liza, 80
Minutemen, 63, 152, 284
misogyny, 409–410
"Misty Morning, Albert Bridge" (Pogues), 287
"Misunderstood" (Wilco), 112–113, 115
Mitchell, Joni, 30, 60, 69, 72
Mix, The (Kraftwerk), 372
"Model, The" (Kraftwerk), 366–367
Mojo (British music magazine), 182n, 195–199, 212

Molloy (Beckett), 3
Monk, Meredith, 60–63, 65–71, 143, 144, 279, 396
Monterey Pop (DVD), 267
Moon, Keith, 180, 182, 187–188, 190, 196, 205, 212, 215, 216, 241, 297
"Moonlight Sonata" (Beethoven), 6
Moore, Thurston, 342–343, 346, 348
Moriarity, Dean. *See* Cassady, Neal
Morris, Butch, 245
Morrison, Sterling, 306, 307, 309, 310, 312, 314
Morrison, Van, 163, 225, 289, 297
Morrow, Bruce (Cousin Brucie), 107
Mothers of Invention, 144, 164, 308, 362
Motown, 96, 206, 327n, 363–364, 378, 394–395
Mouse on Mars, 375
Muldoon, Paul, 5
Mulligan, Gerry, 15
Murcia, Billy, 315, 319
Murray, Sunny, 334
musical theater, 80–81
Music for 18 Musicians (Steve Reich and Musicians), 60
Music for Airports (Eno), 334–335
Music from Big Pink (the Band), 126
Music Omi (music camp), 234–264
  introduction to, 234
  musicians at, 235–237
  performances at, 239–242, 259, 261–264
  work at, 243–259
Musicophilia (Sacks), 373–374
"My Generation" (the Who), 202, 204–205, 208, 231, 385
My Life in the Bush of Ghosts (Byrne and Eno), 60
"My Only Friend" (Magnetic Fields), 83
"Mystery Train" (Presley), 27

Nabokov, Vladimir, 9–10
Naked City, 346
Naked Lunch (Burroughs), 23–24
Name, Billy, 307

Name of This Band Is Talking Heads, The (Talking Heads), 60
Navazio, Mickey, 167
N'Dour, Youssou, 64
Neilson, Benjamin R., Jr. (Jamie), 46–47, 53
Neil Young Bridge School Benefit Concerts, 226–227
Nelson, Steven, 228
Neon Boys, 326
nervous breakdowns, 212–213
NEU (band), 365
New Age music, 279n
New Forms (Reprazent), 411–412
New Picnic Time (Ubu), 89
New Sounds Live Concert Series, 159, 162–163
New Sounds radio program (WNYC public radio), 159, 160, 162, 164
New York Doll (film), 319
New York Dolls, 315, 317–320, 321n, 326, 327n, 348
New York Times, 52, 145
New York underground music, 301–351
  African American music and, 331–335, 339, 340
  avant-garde theater movement and, 316–318
  CBGB-OMFUG club and, 327–328, 327n, 331, 333, 334, 337, 341
  ensemble of Young (La Monte), 304–307
  funk and disco music and, 332–333, 334, 335
  introduction to, 301–305
  jazz and, 333–334, 345–346
  New York City in 1975 and, 321–322
  New York Dolls and, 317–320, 321n
  No Wave movement and, 335–341, 342, 343, 346, 349, 350
  poetry scene and, 322–326
  Sonic Youth and, 343–350
  See also Max's Kansas City; Smith, Patti; Velvet Underground

Next Big Thing, The (radio program), 67, 70
Nico (with Velvet Underground), 308, 309
Nietzsche, Friedrich, 373–375, 376, 382, 383–384, 390, 404, 410
"Night You Can't Remember, The" (Magnetic Fields), 83
Nine Inch Nails, 164
9:30 Club, 76
Nirvana, 93, 312
Nitzsche, Jack, 328n
Nolan, Jerry, 319
No New York (Eno), 334–335
"No One Will Ever Love You" (Magnetic Fields), 82
Noordhuis, Nadje, 239, 240, 242, 251, 255, 262, 264
No Wave (Moore and Coley), 342
No Wave movement, 335–341, 342, 343, 346, 349, 350
Nyro, Laura, 60

Observer, 16
Ocasek, Ric, 337
Oldham, Will, 93, 153
Olsher, Dean, 70
OMD (Orchestra Manoeuvres in the Dark), 376, 376n, 377
Omi International Arts Center (New York), 234
101 (documentary by Pennebaker), 379
Ono, Yoko, 60, 342
On the Road (Kerouac), 19, 21–22, 24, 36
"Ooh La La" (Faces), 189
opera, 80–81
Operation Ore, 176, 228
O'Rourke, Jim, 121
"Ostrich, The" (Reed), 306
"Outtasite (Outta Mind)" (Wilco), 114
Oval (band), 375

Pablo Cruise, 27
"Pale Blue Eyes" (Velvet Underground), 311
Paley, Grace, 54

Pallodino, Chris, 93
"Papa Was a Rodeo" (Magnetic Fields), 83, 84
"Paper Bag and the Sun, A" (Lounge Lizards), 161, 163
Parallel Lines (Blondie), 333
Parker, Charlie (Bird), 15, 16, 24
Parliament-Funkadelic, 364
Parsons, Gram, 239
Pärt, Arvo, 159, 278–279, 282
"Parting Glass, The," 244, 259–260
Partridge, Eric, 16–17, 23, 24, 25, 50
"Passenger Side" (Wilco), 107, 121
"Pavardigar" (Townshend), 208
Pavarotti, Luciano, 209
Peace and Love (Pogues), 287
"Peace" (Depeche Mode), 390
Peanuts cartoons, music for, 93
"Peking O" (Can), 363
Pennebaker, D. A., 379
"People Are People" (Depeche Mode), 379
People's Temple, members of, 41
Pepsi, 31
Pere Ubu, 63, 294
Perkins, E. E. (Edwin), 40
Perkins Product Company, 40
"Personality Crisis" (New York Dolls), 318
"Personal Jesus" (Depeche Mode), 387–389
Peters, Bernadette, 80
P-Funk All Stars, 163
Phair, Liz, 120
Philadelphia, 78–79
Philadelphia Inquirer, 84
Phrenology (Roots), 396–401
Physical Graffiti (Led Zeppelin), 150
"Pictures of Lily" (the Who), 180–181
Pierre, D. J., 407n
"Pinball Wizard" (*Tommy* soundtrack), 178
Pincock, Christian, 240, 241, 242, 247, 249, 250, 251, 253, 257, 262
Pink Floyd, 151
"Piss Factory" (Smith. P.), 325

Place, Pat, 335
Pleasant, Mark, 62
Please Kill Me: The Uncensored Oral History of Punk (McNeil and McCain), 49
Poème Symphonique (Ligeti), 360
poetry project, 322–325
Pogue Mahone (Pogues), 289
Pogues, 258, 283–299
Polk, Brigid, 314
Pomus, Doc, 328n
Pop, Iggy, 49, 297, 314
Popes, the, 289
pornography, 408–409. *See also* child abuse / child pornography
Powerhouse, 358
Pran Nath, Pandit, 237
Prayer for Every Hour, A (Danielson Famile), 101–102, 102n
Presley, Elvis, 26, 27–28, 332
Priestley, F. E. L., 16–17
Process of Weeding Out, The (Black Flag), 152
progressive rock, 144, 144n, 147, 148, 150, 152–153
Project Runway (TV show), 251
Pro Tools, 410–411, 416n
"Providence" (Sonic Youth), 349
Psychoderelict (Townshend), 184, 226
"Punk Love" (Magnetic Fields), 83
punk rock, 48–49, 74, 76, 102, 113, 126, 149, 151, 153–154, 297, 365, 376, 398
    New York underground music and, 309, 312, 321, 327n, 328, 329, 332, 334, 336, 337, 338, 339, 343, 346, 349
"Pure and Easy" (Townshend), 211

Quadrophenia (the Who), 179, 180, 184, 189, 206, 212, 215
Queen, 27
Queen of All Ears (Lounge Lizards), 168, 170
"Quest for Thrills" (Danielson Famile), 95–96

"Quick One, While He's Away, A" (the Who), 145, 185, 186, 189–193, 191n, 231

Radio-Activity (Kraftwerk), 368
"Radio Cure" (Wilco), 123
Radio Ethiopia (Smith, P.), 328, 330
"Rallying the Dominoes" (Danielson Famile), 99
Ramone, Dee Dee, 326, 327n, 330, 343
Ramones, 54, 150, 295, 327, 328, 334n, 368, 371
Ranaldo, Lee, 342–343, 344, 346, 348, 349
Random House Historical Dictionary of American Slang, 50
Ranken, Andrew, 285
rave culture, 401–412, 407n, 413n
"Real Cool Time" (Stooges), 27
"Real Me, The" (the Who), 206
Rebel Without a Cause (film), 54
record clubs, 90–93, 131–145, 142n, 154–157
recovered memory syndrome, 192
Rector, Liam, 256, 257, 258
Redding, Otis, 266–268, 282
Red House Painters, 153
Red Krayola, 163, 295
Reed, Lou, 95, 119, 306–314, 313n, 327n, 343, 345
"Regyptian Strut" (Zappa), 144
Reich, Steve, 335, 342, 346, 360–361
R.E.M., 163
Remain in Light (Talking Heads), 333
Remembering Trauma (McNally), 192
"Reno Dakota" (Magnetic Fields), 84
Rent, 80
Replacements, 50, 63, 76, 112, 138, 140, 284
Reprazent, 411–412
"Respect" (Franklin), 54
Reverby, Martin, 337
Revolver (Beatles), 28
Reynolds, Simon, 403, 404, 405, 407n, 408, 409, 410, 413n
Rhythmicons, 356–357, 357n

Rhythm Synthesizer, 358
Ribot, Marc, 161
Richards, Keith, 203
Richter, Gerhard, 349
Riley, Terry, 64, 340, 346
Rimbaud, Jean Nicolas Arthur, 326
robots, 368–370, 381, 394, 410, 415
"Robots, The" (Kraftwerk), 369
"Rock & Roll" (Velvet Underground), 311
rock and roll music, 26–29, 43–44, 61, 63–64, 73–74, 95, 96, 112, 116–117, 148. *See also* indie rock; New York underground music; progressive rock; punk rock; *names of individual rock bands*
Rocket From the Tombs, 113, 294
Rockmore, Clara, 356
Rockwell, John, 324n
Rolling Stone (magazine), 44, 192–195, 312n
Rolling Stones, 28, 145, 181, 185–186, 288, 396
Rolling Stones Rock and Roll Circus, The (film), 145, 185–186
Romney, Hugh, 42
Ronald Shannon Jackson & the Decoding Society, 345
Roots, 396–401
Roseland Ballroom (New York City), 283–284, 293
"Roses" (Magnetic Fields), 83
Rother, Michael, 365
"Rough Boys" (Townshend), 218–219
Rough Mix (the Who), 210
"Rubbernecker" (Danielson Famile), 98–99
Rugolo, Pete, 15, 16, 17
Rum Sodomy & the Lash (Pogues), 284, 295
Rundgren, Todd, 163, 318
Rush, 273, 282
Rushmore (film/soundtrack), 189

Sacks, Oliver, 373–374
"Sally Simpson" (the Who), 183

Sandinista! (Clash), 288
Sante, Luc, 323
Saunders, George, 4–5
Saunderson, Kevin, 391, 393
Scarpantoni, Jane, 167
Schaefer, John, 159, 160, 161, 162, 165–166, 173–174
Schenkel, John, 252
"Schizophrenia" (Sonic Youth), 347
Schneider, Florian, 364–365, 366, 371, 373
Schwartz, Delmore, 307
Scott, Raymond, 358–359, 362
"Sea Refuses No River, The" (Townshend), 224, 225–226
Semiotext(e), 57
Sertso, Ingrid, 244
Sex Pistols, 48, 52, 140, 149, 218, 319, 330
sexual abuse. *See* child abuse / child pornography
Sharrock, Sonny, 345
Shelley, Steve, 344, 348
"Sheraton Gibson" (Townshend), 208
"She's a Jar" (Wilco), 116, 118–119, 129
"Showroom Dummies" (Kraftwerk), 368
Side Man, 357–358
"Signs and Symbols" (Nabokov), 9–10
Simmons, Adam, 237, 242, 245, 246, 247, 253, 254, 257, 260
Simms, Shirley, 79, 81–82, 88
Simon and Garfunkel, 270–271, 282
Simone, Nina, 30, 208
"Singers Go First" (Danielson Famile), 99
Sister Lovers (Big Star), 118
"Sister Ray" (Velvet Underground), 30, 275, 309–310, 314
Sister (Sonic Youth), 347, 349
6ths, the, 73
sixties, decade of, 30–35
69 Love Songs (Magnetic Fields), 73, 74–75, 77–86
Size, Roni, 411, 412

"Skating Away on the Thin Ice of a New Day" (Jethro Tull), 147
Slaves of New York (Janowitz), 51
Slavin, Julia, 68
Slick, Grace, 82, 143
Slint, 152
"Slip Kid" (the Who), 179
"Slit Skirts" (Townshend), 224
Sly and the Family Stone, 362, 362n, 363, 364
"Smells Like Teen Spirit" (Nirvana), 350
Smile (Beach Boys), 214
Smith, Daniel, 91, 92, 94–99, 101–102, 103
Smith, Patti, 30, 48, 52, 317n, 323–330, 324n, 327n, 331, 334, 336, 341, 342, 343
"Smooth Death" (Danielson Famile), 94
Smothers Brothers Comedy Hour, The (TV show), 204–206
Soderbergh, Steven, 50
Sohl, Richard, 323–324
Some Great Reward (Depeche Mode), 384
"Something in the Way of Things (In Town)" (Roots), 399
Songs of Faith and Devotion (Depeche Mode), 389–390
Sonic Youth, 64, 152, 284, 343–350, 396
Soothing Sounds for Baby album series, 358–359
"Sore Loser" (Katchadourian), 250
soul music genre, 265–267, 363. *See also* celestial music
Soundpainting, 240–242, 243, 245, 246, 247, 249, 250–251, 253, 254, 257, 263
"Sounds of Silence, The" (Simon and Garfunkel), 270
Sparks, 27
"Sparrow" (Simon and Garfunkel), 270–271
Speak & Spell (Depeche Mode), 378
Spector, Phil, 74, 327n, 328, 328n, 334n
Spiderland (Slint), 152

"Spirit of Radio, The" (Rush), 273
spot music, 68
Springsteen, Bruce, 27, 74, 225, 315, 328
Squeeze, 27
"Squeeze Box" (the Who), 146, 180
Stace, Wesley, 5
Stacy, Spider, 288, 293
Stalling, Carl, 358
"Stardom in Acton" (Townshend), 224
Stardust Memories (film), 50
Starr, Ringo, 187–188
Stearns, Matthew, 342n
Stein, Chris, 326
Stein, Gertrude, 59
Stevens, Cat, 153
Steve Reich and Musicians, 60
Stewart, Rod, 220
Stirratt, John, 118
Stockhausen, Karlheinz, 64, 145, 304, 363, 364
Stockholm syndrome, 192
Stoller, Mike, 26
Stonewall riots (1969), 316
Stooges, 27, 49, 316
Stranger Than Paradise (film), 162
"Strawberry Fields Forever" (Beatles), 28
Straw, Syd, 161, 258, 346
Stray Subjects (Durivage and Burnham), 14
Strummer, Joe, 288
"Substitute" (the Who), 180, 181, 189
"Subterranean Homesick Blues" (Dylan), 30
Subterraneans, The (Kerouac), 18
Suicide (musical duo), 337–338
Sumiko (Japanese composer), 238, 242, 243, 253
Summerteeth (Wilco), 116–119, 125
"Summertime Blues" (the Who), 189
Sunday Times (of London), 228
"Sunken Treasure" (Wilco), 114–115, 129
"Sunnyside of the Street, The" (Pogues), 298
"Sunrise" (the Who), 206

Swans (band), 344
Sweetheart of the Rodeo (Byrds), 239
"Sweet Jane" (Velvet Underground), 311
"Sweet-Lovin' Man" (Magnetic Fields), 83
"Sweet Thing" (Morrison), 163
Switched-On Bach (Carlos), 362
Sylvain, Sylvain, 315, 318, 319–320
synthesizers. *See* drum machines

Tabula Rasa (Pärt), 278
Tago Mago (Can), 363
"Take Me to the River" (Green), 333, 389
Talking Heads, 28, 60, 150, 163, 333, 335
Talman, Jeff, 261
"Tattoo" (the Who), 180, 181
Taylor, Cecil, 145
"Tea & Theatre" (the Who), 233
technology, 360–361, 362
Teenage Jesus and the Jerks, 335–336
"Teengenerate" (Dictators), 320
Television (band), 326, 327, 327n, 328, 329, 330, 331, 334
Tell Another Joke at the Ol' Choppin' Block (Danielson Famile), 94–96
Theatre of Eternal Music, 305, 306, 307, 313
Theremin (electronic musical instrument), 356, 357
Theremin, Léon, 356–357
"There's a Heartache Following Me" (Townshend), 207–208
There's a Riot Goin' On (Sly and the Family Stone), 362
"There She Goes Again" (Velvet Underground), 119
Thick as a Brick (Jethro Tull), 146
Thing-Fish (Zappa), 144
Things Fall Apart (Roots), 397, 398
"Things We Did and Didn't Do, The" (Magnetic Fields), 83, 84
Thompson, Ahmir (?uestlove), 396–397
Thompson, Hunter S., 37

Thompson, Walter, 241
"Three Cool Cats" (Coasters), 26
"Through Being Cool" (Devo), 27
Thunders, Johnny, 315, 317–319, 326, 327n
"Tic Toc" (from *Soothing Sounds for Baby* series), 358–359, 359n
"Time Enough for Rocking When We're Old" (Magnetic Fields), 83, 84
tintinnabuli, 278
Tommy (Broadway show), 226
Tommy (film), 178, 179, 182–183, 183n, 190, 191, 201
Tommy (soundtrack album), 178, 179
Tommy (Who album), 178, 181, 183–184, 184n, 210, 212
"Tonight's the Night" (Townshend short story), 220–224
Tortoise (band), 121, 152–153
"Tour de France" (Kraftwerk), 372
Tour de France Soundtracks (Kraftwerk), 372
Tower, Wells, 5
Town and the City, The (Kerouac), 18
Townshend, Betty, 201
Townshend, Pete, 177–180, 184–188, 190, 212–215, 219–221, 231–232
  guitar playing of, 202–206
  Mojo interview, 195–199, 196n, 212
  Rolling Stone interview, 193–195
  singing/voice of, 206–210, 216
  solo career of, 184, 207–208, 210–211, 216–226
  See also child abuse / child pornography
trance/ambient music, 334–335
transcendentalism, 24, 29
Trans-Europe Express (Kraftwerk), 368, 370, 371
Transformer (Bowie), 149
Travolta, John, 255–256
Tri-Danielson Alpha/Omega (Danielson Famile), 98–99
Trocadero (club), 78
Tronzo, Dave, 167, 172

True Stories (Byrne), 28
"Try a Little Tenderness" (Redding), 266–268
Tucker, Maureen, 307, 310, 312, 314
"Turkish Song of the Damned" (Pogues), 285
Turtle Dreams (Monk), 68
Tuvan throat singing, 64
Tweedy, Jeff, 112, 115, 117, 119, 122, 129
23 Minutes Over Brussels (Suicide), 337–338
"Twist and Shout" (Beatles), 28
"Two Kinds of People" (Magnetic Fields), 88
Type, Sam, 229

U2, 164
Ubu, Pere, 89, 284
Ulmer, James "Blood," 345
"Uncle Jerry" (Lounge Lizards), 168
Universal Pictures, 211
Up with People, 82
Use Your Illusion (Guns N' Roses), 74
Utopia, 150

Vaccaro, John, 316, 317
van Tonder, Cobi, 237, 247, 248, 255, 256–257, 259, 263
Varieties of Disturbance (Davis), 3–4
Vega, Alan, 337
Velvet Underground, 30, 118–119, 275, 306–314, 312n, 328, 329, 330, 348, 349
Velvet Underground & Nico, The (Velvet Underground), 308–309
Velvet Underground, The (book by Leigh), 313
Velvet Underground, The (Velvet Underground), 311
"Venus in Furs" (Velvet Underground), 314
Verlaine, Tom, 128, 163, 325–326, 328–329, 331, 343
"Very Funny" (Magnetic Fields), 80
Violator (Depeche Mode), 387, 389, 390, 394

Voice of Chunk (Lounge Lizards), 163, 164, 168, 170
Volcano (film), 52–53

WABC radio, 107
Waits, Tom, 289
Waldman, Anne, 322
Warhol, Andy, 126, 307–308, 309, 316, 369
"(Was I) In Your Dreams" (Wilco), 114
"Washington, D.C." (Magnetic Fields), 82, 83–84
Wave (Smith, P.), 331, 341
Way of the Pilgrim, The, 98
"Way You Say Good-Night, The" (Magnetic Fields), 88
Wednesday Morning, 3 A.M. (Simon and Garfunkel), 270
"We Don't Say Shut Up" (Danielson Famile), 92
"We Got a Hit" (the Who), 233
Welch, Gillian, 148
Westerberg, Paul, 93, 112
Weston, Calvin, 166, 172
West Side Story (Bernstein), 30
"What's Going On?" (Gaye), 30
What's Welsh for Zen (Cale autobiography), 313n
"Wheel Made Man, The" (Danielson Famile), 99
"When My Boy Walks Down the Street" (Magnetic Fields), 83
White Album, The (Beatles), 28, 68, 72–73
White City (Townshend), 184, 226
White, David, 229
White Light/White Heat (Velvet Underground), 309–310, 314, 348
Whitman, Walt, 24
Who Are You (the Who), 215
"Who Are You" (the Who), 218
Who by Numbers, The (the Who), 178–180, 206, 215, 226
Who Came First (Townshend), 180, 207–208, 209, 210–211, 233

Who Sell Out, The (the Who), 180, 206, 216
Who's Next? (the Who), 180, 213–214, 215
Who, the, 28, 145, 146, 186–188, 204–206, 226–227, 233, 292–293. *See also* child abuse/child pornography; Daltrey, Roger; Entwistle, John; Jones, Kenney; Moon, Keith; Townshend, Pete; *names of individual albums and songs*
Wilco, 107–130
Wilder, Alan, 380, 389, 392
Williams, Victoria, 76
Willows, Judy, 234
Will to Power, The (Nietzsche), 374, 376
Wilson, Brian, 208–209
"Wi' Nae Wee Bairn Ye'll Me Beget" (Magnetic Fields), 83
Wingdale Community Singers, 234, 244, 249, 251, 283
Winkel, Dietrich Nikolaus, 354, 354n
"Wishful Thinking" (Wilco), 127
Wish You Were Here (Pink Floyd), 151
"Witch's Promise" (Jethro Tull), 148
WNBC radio, 107
WNYC (New York Public Radio), 66–67, 70, 159
Wolfe, Tom, 34–36, 37–39, 41–42, 43
"Wond'ring Aloud" (Jethro Tull), 147
"Won't Get Fooled Again" (the Who), 183, 188, 206, 208, 210, 213–214
Woo, John, 73, 76, 77, 82, 84

Workingman's Dead (Grateful Dead), 44
Works (Emerson, Lake and Palmer), 149
"World Love" (Magnetic Fields), 83
Worrell, Bernie, 333

Xenakis, Iannis, 145
X (punk rock band), 52
"Xylophone Track" (Magnetic Fields), 83

Yankee Hotel Foxtrot (Wilco), 113, 119–125, 126, 128
"Yeah Yeah Yeah Yeah Yeah" (Pogues), 287–288
Yes (band), 151, 153
yoga, 243, 249
"You Better You Bet" (the Who), 216
Young Fresh Fellows, 163
Young, La Monte, 64, 89, 159, 237, 279, 304–307, 313, 335, 343
Young, Neil, 30, 54, 76, 148
"You're My Only Home" (Magnetic Fields), 76, 84
Yule, Billy, 314
Yule, Doug, 311, 311n, 314

Zappa, Frank, 144–145, 164. *See also* Mothers of Invention
Zazeela, Marian, 305
"Zebra" (Magnetic Fields), 88
Zevon, Warren, 225, 289
Ziggy Stardust (Bowie), 149
Zizek, Slavoj, 50
Zorn, John, 336, 345–346

About the Author

Rick Moody is the author of the novels *Garden State*, *The Ice Storm*, *Purple America*, *The Diviners*, and *The Four Fingers of Death*; two collections of stories, *The Ring of Brightest Angels Around Heaven* and *Demonology*; a collection of novellas, *Right Livelihoods*; and a memoir, *The Black Veil*, winner of the PEN / Martha Albrand Award. Moody has also received the Addison Metcalf Award from the American Academy of Arts and Letters, the *Paris Review*'s Aga Khan Prize, and a Guggenheim Fellowship. He lives in Brooklyn.